The Stoney Creek Recipe Collection

The Stoney Creek Recipe Collection

A Treasury of
Culinary Favorites and
Historical Vignettes

PROVIDENCE HOUSE PUBLISHERS
Franklin, Tennessee

All proceeds from the sale of THE STONEY CREEK RECIPE COLLECTION shall be used solely for the maintenance and preservation of the Stoney Creek Chapel and Cemetery.

Copyright 1994
Stoney Creek Presbyterian Foundation, Inc.

All rights reserved. Written permission must be secured from the publisher to use or reproduce any part of this book, except for brief quotations in critical reviews or articles.

Printed in the United States of America

99 98 97 96 95 94   10 9 8 7 6 5 4 3 2 1

ISBN 1-881576-30-2

The Stoney Creek Chapel and Cemetery photographs used on the cover and on pages 9 and 10 contributed by Lynn McLaren. McLaren is a professional free-lance photographer and photo-journalist. Her credits include National Geographic *and a variety of other periodicals and published works. Most recently she was the author/photographer of the beautiful volume* Ebb Tide—Flood Tide. *She is a member of First Presbyterian Church, Beaufort, South Carolina.*

Published by
PROVIDENCE HOUSE PUBLISHERS
P.O. Box 158
Franklin, Tennessee 37065
800-321-5692

To the faith held by the founders of

*S*toney *C*reek *I*ndependent *P*resbyterian *C*hurch

and to all those who continue in that tradition

by ensuring the preservation of

*S*toney *C*reek *C*hapel and *C*emetery

for present and future generations.

Contents

Introduction	9
Preface and Acknowledgments	13
Terms and Equivalents	15
Part 1. Culinary Favorites	17
1. Beverages—Hors D'Oeuvres—Sandwiches	19
2. Breads—Muffins—Rolls	35
3. Cakes	51
4. Candy—Cookies	73
5. Desserts—Pies	97
6. Eggs and Cheese—Grits	120
7. Fish—Shellfish	128
8. Meats—Entrées and Casseroles	145
9. Poultry—Entrées and Casseroles	173
10. Rice—Beans—Pasta	197
11. Salads	210
12. Sauces—Fruit Dishes—Pickles	238
13. Soups—Stews	246
14. Vegetables	259
Part 2. Historical Vignettes	285
15. Ministry through the Centuries	287
Index	349

Introduction

Stoney Creek Chapel — A Brief History

The Independent Presbyterian Church of Stoney Creek was established May 10, 1743, and served a large colony from the Combahee River and other streams which flowed to the South Carolina coast. This area was known as Prince William's Parish. Stoney Creek Chapel was built in 1832 in the high piney woods of the little village of McPhersonville, South Carolina. It was here that many plantation owners and their families had summer residences where they retreated to escape the unhealthy lowlands during the hotter months of mosquito infestation.

Virtually all local planters of the day were devoted to the cultivation of rice crops which thrived when swamps were drained, diked and properly sluiced. The plantation owners weren't able to leave the malaria infested coastal area for months at a time for business reasons. They needed to be nearby to maintain their crops yet retreat to a safer distance for their health. Many of the planters in the region gave up portions of their property to form one 210-foot-square acre on which the chapel was built, thereby providing a place of worship for the summer months.

U.S. Geological Survey maps indicate that the site of the chapel is approximately eighty-two feet above sea level with neighboring sites within a mile at just seventeen feet above. This difference in elevation was most important to the physical health of the residents who had little in the way of medical treatments.

Stoney Creek Chapel is the only structure which was built prior to the War Between the States remaining in the village of McPhersonville. General Sherman used this Chapel as a federal hospital during the war and tented his troops on the grounds. Although all other churches in the entire area were burned (Sherman was reputed to be Presbyterian), the parent church at Stoney Creek was gradually dismantled over a four year period while Union troops were stationed in the area. Portions were used to construct bridges and to augment living quarters.

The chapel is a rectangular white frame building in the Greek Revival style with later Victorian features. The gable roof has an octagonal steeple which was added around 1890. Four round columns support the pediment. Victorian alterations include arched four-over-four (4/4) light windows with exterior blinds. Above the entrance is a small stained glass window of gold, mauve, and blue.

The sturdy simplicity of the exterior is also present inside the chapel. Worn pews sit on a random-width floor and face a pulpit of white paneled wood augmented by faded bands of gold leaf. Kerosene hanging lamps have been converted to electricity and the Detroit-made Farrand and Votey organ remains in good condition.

Church records indicate that the Reverend James B. Dunwoody, a pastor of the Chapel, performed the marriage of his cousin Martha Bulloch to Theodore Roosevelt in Roswell, Georgia. They were the parents of President Theodore Roosevelt and grandparents of President Franklin Delano Roosevelt. Another pastor was the Reverend S. Edward Axson of Savannah, Georgia, whose daughter Ellen was the first wife of Woodrow Wilson. Many other well-known names appear in church records from throughout the years. The cemetery, at the site of the parent church, contains the graves of many prominent South Carolinians.

Regular worship at the chapel dwindled due to the economy and lack of growth in the community. As a result, the Congregation was dissolved in 1967. Permanent custodianship was assigned by the Charleston Presbytery to the First Presbyterian Church of Beaufort, South Carolina, which serves as the permanent caretaker of this historic church.

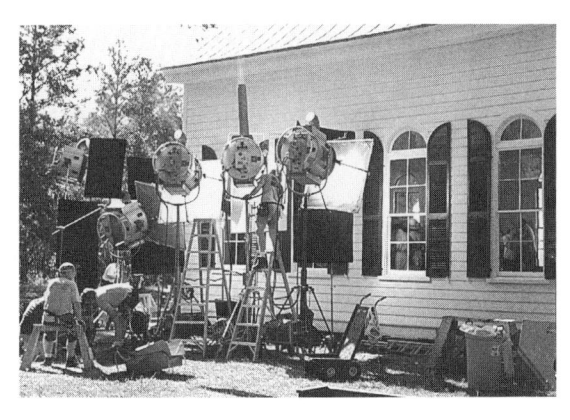

After assessing the costs associated with this responsibility, Stoney Creek Foundation Trustees, comprised of six active members of First Presbyterian, set a goal of $100,000 to be raised. This endowment fund would ensure adequate perpetual care, essential maintenance, and needed restorative improvements for the Stoney Creek Chapel and the cemetery.

In 1993, the chapel was used as a location for scenes in the recent film *Forrest Gump*. Repairs and improvements made by Paramount Studios included: Installation of a deep water well, pump, and pump house; exterior and interior painting; electrical wiring for ceiling lights; restoration of the heart-of-pine floors to their natural wood state; and some sisal rugs for the chapel interior. Trustees of the chapel were grateful for the restorative work done by the studios, but there are many other necessary improvements that must be continued.

Progress toward the financial goal has been achieved through personal donations and from offerings received at the services held at the chapel once or twice each year. Repeat visitors from other denominations, along with a few from among the last remaining members of Stoney Creek, join Beaufort's First Presbyterian congregation in worship. The playing of favorite hymns on the faithful old organ gives those present an opportunity to experience a brief return to less sophisticated times through handed-down remembrances from the past. A sumptuous covered-dish meal follows the service. This time-honored tradition of "dinner on the grounds" inspired THE STONEY CREEK RECIPE COLLECTION.

Preface and Acknowledgments

The Stoney Creek Foundation Trustees, their spouses, and a few other interested persons, after much careful and prayerful deliberation, decided to publish a collection of recipes and church histories from Presbyterian congregations. An informational packet was mailed to Presbyteries and individual churches in the denomination. Members also contacted their previous church homes to garner participation.

The response was tremendous!

The cookbook includes over six hundred recipes from thirty states plus the District of Columbia, the Canadian provinces of Ontario and Saskatchewan, as well as England, Scotland, Ireland, and Harare, Zimbabwe. There are historical sketches from almost two hundred congregations.

A group of talented, dedicated women of the church began the daunting task of organizing the recipes and the histories to avoid duplication and to produce an interesting array of varied offerings for the cookbook.

In some instances, the foreign recipes required conversion of measurements. For example, an English teacup measurement was found to be equivalent to 3/4 cup in American measures. Cooking temperatures also needed to be converted from Celsius to Fahrenheit and some cooking directions needed to be recalculated due to linguistic differences and variations in kitchen equipment.

In order to ensure that the conversions were accurate and that the outcome of the original recipes was not affected it was necessary to test many of them. This was accomplished by a culinarily gifted member of the church, who has published her own cookbook entitled *Strictly For Boys From 8 to 80*, now in its seventh printing. Another volunteer, with a strong culinary background, who owned her own catering business in Southport, Connecticut, cochaired the committee to select the final recipes for inclusion in the cookbook.

In reviewing the selections, an attempt was made to include a wide variety of recipes which could be used for large gatherings such as church suppers or smaller, more intimate gatherings in members' homes. Many recipes came with personal notes indicating that they were "tried and true" and special "old family" offerings.

Acknowledgments

Also, special effort was made to select a variety of geographic locales for inclusion in the cookbook in order to make it a true representation of the many Presbyterian congregations that submitted recipes for consideration.

And in the true spirit of Christian love and giving, members of other denominations, who learned of our project, voluntarily contributed recipes and their church histories to aid in our collection. We are truly grateful for their generosity, along with that of our fellow Presbyterians.

It would be impossible to calculate the number of volunteer hours spent reviewing, testing, and selecting the cookbook contents. Many talented cooks were involved in this project bringing their own kitchen expertise to the effort. The final product reflects tasty choices for everything from potlucks to casual or formal dining in your own home.

Persons involved in THE STONEY CREEK RECIPE COLLECTION project are as follows:

† Charles Aimar	Mary Logan
Barbara Aimar	† Thomas Logan
Fran Barnard	Jeanette Martin
Pat Bassnet	Betsy Merrick
Judy Cannon	† John Myers
Tom Costikyan	Nancy Myers
Dean Cullison	Gretchen Ryan
Mimi Cullison	Jesse Schaudies
Lynn McLaren Demarest	† John Scholer
Dot Erwin	Sally Smith (dec.)
Karlyn Gleason	Shirley Staggs
† Brantley Harvey	Becky Trask
Jim Knight	† Neil Trask, Jr.
Teri Knight	Betty Waskiewicz
Marion Leach	Louise Wilgus

So many people have been helpful that we may have inadvertently overlooked listing someone, if so please forgive us and know that we truly appreciate all the help we've been given.

† *Trustee—Stoney Creek Presbyterian Foundation*

Terms and Equivalents

TERMS

Baking, Beating, or Blending Times—These may vary slightly with different ovens, beaters, or blenders.

Butter—Wherever butter is called for in a recipe, either butter or oleomargarine can be used with equal success.

Can Sizes—Sizes vary slightly with different brands, but similar size cans usually are similar in content. All can sizes given are based on popular brands with national distribution.

Flour—Unless otherwise specified in the recipe, flour means all-purpose white flour.

Herbs—These are dried unless fresh are specifically required.

Oil, Cooking or Salad—In all recipes except those for Salads, cooking oil means liquid corn, safflower, or other vegetable oil, but not olive oil. "Salad oil" means your favorite kind—including olive oil.

Oven Heat—Best results are always achieved by preheating the oven to the temperature required in the recipe. Please read recipe through before you begin to mix ingredients and preheat oven to specified temperature.

Shortening—When a recipe calls for shortening, solid vegetable shortening such as Crisco is meant. Do not use cooking oil, lard, or bacon fat. In a pinch, oleomargarine can be used, as it, too, is solid vegetable shortening, but it is salted, and does have a slightly different taste.

Sour Cream—Where this is called for, the commercial product is meant, not cream soured in your refrigerator.

Spices—These are ground unless whole cloves, crystalline ginger, or stick cinnamon is specified.

Sugar—Sugar always means white granulated sugar; confectioner's sugar and brown sugar are so specified. Where both brown and white sugars are called for, white granulated sugar is referred to as white sugar. Brown sugar measurements are for packed amounts.

Whipped Salad Dressing—A Miracle-Whip-type product.

EQUIVALENTS

1	PINCH OR DASH	1/8	TEASPOON (LESS THAN)
3	TEASPOONS	1	TABLESPOON
2	TABLESPOONS	1	LIQUID OUNCE
4	TABLESPOONS	1/4	CUP
8	TABLESPOONS	1/2	CUP
16	TABLESPOONS	1	CUP
1	CUP	1	GILL (1/2 PINT)
2	CUPS	1	PINT
2	PINTS	1	QUART
4	QUARTS	1	GALLON
2	CUPS LIQUID	1	POUND
2	CUPS BUTTER	1	POUND
2	CUPS GRANULATED SUGAR	1	POUND
4	CUPS FLOUR	1	POUND
1	SQUARE UNSWEETENED CHOCOLATE	1	OUNCE
4	CUPS GRATED CHEESE	1	POUND
8	EGG WHITES	1	CUP (APPROXIMATELY)
16	EGG YOLKS	1	CUP (APPROXIMATELY)
1	LEMON, JUICED	2-3	TABLESPOONS
1	CUP RAW MACARONI	2	CUPS COOKED
1	CUP RAW RICE	3-4	CUPS COOKED
1	CUP WHIPPING (HEAVY) CREAM	2-2 1/2	CUPS WHIPPED CREAM
1	PACKET SUGAR SUBSTITUTE	2	TEASPOONS SUGAR
12	PACKETS SUGAR SUBSTITUTE	1	CUP SUGAR
2	TABLESPOONS LIQUID SWEETENER	1	CUP SUGAR

Part One

Culinary Favorites

Chapter One

Beverages — Hors D'Oeuvres — Sandwiches

BEVERAGES

COFFEE FRAPPÉ

- 1/2 GALLON VANILLA ICE CREAM
- 1/2 GALLON CHOCOLATE ICE CREAM
- 2-4 QUARTS GINGER ALE, CHILLED
- 1/4 CUP STRONG BLACK COFFEE, COOLED

Allow ice cream to soften enough to beat with electric mixer. Add coffee. Gradually add ginger ale until consistency desired. Beat until foamy. Yield: 50 servings.

Sarah Harley—First Presbyterian Church
Beaufort, South Carolina

HOT APPLE DRINK

- 6 CUPS APPLE CIDER
- 2 1/2 CUPS PINEAPPLE JUICE
- 3 TABLESPOONS FRESH LEMON JUICE
- 1 STICK OF CINNAMON
- 1/4 TEASPOON OF ALLSPICE
- 1/4 CUP OF HONEY
- 3 TABLESPOONS SUGAR

Mix all ingredients in a large kettle. Allow to simmer. Drink while hot. Will keep in refrigerator up to 6 weeks.

Pat Cantey—First Presbyterian Church
Marion, North Carolina

Hot Percolator Punch

6	CUPS PINEAPPLE JUICE	1	LEMON, SLICED
6	CUPS CRANBERRY JUICE	4	CINNAMON STICKS
3	CUPS WATER	3	TEASPOONS WHOLE CLOVES
2/3	CUP BROWN SUGAR		

Pour juices and water into the bottom container of percolator. Place all other ingredients into percolator basket and perk. Yield: 12-14 cups.

Eileen Harvey Bakke—Washington Community Fellowship
Washington, D.C.

Huldah's Boiled Custard

Grandmother Currey's homemade miracle—expected every Christmas.

3/4	CUP SUGAR	2	WHOLE EGGS (BEATEN)
1	TABLESPOON FLOUR	6	EGG YOLKS
1	QUART MILK	1	TEASPOON VANILLA
1	DASH SALT	1	DASH NUTMEG

Combine egg yolks with whole eggs in a double boiler. Stir in sugar and flour. Beat well. Add remaining ingredients. Cook at medium heat until mixture coats a silver spoon. Serve with fresh whipped cream if desired.

Katy Currey—Glencliff Presbyterian Church
Nashville, Tennessee

Jingle Bell Punch

2	QUARTS CRANBERRY JUICE, CHILLED	1/2	CUP MARASCHINO CHERRY JUICE
1	(6 OUNCE) CAN LEMONADE, FROZEN	60	OUNCES LEMON-LIME SODA, CHILLED

Combine all ingredients and refrigerate until ready to serve.

Paula Gottlieb—Faith Presbyterian Church
Harrisburg, Pennsylvania

Kris Kringle Punch

1/4	TEASPOON GROUND CINNAMON	4	PINTS CRANBERRY JUICE
1/4	TEASPOON NUTMEG	1	QUART ORANGE JUICE
1/4	TEASPOON ALLSPICE	70	OUNCES OF SPRITE SODA

Combine all ingredients except Sprite. Chill. Add chilled Sprite just before serving. Yield: 42 servings

Paula Gottlieb—Faith Presbyterian Church
Harrisburg, Pennsylvania

LIME PUNCH

- 6 PACKAGES OF LEMON-LIME KOOL-AID OR 3 PACKAGES LIME JELLO
- 2 QUARTS OF GINGER ALE
- 5 POUNDS OF SUGAR
- 6 QUARTS OF WATER
- 3 DOZEN LEMONS, SQUEEZED OR 2 BOTTLES FROZEN CONCENTRATED LEMON JUICE
- 3 LARGE CANS OF PINEAPPLE JUICE
- CHERRIES

Mix well and add 1 additional quart of ginger ale just before serving. Yield: 75 servings

Edmee Boyd—Hampton Presbyterian Church
Hampton, South Carolina

LOW-SUGAR PUNCH

- 2 PACKAGES SUGAR FREE KOOL-AID (STRAWBERRY OR CHERRY PERHAPS)
- 1 PACKAGE KOOL-AID LEMONADE (SUGAR FREE)
- 6 OUNCES FROZEN ORANGE JUICE, UNDILUTED

Place all ingredients in a gallon container. Add water to make 1/2 gallon. Add 2 liter bottle of diet Sprite or 7-Up. (If desired, an ice ring made of regular diluted frozen orange juice may be floated in punch bowl.)

Rosella Hollis Rogers—Central Presbyterian Church
Petersburg, Illinois

PARTY PUNCH

- 7 CUPS PINEAPPLE JUICE
- 1 PINT ORANGE SHERBET
- 1 1/2 PINTS VANILLA ICE CREAM
- 3 CUPS GINGER ALE

Place the first three ingredients in a large mixing bowl. Blend thoroughly with electric mixer at low setting. Add chilled ginger ale when ready to serve. Yield: 24.

Carolyn Souders—Faith Presbyterian Church
Harrisburg, Pennsylvania

Plantation Punch

- 1/4 CUP SUGAR
- 1/3 CUP INSTANT COFFEE CRYSTALS
- DASH OF SALT
- 1 TEASPOON OF VANILLA EXTRACT
- 1 CUP MILK
- 5 CUPS COLD MILK
- 1 PINT VANILLA OR COFFEE ICE CREAM
- WHIPPED TOPPING
- GROUND NUTMEG

Combine first five ingredients. Heat slightly, until dissolved. Add to cold milk and chill. Spoon ice cream into punch bowl. Pour chilled mixture over ice cream. Top with puffs of whipped topping. Sprinkle with nutmeg. Yield: 12 servings.

Robbie Knox—First Presbyterian Church
Aiken, South Carolina

Presbyterian Champagne

- 2 CUPS SUGAR
- 1 QUART WATER
- 4 ORANGES, JUICED
- 4 LEMONS, JUICED
- 2 LEMON RINDS
- 2 CUPS STRONG TEA
- 2 TEASPOONS VANILLA EXTRACT
- 2 TEASPOONS ALMOND EXTRACT
- 1 TWO LITER BOTTLE OF GINGER ALE

Boil sugar and water until sugar dissolves. Allow to cool. Add juice of oranges and lemons. Slice lemon rinds and add to mixture. When ready to serve, add chilled ginger ale. Yield: 24 punch cup servings.

Janie Wheeler—First Presbyterian Church
Fort Lauderdale, Florida

Presbyterian Punch

- 4 CUPS SUGAR
- 1 (46 OUNCE) CAN PINEAPPLE JUICE
- 1 (12 OUNCE) CAN FROZEN ORANGE JUICE, DILUTED
- 2 CANS FROZEN LEMONADE, DILUTED
- 5 MASHED BANANAS
- 2-3 QUARTS GINGER ALE
- 6 CUPS WATER

Boil water and sugar until sugar dissolves. When cool mix all ingredients and freeze in plastic bags. Remove from freezer 2 hours before serving. While partially frozen, beat with mixer, until slushy. To serve add ginger ale. Yield: 60 servings.

Sue Neuhs—Highland Presbyterian Church
Fayetteville, North Carolina

STRAWBERRY PUNCH

4 LARGE BOTTLES OF GINGER ALE	1 ORANGE, SLICED
2 LARGE CANS, FROZEN LEMONADE	1 LEMON, SLICED
2 LARGE PACKAGES, FROZEN STRAWBERRIES WITH SUGAR	1 LIME, SLICED
	1 QUART CRANBERRY JUICE

Mix in a two gallon punch bowl. Chill the ginger ale and add just before serving.

Connie Gezon—Brown Memorial Woodbrook Presbyterian Church
Baltimore, Maryland

SUPER SMOOTHIE

1 CUP OF FRUIT	1/4 CUP YOGURT
3/4 CUP OF FRUIT JUICE	

In an electric blender, mix all ingredients at low speed until smooth and thick.

Laura Cadwallader—Preston Hills Presbyterian Church
Kingsport, Tennessee

RUSSIAN TEA

2 CUPS OF TANG	2 1/2 CUPS SUGAR
1 CUP INSTANT TEA MIX	1 TEASPOON GROUND CINNAMON
1 PACKAGE LEMONADE MIX	1/2 TEASPOON GROUND CLOVES

Mix and store in air-tight container. Use 2 teaspoons per cup, boiling water.

Mederia Rivers Stanley—Harmony Presbyterian Church
Crocketville, South Carolina

HORS D'OEUVRES

ANCHOVY/CELERY COCKTAIL DIP

1/2	POUND PACKAGE CREAM CHEESE		DASH OF PAPRIKA
1/2	TEASPOON WHOLE CELERY SEED	1	TABLESPOON LEMON JUICE
1	TABLESPOON ANCHOVY PASTE	3	TABLESPOONS CREAM
2	TEASPOONS MINCED ONION		

Cream the cheese until smooth. Add remaining ingredients and blend until fluffy. Serve with chips or crackers.

Dorothy King—The Plymouth Church
Framingham Centre, Massachusetts

ARTICHOKE DIP

2	CANS ARTICHOKE HEARTS	1	CUP MAYONNAISE
8	GREEN ONIONS, FINELY CHOPPED	1	CUP COLBY CHEESE
2	CANS GREEN CHILIES		

Drain artichokes. Chop fine. Place in a quiche dish. Sprinkle with chopped onions. Drain and chop green chilies. Arrange chilies in dish over artichokes and onions. Spread mayonnaise over combined ingredients and top with grated cheese. Bake in 325 degree oven for 25 minutes. Serve with chips or small crackers.

Libby Neale—First Presbyterian Church
Homestead, Florida

EASY ARTICHOKE DIP

2	CANS ARTICHOKE HEARTS, CHOPPED	2	CUPS PARMESAN CHEESE
2	CUPS MAYONNAISE		

Mix all three ingredients together well. Bake in 350 degree oven for 1/2 hour or until brown on top. Serve with crackers or chips. Yield: 10-12 servings.

Dial Kitchens—First Presbyterian Church
Columbia, South Carolina

Aunt Kitty's Cheese Straws

1	CUP BUTTER	1	TEASPOON DRY MUSTARD
3	CUPS SHARP CHEDDAR CHEESE, GRATED	1	TEASPOON SALT
2	CUPS FLOUR	1/2	TEASPOON PEPPER
1	TEASPOON BAKING POWDER		

Cream the butter and cheese with mixer or food processor. Combine dry ingredients and add to the mixture. Mix until double ball is formed. On floured surface, roll dough to 1/4 inch thickness. Cut into strips 1 inch wide and 3 inches long. Twist onto cookie sheet. Bake in 400 degree oven for 10 minutes. Sprinkle with paprika while still warm. May also be cut with cookie or biscuit cutters, if desired.

Betsy Brooks Woodford—First Presbyterian Church
Paris, Kentucky

Avocado Dip

8	OUNCES CREAM CHEESE	2	TABLESPOONS CHOPPED PARSLEY
1/4	PINT FRESH CREAM		SALT AND PEPPER TO TASTE
4	TABLESPOONS MAYONNAISE	1	CRUSHED CLOVE OF GARLIC (OPTIONAL)
1	AVOCADO PEAR, PEELED AND MASHED		

Beat cheese with mayonnaise until smooth. Lightly whip cream and stir into mayonnaise mixture. Stir in remaining ingredients. Serve with strips of carrot, celery chips or crackers.

Liz Cushnie—Armagh Road Presbyterian Church
Portadown, Northern Ireland

Beef Balls

1	8-OUNCE PACKAGE CREAM CHEESE, SOFTENED	1	TABLESPOON CHIVES
		1	JAR DRIED BEEF
1/2	CUP NUTS, CHOPPED		

Combine cheese, chives, nuts and shape into balls. Place dried beef in blender and shred. Roll the balls in the beef shreds. May be refrigerated until ready for use. Same day or next day use advised.

Jean Mabe—Hodges Presbyterian Church
Hodges, South Carolina

Beef Sausage

This is a specialty of the Southworths and is always served at their gatherings, sliced thin with crackers.

5	POUNDS LEAN, GROUND BEEF	2	TEASPOONS LEMON PEPPER
2 1/2	TEASPOONS MUSTARD SEED	2	TEASPOONS COARSE GROUND PEPPERCORNS
1/2	TEASPOON GARLIC POWDER	5	HEAPING TEASPOONS MORTON'S
2	TEASPOONS HICKORY SMOKED SALT		"TENDERQUICK"

Mix all ingredients well by hand. Cover and refrigerate for 3 days. Each day, mix well again. Pack tightly before covering and returning to refrigerator. On 4th day, meat should be very dark. Form into small rolls about the size of a 6 ounce frozen orange juice container. Place on the rack of a broiler pan so that grease can drip into the pan while cooking. Bake for 8-10 hours in 150-200 degree oven. Turn once. Allow to cool and wrap in foil. Will keep for about 3 weeks in refrigerator. Freezes well!

Jane and Gene Southworth—First Presbyterian Church
Beaufort, South Carolina

Cheese Ball

- 1 PACKAGE CREAM CHEESE (8 OUNCES)
- 1/4 CUP FINELY CHOPPED GREEN PEPPER
- 1 CUP PINEAPPLE, CRUSHED AND DRAINED
- 2 CUPS CHOPPED NUTS
- 2 TABLESPOONS FINELY CHOPPED ONIONS

Combine first four ingredients and 1 cup pecans in large bowl. Mix well. Shape into a ball. Roll in the remaining pecans. Chill and serve with crackers.

Edna S. Gourley—First Presbyterian Church
Marion, North Carolina

CHEESE AND FRANK ROLLS

1 PACKAGE OF CRESCENT ROLLS
8 FRANKFURTERS
CHEESE

Separate rolls into triangles. Slit frankfurters almost to ends. Insert choice of cheese strips into each frankfurter. Place on each triangle and roll. Place on cookie sheet with cheese sides up. Bake in 375 degree oven for 10-15 minutes.

Mederia Rivers Stanley—Harmony Presbyterian Church
Crocketville, South Carolina

CHEESE SNACKS

1/4 POUND (1 STICK) MARGARINE OR BUTTER
1 CUP GRATED CHEESE
1 TABLESPOON WORCESTERSHIRE SAUCE
1 1/2 CUPS SIFTED FLOUR
1/4 TEASPOON CAYENNE PEPPER
1/4 TEASPOON PAPRIKA
1/2 TEASPOON SALT
PECAN HALVES

Blend butter with grated cheese until smooth. Add Worcestershire sauce. Sift dry ingredients and add to the mixture. Stir thoroughly. Shape into small balls. Place on an ungreased cookie sheet. Press with a fork. Place pecan halves on top of each snack. Bake in 325 degree oven for 25 minutes. Yield: 50 snacks.

Charlotte B. Bone—Ray Memorial Presbyterian Church
Monroe, Georgia

CRABBIES

1 STICK OF BUTTER
1 JAR OLD ENGLISH CHEESE SPREAD
1 1/2 TEASPOON MAYONNAISE
1/2 TEASPOON SEASONED SALT
1/2 TEASPOON GARLIC POWDER
1 CAN CRAB MEAT
ENGLISH MUFFINS

Mix butter and cheese spread. Add mayonnaise and seasonings. Mix well. Add crab and mix lightly. Spread on open halves of English muffins. For appetizers, quarter the muffin halves. Cook in 350 degree oven until hot and bubbly. Note: Double the recipe and cook the crabbies, cool and freeze. Heat in microwave or regular oven.

Susie Neal—Fort Hill Presbyterian Church
Clemson, South Carolina

Crab Dip

1	CAN CRAB MEAT	1	SMALL ONION, CHOPPED FINE
1	CREAM CHEESE (8 OUNCE)	1/2	CUP MAYONNAISE
1	PACKAGE SHREDDED CHEDDAR CHEESE		DASH OF GARLIC POWDER
1/3	CUP PARMESAN CHEESE		SALT AND PEPPER TO TASTE

Mix all ingredients with blender. Chill for several hours. Heat in a 350 degree oven until warm. Serve with rye bread, or chips, or small crackers.

Florence May (from Donna Weiss' recipe)—Fairfax Presbyterian Church
Fairfax, Virginia

Curry Dip for Shrimp

1	CUP MAYONNAISE	1/8	TEASPOON THYME
2	TEASPOONS TARRAGON VINEGAR	1/4	TEASPOON CURRY POWDER
1	DASH BLACK PEPPER	2	TABLESPOONS HEINZ CHILI SAUCE
1/2	TEASPOON SALT	2	TABLESPOONS ONION, CHOPPED FINE

Blend all ingredients and refrigerate. Keeps well, but only if you hide it!

Caroline Wright—Highland Presbyterian Church
Winston-Salem, North Carolina

Dill Dip

1	CONTAINER (16 OUNCES) SOUR CREAM	3	TABLESPOONS ONION
2	CUPS REAL MAYONNAISE		DASH SALT
1	TABLESPOON DILL WEED	1	TEASPOON CELERY SEED
3	TABLESPOONS DRIED PARSLEY		

Combine ingredients and mix well. Refrigerate at least 6 hours before serving. Serve as an appetizer with fresh vegetables or crackers. (2 cups cottage cheese may be substituted for sour cream.)

Becky Gray—Fairfax Presbyterian Church
Fairfax, Virginia

Glorified Onions

5-6	MEDIUM VIDALIA ONIONS (IF VIDALIAS NOT AVAILABLE USE OTHER TYPE)	1	TEASPOON CELERY SEED
		2	CUPS WATER
1/2	CUP VINEGAR	1/2	CUP MAYONNAISE
1	CUP SUGAR	1	TEASPOON CELERY SALT

Combine vinegar, sugar and water. Add very thinly sliced onions. Refrigerate for 2-4 hours. Drain well and toss with mayonnaise and seasonings. Serve on crackers, in a tomato, as a salad or as a condiment. You can keep these in the marinade in the refrigerator for several weeks.

Mrs. Claude Walker, Jr.—First Presbyterian Church
Columbia, South Carolina

Quick Paté

1	(12 OUNCE) ROLL BRAUNSCHWEIGER	1/2	ENVELOPE DRY ONION SOUP MIX
1	(8 OUNCE) PACKAGE CREAM CHEESE		

Combine all ingredients well, if too thick, may thin with small amount of sour cream. Serve with snack crackers or perhaps party rye or pumpernickel bread.

Heart Quick Arno—Pacific Palisades Presbyterian Church
Pacific Palisades, California

Sausage and Cheese Balls

2 1/2	CUPS BISCUIT MIX	8	OUNCES SHARP CHEDDAR CHEESE, GRATED
8	OUNCES HOT OR MILD SAUSAGE		

Cook sausage in large skillet, breaking up with a fork, until no longer pink. About 5-8 minutes. Drain off fat. Spoon into a large bowl, add the cheese, and biscuit mix. Mix with fork until blended. Roll into 1 inch balls. Place on cookie sheet. (May be frozen if desired for later use.) Defrost prior to cooking. Bake in 400 degree oven for 12-15 minutes or until brown.

Mrs. Loma Young—First Presbyterian Church
Savannah, Georgia

Vegetable Pizza

2	CANS REFRIGERATED CRESCENT ROLLS	3/4	CUP CHOPPED BROCCOLI
1	CUP MAYONNAISE	3/4	CUP CHOPPED TOMATO
1	PACKAGE CREAM CHEESE (8 OUNCE)	3/4	SHREDDED CARROT
1	PACKAGE DRY RANCH DRESSING	3/4	CUP SHREDDED SHARP CHEESE

Press crescent rolls onto baking sheet as a solid crust. Bake according to package directions. Mix mayonnaise, cream cheese and dressing thoroughly and spread over cooked crust. Arrange vegetables and shredded cheese over mixture. Refrigerate for 2 hours. Cut into squares and arrange on serving plate.

Margaret C. Tiddy—John Knox Presbyterian Church
Shelby, North Carolina

SANDWICHES

Chicken Salad Party Sandwiches

- 4 LARGE FRYERS, COOKED, DEBONED AND GROUND (8 CUPS CHICKEN)
- 2 CUPS ALMONDS, GROUND
- 2 QUARTS MIRACLE WHIP OR MAYONNAISE-TYPE DRESSING (MAY USE LESS)
- PINCH OF CURRY POWDER
- SALT AND PEPPER TO TASTE

Combine all ingredients well. Cut bread into rounds or squares. Spread mixture over bread to make open face sandwiches. May decorate with strip of pimento or stuffed olive, if desired. Sprinkle with paprika. Yield: 200 sandwiches or 18 dozen.

Charlotte C. Frierson—First Presbyterian Church
Orangeburg, South Carolina

Chipped Beef 'N Cheese

4	OUNCES CREAM CHEESE, SOFTENED	3	TABLESPOONS MAYONNAISE
3/4	CUP CHIPPED BEEF, TORN INTO SMALL PIECES		

Combine cheese, beef and mayonnaise until well mixed. Spread on choice of bread. (Suggestion: rye or pumpernickel bread)

Irene Grant—East Ridge Presbyterian Church
Chattanooga, Tennessee

Fast Fillings for Sandwiches

1 CUP COTTAGE CHEESE MIXED WITH ANY OF THE FOLLOWING COMBINATIONS :
- 1 GRATED CARROT AND 1/4 CUP RAISINS
- 1 TABLESPOON HONEY AND 1/4 CUP COCONUT
- 1/3 CUP CHOPPED APRICOTS
- 1 STEM CHOPPED CELERY AND 1/2 APPLE FINELY CHOPPED
- 1/3 CUP CHOPPED DATES AND 1/4 CUP CHOPPED NUTS

1 CUP GRATED CHEDDAR CHEESE WITH ANY OF THE FOLLOWING COMBINATIONS:
- 1/2 CHOPPED APPLE AND 1/4 CUP RAISINS
- 1 GRATED CARROT AND 2 TABLESPOONS MAYONNAISE

Yield: 4 sandwiches per filling.

Miss H. Dickson—North Church, High Street
Perth, Scotland

Miss Elsie House's Sandwich Mix for Parties

1 CUP RAISINS, CHOPPED OR GROUND	1 LEMON, JUICE AND GRATED RIND
1 CUP SUGAR	1 CUP MAYONNAISE
1 EGG, BEATEN	1 CUP PECANS, CHOPPED
1 LUMP BUTTER (ABOUT 1/2 STICK)	

Cook sugar, egg, butter, lemon juice on low heat until thick. Add raisins and heat again. Remove from heat. Add mayonnaise and pecans.

Barbara Dark—First Presbyterian Church
Marion, North Carolina

Mock Crab Sandwich Filling

1/4 POUND LEAN BACON, FINELY CHOPPED AND COOKED	
1 LARGE ONION, FINELY CHOPPED	1 TEASPOON VINEGAR
2 TOMATOES, FINELY CHOPPED	PEPPER TO TASTE
2 EGGS BEATEN	2 OUNCES CHEDDAR CHEESE, GRATED

Mix well and use open face or on two pieces of bread of choice.

Louise Wilson—Armagh Road Presbyterian Church
Portadown, Northern Ireland

Party Sandwich Loaf

Frosting:

1	LOAF UNSLICED SANDWICH BREAD	2	PACKAGES CREAM CHEESE (8 OUNCES EACH)
	SOFTENED BUTTER OR MARGARINE	1/2	CUP LIGHT CREAM

Shrimp Salad Spread

- 1 (4 1/2 OUNCE) CAN CHOPPED SHRIMP, RINSED AND DRAINED
- 1 HARD-BOILED EGG, MINCED
- 2 TABLESPOONS CELERY, MINCED
- 1 TABLESPOON LEMON JUICE
- SALT AND PEPPER TO TASTE
- 3 TABLESPOONS MAYONNAISE

Olive Nut Spread

- 1 (3 OUNCE) PACKAGE CREAM CHEESE, SOFTENED
- 1/4 CUP CHOPPED PIMENTO STUFFED GREEN OLIVES
- 1/2 CUP FINELY CHOPPED WALNUTS
- 2 TABLESPOONS MILK

Deviled Ham Spread

1	(4 1/2 OUNCE) CAN DEVILED HAM	1	TABLESPOON GRATED ONION
1/4	CUP SOUR CREAM		DASH OF RED PEPPER SAUCE
2	TABLESPOONS SWEET PICKLE RELISH		

Yield for each filling is about 1 cup. Mix each separately and set aside.

Trim crust from loaf of bread. Cut horizontally into 4 equal slices. Spread 3 slices with soft butter or margarine. Place 1 buttered slice on tray or platter. Spread evenly with Shrimp salad. Top with second buttered slice and cover evenly with Olive Nut spread. Top with third slice and spread with Deviled Ham mixture. Top with unbuttered slice. Mix the 2 packages of cream cheese with the light cream. You may add a few drops of food coloring to tint a delicate color, if desired. Frost top and sides of loaf with cream cheese mixture. Chill loaf about 30 minutes until frosting has set. Wrap loaf in a damp cloth and chill for at least 2 1/2 hours. Yield: 12-14 slices.

Note: You may use 1 white and 1 whole wheat loaf and alternate the slices.

First Presbyterian Church, Haddonfield, New Jersey

ORANGE NUT PARTY SANDWICHES

- 2 (8 OUNCE) PACKAGES CREAM CHEESE
- 1/4 CUP GRATED, FRESH ORANGE RIND
- 1 CUP LIGHT OR DARK RAISINS, CHOPPED
- 1/2 CUP ORANGE JUICE

Spread on open faced whole wheat rounds of bread. Garnish with chopped nuts. If mixture is too stiff, add a small amount of mayonnaise. Yield: 4 dozen

Charlotte C. Frierson—First Presbyterian Church
Orangeburg, South Carolina

TUNA PARTY LOAF (SANDWICH SPREAD)

- 2 6 1/8 OUNCE CANS WHITE SOLID PACK TUNA
- 1 8 OUNCE PACKAGE CREAM CHEESE, SOFTENED
- 1 SMALL ONION, SHREDDED OR CHOPPED FINELY
- 2 TEASPOONS PREPARED HORSERADISH
- 1/4 TEASPOON SALT
- 3/4 CUP CHOPPED PECANS
- 4 TABLESPOONS CHOPPED FRESH PARSLEY

Break tuna to fine consistency (food processor off, on, etc.). Remove from processor. Add onion, chop finely. Add cream cheese, salt, and horseradish. Blend, remove from processor. Add tuna to other ingredients mixing by hand to form loaf. Chill one hour. Roll in chopped pecans and parsley. Serve with Triscuits or cracker of choice.

Betsy Dority Collins—First Presbyterian Church
Statesville, North Carolina

ELMIRA B-B-Q

The donor declares that this is one of their standards for parties and picnics.

- 5 POUNDS GROUND BEEF
- 1/2 CUP ONION, CHOPPED
- 3 CUPS KETCHUP
- 1/2 CUP MUSTARD
- 1/4 CUP VINEGAR
- 1/4-1/2 CUP GRANULATED SUGAR

Brown beef and onions together. Drain. Place in a crock pot or dutch oven and heat slowly while mixing in remaining ingredients. Simmer for several hours at very low heat. Stir occasionally. May be served on buns, rolls or bread. Yield: 25 servings

Margaret Page—Elmira United Presbyterian Church
Toulon, Illinois

Sloppy Joes for a Crowd

3	POUNDS GROUND BEEF	3	TABLESPOONS VINEGAR
3	CUPS ONIONS, CHOPPED	3	TABLESPOONS PAPRIKA
3	CUPS CELERY, DICED SMALL	3	TEASPOONS SALT
3	CUPS GREEN PEPPERS, CHOPPED	1/2	TEASPOON BLACK PEPPER
3	CANS (SMALL SIZE) TOMATO PASTE, WITH 3 CANS WATER	1/4	TEASPOON RED PEPPER
		1	TABLESPOON CHILI POWDER
1	CUP CATSUP	2	TABLESPOONS WORCESTERSHIRE SAUCE
3	TABLESPOONS SUGAR		

Brown beef until crumbly and light brown. Drain off grease. In a heavy pan, mix beef with all remaining ingredients. Cover and cook over low heat for 1 hour. Uncover and continue cooking until thick. About 3 hours more. Serve on hamburger buns. Yield: 24 servings. Freezes well.

Mrs. Nedra Greenlee—First Presbyterian Church
Marion, North Carolina

Stromboli Express

1/4	POUND GRATED CHEESE	1	LOAF OF FROZEN BREAD DOUGH, THAWED
6	SLICES HAM (SANDWICH CUTS)		SLICED TOMATOES, OLIVES, AND LETTUCE
1/4 TO 1/2	POUND, FROZEN BROCCOLI PIECES		HONEY MUSTARD

Boil frozen broccoli for 10 minutes and drain well. Roll bread dough to fit 11 x 15 cookie sheet. Spread dough with mustard. Arrange ham slices down center of dough. Top the ham with the broccoli and 3/4 of the cheese. Roll lengthwise as you would a jelly roll. Pinch ends placing seam down on sheet. Bake for 25 minutes in 375 degree oven. Sprinkle with remaining cheese, slice and serve with the lettuce, tomatoes and olives.

Joyce Huizinga—First Presbyterian Church
Demopolis, Alabama

Chapter Two

Breads — Muffins — Rolls

BREADS

APPLE BREAD

4	CUPS ALL PURPOSE FLOUR	1	CUP COOKING OIL
2	TEASPOONS SODA	4	TABLESPOONS SOUR CREAM
2	TEASPOONS CINNAMON	2	TEASPOONS VANILLA
1	TEASPOON SALT	2	CUPS PEELED, CHOPPED APPLES
2	CUPS SUGAR	1	CUP CHOPPED NUTS
4	EGGS, BEATEN	1	CUP RAISINS

Sift flour with soda, cinnamon and salt. Combine sugar with eggs, oil, sour cream, and vanilla. Beat well. Blend in flour mixture. Fold in apples, nuts and raisins. Pour into 2 greased and floured loaf pans. Bake in a 350 degree oven for 1-1 1/2 hours.

Ina N. Good—Olney Presbyterian Church
Gastonia, North Carolina

APPLE HARVEST LOAVES

4	CUPS DICED APPLES	2	EGGS
2	CUPS GRANULATED SUGAR	1	CUP OIL
3	CUPS OF FLOUR	1	TEASPOON VANILLA EXTRACT
2	TEASPOONS BAKING SODA	1	CUP CHOPPED NUTS
1/2	TEASPOON SALT		

Combine apples and sugar. Let stand for 1 hour. Sift flour, soda, and salt together. Add apple mixture. Stir in eggs, oil, vanilla, and nuts. Pour into 2 greased and floured loaf pans. Bake in a 350 degree oven for 60-70 minutes.

Shirley Waller—First Presbyterian Church
Beaufort, South Carolina

Angel Biscuits

2 1/2	CUPS SELF-RISING FLOUR	1	CUP BUTTERMILK
1	TABLESPOON SUGAR	1	PACKAGE YEAST
1/4	CUP SHORTENING		

Dissolve yeast in small amount of hot water. Add the buttermilk to the yeast. Mix with other already blended ingredients as you would regular biscuits. Refrigerate at least 4 hours. Roll out desired size with hands or rolling pin. Brush with melted butter before baking. Bake for 15 minutes in 375 degree oven. Note: Dough will keep in refrigerator for 1 week.

Margorie Hill—Olney Presbyterian Church
Gastonia, North Carolina

Basque Sheepherder's Bread

Early Basque Sheepherders of Nevada baked this bread in a pit. Before serving, a herder would slash the sign of the Cross on top of the loaf, then serve the first piece to his only companion, his indispensable dog.

3	CUPS HOT WATER	2	TEASPOONS SALT
1/2	CUP BUTTER OR MARGARINE	2	PACKAGES ACTIVE DRY YEAST
1/2	CUP SUGAR	9 1/2	CUPS ALL-PURPOSE FLOUR

In a large bowl, combine hot water, butter, sugar, and salt. Stir until butter melts. Cool until slightly warm. Stir in yeast, cover and set in a warm place until bubbly, (5-15 minutes). Add 5 cups of flour and beat with heavy duty electric mixer or large spoon to form a thick batter. With a spoon, stir enough of the remaining flour (about 3 1/2 cups), to form a stiff dough. Place on floured board and knead about 10 minutes. Add flour as needed to prevent sticking. Turn dough over in a greased bowl. Cover and allow to rise in a warm place until doubled, about 1 1/2 hours. Punch down dough and knead to form smooth ball. Grease the inside and lid of Dutch oven. Place dough in pot and cover with lid. Watching closely, allow to rise in warm place until dough pushes up lid, about 1/2 inch. This should take approximately one hour.

Bake covered in 375 degree oven for 12 minutes. Uncover and bake for additional 30-35 minutes until golden brown and sounds hollow when tapped. Remove and turn out on rack to cool. Yield: 12-18.

St. John's Presbyterian Church
Reno, Nevada

BLUEBERRY MONKEY BREAD

2/3	CUP SUGAR, GRANULATED	2/3	CUP BROWN SUGAR
1	TABLESPOON CINNAMON	1 1/4	STICKS OF MARGARINE
4	PACKAGES BUTTERMILK BISCUITS REFRIGERATED (10 OUNCES EACH)	1	TEASPOON VANILLA
		1	TABLESPOON CINNAMON
1 1/4	CUP BLUEBERRIES	1	CUP BLUEBERRIES

Thoroughly grease a 10 x 4 inch tube pan. Mix 2/3 cup white sugar and 1 tablespoon cinnamon. Cut biscuits in quarters. Roll each piece in sugar mixture. Arrange about 1/4 of the biscuit pieces and 1/4 of the blueberries in an even layer in pan. Place blueberries between biscuit pieces, creating a mosaic effect. Repeat 3 more times with biscuit pieces and berries. Covering blueberries of 1 layer with biscuits in the next layer to avoid a column of berries.

In saucepan, combine brown sugar, margarine, vanilla, cinnamon and the additional cup of blueberries. Bring to a boil, reduce heat. Cook, stirring frequently until sugar is dissolved and margarine is melted. Pour over biscuits in pan. Bake in preheated 350 degree oven for approximately 65 minutes. Lift or turn out onto cake plate. Yield: 8 to 10 servings.

United Presbyterian Church
Paterson, New Jersey

BROCCOLI BREAD

1	LARGE ONION CHOPPED FINE	1	BOX JIFFY CORN MUFFIN MIX
1	STICK OF MARGARINE	1	BOX CHOPPED BROCCOLI, DRAINED
4	EGGS, BEATEN	1	TEASPOON SALT
4	OUNCES COTTAGE CHEESE		

Sauté onion in margarine until clear. Mix with all the other ingredients thoroughly. Pour into a 9 x 13 greased pan. Bake in 400 degree oven for 25 minutes.

Ruby Honeycutt—Paint Gap Presbyterian Church
Burnsville, North Carolina

Johnnie's Quick Cheese Bread

5	CUPS BISCUIT MIX (SMALL BOX)	4	TEASPOONS DRY MUSTARD
1 1/2	CUPS WATER	1	POUND SHARP CHEESE, GRATED
4	EGGS (BEATEN)	5	TABLESPOONS MARGARINE

Empty biscuit mix into large bowl. Stir in water and beat with wooden spoon until smooth. Add remaining ingredients, leaving out 1 cup of cheese and 2 tablespoons of margarine. Mix thoroughly. Pour into 2 greased loaf pans. Sprinkle with remaining cup of cheese and margarine. Bake in preheated 350 degree oven for 40-45 minutes. Cool 10 minutes in pan. Remove from pan and cool on rack. Yield: Two loaves.

Charlotte Vedeler—The Old Presbyterian Meeting House
Alexandria, Virginia

Everett's Six Grain Communion Bread

1	CUP CORN	2	CUPS WHITE FLOUR
1	CUP RYE	1/4	TEASPOON SALT
2	CUPS WHEAT	2	TABLESPOONS CORN OIL
1/2	CUP SOY BEAN	2	TABLESPOONS BROWN SUGAR
1/2	CUP SESAME SEED	1	PACKAGE YEAST
1 1/2	CUPS WARM WATER		

Grind together first 5 ingredients. Combine with remaining ingredients. Knead 10 minutes. Let rise. Knead lightly. Let rise. Bake in 450 degree oven for 10 minutes, lower temperature to 350 degrees and bake an additional 20 minutes. Or, for thick crust, place pan of water in oven and bake in 350 degree oven for 40 minutes. Yield: 1 loaf.

Catherine Brown—Westminster Presbyterian Church
St. Louis, Missouri

Cornbread

2	CUPS CORNMEAL	2	TEASPOONS SALT
1	CUP FLOUR	2	TEASPOONS BAKING POWDER
1/2	CUP SHORTENING, MELTED	1 1/2	TEASPOON BAKING SODA
2 1/2	CUPS BUTTERMILK		

Melt shortening in 10 inch iron skillet. Mix all dry ingredients well. Combine melted shortening and buttermilk. Add together, stirring only until dry ingredients are moistened. Pour into hot, well-greased iron skillet. Bake in 425 degree oven for 25 minutes. Yield: 10-12 servings.

Leona Moldenhauer—Crossnore Presbyterian Church
Crossnore, North Carolina

Corn Spoon Bread

1	CUP PLAIN CORNMEAL	1 1/2	TEASPOONS SALT
1	CUP SOUR CREAM	2	TEASPOONS BAKING POWDER
1	16 OUNCE CAN CREAMED CORN	1/2	CUP CORN OIL
2	EGGS		

Pour corn oil into a black round frying pan or an 8 inch square glass pan. Set in the oven and heat until almost smoking. Mix all other ingredients in a large mixing bowl. Pour the hot oil into the batter. Stir quickly. Pour batter into the hot pan. Bake in a 375 degree oven for 30-40 minutes. Yield: 8-10 slices.

Barbara Dark—First Presbyterian Church
Marion, North Carolina

Mrs. Dodd's Bread

1	CUP CRISCO	2	PACKAGES DRY YEAST
3/4	CUP GRANULATED SUGAR	1 1/4	CUPS WARM WATER
1 1/2	CUPS BRAN	6	CUPS FLOUR
2	TEASPOONS SALT	2	EGGS, BEATEN
1 1/4	CUPS BOILING WATER		

Combine first 5 ingredients and stir well. Allow to stand until warm. Dissolve yeast in warm water and allow to cool somewhat. Add 3 cups of flour to the first mixture along with 2 beaten eggs. Beat well. Begin adding remaining flour and alternate with yeast mixture. Knead. Allow to rise in warm place. Make into 3 loaves. Allow to rise again. Bake in 375 degree oven. Should you form dough into rolls, bake in 400 degree oven for 15 minutes.

Catherine Brown (recipe given by Kitty Kerr)—Westminster Presbyterian Church
St. Louis, Missouri

Easy Bread Sticks

Have on hand bread slices or hot dog buns. Butter both sides of the bread, leaving crusts on. Cut into 4 sticks. Bake on a cookie sheet in a 200 degree oven until bread is brown and toasty. May use seasoning or spices as desired, such as garlic, caraway seed, cinnamon, nutmeg, whatever suits individual taste.

Lydia Massingill—First Presbyterian Church
Fairfax, Missouri

Hobo Bread

1	CUP RAISINS	3	CUPS FLOUR
1	CUP CHOPPED DATES	2	TEASPOONS SODA
1 3/4	CUPS WATER	1	TEASPOON CINNAMON
1/4	CUP MOLASSES	1	TEASPOON ALLSPICE
2	TABLESPOONS OIL	1/2	TEASPOON GINGER
1	TEASPOON SALT	2	BEATEN EGGS
1	TEASPOON VANILLA	1 1/4	CUPS GRANULATED SUGAR
1/2	TEASPOON LEMON PEEL	1	CUP CHOPPED NUTS

In a saucepan, combine raisins, dates, water and molasses. Bring to a boil and cook for one minute. Allow to cool. Add oil, salt, vanilla and lemon peel to mixture. In a large bowl, sift together flour, soda, cinnamon, allspice and ginger. Add 2 beaten eggs and sugar to dry mixture. Add liquid mixture to dry ingredients and stir well. Fold in chopped nuts. Pour into 3 coffee cans or 6 soup cans. Bake in a 350 degree oven for 1 hour. Allow to cool for 10 minutes. Remove from cans. Serve with warm butter or cream cheese.

Imogene Holmes—Lillington Presbyterian Church
Lillington, North Carolina

Houston's Bread

Combine the night before:

2	CUPS FLOUR	1/2	CUP SUGAR
2	CUPS WARM WATER	1/2	CUP OIL
1	PACKAGE DRY YEAST		FLOUR
1	TEASPOON SALT		

Combine first 4 ingredients. Cover with foil and leave at room temperature overnight. Next morning, add 1/2 cup sugar and 1/2 cup oil and enough flour to make a fairly stiff dough. Knead 10 minutes. Shape into 2 loaves or 3 small loaves. Place into greased pans and let rise for 1 1/2 hours. Bake in 350 degree oven for 40-45 minutes. Brush tops while warm with melted butter.

For whole wheat bread, substitute 1/2 the white flour for wheat flour and use additional 1/2 package of yeast. (Freezes well.)

Irene Grant—East Ridge Presbyterian Church
Chattanooga, Tennessee

LEMON BREAD

1	CUP SUGAR	2	TEASPOONS BAKING POWDER
6	TABLESPOONS MARGARINE OR BUTTER	1/8	TEASPOON SALT
1/2	CUP MILK	1	TABLESPOON LEMON JUICE
2	EGGS	1	TABLESPOON LEMON ZEST
1 1/2	CUPS FLOUR		

Mix all ingredients in order given. Bake in metal loaf pan for 1 hour in a 350 degree oven, or in glass loaf pan for 1 hour in 325 degree oven. Boil 1/2 cup granulated sugar and 1/4 cup lemon juice. Pour glaze over cooled bread/cake. Keeps well in freezer.

Kathryn Williams—Menlo Park Presbyterian Church
Menlo Park, California

CHINESE PEPPER BREAD

1	PACKAGE DRY YEAST	2	TABLESPOONS SUGAR
1/4	CUP HOTTEST TAP WATER	1	TEASPOON SALT
1	CUP SOUR CREAM	1/4	TEASPOON SODA
1	CUP CHEDDAR CHEESE, GRATED	1/2	TEASPOON BLACK PEPPER
2 1/3	CUPS PLAIN FLOUR		

In a large mixing bowl dissolve yeast in the hot water, add 1 1/3 cups flour, sugar, salt, soda, sour cream and egg. With electric mixer, blend for 30 seconds at low speed setting. Then, beat for 2 minutes at the high speed setting. Stir in remaining flour, cheese and pepper. Mix well with a spoon. Add more flour if necessary for right consistency. Spray 2 one pound coffee cans with Pam, divide the dough between the two cans, put lids on cans and let the dough rise in a warm place for 50 minutes. remove lids, and bake in 350 degree oven for 40 minutes or until brown. Remove from cans immediately. Cool only slightly before slicing.

Mary Logan—First Presbyterian Church
Beaufort, South Carolina

Pistachio Bread

1	PACKAGE DUNCAN HINES YELLOW CAKE MIX	1	CUP SOUR CREAM
		1/4	CUP OIL
1	PACKAGE INSTANT PISTACHIO PUDDING	1/8	CUP WATER
4	EGGS		

Combine all ingredients and mix well with a spoon. Use 2 regular loaf pans or 4 small ones. Grease well and coat with a cinnamon/sugar mixture. Divide mixture evenly between pans. Top with additional cinnamon/sugar mixture. Bake in 350 degree oven for 45 minutes. When cool, wrap in foil and refrigerate. this enhances the flavor. Freezes well!

Florence Daugherty—First Presbyterian Church
Beaufort, South Carolina

Pumpkin Bread

1	CUP SUGAR	1	TEASPOON SALT
1/2	CUP OIL	1/2	TEASPOON GROUND CLOVES
2	EGGS, BEATEN	1	TEASPOON NUTMEG
1	CUP PUMPKIN	1	TEASPOON ALLSPICE
1 3/4	CUPS FLOUR	1/3	CUP RAISINS
1/4	TEASPOON BAKING POWDER	1/3	CUP WATER
1	TEASPOON SODA		

Mix ingredients in order given. Bake in greased and floured bread pan in 350 degree oven for one hour.

Jean Knight—Fairview Presbyterian Church
North Augusta, South Carolina

Redeemer Bread

This bread has been served for communion services and thus named Redeemer Bread. The recipe originated at the First Presbyterian Church in Victoria, Texas.

3/4	CUP GRANULATED SUGAR	2	PACKAGES DRY YEAST
3/4	CUP VEGETABLE OIL	2	EGGS, BEATEN
1	CUP ALL-BRAN	1/2	CUP WARM WATER
1	TABLESPOON SALT		
2	CUPS BOILING WATER		

Mix first 5 ingredients and allow to cool. Dissolve yeast in warm water and add beaten eggs. Combine with cooled first mixture. Stir in 6 1/2 cups flour (may use 2 cups whole wheat, if desired).

Knead on floured board and place into a greased bowl. Allow to rise around 1 1/2 hours, until double in bulk. Divide into 3 parts and place into 3 greased loaf pans. Allow to rise about 45 minutes. Bake in a preheated 325 degree oven for 25-30 minutes. Yield: 3 loaves.

Ann Taylor—University Presbyterian Church
San Antonio, Texas

IRISH SODA BREAD

"Better than any bakery and even some Irish women."

6 1/2 CUPS FLOUR	1 PINT SOUR CREAM
1 CUP SUGAR	3 CUPS BUTTERMILK
2 TABLESPOONS SALT	2 EGGS, SLIGHTLY BEATEN
1 TEASPOON BAKING SODA	3 CUPS RAISINS
2 TABLESPOONS BAKING POWDER	1/2 CUP CARAWAY SEEDS

Mix all ingredients together in a deep bowl. Pour into two greased and floured loaf pans. Make a long indentation in center to allow air to escape as loaves bake. Bake in a 400 degree oven for 1 hour. Cool on side of pan. Yields: 2 loaves.

Mrs. Thomas Cahillane—South Salem Presbyterian Church
South Salem, New York

OATMEAL BREAD

1 CUP THREE MINUTE OATMEAL	1 CUP WHITE GRANULATED SUGAR
1 STICK OF MARGARINE	1 1/2 CUPS FLOUR
3/4 CUP RAISINS	1 TEASPOON SALT
1 1/4 CUPS BOILING WATER	1 TEASPOON SODA
2 EGGS	1 TEASPOON NUTMEG
1 CUP DARK BROWN SUGAR	1 TEASPOON CINNAMON

Pour boiling water over first 3 ingredients. Beat together eggs and both sugars and add to mixture. Sift together flour, soda and spices. Add all ingredients together and mix well. Pour into two loaf pans and bake in a 325 degree oven for 1 hour, perhaps even 5 minutes more. Yields: 3 loaves. Freezes well.

Peggy B. Miller—First Presbyterian Church
Savannah, Georgia

Sourdough Bread Starter

1 PACKAGE DRY YEAST	3 TABLESPOONS SUGAR
1/2 CUP WARM WATER (105°–115°)	1 TEASPOON SALT
2 CUPS ALL-PURPOSE FLOUR	2 CUPS WARM WATER (105°–115°)

Dissolve yeast in 1/2 cup warm water—allow to stand for 5 minutes. Combine flour, sugar, and salt in medium size glass bowl and stir well. Gradually stir in 2 cups warm water. Add yeast mixture and stir well.

Cover loosely with plastic wrap or cheesecloth and allow to set in a warm place (85 degrees), for 72 hours, stirring 2-3 times daily. Place fermented mixture in refrigerator and stir once daily. Use within 11 days.

TO USE: Remove from refrigerator and allow to stand at room temperature at least 1 hour

Stir starter well and measure amount needed for recipe. Replenish starter with starter food and return to refrigerator.

Starter Food

1/2 CUP SUGAR	1 CUP MILK
1 CUP ALL-PURPOSE FLOUR	

Sourdough Bread

2 PACKAGES DRY YEAST	1/4 CUP GRANULATED SUGAR
1 1/4 CUPS WARM WATER	2 TEASPOONS SALT
1 CUP SOURDOUGH STARTER	2 EGGS, BEATEN
1/4 CUP VEGETABLE OIL	6 CUPS BREAD FLOUR

Dissolve yeast in warm water in a large non-metal bowl. Allow to stand 5 minutes. Stir in Sourdough Starter, 1/4 cup oil, sugar, salt, eggs, and 3 cups flour. Gradually stir in enough remaining flour to make soft dough.

Turn dough onto floured surface and knead until smooth and elastic (8-10 minutes). Place in well-greased bowl, turning to grease top. Cover and let rise in warm place until doubled in bulk. Punch down dough and divide in half. Place into 2 prepared pans. May use non-stick pans, sprayed with Pam or grease standard bread loaf pans. Cover and allow to rise until double, about 1 hour. Bake in 375 degree oven for 30-35 minutes until loaves sound hollow when tapped. Remove loaves from pans immediately and brush with melted butter. (Do not freeze.)

Faye McGowan—First Presbyterian Church
Beaufort, South Carolina

Hearty Whole Wheat Bread

3 1/2	CUPS WHOLE WHEAT FLOUR	1/4	CUP HONEY
1/2	CUP WHEAT BRAN	3 1/4	CUPS WARM WATER (110°)
2	ENVELOPES DRY YEAST	4 1/2	CUPS WHITE FLOUR
1/2	CUP INSTANT DRY MILK		

Place flour, bran, yeast. and milk in a bowl and mix thoroughly. Mix honey and water together. Pour honey-water into dry ingredients all at once. Stir well to mix. Add enough white unbleached flour and stir until too stiff to handle with spoon. Turn out onto a floured surface and knead, adding additional white unbleached flour. Knead 10-15 minutes until dough is firm. Leave in a warm place to rise until double in bulk, about 1 hour. Punch down, knead for 5 minutes more. Cut dough in half. Shape and place into 5" x 9" bread pans. Allow to rise again until double in bulk before baking. Bake immediately in a 375 degree oven for 30-35 minutes.

John W. Meyers, Trustee
Stoney Creek Foundation

Whole Wheat Quick Bread

1	EGG, BEATEN	1	TEASPOON BAKING SODA
2	CUPS BUTTERMILK	2	TEASPOONS BAKING POWDER
1 1/2	TABLESPOONS MELTED BUTTER	1/2	TEASPOON SALT
2	CUPS WHOLE WHEAT FLOUR	1/2	CUP SHELLED WALNUTS
3	TABLESPOONS MOLASSES OR HONEY	1/2	CUP RAISINS

Combine beaten egg with buttermilk, molasses or honey and butter. Mix all the dry ingredients together well. Add buttermilk mixture. Stir in walnuts and raisins. Spoon into greased loaf pan (9x5x3 inches) or 2 smaller pans, (5x3x2 inches). Bake in preheated 400 degree oven for 1 hour.

Fairfax Presbyterian Church, Fairfax, Virginia

MUFFINS

English Muffins

1	YEAST CAKE	1	TEASPOON SALT
	FLOUR TO MAKE A RATHER STIFF BATTER	1	PINT OF MILK

Mix together and allow to rise for 10 hours. When ready to bake, stir in two eggs and 1 tablespoon melted butter. Bake on griddle in rings, turning like pancakes.

Warm Springs Presbyterian Church
Warm Springs, Virginia

Pat's Fresh Apple Loaf/Muffins

"Great for breakfast, tailgate, even dessert or after school snacks."

3	CUPS ALL-PURPOSE FLOUR	1	CUP CHOPPED NUTS (WALNUTS/PECANS)
2 1/2	CUPS SUGAR	2	TEASPOON VANILLA
1	TEASPOON SODA	2	EGGS
1	TEASPOON CINNAMON	1 1/4	CUPS WESSON OIL
1	TEASPOON APPLE PIE SPICE	3	CUPS GRATED AND PEELED APPLES
1/2	TEASPOON SALT		(TART, SUCH AS GRANNY SMITH)

Mix all together thoroughly. Pour into paper muffin cups or tins. Bake in a 350 degree oven for 20-25 minutes. Cool on racks. May be iced with recipe below but just as delicious without. Yield: 24 muffins or 1 small loaf.

Icing:

1	CUP BROWN SUGAR	1	TEASPOON VANILLA
1/2	CUP MARGARINE	1/4	CUP EVAPORATED MILK

Boil all ingredients to soft ball stage, about 5 minutes. Spread on muffins and sprinkle shredded coconut and more nuts on top. This freezes well.

Charlotte C. Frierson (Mrs. Henry F.)—First Presbyterian Church
Orangeburg, South Carolina

Corny Mini-Muffins

3/4	CUP YELLOW CORNMEAL	1/4	TEASPOON SALT
3/4	CUP ALL-PURPOSE FLOUR	1	EGG, LIGHTLY BEATEN
2	TABLESPOONS SUGAR	1	CUP BUTTERMILK
1 1/2	TEASPOONS BAKING POWDER	1/4	CUP CORN OR LIGHT OIL
1/2	TEASPOON BAKING SODA	3/4	CUP CANNED CORN, DRAINED

In a medium bowl, combine cornmeal, flour, sugar, baking powder, baking soda and salt. Stir until blended. Make a well in center. In small bowl, beat together egg, buttermilk and oil. Pour mixture into well in the dry ingredients. Add drained canned corn and stir to blend. Do not over mix. Lumps should remain. Fill greased mini-muffin tins about 3/4 full with heaping teaspoons of batter. Bake in 425 degree oven until lightly browned, about 15 minutes. Serve warm or at room temperature. Yield: 3 dozen. Freezes well.

Irene Grant—East Ridge Presbyterian Church
Chattanooga, Tennessee

COUNTRY MUFFINS

2	CUPS WHOLE WHEAT FLOUR	1/2	CUP OIL
1	TEASPOON BAKING SODA	1/2	CUP HONEY
1	TEASPOON BAKING POWDER	1/2	CUP WATER
2	EGGS		

Mix all ingredients, adding enough water to make a good consistency. Bake in greased and floured muffin tins in a 350 degree oven for 15 minutes.

Henri Ann Logan—First Presbyterian Church
Beaufort, South Carolina

QUICK HOLIDAY MUFFINS

1	EGG, SLIGHTLY BEATEN	2	TABLESPOONS SUGAR
1	CUP MILK	1	CUP CHOPPED CANDIED MIXED FRUIT
2	CUPS BISQUICK		

Add sugar to Bisquick. Stir in egg and milk mixture. Fold in fruit. Use greased muffin tins. Bake in 400 degree oven for 20 minutes. Yield: 1 dozen. Freezes well.

Arlene Fawns—First Presbyterian Church
Blackwood, New Jersey

DELICIOUS LOW FAT MUFFINS

1	EGG, BEATEN	1	CUP QUICK OATS
3/4	CUP RAISINS	1/3	CUP SUGAR (GRANULATED)
1	CHOPPED APPLE	3	TEASPOONS BAKING POWDER
1/2	CUP CANOLA OIL	1	TEASPOON SALT
1	CUP FLOUR	1	TEASPOON ALLSPICE OR NUTMEG
3/4	CUP SKIM MILK	2	TEASPOONS CINNAMON

Mix all ingredients just to moisten. Pour into greased muffin tins until 3/4 full. Bake in 400 degree oven for 15-20 minutes. Serve piping hot or cool. Freezes well.

Elizabeth Caldwell (Mrs. James D.)—First Presbyterian Church
Beaufort, South Carolina

Party Muffins

1	STICK OLEO MARGARINE	2	CUPS BISQUICK
1	8 OUNCE CARTON SOUR CREAM		

Mix margarine and sour cream well. Add the Bisquick and mix thoroughly. Use small muffin tins and fill with a teaspoon. Bake in a 400 degree oven until brown.

Edmee Boyd—Hampton Presbyterian Church
Hampton, South Carolina

Easy Breakfast Ring

1/2	CUP PECANS OR WALNUTS	1	3 1/2 OUNCE PACKAGE VANILLA PUDDING MIX
1	PACKAGE RICH'S FROZEN ROLL DOUGH		(NOT INSTANT)
3/4	CUP BROWN SUGAR	6	TABLESPOONS MELTED MARGARINE
1	TEASPOON CINNAMON		

Sprinkle bottom of greased bundt pan with chopped nuts. Line frozen rolls closely together in pan. Mix sugar, pudding, and cinnamon together and sprinkle over rolls. Pour butter or margarine over all. Cover with foil (or a towel) and let stand overnight. Next morning, bake 30 minutes in a 350 degree oven. Invert onto plate so that the caramel drizzles over it. Freezes well.

Audrey Bickenbach—First Presbyterian Church
Beaufort, South Carolina

Orange Buttermilk Scones

3	CUPS ALL-PURPOSE FLOUR	2	TEASPOONS GRATED ORANGE PEEL
3/4	CUP GRANULATED SUGAR	1/2	CUP BUTTER OR MARGARINE
1/2	TEASPOON BAKING POWDER	3/4	CUP BUTTERMILK
1	TEASPOON BAKING SODA	3/4	CUP CURRANTS OR RAISINS

In a large bowl, stir together flour, sugar, baking soda, baking powder and orange peel. With pastry blender or fingers, work in butter until fine crumbs form. Stir in raisins or currants. Add buttermilk and mix until evenly moistened. Knead 10 turns on a floured board. Pat into a 9 inch round and place into a greased 9 inch round cake pan. Sprinkle lightly with sugar and cinnamon. Bake in a 400 degree oven for 40 minutes. Yield: 8 servings.

St. John's Presbyterian Church, Reno, Nevada

COFFEE CAKE

1/2	CUP SHORTENING	1/2	PINT (8 OUNCES) SOUR CREAM
3/4	CUP SUGAR	6	TABLESPOONS BUTTER
1	TEASPOON VANILLA	1	CUP FIRMLY PACKED BROWN SUGAR
3	EGGS	2	TEASPOONS CINNAMON
2	CUPS SIFTED FLOUR	1	CUP CHOPPED NUTS
1	TEASPOON BAKING POWDER		
1	TEASPOON BAKING SODA		

Cream shortening, sugar, and vanilla. Add eggs one at a time. Beat well after each addition. Sift flour, baking powder, and baking soda together. Add to creamed mixture, alternately with sour cream. Blend after each addition. Spread half of batter in 10 inch tube pan that has been greased and lined on bottom with waxed paper. Cream butter, brown sugar and cinnamon together. Add nuts and mix well. Dot butter in pan evenly with half of the nut mixture. Cover with remaining batter. Dot with remaining mixture. Bake in a 350 degree oven for about 50 minutes. Cool 10 minutes in pan before removing.

Winkie Keith (Coral's mother)—First Presbyterian Church
New Vernon, New Jersey

❖ ROLLS ❖

DIFFERENT ANGEL ROLLS

1	PACKAGE DRY YEAST	2	TABLESPOONS SUGAR
1/2	CUP WARM WATER	1	TEASPOON SALT
2 1/2–3	CUPS ALL PURPOSE FLOUR	1/2	CUP VEGETABLE OIL
1	TEASPOON BAKING POWDER	1	CUP BUTTERMILK
1/2	TEASPOON BAKING SODA		

Dissolve yeast in warm water. Let stand for 5 minutes. Mix flour, baking powder, soda, sugar, and salt in large bowl. Make a well in center of mixture. Combine oil, buttermilk, and yeast mixture; add to dry ingredients. Stir until moist (dough will be slightly sticky). Roll dough to 1/2 inch thickness on a lightly floured board. Cut with 2 1/2 inch biscuit cutter. Place rolls on an ungreased baking sheet. Bake in a 350 degree oven for 16 minutes or until golden. Yield: 2 dozen rolls.

Irene Grant—East Ridge Presbyterian Church
Chattanooga, Tennessee

Yeast Rolls I

1	PACKAGE DRY YEAST	1	TEASPOON SALT
3/4	CUP SCALDED MILK	1/4	CUP GRANULATED SUGAR
1/3	CUP SHORTENING	1	EGG
1/2	CUP COOKED AND MASHED POTATOES		PLAIN FLOUR

Place sugar, shortening and salt into a large bowl. Add the warm mashed potatoes and mix well. Add the egg to the warm milk and mix again. Add the yeast to 2 cups of the flour and gradually add to the mixture. Beat well as you add. Add enough flour to knead. Allow to rise until double in bulk. Mash down and place in refrigerator until needed. (Or allow to rise and bake the same day.) Bake in a 400 degree oven for 10 minutes. Brush tops of rolls after baking with melted butter if desired. Yield: about 2 dozen. Freezes well.

Miriam A. Broome—First Presbyterian Church
Marion, North Carolina

Yeast Rolls II

"This recipe rises overnight in the refrigerator."

1/2	CUP SHORTENING	1/2	CUP WATER
1	CUP SUGAR	1	EGG
1/2	CUP BOILING WATER	3	CUPS PRESIFTED FLOUR
1/2	PACKAGE DRY YEAST	1	TEASPOON SALT

Cream shortening with sugar. Slowly add boiling water. Dissolve yeast in 1/2 cup water and add to mixture. Beat egg well and stir in flour and salt. Gradually add this to yeast mixture and mix well. Cover and refrigerate overnight.

About 2 hours before use, place 3 small dough balls into each cup of well-greased muffin tins. Fill just below top of each section. Allow to rise about 2 hours before baking. Bake in a preheated oven at 425 degrees for about 8-10 minutes. Check to see when browned. Makes bout 2 dozen rolls, depending on section sizes.

Kitty Roberts (Fran Barnard's sister)—First Presbyterian Church
Spartanburg, South Carolina

Chapter Three

Cakes

CAKES

APPLE CAKE (OR MUFFINS)

"I like to pour the sauce on the cake, hot from the oven and serve warm with Cool Whip."

2	CUPS FLOUR	1	TEASPOON CINNAMON
2	CUPS SUGAR	1 1/2	CUPS NUTS, CHOPPED
3	CUPS CHOPPED APPLES	1/2	TEASPOON NUTMEG (OPTIONAL)
1	CUP OIL	1/4	TEASPOON CLOVES (OPTIONAL)
1 1/2	TEASPOONS BAKING SODA	1	TEASPOON VANILLA
2	EGGS	1	TEASPOON SALT

Sauce:

1/2	CUP BUTTER	1/2	CUP BROWN SUGAR
1/2	CUP HALF-AND-HALF	1	TEASPOON VANILLA
1/2	CUP SUGAR		

Blend apples with sugar. Add the remaining ingredients. Bake in a 350 degree oven for 45 minutes, for muffins, 25 minutes, or until a toothpick comes out clean. Mix together sauce ingredients and boil 2 minutes. Serve over cake with Cool Whip.

Sandra Stoehr—Ray Memorial Presbyterian Church
Monroe, Georgia

Fresh Apple Cake

1	CUP VEGETABLE OIL	1	TEASPOON SALT
2	CUPS SUGAR	1	TEASPOON SODA
3	EGGS	2	TEASPOONS BAKING POWDER
2 1/2	CUPS PLAIN FLOUR	4	CUPS CHOPPED APPLES (GRANNY SMITH)

Grease 9 X 13" pan. Beat oil and sugar with mixer until thick. Add eggs one at a time and beat well. Sift together flour, salt, soda and baking powder. Add to egg mixture gradually and beat well. (Batter will be very thick.) Stir in apples. Pour into greased pan and bake 40 to 50 minutes. Pour topping over hot cake.

Topping:

1/2	CUP MARGARINE	1	CUP FIRMLY PACKED BROWN SUGAR
1	TEASPOON VANILLA	1/2	CUP MILK

Combine and cook until thick, about 2 1/2–3 minutes.

Susan Mills—Guilford Park Presbyterian Church
Greensboro, North Carolina

Kay's Apple Cake

1 3/4	CUPS SUGAR	1	TEASPOON SALT
3	EGGS	1	TEASPOON CINNAMON
1	TEASPOON VANILLA	1	TEASPOON BAKING POWDER
1	CUP OIL	3	CUPS TART MEDIUM APPLES, CHOPPED
2	CUPS FLOUR	1/2	CUP NUTS (OPTIONAL)

Beat sugar, eggs, vanilla, and oil. Add sifted dry ingredients. Mix in apples and nuts. In a greased 9x13" pan, bake in a 350 degree oven for 40 minutes.

Mrs. K. F. Forsberg—South Salem Presbyterian Church
South Salem, New York

Special Apple Coffee Cake

2	CUPS FLOUR	2	EGGS
1	TEASPOON SODA	2/3	CUP OIL
1/2	TEASPOON BAKING POWDER	1	TEASPOON VANILLA
1	CUP SUGAR	1	CAN COMSTOCK PIE FILLING
1	TEASPOON SALT	2/3	CUP CHOPPED PECANS

Topping:

1	CUP SUGAR	1/2	CUP SOUR CREAM
1/2	TEASPOON BAKING SODA		

Mix flour, soda, baking powder, sugar and salt. Beat and add the eggs and oil, and vanilla. Add the flour mixture and pecans. Mix well and fold in the pie filling. Pour into 9x13" pan and bake in a 350 degree oven for 40-45 minutes. Cook topping ingredients over low heat to a boil. Pour topping over warm cake and sprinkle with more pecans.

Alice Arntsen—Menlo Park Presbyterian Church
Menlo Park, California

NO-SUGAR BANANA CAKE

2	CUPS GROUND OATMEAL	2	RIPE BANANAS
1/2	CUP RAISINS	1/2	CUP OIL
1/2	CUP CHOPPED DATES		PINCH SODA
1	TEASPOON BAKING SODA	1/2	CUP UNSWEETENED APPLESAUCE
1	TEASPOON VANILLA		

Mash bananas and mix well with cooking oil and pinch of soda. Stir into dry ingredients. Add 1/2 cup unsweetened applesauce and vanilla. Bake in a 325 degree oven for 25-30 minutes. Use a 9x12" Pyrex pan. Do not grease or flour pan.

Monica McGregor—Fort Hill Presbyterian Church
Clemson, South Carolina

BELGIAN LOAF

1	STICK MARGARINE	3/4	CUP MILK
3/4	CUP SUGAR	1	MEDIUM EGG
3/4	CUP SULTANAS (GOLDEN RAISINS)	1 1/2	CUPS SELF-RISING FLOUR

Mix together the margarine, sugar, sultanas and milk, bring to a boil. Simmer three minutes, allow to cool. Add the egg, flour and mix well. Pour into loaf pan and bake 1 hour in a 400 degree oven.

Mrs. L. Macphail—Perth North Church
Perth, Scotland

CHUKKA'S BLUEBERRY CAKE

1	BOX (2 LAYER) WHITE CAKE MIX	1	CAN BLUEBERRY PIE FILLING
1/4	POUND MARGARINE		

Spray a 9x13" pan with cooking spray. Spread the pie filling evenly in the pan. Sprinkle the dry cake mix evenly over the pie filling. Dot evenly with the margarine. Bake in a 350 degree oven for 30-40 minutes or until golden.

Pam Thompson—Faith Presbyterian Church
Harrisburg, Pennsylvania

All-Bran Cake

1	CUP ALL-BRAN	1	CUP MIXED DRIED FRUIT
1	CUP BROWN SUGAR	1	CUP SELF-RISING FLOUR
1	CUP MILK	1	EGG, BEATEN

Mix bran, sugar, milk and fruit, let stand overnight. Mix in the flour and beaten egg, pour into a 6 cup loaf pan and bake in a 325 degree oven for 1 1/4 hours. Cool on wire rack.

Letchworth Free Church
Letchworth, England

Bride's Cake

1	POUND OF LOVE	1	OUNCE POUNDED WIT
1/2	POUND OF BUTTER OF YOUTH	1	OUNCE OF DRY HUMOR
1/2	POUND GOOD LOOKS	2	TABLESPOONS OF SWEET ARGUMENT
1	POUND SWEET TEMPER	1	PINT OF RIPPLING LAUGHTER
1/2	POUND BLUNDER OF FAULTS	1 1/2	WINE-GLASSES OF COMMON SENSE.
1	POUND SELF-FORGETFULNESS		

Mix the love, looks and sweet temper into a well furnished house, beat the butter to a cream, mix these ingredients well together with the blunder of faults and self-forgetfulness, stir the pounded wit and dry humor with the sweet argument, then add it to the above. Pour in gently the rippling laughter and common sense, and thoroughly mix. Bake well for ever.

This, of course, is not a recipe as such, but someone about to get married might like this. Also from Gm's very old and tattered cookbook.

Charlotte Vedeler—The Old Presbyterian Meeting House
Alexandria, Virginia

Carrot Cake

2 1/2	CUPS UNSIFTED WHOLE WHEAT FLOUR	1	CUP SUGAR
1	TEASPOON BAKING POWDER	1	CUP BROWN SUGAR
1	TEASPOON BAKING SODA	1	CUP VEGETABLE OIL
1 1/2	TEASPOONS CINNAMON	2 1/2	CUPS COARSELY SHREDDED CARROTS
1 1/2	TEASPOONS NUTMEG	1	CUP RAISINS
4	EGGS	1	CUP COARSELY CHOPPED NUTS

Combine dry ingredients. Mix thoroughly with a fork. Beat eggs with sugar in large bowl until light and fluffy. Gradually beat in oil until mixture is thoroughly combined. Add dry ingredients, stirring until well blended. Stir in carrots, raisins and nuts. Pour into a well-greased 9 inch tube pan. Bake in a 350 degree oven for 1 hour or until top springs back. Cool 10 minutes, remove and finish cooling. This cake is very good with orange or lemon butter cream frosting, and it freezes well.

Eunice M. Rogers—Christ Presbyterian Church
Camp Hill, Pennsylvania

PINK MOUNTAIN CHERRY CAKE

1 1/2	STICKS MARGARINE	1/2	TEASPOON LEMON FLAVORING
1	BOX WHITE CAKE MIX WITH PUDDING	1	21 OUNCE CAN CHERRY PIE FILLING
4	EGGS		

Glaze:

| 1 | TABLESPOON MARGARINE | 1/4 | TEASPOON LEMON EXTRACT |
| 2 | TEASPOONS WATER | 1 1/4 | CUP POWDERED SUGAR |

Melt margarine, pour into cake mix and stir. Add eggs and extract. Stir in pie filling and blend well. Pour into 10 inch tube pan. Bake in a 350 degree oven for 50 minutes. Cool in pan and turn out. Drizzle glaze over top.

Catherine P. Spangler—John Knox Presbyterian Church
Shelby, North Carolina

CHOCOLATE CAKE

1/2	CUP CASTER SUGAR (GRANULATED)	2	EGGS
3/4	STICK MARGARINE	1/4	CUP COCOA
1	CUP SELF-RISING FLOUR	2	TABLESPOONS HOT WATER

Beat margarine and sugar, add egg yolks, then add chocolate mixed with hot water. Sift in flour, fold in the stiffly beaten egg whites. Turn into a greased 8" cake pan and bake in a 350 degree oven for 40 minutes.

Margery Fennell—The Bethel Reformed Church
Chester-le-Street, England

Chocolate Chocolate Chip Cake

"True chocolate lovers died-and-gone-to-heaven cake."

1	PACKAGE DEVIL'S FOOD CAKE MIX	4	EGGS, BEATEN
1	(6 OUNCE) BOX INSTANT CHOCOLATE PUDDING MIX	1/2	CUP WARM WATER
		1	CUP SOUR CREAM
1	(12 OUNCE) BAG SEMI-SWEET CHOCOLATE CHIPS	1	CUP VEGETABLE OIL

Mix all together. Add chocolate chips. Pour into a buttered bundt cake pan. Bake in a 350 degree oven for about 1 hour. Do not over bake. Cool 5 minutes and turn out onto a plate. Sprinkle with powdered sugar or drizzle with icing. Yield: 15 servings.

Virginia Henderson—The Presbyterian Church of Cadiz
Cadiz, Ohio

Chocolate Eclair Cake

1	LARGE BOX (OR 2 SMALL) INSTANT VANILLA PUDDING		BOX GRAHAM CRACKERS
		8	OUNCES COOL WHIP
3	CUPS MILK		

Chocolate icing:

1 1/2	CUPS SUGAR	1/2	STICK BUTTER OR MARGARINE
1/2	CUP COCOA	1	TEASPOON VANILLA
1/4	CUP MILK	1	DASH SALT

Mix icing ingredients together. Cook, stirring constantly, until mixture thickens to consistency of heavy chocolate syrup. Remove from stove and add butter and vanilla. Mix well; cool. Set aside. Combine pudding mix with three cups of milk and beat until thick (approximately 3 minutes). Fold in the Cool Whip. Line the bottom of a 9 x 13" baking pan or dish with whole graham crackers. Spoon 1/2 pudding mixture on top; add another layer of whole graham crackers, and another layer of pudding mixture until used up. Pour icing over cake. Refrigerate, preferably overnight. Yield: 12 servings.

Louise Robinson—United Presbyterian Church, Lenoir, North Carolina
Similar recipe from: Peachtree Presbyterian Church, Atlanta, Georgia

Chocolate Shortcake

- 2 CUPS FLOUR
- 2 CUPS SUGAR
- 1 STICK MARGARINE
- 4 TABLESPOONS COCOA
- 1 CUP WATER
- 1/2 CUP CRISCO
- 1/2 CUP BUTTERMILK
- 2 UNBEATEN EGGS
- 1 TEASPOON SODA
- 1 TEASPOON VANILLA
- 1/2 TEASPOON SALT

Mix flour and sugar. Place margarine, cocoa, water, and Crisco in a pan and let come to a boil. Pour over dry ingredients. Add buttermilk, eggs, soda, vanilla and salt. Mix well. Grease and flour an 11 x 15" sheetcake pan. Pour batter into pan. Bake in a 350 degree oven for 25 to 30 minutes. Cool 5 minutes and top with icing.

Icing:

- 1 STICK MARGARINE
- 4 TABLESPOONS COCOA
- 6 TABLESPOONS MILK OR COFFEE
- 1 BOX CONFRCTIONER'S SUGAR
- 3/4 CUP CHOPPED PECANS
- 1 TEASPOON VANILLA

Bring margarine, cocoa, and milk/coffee to a boil. Add sugar and pecans and vanilla. Spread over cake.

Fran Barnard—First Presbyterian Church
Beaufort, South Carolina

Chocolate Surprise Bundt Cake

- 1/2 CUP DRIED APRICOTS, CHOPPED
- 1/2 CUP MINI CHOCOLATE CHIPS
- 1/2 CUP CHOPPED WALNUTS
- 1 TABLESPOON CORNSTARCH
- 1 BOX DUNCAN HINES DEVIL'S FOOD CAKE MIX
- 2 EGGS
- 1 1/2 CUPS LOW FAT BUTTERMILK
- POWDERED SUGAR

Lightly grease and flour a 12-cup bundt pan or angel food cake pan. Combine apricots, chocolate chips, walnuts, and cornstarch in a small bowl; stir to coat and set aside. Combine remaining ingredients in a large bowl; mix with electric mixer at slow speed setting until blended. Fold in apricot mixture until combined mixture is no longer white in color. Pour into pan and bake in a (preheated) 350 degree oven for 40-50 minutes. Cool for 25 minutes, then turn out on a rack and cool completely. Sprinkle top with powdered sugar before serving. Yield: 16 servings.

Patricia T. Kirkpatrick—Alamo Heights Presbyterian Church
San Antonio, Texas

Chocolate Cake Icing

2	CUPS SUGAR	1	STICK BUTTER OR MARGARINE
1/2	CUP MILK	1	TEASPOON VANILLA
1/2	CUP COCOA		

Put all ingredients together in large pan and mix well. Bring to boil and boil for 2 minutes. Let cool, then beat until of spreading consistency.

Hazel Sparks—Fort Hill Presbyterian Church
Clemson, South Carolina

Date and Walnut Cake

1/2	CUP BROWN SUGAR	4	OUNCES DATES, CHOPPED
1	STICK MARGARINE	1	EGG, LARGE, BEATEN
2	CUPS SELF-RISING FLOUR	5	TABLESPOONS MILK
	PINCH OF SALT	1/2	CUP WALNUTS, CHOPPED

Cream margarine and sugar. Add egg and milk. Add other ingredients, mix well. Pour into a greased 7" cake pan. Bake 1 1/2 hours in a 325 degree oven.

Letchworth Free Church, Letchworth, England

Earthquake Cake

1 1/2	CUPS CHOPPED PECANS	1	BOX POWDERED SUGAR
1	BOX GERMAN CHOCOLATE CAKE MIX	1	3 OUNCE CAN COCONUT
1	8 OUNCE PACKAGE CREAM CHEESE	1	STICK OLEO

Prepare cake mix according to directions. Sprinkle bottom of 9x13" greased baking pan with chopped pecans. Sprinkle coconut over. Pour prepared cake mix over this. Melt oleo and cream cheese together; add powdered sugar and mix well. Pour mixture over cake batter. Bake in a 350 degree oven for 45 minutes. Remove from oven, cool, cut into squares. Yield: 24 squares.

Faye Hannah—Hodges Presbyterian Church
Hodges, South Carolina

Fruit Cocktail Cake

1 1/2	CUP SUGAR	1/2	TEASPOON SALT
2	EGGS	2	TEASPOONS SODA
1/2	CUP OIL	1	MEDIUM CAN FRUIT COCKTAIL
2	CUPS FLOUR		

Beat sugar, eggs and oil together. Add flour, salt and soda, and fruit cocktail with juice. Pour into oblong pan and sprinkle 1/2 cup coconut over top. Bake in a 350 degree oven for 45 minutes.

Pat Newbraugh—St. Andrew Presbyterian Church
Williamsport, Maryland

FRUIT LOAF

1	CUP SULTANAS (GOLDEN RAISINS)	1	CUP COLD TEA
1	CUP RAISINS	1	EGG, BEATEN
1	CUP BROWN SUGAR	2	CUPS SELF-RISING FLOUR

Soak sultanas, raisins and sugar in the tea overnight. Next day mix in the egg and flour. Pour into a 8 1/2 x 3 5/8 x 2 5/8" loaf pan, bake in a 350 degree oven for 60 minutes.

M.B.S.—Isle of Cumbrae Parish Church
Isle of Cumbrae, Scotland

FLUFFY GINGERBREAD

2	CUPS PLAIN FLOUR	2	EGGS
1 1/2	TEASPOONS BAKING SODA	3/4	CUP SYRUP
1	TEASPOON CINNAMON	1/2	CUP SUGAR
1/2	TEASPOON CLOVES	1/2	CUP SHORTENING
2	TEASPOONS GINGER	1	CUP BOILING WATER

Mix all dry ingredients. Cream sugar and shortening. Add eggs and syrup. Mix with dry ingredients. Add boiling water. Pour into a greased and floured 8x12x1" baking dish. Bake in a 375 degree oven for 25 minutes or until cake tester comes out clean. Serve with hot lemon sauce.

Sauce:

1/2	CUP MARGARINE	1/4	CUP FLOUR
3/4	CUP SUGAR	1	LEMON (JUICE)

In top of double boiler put margarine, sugar, flour, and lemon juice. Stir until thick, adding hot water if necessary for right consistency.

Mary Jo Dally Whitley—Ray Memorial Presbyterian Church
Monroe, Georgia

Ginger Bread

3/4	STICK MARGARINE	1/2	TEASPOON BAKING SODA
1/4	CUP BROWN SUGAR	2	TEASPOONS GROUND GINGER
1	CUP MOLASSES	2	CUPS PLAIN FLOUR
1	CUP MILK		

Melt sugar, margarine and syrup in a sauce pan, do not boil. Stir in the dry ingredients. Add soda to milk and stir in quickly. Turn into a greased 7" square pan. Bake 45 minutes, in a 350 degree oven.

Letchworth Free Church, Letchworth, England

Recipe for a Happy Home

4	CUPS LOVE	1	SMALL PINCH IN-LAWS
2	CUPS LOYALTY		A GENEROUS DASH COOPERATION
5	TABLESPOONS HOPE	1	CUP BLINDNESS TO THE OTHER'S FAULTS
2	TABLESPOONS TENDERNESS	2	CUPS PRAISE
1	CUP CONSIDERATION	1	LARGE AND SEVERAL SMALL HOBBIES
4	OUNCES FORGIVENESS	2	CUPS MILK OF HUMAN KINDNESS
3	TEASPOONS EXTRACT OF "I AM SORRY"	2	CUPS FLATTERY-CAREFULLY CONCEALED
1	QUART FAITH IN EACH OTHER		SPRINKLE OF APPRECIATION

Flavor with frequent portions of recreation and a dash of happy memories. Stir well and remove any specks of jealousy, temper or criticism. Sweeten well with a generous portion of love and keep warm with a steady flame of devotion. Blend with tenderness and hope, sprinkle abundantly with laughter. Bake with sunshine.

Never serve with cold shoulder or hot tongue. (Author Unknown)

Charlotte Vedeler—The Old Presbyterian Meeting House
Alexandria, Virginia

Hawaiian Pizza Cake

- 1 LARGE YELLOW CAKE MIX
- 1/4 CUP BROWN SUGAR
- 1/4 CUP WATER
- 1/4 CUP SOYBEAN OIL MARGARINE (MELTED)
- 2 EGGS
- 1 1/2 CUPS CHOPPED NUTS

Topping:

- COOL WHIP OR WHIPPED CREAM OR CREAM CHEESE
- GARNISH OF FRESH FRUIT (SEE BELOW)

Mix cake mix, sugar, water, melted margarine, eggs and nuts. Spread mixture, (which should be rather stiff), on 2 pizza pans. Bake in a 350 degree oven for 15 minutes. Cool well. Spread Cool Whip, whipped cream, or cream cheese on top of crust. Garnish with rings of fruit: strawberries, raspberries, pineapple, mandarin oranges, bananas, blueberries, green grapes and/or kiwi fruit.

Sparta Presbyterian Church, Sparta, North Carolina

Hawaiian Wedding Cake

- 2 CUPS SIFTED FLOUR
- 1 TEASPOON BAKING SODA
- 1 CUP NUTS, CRUSHED
- 1 CAN (20 OUNCE) CRUSHED PINEAPPLE
- 2 CUPS SUGAR
- 2 EGGS, BEATEN
- 1 CUP FLAKED COCONUT

Sift dry ingredients together. Mix remaining ingredients in lightly. Bake in a greased and floured 13x9" pan in a 350 degree oven for 45 minutes.

Icing:

- 1 (8 OUNCE) PACKAGE OF CREAM CHEESE
- 1/2 CUP BUTTER OR MARGARINE, SOFTENED
- 1 TEASPOON VANILLA
- 1 1/2 CUPS POWDERED SUGAR

Mix well. Frost cake while still warm.

Florence Daugherty, a new member—First Presbyterian Church
Beaufort, South Carolina
[former member of First Presbyterian Church, Fort Wayne, Indiana]

Kentucky Jam Cake

1 3/4	CUPS ALL-PURPOSE FLOUR	1	TEASPOON CINNAMON
1 1/2	CUPS SUGAR	2	TEASPOONS NUTMEG
1	CUP SALAD OIL	1	TEASPOON ALLSPICE
1	CUP BUTTERMILK	1/2	TEASPOON GROUND CLOVES
1	CUP BLACKBERRY JAM	1	TEASPOON VANILLA
1	TEASPOON BAKING SODA	1/2	TEASPOON SALT
1	TEASPOON DOUBLE-ACTING BAKING POWDER	1	CUP FINELY CHOPPED PECANS
		3	EGGS

Preheat oven to 350 degrees. Grease and flour two 9x9" baking pans. Into large bowl, measure all ingredients except pecans and icing. With mixer at low speed, beat ingredients until just mixed; increase speed to high and beat about 8 minutes or until sugar is dissolved. (You may add more pecans to cake mixture, if desired). Pour cake mixture into prepared pans and bake in a preheated, 350 degree oven for 40 minutes. Use buttermilk icing between layers and to frost cake. Yield: 24 servings.

Buttermilk Icing:

3	CUPS SUGAR	2	TABLESPOONS LIGHT CORN SYRUP
1	CUP BUTTER OR MARGARINE	1	TEASPOON BAKING SODA
1	CUP BUTTERMILK		

Mix together in 4-quart saucepan and cook over medium heat until a spoonful of mixture dropped into cold water forms a soft ball. Pour mixture into large bowl and beat until of spreading consistency. Fold in pecans.

Mrs. John C. Douthat—Timber Ridge Presbyterian Church
Greeneville, Tennessee

Lemon/Vanilla Tea Bread

3/4	STICK MARGARINE	1/4	TEASPOON SALT
3/4	CUP SUGAR (FINE GRANULATED)	1	TEASPOON VANILLA
1	EGG	1	LEMON (JUICE AND GRATED RIND)
2	CUPS SELF-RISING FLOUR		

Place all ingredients in a large bowl and beat thoroughly, mix about two minutes. Turn into a lightly greased 1 pound loaf pan. Bake in a preheated, 375 degree oven for 50 to 55 minutes until golden brown and well risen. Cool on wire rack.

Letchworth Free Church, Letchworth, England

Lemon Stuffed Cake

2/3	CUP BUTTER OR MARGARINE	3	CUPS SIFTED CAKE FLOUR
1 3/4	CUPS SUGAR	1	TEASPOON SALT
2	EGGS	1 1/2	CUPS MILK
1 1/2	TEASPOON VANILLA		

Cream butter. Add sugar gradually, creaming until light. Add eggs and vanilla and beat until light and fluffy. Sift dry ingredients together and add alternately with milk, beating after each addition. Beat 1 minute. Bake in 2 greased and floured round 8 x 1 1/2" cake pans. Bake in a 350 degree oven for 30-35 minutes. Remove from pans. Frost bottom layer with lemon filling (below). Top with second layer and frost with 7-minute frosting. Sprinkle top with coconut.

Lemon filling:

3/4	CUP SUGAR	1	TABLESPOON BUTTER OR MARGARINE
2	TABLESPOONS CORNSTARCH	2	EGG YOLKS, SLIGHTLY BEATEN
	DASH OF SALT	3	TABLESPOONS LEMON JUICE
3/4	CUP WATER	1	TEASPOON LEMON PEEL, GRATED

Combine sugar, cornstarch, and salt in heavy saucepan. Add water, egg yolks and lemon juice. Cook over medium heat until thick, stirring constantly. Remove from heat; add lemon peel and butter or margarine. Cool. Fill cake layers as above.

Mederia Rivers Stanley—Harmony Presbyterian Church
Crocketville, North Carolina

B. Huber's Mayonnaise Cake

- 1 CUP SUGAR
- 1 CUP MAYONNAISE (REGULAR)
- 2 CUPS FLOUR
- 4 TABLESPOONS COCOA
- 1 CUP WATER
- 2 TEASPOONS BAKING SODA
- 1 TEASPOON VANILLA

Mix all ingredients together thoroughly. Bake in a greased 9x13" baking pan for 30 minutes at 375 degrees. This is a moist, long-lasting cake. (The mayonnaise takes the place of eggs, shortening and milk).

Pat Basnett—First Presbyterian Church
Beaufort, South Carolina

Miracle Cake

- 2 STICKS BUTTER
- 1 3/4 CUPS SUGAR
- 5 EGGS
- 2 CUPS PLAIN FLOUR
- 1 TEASPOON BUTTER FLAVORING

Cream butter and sugar well. Add eggs one at a time, then add flour and flavoring. Bake in a tube pan in preheated 325 degree oven for about 1 hour. This cake freezes well, and is even better!

Mrs. Annie Bowers (our oldest living member)—First Presbyterian Church
Beaufort, South Carolina

Sunburst Miniature Muffins

- 1 BOX LEMON SUPREME CAKE MIX
- 1 3 3/4 OUNCES PACKAGE INSTANT LEMON PUDDING MIX
- 1 CUP BUTTERMILK
- 1/2 CUP VEGETABLE OIL
- 4 EGGS

Glaze:

- 3 TABLESPOONS FRESH LEMON JUICE
- 6 TABLESPOONS FRESH ORANGE JUICE
- 1 1/2 TEASPOONS VANILLA
- 3 1/2 CUPS CONFECTIONERS SUGAR

Grease miniature muffin pans. Mix muffin ingredients and pour into pans. Fill 1/2 full. Bake for 10 minutes. Mix glaze ingredients. With tongs, dip warm muffins into glaze, coating all over. Place on cake rack to drain. (Make more glaze recipe for extra glaze.)

Claire Wollenhaupt—Crossnore Presbyterian Church
Crossnore, North Carolina

OATMEAL CAKE

1 1/3	CUPS HOT WATER	1	TEASPOON VANILLA
1	CUP OATMEAL	2	CUPS FLOUR
1	STICK BUTTER OR MARGARINE	1	TEASPOON BAKING SODA
1	CUP WHITE SUGAR	1	TEASPOON BAKING POWDER
1	CUP BROWN SUGAR	1	TEASPOON CINNAMON
2	EGGS	1/4	TEASPOON SALT

Topping

1	STICK BUTTER OR MARGARINE	1/2	CUP COCONUT
1	CUP BROWN SUGAR	1/2	CUP PECANS

Combine hot water and oatmeal. Let stand 20 minutes. Cream 1 stick butter with the brown and white sugars. Add eggs and vanilla. Blend well. Then add cooled oatmeal to the creamed mixture. Stir dry ingredients together. Blend them into the batter. Pour into 11x13 inch pan and bake in a preheated 350 degree oven for 35 minutes. Combine topping ingredients. Remove cake from oven. Sprinkle topping on hot cake. Return to oven for 15 minutes. Cool. Yield: 18 servings.

Ellen Barnard—Oakland Avenue Presbyterian Church
Rock Hill, South Carolina

FRESH ORANGE CAKE

1	STICK BUTTER OR MARGARINE		PINCH OF SALT
3/4	CUP SUGAR	2	LARGE EGGS, BEATEN
1	ORANGE (JUICE AND FINELY GRATED RIND)	2	TABLESPOONS MILK
1 1/2	CUPS SELF-RISING FLOUR		

Topping:

WHIPPED CREAM	FRESH ORANGE SEGMENTS

Cream butter and sugar. Add orange and beat until light and fluffy. Sift the flour and salt and set aside. Add eggs and milk alternately with the flour, mix well. Pour into a well-greased 7" cake pan. Bake in a 350 degree oven for 30 minutes or until lightly brown. Remove from pan when cool. Spread with whipped cream and decorate with orange segments.

Letchworth Free Church, Letchworth, England

Peach Glaze Cake

- 1 CUP BUTTER
- 2 TABLESPOONS SUGAR
- 2 EGGS
- 2 CUPS FLOUR
- 4 TEASPOONS BAKING POWDER
- 1 CUP MILK
- 1 TEASPOON VANILLA
- 3-4 PEACHES
- 1 CUP CONFECTIONERS SUGAR
- 1 TABLESPOON ALMOND EXTRACT
- 1 TABLESPOON LEMON JUICE

Cream butter and sugar; add beaten eggs. Sift together the dry ingredients and add to creamed mixture alternately with the milk and vanilla. Spread into a greased, 8x10", cake pan. Slice peaches over top. Bake until done, about 35-40 minutes, in a 350 degree oven. While cake is warm, drizzle over it a glaze made of the confectioners sugar and almond and lemon flavorings.

Marilyn Bathrick—First Presbyterian Church
Attica, New York

Pineapple Do-Nothing Cake

- 2 CUPS FLOUR
- 2 CUPS SUGAR
- 2 EGGS
- 1/3 CUP OIL
- 1 TEASPOON BAKING POWDER
- 3/4 TEASPOON SALT
- 1 TEASPOON VANILLA
- 1 (20 OUNCE) CAN CRUSHED PINEAPPLE

Mix all ingredients together and pour into well-greased and floured 9"x14" pan. Bake in a 350 degree oven for 40 minutes.

Icing

- 3/4 STICK BUTTER OR MARGARINE
- 1 CUP SUGAR
- 2/3 CUP EVAPORATED MILK (SMALL CAN)

Melt butter over low heat. Add sugar and milk. Increase heat and cook for 5 minutes. Remove from heat and add: 1 cup coconut, 1 cup chopped pecans, 1 teaspoon vanilla. Pour on cake and spread evenly.

Hazel Scheidt—First Presbyterian Church
Beaufort, South Carolina

PINEAPPLE FRUIT CAKE

1	STICK BUTTER	12	OUNCES MIXED FRUIT
3/4	CUP BROWN SUGAR	8	OUNCE CAN CRUSHED PINEAPPLE
2	CUPS SELF-RISING FLOUR	1/2	TEASPOON MIXED SPICE
2	EGGS, BEATEN		FEW DROPS LEMON FLAVORING
4	OUNCES CANDIED CHERRIES, CHOPPED		

Roll chopped cherries in a little flour. Place cherries, butter, brown sugar, mixed fruit, pineapple, spice and lemon flavoring in a saucepan, bring to a boil. Remove from heat and let cool. Add eggs and flour and mix well, turn into a small greased tube pan and bake in a 325 degree oven for 1 1/2 to 2 hours.

Letchworth Free Church, Letchworth, England

POPPYSEED ALMOND CAKE

1	BOX YELLOW CAKE MIX	4	EGGS (ADD ONE AT A TIME)
1	PACKAGE INSTANT LEMON PUDDING MIX	1	TEASPOON ALMOND EXTRACT
1	CUP WATER	4	TABLESPOONS POPPYSEED
1/2	CUP OIL	1	SMALL PACKAGE SLIVERED ALMONDS,

Lightly toast almond slivers and set aside. Mix cake mix and pudding mix together in large mixer bowl; add water and oil and mix; add eggs, one at a time; turn electric mixer to the medium high setting, and beat mixture 6 minutes; turn mixer down and blend in extract and poppy seed. Turn mixer off, and stir in almonds. Pour into bundt pan sprayed with Pam and floured. Bake in a 350 degree oven for 50-60 minutes.

Icing:

1	CUP POWDERED SUGAR	1/2	TEASPOON ALMOND EXTRACT
	JUICE FROM 1/2 SMALL LEMON	2	TABLESPOONS MELTED MARGARINE

Mix well and drizzle over warm cake.

Mrs. Frank Elliott—First Central Presbyterian Church
Abilene, Texas

4-Banana Pound Cake

1	PACKAGE YELLOW CAKE MIX	1 1/3	CUP MASHED RIPE BANANAS
4	EGGS (ROOM TEMPERATURE)	1	PACKAGE (3 3/4 OUNCES) INSTANT VANILLA PUDDING MIX
1/2	TEASPOON NUTMEG		
1/3	CUP SALAD OIL	1/2	TEASPOON CINNAMON
1/2	CUP WATER		

Combine all ingredients in large bowl. Mix until blended, then beat with electric mixer, at medium speed for 4 minutes. Turn batter into greased and lightly floured 10" bundt cake pan or 10" tube pan. Bake in a 350 degree oven for 1 hour, or until cake tester inserted in cake comes out clean. Cool in pan 10 minutes, then turn onto rack and cool completely. If desired, dust with confectioner's sugar.

Irene Grant—East Ridge Presbyterian Church
Chattanooga, Tennessee

Buttermilk Pound Cake

1 1/4	CUPS BUTTER	3	CUPS ALL-PURPOSE FLOUR
3	CUPS SUGAR	1/2	TEASPOON SALT
5	EGGS	1/4	TEASPOON BAKING POWDER
1	CUP BUTTERMILK	2	TEASPOONS VANILLA

Combine dry ingredients. Cream butter and sugar until light. Add eggs one at a time, beating after each one. Add the dry ingredients, alternating with the buttermilk, beginning and ending with dry ingredients. Add vanilla. Pour into greased and floured tube pan. Bake in a 325 degree oven for 1 1/2 to 1 3/4 hours. (Check with a straw after 1 1/2 hours—it usually takes another 15 minutes.)

Edith Read Boon—Trinity Avenue Presbyterian Church
Durham, North Carolina

Cold Oven Pound Cake

2	STICKS BUTTER	1/2	CUP SELF-RISING FLOUR
1/2	CUP CRISCO	6	EGGS
3	CUPS SUGAR	2	TABLESPOONS BUTTERNUT FLAVORING
2 1/2	CUPS CAKE FLOUR	1	CUP MILK

Mix all ingredients. Place in cold oven set for 325 degrees. Bake 1 3/4 hours. Mix 1/2 box powdered sugar, 1/2 stick oleo and 2 ounces lemon juice. Pour over hot cake. Seal in cake keeper a couple of days before serving.

Gwendolyn K. Polk—Harmony Presbyterian Church
Crocketville, South Carolina

POUND CAKE

1/2	POUND BUTTER OR MARGARINE	1/8	TEASPOON SALT
1/2	CUP VEGETABLE SHORTENING (CRISCO)	1	CUP MILK
3	CUPS SUGAR	5	EGGS
3	CUPS FLOUR	1	TEASPOON VANILLA
1	TEASPOON BAKING POWDER	1	TEASPOON LEMON

Lightly grease and flour 1 large tube pan or 1 bundt pan and 1 loaf pan. Cream butter and shortening. Add sugar and blend; beat until light and fluffy. Add whole eggs, one at a time, beating after each. Sift dry ingredients together and add alternately with milk. Blend thoroughly, add flavorings and beat 1 minute longer. All ingredients should be at room temperature before mixing. Bake in a 350 degree oven for 1 hour and 15 minutes for tube pan or 40-45 minutes for bundt or loaf pan. Do not open oven during baking.

Hazel Sparks—Fort Hill Presbyterian Church
Clemson, South Carolina

THELMA HARVEY'S SOUR CREAM POUND CAKE

1	CUP BUTTER	1/4	TEASPOON SALT
3	CUPS SUGAR	1/4	TEASPOON SODA
6	EGGS, SEPARATED	1/4	TEASPOON BAKING POWDER
8	OUNCES SOUR CREAM	1/4	TEASPOON MACE
3	CUPS FLOUR	1	TEASPOON LEMON JUICE

Cream butter and sugar. Add egg yolks and mix well. Sift flour, salt, soda and baking powder. Add flour mixture and sour cream alternately to butter mixture. Season with mace and lemon juice. Beat egg whites until stiff and fold into mixture. Bake in a greased tube pan in a 300 degree oven for 1 1/2 hours.

Eileen Harvey Bakke—Washington Community Fellowship
Washington, D.C.

Pumpkin Cake Roll

3	EGGS	2	TEASPOONS CINNAMON
1	CUP SUGAR	1/2	TEASPOON NUTMEG
2/3	CUP PUMPKIN	1	TEASPOON BAKING POWDER
1	TEASPOON LEMON JUICE	1	TEASPOON GINGER
3/4	CUP FLOUR	1/2	TEASPOON SALT

Beat eggs with electric mixer at high speed for 5 minutes. Heat in small saucepan on top of stove the sugar. Stir in 2/3 cup pumpkin until sugar dissolves. Mixture should be barely warm. Add lemon juice and mix well. Stir together the flour and spices, and add to the liquid ingredients. Spread batter on greased cookie sheet (15x9x1). Top with 1 cup of chopped nuts (optional). Bake in a 375 degree oven for 15 minutes. Turn onto towel, sprinkled with powdered sugar. Roll up lengthwise together with towel. Refrigerate 1/2 hour, unroll and fill.

Filling:

1	CUP POWDERED SUGAR	6 OR 8	OUNCES CREAM CHEESE
1/2	TEASPOON VANILLA	4	TABLESPOONS BUTTER

Mix together and spread over cake. Roll and chill. Keep in freezer. Slice as needed.

Central Presbyterian Church, Fort Smith, Arkansas

Punch Bowl Cake

2	YELLOW CAKE LAYERS	16	OUNCE CAN CRUSHED PINEAPPLE, DRAINED
2	SMALL PACKAGES INSTANT VANILLA PUDDING	1 1/2	CUPS CHOPPED NUTS
		2	PACKAGES (6 OUNCES) FROZEN COCONUT
1	CAN CHERRY PIE FILLING	2	8 OUNCE CARTONS COOL WHIP
16	OUNCE CAN FRUIT COCKTAIL, DRAINED		

Make cake layers. Cool. Prepare instant pudding according to directions on package. Refrigerate to set up. Place one cake layer in bottom of 6 quart punch bowl. Add in layers one-half of each ingredient in this order: Pudding, cherry pie filling, fruit cocktail, pineapple, nuts, coconut and Cool Whip. Add second layers, using remaining ingredients in the order given. Garnish top with cherries, nuts and with more coconut. Refrigerate. Yield: 35 servings.

Pauline Ledford—Paint Gap Presbyterian Church, Burnsville, North Carolina
Betsy Henderson—First Presbyterian Church, Aiken, South Carolina

Scripture Cake

1	CUP JUDGES 5:25 (LAST CLAUSE)	2	CUPS 1 KINGS 4:22
1	CUP JEREMIAH 6:20	2	CHRONICLES 9:9 TO TASTE
1	TABLESPOON 1 SAMUEL 14:25		PINCH LEVITICUS 2:13
3	JEREMIAH 17:11	1	TEASPOON AMOS 4:5
1	CUP 1 SAMUEL 30:12 (SECOND FOOD)	3	TABLESPOONS JUDGES 4:19 (LAST SENTENCE)
1	CUP NAHUM 3:12 (CHOPPED)		
1/4	CUP NUMBERS 17:8 (BLANCHED, CHOPPED)		

Cream first 3 ingredients. Beat in the 3 Jeremiahs, one at a time. Add next 3 ingredients and beat again. Sift together Kings, 2 Chronicles, Leviticus, and Amos. Add to first mixture. Lastly add Judges. Bake in a 325 degree oven for 1 1/2 hours or until done.

The Old Presbyterian Meeting House, Alexandria, Virginia

Shoo-Fly Cake

4	CUPS FLOUR	1	CUP DARK MOLASSES
3/4	CUPS SHORTENING	1	TABLESPOON SODA
2	CUPS BROWN SUGAR (DARK)	2	CUPS HOT WATER
1	TEASPOON SALT		

Mix flour, shortening, sugar, and salt. Set aside one cup of crumb mixture. Mix the molasses, soda, and water and combine with the remaining crumbs. Pour into a greased 9x12" oblong pan. Sprinkle 1 cup of crumbs over the top; bake in a 350 degree oven for 45-50 minutes. Bottom will be moist like shoo-fly pie in this moist, Pennsylvania Dutch recipe.

Jane Brindle—Paxton Presbyterian Church
Harrisburg, Pennsylvania

Sultana Cake

2	STICKS BUTTER	1/2	CUP MILK
3/4	CUP SUGAR (FINE GRANULATED)	1/2	POUND SULTANAS (GOLDEN RAISINS)
4	EGGS	1	CUP SELF-RISING FLOUR
2	CUPS PLAIN FLOUR		

Beat butter and sugar to a cream, beat in eggs one at a time, add a little flour then the milk. Add sultanas, then the rest of the flour. Keep mixture rather soft. Turn into a loaf pan, 4"x5"x9" and bake in a 325 degree oven for about 2 hours.

Mrs. L. MacPhail—North Church High Street
Perth, Scotland

Kate's Upsidedown Cake

1/2	CUP BUTTER	1	CUP SUGAR
1	CUP BROWN SUGAR	5	TABLESPOONS PINEAPPLE JUICE
1	LARGE CAN PINEAPPLE	1	CUP FLOUR
3	EGG YOLKS	1	TEASPOON BAKING POWDER
3	EGG WHITES, BEATEN		RED CHERRIES TO GARNISH

Melt butter in frying pan, add brown sugar; spread evenly over pan. Lay pineapple in rings or use crushed pineapple. Place cherries over pineapple. Beat egg yolks, add sugar and pineapple juice. Sift in flour and baking powder. Fold into stiffly beaten egg whites. Pour over fruit. Bake in a 350 degree oven for 45 minutes.

Mrs. C.L. Wooddell—First Presbyterian Church
Charleston, West Virginia

Wine Cake

1	BOX DUNCAN HINES GOLDEN CAKE MIX	1/2	CUP WATER
1	(3 1/2 OUNCE) PACKAGE INSTANT FRENCH VANILLA PUDDING MIX	1/2	CUP OIL
		4	EGGS (ROOM TEMPERATURE)
1/2	CUP WHITE TABLE WINE		

Glaze:

1	STICK MARGARINE	1	CUP WHITE SUGAR
1/4	CUP WHITE WINE		

Mix all cake ingredients together thoroughly. Grease and flour an angel food cake pan. Bake in a 350 degree oven for 50 minutes. Combine glaze ingredients in a small saucepan and bring to boil. Let boil rapidly, stirring, for 1 minute. Pour over cake while it is hot. Leave glazed cake in pan until cold.

Nellie and Bob Newman—First Presbyterian Church
Beaufort, South Carolina

Chapter Four

Candy—Cookies

CANDY

BICKENBACH CANDY

1	CUP SUGAR	2	SQUARES CHOCOLATE
1/2	CUP BUTTER	3/4	CUP MILK
1	CUP KARO SYRUP	1/2	CUP CHOPPED NUTS
	PINCH OF SALT		

Mix together all ingredients except nuts, creaming sugar and butter. Cook, stirring constantly, until mixture forms a hard ball in water. Watch for burning toward end of cooking. Remove from heat and add chopped nuts. Pour into buttered pan. Start to cut in squares as soon as candy starts to set. Wrap in waxed paper.

Audrey Bickenbach—First Presbyterian Church
Beaufort, South Carolina

BUCKEYES CANDY

2	CUPS PEANUT BUTTER	1/2	POUND MARGARINE
1 1/2	POUNDS CONFECTIONERS SUGAR	1	(12 OUNCE) PACKAGE CHOCOLATE CHIPS
3/8-1/2	BAR PARAFFIN WAX		

In a bowl, mix peanut butter, sugar and margarine. Roll into balls, chill for 1/2 hour. Melt one 12 ounce package of chocolate chips and 3/8-1/2 bar paraffin wax. Dip ball with toothpick into chocolate mixture, covering 3/4 of the way. Place on waxed paper. Keep refrigerated. Yield: 90.

Melanie and Jan Eachus—Pittsgrove Presbyterian Church
Daretown, New Jersey

Black Walnut Divinity

3 CUPS WHITE SUGAR	2 EGG WHITES
1 CUP COLD WATER	1 TEASPOON VANILLA
2 TEASPOONS WHITE VINEGAR	1/2 CUP CHOPPED BLACK WALNUTS
1/8 TEASPOON SALT	

Combine sugar, water, vinegar and salt in a sauce pan. Heat slowly, stirring constantly until sugar is dissolved. Then cook rapidly, without stirring, to soft ball stage (234-240 degrees). Beat egg whites until stiff, but not dry. Add hot syrup gradually, beating until mixture is creamy and set, and holds its shape. Add vanilla and nuts. Drop by teaspoons on waxed paper. Let stand until set.

Marion Daniels—Piedmont Presbyterian Church
Piedmont, West Virginia

Tillie's Fudge

Cook to soft ball stage, stirring constantly:

4 CUPS SUGAR	PINCH SALT
1 CUP BUTTER	1 CUP EVAPORATED MILK

Remove from heat and add:

12 OUNCES SEMI-SWEET CHOCOLATE BITS	VANILLA TO TASTE
1 PINT MARSHMALLOW WHIP	

Stir constantly until dissolved. Beat with mixer every once in a while until cool. Pour into buttered pan.

Anne Skinner—Pittsgrove Presbyterian Church
Daretown, New Jersey

Peanut Butter Easter Eggs

2	STICKS MARGARINE	1	LARGE BAG SEMI-SWEET CHOCOLATE CHIPS
1 1/2	POUNDS PEANUT BUTTER (2 3/4 CUPS)	1	INCH SQUARE OF PARAFFIN
2	POUNDS POWDERED SUGAR (2 BOXES)	1	SQUARE UNSWEETENED CHOCOLATE
1	TABLESPOON VANILLA		

Mix first four ingredients together. With your hands, shape into "eggs". Make sure they are very firm. In double boiler, melt 1 inch square paraffin, 1 square unsweetened chocolate and 1 large bag semi-sweet chocolate chips. Dip eggs into chocolate to coat. Place on waxed paper or greased cookie sheet. Chill.

Mrs. Frank Sells—Low Country Presbyterian Church
Bluffton, South Carolina

Peanut Butter Fudge I

2	CUPS SUGAR	1	CUP SKIPPY CHUNKY PEANUT BUTTER
1	BOX LIGHT BROWN SUGAR	1	16 OUNCE JAR MARSHMALLOW FLUFF
1 1/2	CUPS EVAPORATED MILK	1	TEASPOON VANILLA
4	TABLESPOONS BUTTER	1	TEASPOON ALMOND EXTRACT

Boil sugar, brown sugar and milk for 10 minutes, stirring constantly. In a large bowl, combine remaining ingredients. Pour sugar mixture over peanut butter mixture. Beat until creamy. Pour into 9x13" pan to cool.

Kitty Smith—Pittsgrove Presbyterian Church
Daretown, New Jersey

Peanut Butter Fudge II

3	CUPS WHITE SUGAR	3	TABLESPOONS COCOA
3/4	CUP MILK		LUMP OF BUTTER THE SIZE OF A WALNUT

Mix all ingredients together. Boil hard for 3 minutes. Take off heat and add a 12 ounce jar of peanut butter and 1 small jar of marshmallow cream. Pour into a pan and cool.

Pat Newbrough—St. Andrew Presbyterian Church
Williamsport, Maryland

Old-Time Penuche

4 1/2 CUPS PACKED LIGHT BROWN SUGAR	1/4 TEASPOON SALT
1 CUP EVAPORATED MILK	1 TEASPOON VANILLA
1/4 POUND BUTTER	2 CUPS CHOPPED NUTS (WALNUTS OR PECANS)

Cook, stirring, until sugar is dissolved. Continue cooking until a soft ball forms (238 degrees on candy thermometer). Remove from heat and let stand until lukewarm (110 degrees). Add vanilla and nuts. Beat until thick and mixture loses its gloss. Pour into 9x9x2" buttered pan. Cut when firm.

Marion Daniels—Piedmont Presbyterian Church
Piedmont, West Virginia

Toffee Bars

1 STICK BUTTER	48 GRAHAM CRACKERS
1 STICK MARGARINE	1/2 CUP CHOPPED PECANS
1/2 CUP SUGAR	

Boil butter, margarine and sugar for 2 minutes. Place 48 graham crackers on foil-lined cookie sheet (apart but close together). Pour mixture over top. Sprinkle with chopped nuts. Bake in a 350 degree oven for 10 minutes; cool and break apart.

Lanna Hitchcock—Presbyterian Church, Jewett, New York
Miriam (Mickey) Broome—First Presbyterian Church, Marion, North Carolina

English Toffee

1 POUND SUGAR (2 CUPS)	PINCH OF SALT
1 POUND BUTTER	2 6 OUNCE BAGS CHOCOLATE CHIPS
1/2 POUND CHOPPED NUTS (PECANS)	1/2 POUND PULVERIZED PECANS
2 TABLESPOONS LIGHT KARO SYRUP	

Combine sugar, butter, pecans, syrup and salt in heavy pan. Over low heat, cook until melted and mixed together. Increase the heat. Stir constantly until it reaches temperature 310 degrees. Pour into flat buttered pan, spreading thin. Let cool and harden. Melt one bag of chips and spread over cooled candy. Press half of the pulverized pecans into the chocolate until they stick. Let harden and then repeat on the other side with the other bag of chips and the rest of the pulverized nuts. Break into pieces and store in airtight containers.

Mrs. Frank Sells—Low Country Presbyterian Church
Bluffton, South Carolina

Toffee

3	STICKS BUTTER	8	OUNCES SLICED ALMONDS
2 1/2	CUPS SUGAR	1	LARGE MILK CHOCOLATE BAR

Put butter, almonds and sugar into heavy cast-iron pot. Cook to hard crack stage, stirring constantly, until almonds are roasted. Quickly pour candy onto inverted cookie sheets and spread. Work carefully because candy is extremely hot! When slightly firm, place milk chocolate onto toffee and allow to melt. Put in a cool place until chocolate sets. Break into bite-sized pieces and store in a tightly covered container.

Faye McGowan—First Presbyterian Church
Beaufort, South Carolina

COOKIES

Chewy Apricot Squares

6	OUNCES DRIED APRICOTS, SNIPPED	2	TABLESPOONS WHOLE WHEAT FLOUR
1/2	CUP PACKED BROWN SUGAR	1	TEASPOON VANILLA
3/4	TEASPOON GROUND CORIANDER		

Cook apricots covered in 1 cup water for 20-25 minutes. Combine sugar, 2 tablespoons flour and coriander. Stir into apricot mixture. Cook until bubbly. Cook one minute more. Remove from heat and stir in vanilla.

1/2	CUP WHOLE WHEAT FLOUR	1/3	CUP MARGARINE
1/3	CUP WHOLE BRAN CEREAL	3	TABLESPOONS WATER
1/2	CUP QUICK QUAKER OATS		

Combine flour, oats, and cereal. Cut in margarine until crumbly. Set aside 1/2 cup of this mixture. Stir water into remaining crumb mixture; press onto bottom of ungreased 8x8x2" baking dish. Top with apricot mixture. Sprinkle reserved crumbs on top and press lightly. Bake at 350 degrees 30-35 minutes. Cool and cut into bars. Makes 24.

Anna Louise Larson Fisher—Westminster Presbyterian Church
St. Louis, Missouri

Australian Crunchies

1 1/2	STICKS MARGARINE	2/3	CUP SUGAR (GRANULATED)
3/4	CUP COCONUT	1 1/2	CUPS CRUSHED CORNFLAKES
1	TABLESPOON COCOA	1 1/4	CUPS SELF-RISING FLOUR

Melt margarine over low heat. Stir in cocoa, sugar, coconut and cornflakes. Gradually, stir in the flour, spread evenly in a greased 8" square cake pan. Bake in a 350 degree oven for 30 minutes. Cut into triangles while warm. When cold, cover with melted chocolate.

Evelyn Watt—The Bethel Reformed Church
Chester-le-Street, England

Basic Cookie

3/4	CUP WHITE SUGAR	2 1/2	CUPS PLAIN FLOUR
3/4	CUP BROWN SUGAR	1	TEASPOON SALT
2	STICKS BUTTER OR MARGARINE (ROOM TEMPERATURE)	1	TEASPOON SODA
		1	TEASPOON VANILLA
2	LARGE EGGS	1	CUP NUTS, CHOPPED (OPTIONAL)

Cream sugars and butter or margarine. Add eggs, one at a time, beating after each. Gradually, stir in flour. Add salt, soda, vanilla and nuts. Drop by teaspoonful two inches apart on ungreased cookie sheet and bake in a 375 degree oven for 7-8 minutes. Note: A 12-ounce package of chocolate bits, 2 cups of raisins or dates, etc., may be added or these may be baked plain.

Ruby Campen—Highland Presbyterian Church
Fayetteville, North Carolina

"Mother's" Brownies

"Mother" was Mrs. Anthony Fuller, Becky's mother.

1	CUP SUGAR	3	EGGS
1/2	CUP FLOUR	1	TEASPOON VANILLA
1/2	CUP COCOA	1	CUP BROKEN PECANS
1	STICK BUTTER OR MARGARINE, MELTED		POWDERED SUGAR

Combine cocoa and flour. Mix beaten eggs and sugar. Mix well with cocoa and flour. Add melted butter and mix well. Add vanilla and nuts. Place batter in 7"x11" pan that has been prepared with cooking spray to keep batter from sticking to pan. Place in a preheated 350 degree oven and bake 20-25 minutes. As batter bakes, open oven door and move baking rack on which pan is located up and down several times rapidly! This will result in a chewy brownie. When done, dust with powdered sugar. Cool. Cut into bars. Enjoy.

Rebecca Fuller Trask (Mrs. Neil, Jr.)—First Presbyterian Church
Beaufort, South Carolina

BUTTER SQUARES

- 1 BOX DROMEDARY OR BETTY CROCKER POUND CAKE MIX
- 1 STICK BUTTER, MELTED
- 2 JUMBO EGGS, BEATEN
- 8 OUNCES CREAM CHEESE, SOFTENED
- 2 JUMBO EGGS
- 1 BOX POWDERED SUGAR

Stir first 3 ingredients by hand, pat into a greased 9x13" pan. Mix cream cheese, 2 eggs and confectioners sugar in blender and pour over the top. Bake in a 325 degree oven for 40 minutes. Cool and cut into 64 small squares.

Helen Harvey Laffitte—First Presbyterian Church of Columbia
Columbia, South Carolina

CARAMEL BARS

- 2 STICKS MARGARINE
- 1 BOX LIGHT BROWN SUGAR
- 2 EGGS
- 2 CUPS PLAIN FLOUR
- 1 TEASPOONS BAKING POWDER
- 1 TEASPOON VANILLA
- 1 TEASPOON ALMOND FLAVORING
- 1/2 TEASPOON SALT
- 1/2 CUP BROKEN PECANS

Cream margarine and sugar. Add eggs, then dry ingredients, flavoring and nuts. Bake in a well-greased pan (9x12") for 30 minutes in a 300-350 degree oven. Do not overbake. Turn out on cookie sheet and cut into squares while hot.

Mary Lois Miller—First Presbyterian Church
Marion, North Carolina

CARAMEL CRACKER COOKIES

40	SALTINE CRACKERS	1	(12 OUNCE) BAG CHOCOLATE CHIPS
1	CUP DARK BROWN SUGAR	2	STICKS BUTTER (NOT MARGARINE)

Cover cookie pan with foil. Place crackers on foil. Boil sugar and butter for 3 minutes. Pour this mixture over crackers and bake at 400 degrees for 5 minutes. Remove from oven and quickly spread chocolate chips over all; add nuts if desired. Chill in refrigerator and remove when cool. Break into cookie-sized pieces.

Harold J. Rogers—Central Presbyterian Church, Petersburg, Illinois
Evelyn Rabey—Fort Hill Presbyterian Church, Clemson, South Carolina

CHESS SQUARES

1	BOX CAKE MIX (BUTTER, LEMON, CHOCOLATE, ETC.)	2	TEASPOONS VANILLA
		8	OUNCES CREAM CHEESE, SOFTENED
1	BEATEN EGG	3	BEATEN EGGS
1	STICK BUTTER, MELTED	1	BOX POWDERED SUGAR

Mix cake mix, egg, and melted butter well. Pat onto bottom of greased 9 1/2x15" pan. Mix together cream cheese, eggs, powdered sugar, and vanilla. Pour over cake mix. Bake in a 350 degree oven for 30-40 minutes, or until brown on top. Cut into squares.

Barbara Covington—Sea Island Presbyterian Church
Beaufort, South Carolina

CHOCOLATE CHEWS

3	EGGS	1	TEASPOON BAKING POWDER
2/3	CUP SALAD OIL	1	CUP NUTS, CHOPPED
1	POUND BROWN SUGAR	1	PACKAGE CHOCOLATE CHIPS
2 1/2	CUPS FLOUR		

Beat eggs; add oil and sugar. Mix flour and baking powder. Add to first mixture. Add nuts, chips, and mix. Mixture will be stiff. Spread in 9x13" pan. Bake in a 350 degree oven for 30-35 minutes at 350 degrees.

Mrs. Bill Spencer—First Central Presbyterian Church
Abilene, Texas

Chocolate Crinkles

- 1/2 CUP VEGETABLE OIL
- 4 OUNCES UNSWEETENED CHOCOLATE
- 2 CUPS SUGAR
- 4 EGGS
- 2 TEASPOONS VANILLA
- 2 CUPS FLOUR
- 2 TEASPOONS BAKING POWDER
- 1/2 TEASPOON SALT
- 1 CUP CONFECTIONERS SUGAR

Melt the chocolate in microwave. Add oil and sugar. Blend in one egg at a time. Add vanilla. Stir flour, baking powder, and salt into mixture. Chill overnight or at least several hours. Drop teaspoonfuls of dough into confectioner,s sugar, roll well and then shape into balls. Place 2 inches apart on greased cookie sheet. Bake in preheated 350 degree oven for 8-10 minutes. Do not overbake!

Clara Thompson—Presbyterian Church
Jewett, New York

Church Windows

- 1 STICK BUTTER
- 1 10 1/2 OUNCE PACKAGE COLORED MARSHMALLOWS
- 12 OUNCES CHOCOLATE BITS
- 1 CUP WALNUTS, CHOPPED

Melt butter and chocolate bits in double boiler; cool. Add colored marshmallows and walnuts. Mix well, until marshmallows begin to dissolve. Separate into 3 mounds on waxed paper. Shape into oblong logs. Chill for 8 hours. Slice 1/4 inch thick.

Karolyn Davey—First Congregational Church
Medfield, Massachusetts

Christmas Cookies

3	CUPS FLOUR	1	POUND WHITE RAISINS
1	TEASPOON CLOVES	1	POUND CANDIED PINEAPPLE, FINELY CUT
1	TEASPOON ALLSPICE	1	POUND CANDIED CHERRIES, FINELY CUT
1	TEASPOON CINNAMON	1/2	CUP WHISKEY
1	CUP BROWN SUGAR	1	TEASPOON SODA DISSOLVED IN
1/2	CUP BUTTER		3 TABLESPOONS BUTTERMILK
4	EGGS	2	POUNDS PECAN HALVES

Mix flour and spices. Stir about 1 cup of mixture into fruit to separate. Cream butter and sugar; add rest of liquid ingredients. Mix into fruit and add the rest of the flour mixture. Add pecans. Drop by small teaspoonfuls onto greased cookie sheet. Bake in a 250 degree oven for 20-25 minutes.

Brantley Harvey, Jr., Trustee
Stoney Creek Foundation

Red and Green Christmas Ball Cookies

1/2	CUP BUTTER	1 1/4	CUPS SIFTED FLOUR
1/3	CUP SIFTED CONFECTIONERS SUGAR		DASH OF SALT
1	TABLESPOON WATER	1/2	CUP CHOPPED NUTS
1	TEASPOON VANILLA		GREEN AND RED SUGARS

Cream butter and sugar. Stir in water and vanilla. Add flour and salt; mix. Stir in nuts. Shape into 1 inch balls. Roll in colored sugar. Place 1 inch apart on ungreased baking sheet. Bake in a 300 degree oven for 20 minutes, or until set but not brown. Cool slightly before removing from pan. Yield: 2 dozen.

Peggy Brown—Bryson Presbyterian Church
Bryson City, North Carolina

Crispy Balls

1	CUP KARO SYRUP	14	OUNCES PEANUT BUTTER
1	CUP SUGAR (GRANULATED)	5	CUPS RICE KRISPIES CEREAL

Warm the Karo and sugar. Add the peanut butter and stir well. Add to the cereal. Mix well. Form into 1" balls and lay on wax paper.

Margaret Botsford—First Presbyterian Church
Casa Grande, Arizona

Coconut Macaroons

1 1/3	CUPS FLAKED COCONUT	2	EGG WHITES
1/3	CUP SUGAR	1/2	TEASPOON ALMOND EXTRACT
2	TABLESPOONS FLOUR		

Combine coconut, sugar and flour in bowl. Stir in unbeaten egg white and almond extract. Drop by spoonfuls onto greased and floured baking sheets. Bake in a 325 degree oven for 20 minutes or until edges are browned. Remove from cookie sheets at once. Yield: 1 1/2 dozen cookies.

Mederia Rivers Stanley—Harmony Presbyterian Church
Crocketville, South Carolina

Crumb Cookies

1	CUP SHORTENING	2	TEASPOONS SODA
3	EGGS	1	TEASPOON SALT
2	TEASPOONS BAKING POWDER	3/4	TEASPOONS CLOVES
2	TEASPOONS CINNAMON	1/2	CUP CHOPPED NUTS
1	CUP GROUND RAISINS	1	POUND COOKIE CRUMBS, ANY KIND (4 CUPS)
1 1/2	CUP SUGAR	1/4	CUP MILK
5	CUPS FLOUR	1	CUP MOLASSES

Cream shortening, sugar and eggs. Mix flour, soda, baking powder, salt and spices. Stir ground raisins into mixture. Mix all ingredients together, alternating flour mixture, cookie crumbs with milk and molasses. Chill overnight. Roll 3/8" thick and cut with large cookie cutter (3/4"). Sprinkle with sugar on top before baking in a 350 degree oven for 10-15 minutes. Do not roll any thinner than 3/8". These freeze well.

Connie Martin—Fairfax Presbyterian Church
Fairfax, Virginia

Decadent 3-C Bars

1	PACKAGE (21.5 OUNCES) FUDGE BROWNIE MIX (GENERIC WILL DO!)	1	CAN (14 OUNCES) SWEETENED CONDENSED MILK)
2	TEASPOONS VANILLA	1	8 OUNCE BAR CREAM CHEESE, SOFTENED
1	EGG	1	CAN CHERRY PIE FILLING

Prepare brownie mix in 9x13" pan as directed on package, except bake only 20 minutes. Beat vanilla, egg, sweetened condensed milk and cream cheese together until smooth. Spread over the partially-baked brownie mix. Bake 25 minutes or until the top has set. Cool 2 hours. Spread cherry pie filling over. Cut into squares. Store in the refrigerator.

Pam Thompson—Faith Presbyterian Church
Harrisburg, Pennsylvania

Empire Biscuits or Cookies

2 1/2	CUPS PLAIN FLOUR	2	STICKS SOFT MARGARINE
1/2	CUP ICING SUGAR		

Brown margarine and sugar. Add flour. Roll out on a lightly floured board approximately, 1/8" thick. Cut into rounds and place on baking tray. Bake 15-20 minutes in a 325 degree oven. Sandwich two together when cold with strawberry jam. Ice top with icing sugar and water mixed to a fairly stiff consistency.

Effie H. Kerr—Isle of Cumbrae Parish Church
Isle of Cumbrae, Scotland

Fennel Cookies

This is a great Christmas cookie!

1	CUP SOFTENED BUTTER	2	TABLESPOONS AMARETTO
1 1/2	CUPS SUGAR	2	CUPS FLOUR
1	EGG	1	TEASPOON BAKING POWDER
2	TEASPOONS FENNEL SEEDS	1/2	TEASPOON SALT
1	TABLESPOON LEMON PEEL	1/2	CUP CHOPPED PISTACHIO NUTS

Cream butter and sugar, add fennel seeds, lemon peel and Amaretto. Gradually add flour, baking powder, salt and nuts. This makes a stiff dough. Roll dough into balls the size of a marble and place on ungreased cookie sheet. Bake in a 350 degree oven for 10-13 minutes.

Charlotte Vedeler—The Old Presbyterian Meeting House
Alexandria, Virginia

GINGER COOKIES

2 1/2	CUPS OF CAKE FLOUR	1	CUP SUGAR
2	TEASPOONS BAKING SODA	3/4	CUP BUTTER OR MARGARINE
1	TEASPOON GINGER	1	EGG, BEATEN
1	TEASPOON GROUND CLOVES	4	TABLESPOONS MOLASSES
1	TEASPOON CINNAMON		

Sift together the dry ingredients. Work in the shortening with beater at low speed. Add egg and molasses. Mix well. Place in the refrigerator for 3-4 hours. Roll into small balls about 1-1 1/2 inches in diameter. Roll in additional sugar. Bake on greased cookie sheet in a 375 degree oven for 10-12 minutes.

Barbara Schott—West Side Presbyterian Church
Ridgewood, New Jersey

GINGER SHORTCAKE

1	STICK BUTTER	1	TEASPOON GROUND GINGER
1/4	CUP SUGAR (FINE GRANULATED)	1 1/4	CUPS PLAIN FLOUR
1	TEASPOON BAKING POWDER		

Cream butter and sugar together. Sift in flour, baking powder, and ginger. Spread the mixture into a greased 8" cake pan. Bake in a 350 degree oven for 30-40 minutes. While the shortcake is baking, make the icing.

Icing:

1/4	CUP POWDERED SUGAR	1/2	STICK BUTTER
1	TEASPOON GROUND GINGER	3	TEASPOONS GOLDEN SYRUP

Melt the butter over gentle heat then add remaining ingredients. Pour over shortcake while it is still warm. Cut into slices while still warm, but leave in the pan until cool.

Sybil Chandler—Ash United Reformed Church
Kent, England

Graham Cracker Dessert Cookies

This recipe is submitted by the Stoney Creek Cookbook Committee to honor Martha Ann McCaskill, wife of our former minister who now is Pastor of Indiantown Presbyterian Church, Hemingway, South Carolina. Martha Ann was active throughout our church and started the Serendipity Sunday School Class which remains one of the most popular in the church.

1	STICK MARGARINE	2	EGGS, SLIGHTLY BEATEN
2	CUPS GRAHAM CRACKER CRUMBS	3/4	CUP CHOPPED PECANS
1	CUP GRANULATED SUGAR	1	TEASPOON VANILLA

Melt the margarine and pour it over the graham cracker crumbs, mixing well. Add the sugar and slightly beaten eggs. When mixed well, add pecans and vanilla. Spread in greased square pan (8"x8"). Bake in a 340 degree oven for 25 minutes. (No more, as these are supposed to be soft.) The reason they are called "dessert cookies" is because they can be cut in large squares (8 or 9 pieces) and served with whipped cream or vanilla ice cream for dessert or cut into small squares as soft cookies. Delicious!

Fran Barnard (Stoney Creek Cookbook Committee)—Indiantown Presbyterian Church
Hemingway, South Carolina

Heath Bars

2	CUPS BROWN SUGAR	1	EGG
2	CUPS FLOUR	1	CUP MILK
1/2	CUP BUTTER	1	TEASPOON SODA
6	HEATH CANDY BARS	1	TEASPOON VANILLA

Mix brown sugar, flour and butter together. Save 1 cup of this mixture for topping. Mix egg, milk, soda, and vanilla together and add to the dry ingredients. Pour into 9x13" pan. Sprinkle crumb mixture on top. Cut up 6 Heath bars over the crumb mixture. (Fewer candy bars may be used.) Bake in a 350 degree oven for 25 minutes or until done.

Marilyn Johnson—First Presbyterian Church
Belle Plaine, Minnesota

IMPERIAL BISCUITS

2	CUPS FLOUR	1/2	TEASPOON BAKING POWDER
1	STICK BUTTER	1	TEASPOON CINNAMON
1/2	CUP SUGAR		JAM AND WATER ICING
1	EGG		

Cream the butter and sugar. Beat in egg. Sift in flour, cinnamon, and baking powder and work until smooth. Dough will be stiff. Refrigerate to keep stiff. Roll out thinly and cut into shapes. Bake 10 minutes on cookie sheets in a 350 degree oven. When cool, spread one biscuit with raspberry jam and put another on top. Ice with powdered sugar and water icing. Flavor with a drop of almond flavoring. Color as desired.

Sheila Cawns—Westminster Presbyterian Church
St. Louis, Missouri

MAMA'S ICE BOX COOKIES

"Mama" is Grace B. Coggeshall, Darlington, South Carolina.

1	CUP BROWN SUGAR	1	TEASPOON SALT
1	CUP WHITE SUGAR	2	TEASPOONS SODA
1 1/2	CUPS CRISCO	2	TEASPOONS CINNAMON
3	EGGS	1	CUP BROKEN PECANS
5	CUPS FLOUR		

Cream Crisco and sugars, then add eggs one at a time. Sift flour before measuring. Stir in salt, soda, and cinnamon. fold into creamed mixture. Add pecans. Form into rolls and refrigerate for at least 24 hours. Slice and bake in a 375 degree oven for 10 minutes. Note: "It is hard to get these sliced thin enough. I put them in the freezer for a couple of hours or longer and then they cut better. It does not seem to change the taste."

Helen Harvey—First Presbyterian Church
Beaufort, South Carolina

Lemon Squares I

This recipe is from our church cookbook, "Divine Dishes," published in 1983.

- 2 CUPS FLOUR
- 1/2 CUP CONFECTIONER'S SUGAR
- 1 CUP BUTTER

Mix and press into 9x13" pan. Bake 15-20 minutes until lightly brown.

Filling:

- 4 EGGS
- 2 CUPS GRANULATED SUGAR
- 1/3 CUP LEMON JUICE
- 1/4 CUP FLOUR
- 1/2 TEASPOON BAKING POWDER

Beat eggs; add other ingredients. Pour over crust. Bake 20 minutes more. Cool and sprinkle with confectioner's sugar; cut into squares.

Irene Childs (deceased)—First Presbyterian Church, Easton, Maryland
Ernestine Philpott—East Ridge Presbyterian Church, Chattanooga, Tennessee

Lemon Squares II

- 1 BOX LEMON CAKE MIX
- 1 STICK MARGARINE
- 1 EGG
- 8 OUNCES CREAM CHEESE, SOFTENED
- 2 EGGS, BEATEN
- 1 BOX POWDERED SUGAR

Mix first 3 ingredients and pat into 9x13" pan. Mix and spread the next three ingredients over the lemon cake mixture. Bake in a 350 degree oven for 30 minutes or until brown. Cut into squares.

Edmee Boyd—Hampton Presbyterian Church
Hampton, South Carolina

LETHAL LAYERS

1/2	CUP UNSALTED BUTTER	1	TEASPOON VANILLA
1/2	CUP DARK BROWN SUGAR	1/2	TEASPOON SALT
1	CUP ALL-PURPOSE FLOUR	1	TEASPOON BAKING POWDER
1	CUP PECAN HALVES		ALL-PURPOSE FLOUR (SEE DIRECTIONS)
2	EGGS	1	CUP CHOCOLATE CHIPS
1	CUP FIRMLY PACKED DARK BROWN SUGAR		

In a food processor, combine first 3 ingredients with metal blade until crumbly. This can also be done with 2 pastry knives or a pastry cutter. Place crust into a buttered 9x13" pan and bake for 10 minutes. When crust is cool, spread pecans evenly over surface. Beat eggs with brown sugar until thick. Add vanilla. Put salt and baking powder in bottom of 1/4 cup measure; fill rest of measure with flour. Stir into egg mixture. Pour over crust; sprinkle chocolate chips evenly over mixture. Bake in a 375 degree oven for 20 minutes or until center is baked. Cool; cut into 32 squares.

Susan Boutwell—Fairfax Presbyterian Church
Fairfax, Virginia

MONSTER COOKIES

This recipe makes enough cookies for a "monster" crowd at Youth Fellowship or Vacation Bible School!

1	POUND BUTTER	3	POUNDS PEANUT BUTTER
2	POUNDS BROWN SUGAR	18	CUPS OATMEAL
4	CUPS WHITE SUGAR	8	TEASPOONS BAKING SODA
12	EGGS	1	POUND CHOCOLATE CHIPS
1	TABLESPOON VANILLA	1	POUND M&M PLAIN CANDIES
1	TABLESPOON LIGHT CORN SYRUP		

Cream butter well with brown and white sugars. Add eggs and mix well. Add peanut butter, vanilla and light corn syrup and beat well. Mix oatmeal and baking soda in large bowl. Pour in the butter and sugar and peanut butter mixture and mix well by hand or with a large spoon. Mix in the chips. Drop by tablespoons onto greased cookie sheet and press down a bit with a large spoon or ice cream scoop. Bake in a 350 degree oven for 10-12 minutes. Cool on rack.

Catherine Hanahan—First Presbyterian Church, Valdosta, Georgia
Loma Young—First Presbyterian Church, Savannah, Georgia

Morning Cookies

1	CUP BROWN SUGAR	1	TEASPOON SODA
1/2	CUP MARGARINE	1	TEASPOON CINNAMON
1 1/2	CUPS WHOLE WHEAT FLOUR	1/2	TEASPOON BAKING POWDER
1 1/2	CUPS APPLESAUCE	1/2	TEASPOON SALT
1	CUP ROLLED OATS	1/4	TEASPOON CLOVES
2/3	CUP WHEAT BRAN	1	CUP RAISINS
2	EGG WHITES	1	CUP CHOPPED NUTS
1/2	CUP DRIED MILK		

Cream margarine and brown sugar. Mix well. Mix dry ingredients together, add to creamed mixture with egg whites. Drop by rounded tablespoons 2 inches apart onto baking sheet. Bake in a 375 degree oven for 10 minutes. Make into sandwiches using cream cheese or butter.

Elizabeth C. Robertson—First Presbyterian Church
Beaufort, South Carolina

No-bake Cookies

1	CUP WHITE SUGAR	1	CUP CRUNCHY PEANUT BUTTER
1	CUP WHITE KARO SYRUP	6	CUPS SPECIAL K CEREAL
1	TEASPOON VANILLA	1	CUP BUTTERSCOTCH CHIPS
	DASH SALT	1	CUP CHOCOLATE CHIPS

In a large saucepan boil sugar and syrup long enough to melt sugar. Remove from heat, add peanut butter, and stir to dissolve peanut butter. Pour syrup over cereal in a 9x12" pan. (Crunch cereal with your hands just enough so that flakes will not be so big.) Melt, over hot water, the butterscotch and chocolate chips. Spread over top of hot cereal and syrup mixture. Let stand 3 hours, then cut.

Mrs. Jack Connor—First Central Presbyterian Church
Abilene, Texas

Nut Crust Cookies

1 1/2	POUNDS FLOUR	1	EGG
1 1/4	POUNDS SUGAR (2 3/4 CUPS)	1	POUND LARD
	PINCH OF BAKING SODA	1	CUP PEANUT HALVES

Mix all ingredients together except peanut halves. Place by spoonfuls on cookie sheet. Place several peanut halves on top of cookie for decoration. Bake in a 400 degree oven for 10 minutes.

Leila Ming—St. Stephens Presbyterian Church
Scarborough, Ontario, Canada

OATMEAL CRISPIES

1	CUP SHORTENING (CRISCO)	1 1/2	CUPS FLOUR
1	CUP BROWN SUGAR, PACKED	1	TEASPOON SALT
1	CUP GRANULATED SUGAR	1	TEASPOON BAKING SODA
2	BEATEN EGGS	3	CUPS OATMEAL
1	TEASPOON VANILLA	1/2	CUP CHOPPED WALNUTS

Cream shortening and sugar, add eggs and vanilla. Beat well. Add sifted dry ingredients. Add oatmeal and walnuts. Mix well. Shape into a log 2" by 3" in diameter, wrap in waxed paper and chill thoroughly or overnight. Slice 1/4 inch thick. Bake in a 350 degree oven for 10 minutes.

Melody Baker—Valley Community Presbyterian Church, Golden Valley, Minnesota
Martha Pritchard—Crossnore Presbyterian Church, Crossnore, North Carolina

ORANGE COOKIES

1 1/2	CUPS SUGAR	2	TEASPOONS BAKING POWDER
1	CUP SHORTENING	4	CUPS ALL PURPOSE FLOUR
2	EGGS		GRATED RIND AND JUICE OF ONE ORANGE
1	CUP SOUR MILK		VANILLA TO TASTE
1	TEASPOON SODA		

Icing:

3/4	CUP POWDERED SUGAR		GRATED RIND AND JUICE OF ONE ORANGE

Mix sugar and shortening, add eggs, sour milk and soda. Mix flour, baking powder and salt. Add to other ingredients. Add orange juice and vanilla to mixture. Let stand 15 minutes in a cool place. Drop by teaspoonsful on cookie sheet. Bake in a 350 degree oven for 12-15 minutes. Ice while hot with: 3/4 cup powdered sugar, grated rind and juice of one orange. (You may have to add more sugar.) Yield: 7 dozen.

Mary Runkle—Kings Grant Presbyterian Church
Virginia Beach, Virginia

Parkins

4	CUPS PLAIN FLOUR	2	TEASPOONS GROUND GINGER
6	CUPS OATMEAL	1	TEASPOON GROUND CINNAMON
1	CUP LIGHT SYRUP	3	TEASPOONS BAKING SODA
1 2/3	CUPS SUGAR	2	EGGS
3	STICKS MARGARINE		

Mix all dry ingredients. Melt syrup and margarine. Add to dry ingredients, mix well to a stiff dough. Allow to cool for 1 hour. Form into small balls the size of walnuts. Place on well-greased cookie sheet leaving room to spread. Bake for 10-15 minutes in a 350 degree oven. Cool slightly. Place on wire rack to cool and become crisp. Yield: 100

H. Leach—Letchworth Free Church
Letchworth, England

Peanut Butter Oatmeal Cookies

3	CUPS SUGAR	1	BLOCK BUTTER
1/4	CUP CHOCOLATE	3	CUPS OATMEAL
1/2	CUP MILK	1/4	CUP PEANUT BUTTER

Combine all ingredients and cook for 1 1/2 minutes. Stir in 3 cups oatmeal, 1/4 cup peanut butter. Drop by spoonfuls onto waxed paper. Store in tightly covered container.

Angela Lyleet Stanley—Harmony Presbyterian Church
Crocketville, South Carolina

Pecan Bars

1	STICK MARGARINE	1	CUP LIGHT BROWN SUGAR
2	EGGS	1	CUP PECANS, CHOPPED
3/4	CUP FLOUR (PLAIN)	1	TEASPOON VANILLA

Melt margarine. Add all other ingredients and mix. Pour into shallow, greased or wax-papered pan about 1/2 inch thick. Bake about 20 minutes in a 350 degree oven. Cool, cut into small bars and dust with powdered sugar.

Rebecca O. Bennett—Dahlonega Presbyterian Church
Dahlonega, Georgia

PITCAITHLY BANNOCK

4	CUPS PLAIN FLOUR	2	OUNCES CHOPPED ORANGE OR LEMON PEEL
2 1/2	STICKS BUTTER	2	OUNCES CHOPPED ALMONDS
1/2	CUP SUGAR		

Cream sugar and butter. Work in flour, peel, and almonds. Form into two rounds about 1/2" thick. Trim around the edges and prick all over with a fork. Bake on greased baking sheet in a 350 degree oven until firm and crispy, about 30 minutes. Cut while warm, store in tight container when cool.

Mrs. Edith Hay—Auchtergaven & Moneydie Parish Church
Perth, Scotland

THE PRACTICALLY PERFECT COOKIE

My step-daughter won a blue ribbon at the County Fair with this recipe. This cookie has a chewy interior, crunchy edges and well-blended flavor. It has a high overall chocolate impact to give a sensuous rush to the chocoholic.

2 1/4	CUPS FLOUR	2	STICKS (1/2 POUND) BUTTER (SOFTENED)
1	LEVEL TEASPOON BAKING SODA	1	TEASPOON VANILLA EXTRACT
1	LEVEL TEASPOON SALT	2	LARGE EGGS
3/4	CUP WHITE SUGAR	1	12 OUNCE PACKAGE NESTLE
3/4	CUP DARK BROWN SUGAR, PACKED		SEMI-SWEET CHOCOLATE CHIPS

Mix the flour, baking soda and salt in a bowl and set aside. Mix the sugars briefly, add butter in small goblets and mix, first at low speed and then at high speed. Beat until mix is pale, light, and very fluffy. Add vanilla and beat; add eggs at low speed, then beat at high speed. Mix should look creamed, not curdled. Add flour, baking soda and salt, 1/2 cup at a time, mixing at low, and then high speed, scraping sides of bowl. Stir in chocolate chips. Drop by tablespoonfuls onto an ungreased cookie sheet. Bake in a preheated 375 degree oven until the cookies are pale golden brown, 9 minutes in an electric oven, 10-11 minutes in a gas oven. Cool on a rack. Enjoy!

Henry Loble—First Presbyterian Church
Helena, Montana

Pumpkin Cookies

3/4	CUP HONEY	2 1/2	CUPS FLOUR
1	STICK BUTTER (1/2 CUP)	1	TEASPOON BAKING SODA
1	EGG	1	TEASPOON BAKING POWDER
1	CUP PUMPKIN	1	TEASPOON CINNAMON
1	TEASPOON VANILLA	1	TEASPOON NUTMEG

Mix butter, honey, egg, pumpkin and vanilla. Stir in the dry ingredients. Drop by small teaspoonfuls on greased baking sheet. Bake in a 350 degree oven for 12-15 minutes.

Lanna Hitchcock—Presbyterian Church
Jewett, New York

Highland Shortbread

1 1/2	CUPS PLAIN FLOUR	2/3	CUP POWDERED SUGAR
1 1/2	STICKS BUTTER (NOT MARGARINE)	1/2	CUP CORN STARCH

Sift all dry ingredients, knead butter into mixture. Keep mixing by hand until it forms a firm paste. Divide between two 8" cake pans, press down and prick all over with a fork. Bake in a 325 degree oven for 30 minutes or until golden brown. Cut into wedges while warm. Sprinkle with sugar. Leave in pans until cool.

Dorothy Kennedy—North Church, Perth, Tayside, Scotland
Isabel M. Laing—Letchworth Free Church, Letchworth, England
Effie Kerr—Isle of Cumbrae Parish Church, Isle of Cumbrae, Scotland
Joan Polumbo—Highland Presbyterian Church, Fayetteville, North Carolina
Mrs. Mark Patek—South Salem Presbyterian Church, South Salem, New York
Jean Cameron—North Church, Perth, Scotland

Good Spice Cookies-Molasses

2 1/4	CUPS FLOUR	1/2	TEASPOON CLOVES
2	TEASPOONS BAKING SODA	1	CUP FIRMLY PACKED BROWN SUGAR
1/4	TEASPOON SALT	3/4	CUP (1 1/2 STICKS) MARGARINE
1	TEASPOON CINNAMON	1/3	CUP MOLASSES
1	TEASPOON GINGER	1	EGG

Mix together well. Add dry ingredients. Use a teaspoon to scoop up; dip tops in regular sugar and lay on greased cookie sheets. Bake in a 350 degree oven, about 12 minutes.

Polly Russak—Bryson City Presbyterian Church
Bryson City, North Carolina

BIG SOFT SUGAR COOKIES

1	CUP BUTTER OR MARGARINE	1	TEASPOON BAKING POWDER
2	CUPS WHITE SUGAR	4	CUPS FLOUR
2	EGGS	1	TEASPOON VANILLA
1	CUP BUTTERMILK	1/2	TEASPOON VANILLA
1	TEASPOON SODA		

Cream shortening, sugar and eggs. Add buttermilk and dry ingredients. Drop dough by big tablespoons on greased cookie sheet, press down with a glass dipped in water. Sprinkle with sugar and bake in a 350 degree oven for 10-12 minutes.

Beth Seelau—Corfu United Presbyterian Church
Corfu, New York

STREUSEL FINGERS

1 1/2	CUPS PLAIN FLOUR	1	EGG, WELL BEATEN
2	TEASPOONS BAKING POWDER	1/4	CUP BROWN SUGAR
	PINCH OF SALT	2	TABLESPOONS BUTTER
3/4	CUP SUGAR	2	TABLESPOONS PLAIN FLOUR
1/2	STICK OF MARGARINE	1	TEASPOON GROUND CINNAMON
4	TABLESPOONS MILK	1/4	CUP CHOPPED WALNUTS

Sift together flour, baking powder and salt. Cream the margarine and sugar, add beaten egg. Add milk and fold in flour. Pour 1/2 the batter into a greased 8"x12" pan, spread out evenly. Mix topping, it will be crumbly. Sprinkle 1/2 of the topping over the batter. Repeat the layers with remaining batter and topping. Bake in a 350 degree oven for 35 minutes. Cut into fingers when cool.

Isle of Cumbrae Parish Church, Isle of Cumbrae, Scotland

SURVIVAL COOKIES

These cookies are excellent to stow away when traveling as no refrigeration is required and they don't crumble!

2	CUPS FLOUR	2	TEASPOONS VANILLA
1	TEASPOON SALT	3/4	CUP WHITE SUGAR
1	TEASPOON BAKING POWDER	3/4	CUP CANOLA OIL
2	TEASPOONS CINNAMON	3	CUPS ROLLED OATS
1	TEASPOON SODA	1	CUP RAISINS
3/4	CUP DARK BROWN SUGAR	3/4	CUP PECANS, CHOPPED
2	TABLESPOONS WATER	1/2	CUP CANDIED CHERRIES
2	LARGE EGGS	1/2	CUP FRUITCAKE MIXED FRUIT

Sift flour, salt, baking powder, cinnamon, baking soda and sugar into a large bowl. Add eggs, water, vanilla, and shortening and beat until smooth with electric beater. Fold in remaining ingredients. This mixture will be very stiff and a wooden spoon is helpful in mixing. You may use more or less of the fruit mixture; adjust liquid accordingly. Roll into balls, press out slightly on cookie sheet, approximately 2 inches apart, on greased cookie sheet. Bake in a 375 degree oven for 12-15 minutes. You may use egg substitute, or less sugar.

Julia O. Ramsey—Highland Presbyterian Church
Fayetteville, North Carolina

TEATIME SPECIAL

1/2	CUP SHORTENING	2	CUPS SELF-RISING FLOUR
1/2	CUP SUGAR	3/4	CUP CURRANTS
	MILK		

Cut shortening and sugar into the flour, add currants and enough milk to make stiff dough. Spread evenly on a greased cookie sheet to about 3/4 thickness, bake in a 350 degree oven for 30 minutes. Cool before cutting into squares.

Letchworth Free Church, Letchworth, England

Chapter Five

Desserts — Pies

DESSERTS

APPLE CRUMBLE

2	CUPS SELF-RISING FLOUR	1	EGG, BEATEN
2/3	CUP GRANULATED SUGAR	1	TEASPOON VANILLA EXTRACT
1	STICK MARGARINE	1	TEASPOON ALMOND EXTRACT
2	POUNDS APPLES	1/2	TEASPOON CINNAMON
1/2	CUP RAISINS		

Mix the flour with 1/2 cup sugar and rub in the margarine. Add beaten egg, vanilla and, almond extract, and mix well. Press half of this mixture into a 9" pie pan. Grate the peeled and cored apples and mix in raisins, cinnamon, and the remaining sugar. Place this on top of the flour, sugar, and margarine mixture, crumble the remaining mixture on top of the apples. Bake in a 375 degree oven for 35 minutes. Yield: 8 to 10 servings.

Doreen Knight—Letchworth United Reformed Church
Letchworth, England

APPLE FINGERS

2 1/2	CUPS SELF-RISING FLOUR	1	EGG
1 1/4	STICK MARGARINE	1	TABLESPOON MILK
2/3	CUP BROWN SUGAR		SUGAR (FINELY GRANULATED)
1	POUND COOKING APPLES		PINCH OF SALT

Sift flour and salt, cut in margarine until mixture is like bread crumbs. Peel core and chop apples into small pieces, add to mixture. Stir in beaten egg and milk. Turn into a greased 9"x12" and spread evenly. Bake in a 400 degree oven for 35 to 40 minutes. Dust with sugar and cut into fingers. Serve hot or cold.

Eloise Rhodes—Letchworth Free Church
Letchworth, England

John's Boy Scout Blueberry Dessert

1	JIFFY YELLOW CAKE MIX	1/2	STICK MARGARINE
1	CAN BLUEBERRY PIE FILLING		

Lightly grease a 6"x10" baking pan. Pour blueberry pie filling in pan and spread evenly. Sprinkle cake mix over the top. Thinly slice margarine and dot over cake mix. Bake in a 325 degree oven until top is golden brown, about 20 minutes. Yield: 12 to 16 servings. You may use apple pie filling. Delicious served hot with a scoop of vanilla ice cream.

Mederia Rivers Stanley—Harmony Presbyterian Church
Crocketville, South Carolina

New Orleans Bread Pudding

You've eaten bread pudding before, but this will be the best.

2	QUARTS STALE FRENCH BREAD, CUBED	1/8	TEASPOON SALT
1	QUART SWEET MILK	5	EGGS, SLIGHTLY BEATEN
1	TALL CAN EVAPORATED MILK	1/2	CUP RAISINS, SOAKED IN MILK
1 1/2	CUPS SUGAR		VANILLA TO TASTE
1/2	STICK MARGARINE, MELTED		

Mix all ingredients together and let stand 30 minutes or longer. Pour into buttered baking dish, set in larger pan in 1" of water. Bake in a 350 degree oven for 1 hour, or until knife comes out clean.

Sauce: (optional)

1	STICK MARGARINE	1	EGG, BEATEN
1	CUP SUGAR	1/4	CUP RUM OR BOURBON
1/4	CUP WATER		

Cook margarine, sugar and water until sugar dissolves. Remove from heat. Slowly add the beaten egg, stirring constantly. Return to heat, cook one minute, add the rum or bourbon.

Bonnie Mahaffey—First Presbyterian Church
Baton Rouge, Louisiana

Wonderful Bread Pudding

4	CUPS MILK	1	TEASPOON VANILLA OR NUTMEG
2	EGGS	3/4	CUP SUGAR
5	SLICES BREAD OR ROLLS	4	TABLESPOONS MELTED BUTTER

Soak bread in warm milk. Beat until well-mixed. Add rest of ingredients. Put in baking dish 8 1/2 inches square. Bake in a 350 degree oven until set, or a silver knife comes out clean. Yield: 10 to 12 servings.

Mrs. Annie Bowers (our dear member of longest membership)—First Presbyterian Church
Beaufort, South Carolina

Cheesecake

An easy classic cheesecake your friends will love!

3	8 OUNCE PACKAGES CREAM CHEESE	1	TEASPOON VANILLA
1	CUP SUGAR	2	GRAHAM CRACKER CRUSTS
3	EGGS	1	CAN CHERRY PIE FILLING
2	TABLESPOONS FLOUR		

Cream sugar and cream cheese until fluffy. Add eggs beating in one at a time. Beat in the flour and vanilla. Pour into prepared crusts. Bake in a 350 degree oven for 45 minutes. Cool and top with cherry pie filling.

Patty Waller—Christian Assembly of God
Greenville, South Carolina

Cheese Pie Dessert

2	8 OUNCE PACKAGES CREAM CHEESE	1/2	PINT SOUR CREAM
2/3	CUPS SUGAR	1	TEASPOON VANILLA
3	EGGS	3	TABLESPOONS SUGAR
1/2	TEASPOON ALMOND EXTRACT		

Beat cream cheese, 2/3 cup sugar, eggs and almond extract until well blended. Place in a buttered 9" pie pan. Bake 35 minutes in a 350 degree oven. Cool 20 minutes. Combine the sour cream, vanilla and 3 tablespoons sugar. Spread on top of pie. Bake 10 minutes longer. Top with coconut, toasted almonds or chocolate swirls. Yield: 8 servings.

Bobbie Rubin—Pacific Palisades Presbyterian Church
Pacific Palisades, California

Charlotte Rousse

This recipe was my Grandmother's—Leonora Howze Bryan, wife of the Rev. Dr. James Alexander Bryan, pastor of the Third Presbyterian Church of Birmingham, Alabama, from 1889 to 1941, and Chaplain of the City of Birmingham.

- 4 TABLESPOONS MILK
- 1 1/4 OUNCE PACKAGE UNFLAVORED GELATIN
- 5 TABLESPOONS SWEET SHERRY
- 6 EGGS, SEPARATED
- 5 TABLESPOONS SUGAR
- 1 TEASPOON VANILLA EXTRACT
- 1 PINT HEAVY CREAM

Dissolve gelatin in milk in top of a double boiler over low heat. Cool and add sherry. Beat egg yolks and 1 tablespoon sugar and vanilla together. Add this mixture to the milk mixture. Cool and set aside. Beat egg whites until stiff and gradually add 3 tablespoons sugar. In another bowl, beat cream until stiff and add 1 tablespoon sugar. Fold whipped cream and egg whites into the yolk mixture. Pour into a bowl and chill for 3 hours. Yield: 10 to 12 servings.

Frances Bryan Brewer—First Presbyterian Church
Beaufort, South Carolina

Chocolate Eclair Dessert

- 1 BOX GRAHAM CRACKERS (USE WHOLE)
- 1 LARGE (5 1/2 OUNCE) PACKAGE INSTANT VANILLA PUDDING
- 3 CUPS MILK
- 1 9 OUNCE CARTON COOL WHIP

Topping:

- 1 TABLESPOON VANILLA
- 3 TABLESPOONS BUTTER, MELTED
- 2 TABLESPOONS CORN SYRUP
- 2 SQUARES SEMI-SWEET BAKING CHOCOLATE
- 1 1/2 CUPS POWDERED SUGAR
- 3 TABLESPOONS MILK

Mix pudding mix and milk. Fold into Cool Whip. Layer graham crackers on bottom 9x13 inch pan. Pour over half pudding mix. Make another layer of crackers and cover with rest of pudding. Add a third layer of crackers. For topping, melt chocolate and butter together and combine other ingredients. Add topping. Yield: 16-20 servings.

Julia Randel—First Presbyterian Church, Beaufort, South Carolina
Joan Matteson—Providence Presbyterian Church, Fairfax, Virginia

Chocolate Layer Dessert

First layer:

| 1 | STICK MARGARINE | 1 | CUP CHOPPED NUTS |
| 1 | CUP FLOUR | | |

Second layer:

| 1 | LARGE, 8 OUNCE CREAM CHEESE | 8 | OUNCES COOL WHIP |
| 1 | CUP POWDERED SUGAR | 1 | TEASPOON VANILLA |

Third layer:

| 2 | SMALL INSTANT CHOCOLATE PUDDING | 8 | OUNCES COOL WHIP |

First layer, mix ingredients, press into a 9"x13" pan. Bake in a 350 degree oven for 15 minutes. Cool. Second layer, mix ingredients and spread over first layer. Third layer, mix chocolate pudding according to package directions and spread over second layer. Cover with the Cool Whip. Chill overnight. Yield: 15-18 servings.

Mrs. Loma Young—First Presbyterian Church
Savannah, Georgia

Cloutie Dumpling

1	CUP SELF-RISING FLOUR	1	APPLE, GRATED
3/4	CUP SUGAR	1 1/2	CUPS CURRANTS
3/4	CUP SUET, FINELY CHOPPED	2 1/4	CUPS RAISINS
3/4	CUP BREAD CRUMBS	1	TABLESPOON MOLASSES
1 1/4	CUPS MILK		

Mix all ingredients together. Scald a pudding cloth in boiling water. Drain well, then lay out flat and flour the cloth and sprinkle with sugar. (This forms the characteristic skin). Place the mixture onto the cloth and tie securely, allowing for expansion. Place on a plate in the bottom of a large saucepan. Pour in boiling water to cover, then simmer for 2 1/2 to 3 hours. Turn out carefully and dry off in oven. (If dipped in cold water, the skin should not stick to the cloth.) Serve with custard or cream.

Mrs. Alison McGregor—Auchtergaven & Moneydie Parish Church, Perth, Scotland
Mrs. Anne K. Mitchell—Perth North Church, Perth, Scotland

COCONUT TORTE

(World's Best Dessert) This recipe was given to me especially for this cookbook by my friend, Lib Yingling of St. Thomas Episcopal Church, Savannah, Georgia.

1/4	CUP MARGARINE, SOFTENED	2	PACKAGES REGULAR JELLO (NOT INSTANT) COCONUT CREAM PUDDING
2	TABLESPOONS SUGAR		
1	CUP FLOUR	3	CUPS MILK
1/2	CUP PECANS, BROKEN	1/2	CUP ANGEL FLAKE COCONUT
1	CUP COOL WHIP	8	OUNCES CREAM CHEESE, SOFTENED
1 1/2	CUPS POWDERED SUGAR	1	16 OUNCE CONTAINER COOL WHIP

Mix margarine, sugar, flour, and pecans. Pat into a 9x13" pan. Bake for 15 minutes in a preheated 350 degree oven. Cool. Mix cream cheese, Cool Whip (1 cup), and powdered sugar. Spread over cooled crust. Cook pudding and milk. Add coconut to pudding. Cool and then spread over cream cheese/Cool Whip layer. Top with container of Cool Whip. Sprinkle with more coconut. Refigerate until time to serve. Cut into squares. Yield: 10 servings. Freezes well.

Nancy Myers—First Presbyterian Church
Beaufort, South Carolina

CRANACHAN

1	POUND RASPBERRIES		SUGAR TO TASTE
1 1/4	CUPS WHIPPING CREAM	2	OUNCES MINIATURE OF DRAMBUIE
1/4	CUP TOASTED ROLLED OATS		

Whip cream until slightly thickened, add raspberries, toasted oats, Drambuie and sugar, fold in carefully. Serve immediately in sundae glasses.

Mrs. Margorie McFarlane—Auchtergaven & Moneydie Parish Church
Perth, Scotland

CRANBERRY-APPLE CASSEROLE

- 4 CUPS TART APPLES, PEELED AND DICED
- 2 CUPS FRESH, WHOLE CRANBERRIES
- 1 CUP SUGAR

Mix ingredients and put in 10x13 inch pan.

Topping

- 1 CUP CHOPPED PECANS
- 1/3 CUP FLOUR
- 1/2 CUP MELTED BUTTER
- 1/2 CUP BROWN SUGAR
- 1/2 CUP OATMEAL

Mix together and sprinkle over fruit. Bake in a 325 degree oven for 1 hour.

Susie Neal—Fort Hill Presbyterian Church, Clemson, South Carolina
Charlotte Vedeler—The Old Presbyterian Meeting House, Alexandria, Virginia

CROWN JEWEL DESSERT

- 1 3 OUNCE PACKAGE LIME JELLO
- 1 3 OUNCE PACKAGE ORANGE JELLO
- 1 3 OUNCE PACKAGE RASPBERRY JELLO
- 1 1/2 CUPS COLD WATER
- 1 CUP PINEAPPLE JUICE
- 1/4 CUP SUGAR
- 1 PACKAGE LEMON JELLO
- 1/2 CUP COLD WATER
- 18-20 WHOLE LADYFINGERS, SEPARATED
- 16 OUNCES COOL WHIP

Prepare lime, orange and raspberry Jello (each in separate 8x8 inch pan) using 1 cup boiling water and 1/2 cup cold water for each package. Chill until firm. Cut into 1/2 inch squares. Heat pineapple juice to boiling point, remove from heat, add lemon Jello, add sugar and stir until dissolved, add remaining 1/2 cup of cold water. Chill until syrupy. Line bottom and sides of trifle bowl (glass bowl) with lady fingers. Set aside. Fold syrupy lemon Jello into the Cool Whip. Then fold in Jello cubes. Pour this into a glass bowl. Chill for 8 hours or overnight.

Charlotte Vedeler—The Old Presbyterian Meeting House
Alexandria, Virginia

Easy Cheese Cake

Filling:

- 3 8 OUNCE PACKAGES CREAM CHEESE
- 3 CUPS SUGAR
- 6 CUPS COOL WHIP
- 1 TEASPOON SALT
- 9 EGGS, SEPARATED

Crust:

- 2 1/2 CUPS GRAHAM CRACKER CRUMBS
- 1/2 CUP SUGAR
- 1/2 CUP MARGARINE

Mix the crust ingredients together well and press into two 9"x13" baking dishes. Bake in a 375 degree oven for 8 minutes. Cool. Make the filling by creaming the sugar and egg yolks, salt and cheese until smooth, then add Cool Whip. Beat egg whites until very stiff and fold into the sugar mixture. Pour into the cooled crusts. Sprinkle more crumbs over the top, cover with plastic wrap and freeze. Keep frozen until ready to serve. Serve with any kind of fruit in season or use canned pie filling. Yield: 48 servings.

Dr. Mildred K. Ellis—The National Presbyterian Church
Washington, D.C.

Fairy Torte

- 1 1/2 CUPS SUGAR
- 1 STICK BUTTER
- 4 EGGS, SEPARATED
- 1 TEASPOON VANILLA
- 1/2 CUP FLOUR
- 4 TABLESPOONS MILK
- 1 TEASPOON BAKING POWDER
- 1 CUP WHIPPED CREAM
- SLICED STRAWBERRIES OR DRAINED CRUSHED PINEAPPLE

Cream 1/2 cup of the sugar with the butter, add the egg yolks to the creamed mixture. Add the flour, baking powder, and milk to the creamed mixture (alternate, a little, flour then a little milk until all is used). Pour into 2 buttered layer pans. Beat the egg whites until peaks form, then beat in the vanilla and remaining sugar, 2 tablespoons at a time, until all the sugar is used. Then beat until very stiff, divide this mixture between the two pans and spread evenly over the batter. Bake 25 minutes in a 375 degree oven. Cool, remove from pans. When putting together, arrange with one meringue down on the plate, spread with whipped cream mixed with the strawberries or pineapple. Place top layer on with the meringue on top. The meringue may be sprinkled with chopped nuts before baking if desired.

Jean Nevius—Hampton Presbyterian Church
Hampton, South Carolina

Free Kirk Pudding

1 1/4	CUPS PLAIN FLOUR	1/4	STICK BUTTER
1/4	CUP TAPIOCA	1/4	CUP SUGAR
1/4	CUP RAISINS	1	TEASPOON BAKING SODA
2 1/2	CUPS BOILING MILK	1/2	TEASPOON GROUND NUTMEG

Melt butter in milk, add all other ingredients, mixing well. Place in a well-buttered pudding basin (any heat proof bowl), cover with 2 layers of greased, greaseproof paper with a fold over the top to allow for expansion. Steam in a pot of boiling water for 2 hours. Serve with cream or custard sauce.

Miss Lena Ritchie—Auchtergaven & Moneydie Parish Church
Perth, Scotland

Fruit Sherbet

- 1 LARGE CAN SLICED PEACHES, CRUSHED WITH JUICE
- 1 SMALL CAN CRUSHED PINEAPPLE WITH JUICE
- 1 CUP SUGAR
- 1 SMALL BOTTLE CHERRIES, DRAINED, CUT UP
- JUICE OF 2 LEMONS

Mix and put in container to freeze. Take out of freezer about 15 minutes before serving.

Marion Vaughan—Hampton Presbyterian Church
Hampton, South Carolina

Lemon Delicacy

2	TABLESPOONS BUTTER	1	CUP MILK
3/4	CUP SUGAR	2	TABLESPOONS FLOUR
1	LEMON (JUICE)	1/2	LEMON (GRATED RIND)
2	EGGS		

Cream butter and sugar gradually and cream well. Add well beaten egg yolks, flour, lemon juice, and rind. Add milk and stiffly beaten egg whites; pour into greased baking dish. Place in pan of hot water and bake in a 325-350 degree oven for 45 minutes. A delicate crust will form on top and the pudding will supply its own sauce. Yield: 6 servings.

Jeanne Sams Aimar—First Presbyterian Church, Beaufort, South Carolina
Clara Thompson—Presbyterian Church, Jewett, New York

Marshmallow/Pineapple Dessert

1	POUND MARSHMALLOW	1	#2 CAN CRUSHED PINEAPPLE
1	PINT WHIPPING CREAM OR	1	CUP CHOPPED NUTS
1	LARGE COOL WHIP		GRAHAM CRACKER CRUMBS

Drain pineapple juice and heat. Melt marshmallows in juice. Set aside to cool, then chill in refrigerator. Whip cream (or use Cool Whip), add marshmallow mixture, pineapple and nuts. Spread in large rectangular pan lined with graham cracker crumbs. Chill a few hours before serving. Will keep indefinitely in refrigerator. Yield: 15 servings.

Mrs. Coy Warren—First Central Presbyterian Church
Abilene, Texas

Mary, Queen of Scots, Tart

1/2	STICK BUTTER	1/4	CUP RAISINS
1/4	SUGAR	2	EGGS, BEATEN
2	OUNCES CHOPPED CANDIED PEEL		

Grease an 8" cake pan and line with puff pastry. Melt the butter and sugar together, add the candied peel, raisins and eggs. Pour into the lined pan and bake for 30-40 minutes in a 375 degree oven. When cold, the top may be covered with a light icing. Yield: 8-10 servings.

Jenny Orr—Isle of Cumbrae Parish Church
Isle of Cumbrae, Scotland

Mint Mousse

36	LARGE MARSHMALLOWS	1	LARGE CARTON WHIPPED TOPPING
2/3	CUP CREME DE MENTHE	1	SMALL CAN CHOCOLATE SYRUP

Melt marshmallows in creme de menthe in top of double boiler, over simmering water. Cool. Fold in whipped topping. Pour into a 2 quart mold and freeze. Unmold on plate by dipping mold into hot water, return to freezer. When serving, pass the chocolate syrup in a small pitcher to drizzle over the mousse.

Mrs. Sam Huhn—First Presbyterian Church
Beaufort, South Carolina

PEACH COBBLER

1 CUP SUGAR	1 STICK MARGARINE, MELTED
1 CUP SELF-RISING FLOUR	4 CUPS FRESH PEACHES (FROZEN OR CANNED FRUIT SUCH AS BLUEBERRIES OR CHERRIES MAY BE USED.)
1 CUP MILK	

Melt margarine in bottom of 8"x12" pan. Make a batter of the sugar, flour, and milk. Pour into the middle of the margarine. Pour the peaches into middle of batter. Bake in a 400 degree oven for about 25 minutes. Yield: 8 servings.

Madlyn Webb McElveen—First Presbyterian Church, Beaufort, South Carolina
Edmee Boyd—Hampton Presbyterian Church, Hampton, South Carolina
Lilie Allred—Harmony Presbyterian Church, Crocketville, South Carolina

PINA COLADA DESSERT SQUARES

2 CUPS VANILLA WAFER CRUMBS	1 8 OUNCE FROZEN WHIPPED TOPPING, THAWED
1/3 CUP MARGARINE, MELTED	1 8 OUNCE CAN CRUSHED PINEAPPLE, DRAINED
1 8 3/4 OUNCE CAN COCO GOYA CREAM OF COCONUT	1/2 CUP CHOPPED MARASCHINO CHERRIES, DRAINED
2 8 OUNCE PACKAGES CREAM CHEESE SOFTENED	1/2 CUP CHOPPED NUTS
1 TEASPOON RUM FLAVORING	1/2 CUP FLAKED COCONUT, TOASTED

Combine crumbs, margarine, press into bottom of 13x9 inch pan. Gradually add cream of coconut to cream cheese, mixing at medium speed of electric mixer until well-blended. Stir in rum. Fold in whipped topping, pineapple, cherries and nuts. Spread over crust. Sprinkle with coconut. Chill several hours or overnight. Yield: 15 servings.

Illyf Nichols—First Presbyterian Church
Blackwood, New Jersey

Plum Pudding

2	POUNDS RAISINS	1/2	POUND CANDIED PEEL
1	POUND SULTANAS (GOLDEN RAISINS)	6	EGGS
1	POUND CURRANTS	2	TEASPOONS NUTMEG
1	POUND SUET, FINELY CHOPPED	1/2	TEASPOON SALT
6	CUPS BREAD CRUMBS	3/4	CUP MILK
1	CUP FLOUR	2	TABLESPOONS BRANDY
3/4	CUP BROWN SUGAR		RIND AND JUICE OF 1 LEMON

Beat eggs. Add milk and brandy. Add to dry ingredients and mix well. Pour into greased pudding basins, any heat proof bowl, and tie a cloth over the top of the bowl. Set bowl on a rack in a large sauce pan. Add water to pan, cover and steam the pudding for 3 hours. Be sure pan does not boil dry. Store in a cool place. When ready to serve, steam again to heat. Turn out of bowl and serve warm with custard or brown sugar sauce. Yield: 3 puddings, 8-9 servings each.

Vera Forde—St. Andrews Presbyterian Church
Saskatoon, Saskatchewan, Canada

Layered Raspberry Dessert

"Served at our Presbyterian Women (PW) luncheons."

Layer 1:

1	CUP BUTTER, MELTED	2	TABLESPOONS SUGAR
1 1/2	CUPS FLOUR		

Mix ingredients together, spread in greased 9"x13" pan. Bake in a 350 degree oven for 20-25 minutes. Cool completely.

Layer 2:

6	OUNCES CREAM CHEESE, SOFTENED	2	CUPS POWDERED SUGAR
1/2	CUP BUTTER, MELTED		

Mix cream cheese and butter. Add sugar and mix well. Spread over first layer.

Layer 3:

1   CUP CHOPPED PECANS

Sprinkle nuts over second layer.

Layer 4:

1   3 OUNCE PACKAGE RASPBERRY GELATIN
1   CUP BOILING WATER
    WHIPPED CREAM OR COOL WHIP
2   10 OUNCE PACKAGES FROZEN RASPBERRIES, THAWED

Mix gelatin and water, add raspberries in heavy syrup. Refrigerate until gelatin has started to thicken. Spoon over third layer, chill. To serve, cut into squares and top with whipped cream. Yield: 24 servings. (Frozen strawberries, also in heavy syrup may be used with strawberry gelatin.)

First Presbyterian Church
Wyoming, New York

FROSTY STRAWBERRY SQUARES

1   CUP FLOUR
1/2   CUP CHOPPED NUTS
1/2   CUP BROWN SUGAR
1/2   CUP MARGARINE
2   EGG WHITES
2   TABLESPOONS LEMON JUICE
1   CARTON COOL WHIP
1/2   CUP SUGAR
2   CUPS STRAWBERRIES (FROZEN OR FRESH)

Mix flour, chopped nuts, brown sugar, and margarine together and spread in 9x13 inch pan. Bake and turn in a 300 degree oven for 15 minutes. Reserve 1/3 of crumbs for top of dessert. Beat egg whites until stiff. Add sugar and lemon juice. Fold in crushed strawberries and Cool Whip. Spoon over crumbs. Top with crumbs. Freeze. Cut in squares to serve and let thaw at room temperature for an hour before serving. Garnish with whipped cream or a fresh strawberry. Yield: 24 servings.

Mrs. Bill Spencer—First Central Presbyterian Church
Abilene, Texas

TRIFLE

- 1 ANGEL FOOD CAKE
- 2 LARGE INSTANT PUDDING, VANILLA
- CUT UP FRUIT, BANANAS, STRAWBERRIES, ETC.

Tear cake into pieces. Prepare the pudding. Put 1/3 of the cake into a serving bowl, pour 1/3 of the pudding over the cake, add a layer of fruit. Repeat cake, pudding, and fruit until bowl is full. A little sherry sprinkled over the top of dessert will add sparkle. Yield: 12 to 15 servings.

Martha Carpenter—Westminster Presbyterian Church
Greenville, South Carolina

WELSH CAKES

- 2 CUPS SELF-RISING FLOUR
- 1/2 STICK MARGARINE OR BUTTER
- 1/4 CUP SHORTENING
- MILK
- 1/4 CUP SUGAR
- 1/2 CUP CURRANTS
- 1 EGG
- PINCH OF NUTMEG, IF DESIRED

Heat griddle or heavy frying pan. Work butter and shortening into flour until mixture resembles bread crumbs. Stir in sugar and currants, beat egg and add to mixture with just enough milk to make a firm dough. Roll out on floured surface and cut into rounds, bake on greased griddle on low heat for about 3 minutes on each side until golden brown. Cool on wire rack and serve with a dusting of sugar.

Phyllis Fernyn—Letchworth Free Church
Letchworth, England

PIES

AMBROSIA PIE

- 2 BAKED PIE SHELLS
- 1 #2 CAN CRUSHED PINEAPPLE
- 6 TABLESPOONS FLOUR
- 1 1/2 CUPS SUGAR
- 3 BANANAS
- 1 CUP CHOPPED NUTS
- COCONUT TO SPRINKLE OVER 2 PIES
- 1/2 PINT WHIPPING CREAM OR COOL WHIP

Combine undrained pineapple, flour, and sugar. Cool until thick, and set aside to cool. Place cut bananas in bottom of 2 baked pie crusts. Sprinkle nuts evenly over the 2 pies. Pour cooled pineapple mixture over all. Sprinkle with coconut. Top with whipped cream or Cool Whip. Yield: 2 pies.

Julie LaGrone—First Presbyterian Church
Beaufort, South Carolina

Apple Crumb Pie

6	LARGE TART APPLES	1/3 TO 1/2	CUP SUGAR
1	DEEP-DISH PIE CRUST	3/4	CUP FLOUR
1/2	CUP SUGAR	1/3	CUP MARGARINE
1	TEASPOON CINNAMON		

Peel apples, slice and arrange in deep-dish crust. Mix 1/2 cup sugar with cinnamon, sprinkle over apples. Sift 1/3 to 1/2 cup sugar with flour, cut in margarine till crumbly. Sprinkle over apples. Bake in center of oven with baking sheet on lower rack to catch drips.

Jo Ann C. Leist—Ray Memorial Presbyterian Church
Monroe, Georgia

Apple Pecan Pie

2	CUPS DICED APPLES	1	EGG
1/2	CUP WHITE SUGAR	1/2	CUP PECANS
1/2	CUP BROWN SUGAR	1	TEASPOON VANILLA
1/3	CUP FLOUR (ALL-PURPOSE)		DASH SALT
1	TEASPOON BAKING POWDER		

Mix ingredients in order given and pour into unbaked pie crust (9"). Preheat oven to 375 degrees. After pie browns, (about 25 minutes), lower heat to 325 degrees and bake for 35-40 minutes longer. If crust edge gets too brown, cover with strip of foil. Cool on wire rack. Can be served warm or cold. Delicious with a scoop of vanilla ice cream.

Virginia Foster (This recipe came from my mother.)—Fairfax Presbyterian Church
Fairfax, Virginia

Sour Cream Apple Pie

9"	UNBAKED PIE SHELL	1	TEASPOON VANILLA
1	CUP SOUR CREAM	1	EGG
1/3	CUP PLUS 2 TABLESPOONS FLOUR	3	CUPS DICED APPLES (TART)
1	CUP SUGAR	1/2	CUP BROWN SUGAR
1/4	TEASPOON SALT	1/4	CUP BUTTER, SOFTENED

Beat together sour cream, two tablespoons flour, sugar, salt, vanilla, and egg. Mix in apples and place in pie shell. Bake 25 minutes in a 375 degree oven. Combine brown sugar, butter, and 1/3 cup flour, sprinkle on top of pie. Bake additional 20 minutes. Serve warm or cold. Yield: 8 servings.

Myrtie Dunn—First Presbyterian Church
Cuero, Texas

Buttermilk Pie

3	EGGS	3	TABLESPOONS FLOUR
1	CUP SUGAR	1/2	STICK MELTED BUTTER
1	CUP BUTTERMILK	1	LEMON (JUICE)
1	UNBAKED 9" PIE SHELL		

Beat eggs well, add sugar and mix well. Add remaining ingredients and pour into pie shell. Bake in a 350 degree oven for 55-60 minutes. Yield: 8 servings.

Blanche E. Bauer—First Presbyterian Church
Cuero, Texas

Chess Pie (Miss Eva Keeter's)

1	STICK BUTTER	1	TEASPOON NUTMEG
1 3/4	CUPS SUGAR	1	TEASPOON VANILLA
1/4	CUP PLAIN WHITE CORNMEAL	2	EGGS
1/4	CUP PLAIN FLOUR, SIFTED	1 1/2	CUPS MILK
1	TEASPOON SALT	1	UNBAKED PIE SHELL

Mix first seven ingredients, in exact order. Add eggs and milk and beat with a spoon. Let stand one hour. Pour into the unbaked pie shell. Bake in a 350 degree oven for 45 minutes or longer. Yield: 8 servings.

Barbara Dark—First Presbyterian Church
Marion, North Carolina

Coconut Macaroon Pie

1	CUP COCONUT	1/4	TEASPOON VANILLA FLAVORING
1	CUP GRAHAM CRACKER CRUMBS	2	DROPS BLACK WALNUT FLAVORING
1	CUP PECANS	2	DROPS COCONUT FLAVORING
1	CUP SUGAR	1	PINT COOL WHIP
4	EGG WHITES		

Beat egg whites until stiff. Fold in coconut, cracker crumbs, pecans sugar and all flavorings. Put in 8 inch pie pan. Bake for 25 minutes, in a 325 degree oven. Let cool. Spread Cool Whip over top. Place about 5 pecans on top. Keep in refrigerator overnight. This pie will keep at least a week.

Irene Grant—East Ridge Presbyterian Church
Chattanooga, Tennessee

E-Z COCONUT PIE

4	EGGS	1	LARGE CAN EVAPORATED MILK
3/4	CUP SUGAR	3/4	STICK MARGARINE
1	TABLESPOON SELF-RISING FLOUR	1	TEASPOON VANILLA
1	PACKAGE (6 OUNCE) FROZEN COCONUT		

Melt margarine. Mix with sugar and flour. Beat well. Add eggs, milk, vanilla, and coconut. Place in greased and floured 10-inch pie pan. Freezes well.

Idelle E. Dowling—First Presbyterian Church, Greenwood, South Carolina
Mary Altman—Harmony Presbyterian Church, Crocketville, South Carolina

COFFEE TOFFEE PIE

1	PACKAGE PIE CRUST MIX	1	SQUARE UNSWEETENED CHOCOLATE
1/4	CUP LIGHT BROWN SUGAR FIRMLY PACKED	1	TEASPOON VANILLA
3/4	CUP FINELY CHOPPED WALNUTS	1	TABLESPOON WATER

In medium bowl, combine pie crust mix with brown sugar, walnuts, and chocolate. Add water and vanilla. Blend well with fork. Press firmly into bottom and sides of greased pie pan. Bake in preheated 375 degree oven 15 minutes. Cool pastry shell in pie tin on wire rack.

Filling:

1/2	CUP SOFT BUTTER OR MARGARINE	2	TABLESPOONS INSTANT COFFEE
3/4	CUP GRANULATED SUGAR	2	EGGS
1	SQUARE UNSWEETENED CHOCOLATE,		

In small bowl, mix butter at medium speed until creamy. Gradually add sugar, beating until light. Blend in cool melted chocolate and instant coffee. Add one egg and beat for 5 minutes. Add remaining egg and beat 5 minutes. Pour into baked pie shell and refrigerate, covered overnight.

Topping:

2	CUPS HEAVY CREAM	1/2	CONFECTIONER'S SUGAR
2	TABLESPOONS INSTANT COFFEE		CHOCOLATE CURLS

Next day, in large bowl, combine cream with coffee and the sugar. Refrigerate mixture, covered 1 hour and then beat mixture until stiff. Decorate pie with topping. Garnish with chocolate curls. Refrigerate the pie at least 2 hours. Yield: 8 servings. May be served frozen.

Alice Arntsen—Menlo Park Presbyterian
Menlo Park, California

Fudgey Pecan Pie

9	INCH UNBAKED PASTRY SHELL	3	EGGS LIGHTLY BEATEN
1/3	CUP BUTTER BLEND	3/4	CUP LIGHT CORN SYRUP
1/3	CUP COCOA	1	CUP BROKEN PECANS
2/3	CUP SUGAR		SWEETENED WHIPPED CREAM
1/4	TEASPOON SALT		PECAN HALVES (OPTIONAL)

Prepare pastry shell; set aside. In medium saucepan, over low heat, melt butter blend; add cocoa and stir until mixture is smooth. Remove from heat, cool slightly. Stir in sugar, salt, eggs, and corn syrup; blend thoroughly. Stir in pecans. Pour into unbaked pastry shell. Bake in a 350 degree oven for 40 minutes. Cool. Cover and let stand at room temperature for about 8 hours before serving. Garnish with whipped cream and pecan halves, if desired. Yield: 8 servings. Freezes well.

Sweetened Whipped Cream:

Combine 1/2 cup chilled heavy or whipping cream, 1 tablespoon confectioner's sugar, and 1/4 teaspoon vanilla in small mixer bowl; beat until stiff.

Irene Grant—East Ridge Presbyterian Church
Chattanooga, Tennessee

Japanese Fruit Pie

1	CUP WHITE SUGAR	1/2	CUP PECANS
1	STICK BUTTER, MELTED	1/2	CUP RAISINS
2	EGGS	1	TEASPOON VANILLA
1/2	CUP COCONUT		

Mix all ingredients well. Bake in a 300 degree oven in unbaked pie shell for 40 minutes.

Daisy Summels—Highland Presbyterian Church
Fayetteville, North Carolina

Lemon Pie

1 1/2	CUPS SUGAR	3/4	STICK BUTTER
4	EGGS	1	TABLESPOON FLOUR
1	LEMON	1	PINCH OF SALT

Mix sugar, flour and salt. Add melted butter and mix well, add juice and grated rind of the lemon. Stir, do not beat, each egg into the mixture. Pour into a 9-inch pie shell and bake in a 350 degree oven for 30-35 minutes. Yield: 8 servings.

Almetto Mencer—First Presbyterian Church, Apopka, Florida
First Presbyterian Church, LeRoy, New York

NANTUCKET PIE

2	CUPS RAW CRANBERRIES	1	CUP FLOUR
1/2	CUP SUGAR	1	TEASPOON ALMOND EXTRACT
1/2	CUP CHOPPED WALNUTS	2	EGGS, BEATEN
1 1/2	STICK OLEO	1	CUP SUGAR

Grease a 10 inch pie plate or 7x11 oblong pan. Wash and pick over cranberries. Put cranberries on bottom of pie plate, sprinkle with the 1/2 cup of sugar and walnuts. Make a batter of the cup of sugar, melted margarine, eggs, flour and flavoring. Mix the sugar, oleo together, then add remaining ingredients. Pour the batter over the cranberries. Bake in a 325 degree oven for 35-40 minutes. Serve with Cool Whip or whipped cream. Place on top rack. Yield: 8 servings.

Marion Brauneis—Waquoit Congregational Church
Falmouth, Massachusetts

OATMEAL PIE

1/4	CUP BUTTER	1/4	TEASPOON SALT
1/2	CUP SUGAR	1	CUP DARK CORN SYRUP
1/2	TEASPOON CINNAMON	3	EGGS
1/2	TEASPOON CLOVES	1	CUP QUICK-COOKING ROLLED OATS
1	9-INCH UNBAKED PASTRY SHELL		

Cream butter and sugar together. Add cinnamon, cloves and salt. Stir in syrup. Add eggs, one at a time, stirring well after each egg is added. Stir in rolled oats. Pour into 9-inch pastry shell. Bake in a 350 degree oven for 60 minutes—or until a knife comes out clean. The oatmeal will form a chewy "crust" on the top of pie.

First Presbyterian Church of Coalinga, Coalinga, California

Peanut Butter Pie

- 1 (8 OUNCE) CREAM CHEESE BAR SOFTENED AT ROOM TEMPERATURE
- 1/2 CUP PEANUT BUTTER
- 1 CUP CONFECTIONER'S SUGAR
- 1/2 CUP MILK
- 1 8 OUNCE CARTON FROZEN NON-DAIRY TOPPING, THAWED
- 1 GRAHAM CRACKER OR CHOCOLATE PIE SHELL, 9 INCH

Whip cream cheese until soft and fluffy. Beat in peanut butter and sugar and slowly add milk, beating until well blended. Fold topping into mixture and ladle into pie shell. Freeze until firm. Serve frozen, store leftovers in freezer. (If using 8-inch pie shells, double recipe—making 3 pies.)

Nedra M. Greenlee—First Presbyterian Church
Marion, North Carolina

Pear Pie

- 2/3 CUP PEARS (GRATED)
- 1/2 STICK OLEO
- 1 EGG
- 2 TABLESPOONS SELF-RISING FLOUR
- 1 CUP SUGAR
- 1 CUP COCONUT
- 1 TEASPOON VANILLA

Pour in raw crust. Use second crust as strips across pie. Bake in a 450 degree oven for 10 minutes, reduce heat to 350 degrees and bake 30 minutes. You can mix the ingredients for pie and freeze. Remove, thaw, and pour in raw crust. Apples or other fruits can be used.

Edmee Boyd—Hampton Presbyterian Church
Hampton, South Carolina

Pecan Pie

- 3 EGGS
- 3/4 CUP DARK CORN SYRUP
- 1/4 CUP BUTTER, MELTED
- 1/4 TEASPOON SALT
- 1 CUP COARSELY CHOPPED PECANS
- 1/2 CUP QUICK ROLLED OATS
- 3/4 CUP SUGAR

Beat eggs until foamy and add corn syrup, sugar, salt and butter. Stir in pecans and oats. Pour into pie shell and bake in a 350 degree oven for 45-50 minutes. Cool and cut.

Rev. Beth Braxton—Burke Presbyterian Church
Burke, Virginia

New Orleans Pecan Pie

2	TABLESPOONS CORN STARCH		1/4	TEASPOON LEMON FLAVORING
3	EGG YOLKS		1	CUP SUGAR
1	SMALL CARTON SOUR CREAM		1	PINCH SALT

Topping:

3	EGG WHITES		1	CUP CHOPPED PECANS
1	CUP BROWN SUGAR			

Mix first 6 ingredients and cook together in double boiler. Stir constantly and cook until thick. Pour into baked pie shell. Beat egg whites and brown sugar until peaks. Stir in pecans. Place on filling in pie shell, spreading until it covers the top. Cook in a 350 degree oven for 10 minutes or until golden brown. (Be sure and stir in pecans rather than beating them in.)

Rosemary Hutchins—First Presbyterian Church
Marion, North Carolina

Easy Pineapple Pie

3/4	CUP SUGAR		2	EGGS
1/4	CUP CORN STARCH		1	TEASPOON VANILLA
1	CUP WATER		1	SMALL CAN CRUSHED PINEAPPLE DRAINED
1	TABLESPOON BUTTER			

Mix sugar and cornstarch together. Add water and butter. Stir and cook until thick, stirring constantly. Add the two eggs, well beaten. Cook slowly until it boils. Remove from heat and add pineapple and vanilla. Pour into unbaked pie shell and bake in a 325 degree oven for 25-30 minutes.

Lois Hirst—First Presbyterian Church
Fort Lauderdale, Florida

Refrigerator Fruit Pie

World's easiest pie.

1	CUP MILK	1	GRAHAM CRACKER PIE CRUST
1	PINT SOUR CREAM	1	SMALL PACKAGE VANILLA INSTANT PUDDING

Beat milk, sour cream, and pudding together, pour into pie shell. It will set almost immediately. Top with cherry or blueberry pie filling and chill well before serving.

Hilda Williams—Pittsgrove Presbyterian Church
Daretown, New Jersey

Refrigerator Pie

2	GRAHAM CRACKER PIE CRUSTS	1/3	CUP LEMON JUICE
1	CAN EAGLE BRAND CONDENSED MILK	1/2	CUP PECANS OR WALNUTS
1	LARGE COOL WHIP	1	LARGE CAN CRUSHED PINEAPPLE

Combine lemon juice and milk. Fold in Cool Whip, drained pineapple, and nuts. Divide equally in 2 pie crusts. Refrigerate. Ready to serve in one hour.

Janice Hankey—Estill Presbyterian Church
Estill, South Carolina

Rhubarb Cream Pie

1 1/2	CUPS SUGAR	2	EGGS, WELL BEATEN
3	TABLESPOONS ENRICHED FLOUR	3	CUPS CUT RHUBARB
1/2	TEASPOON NUTMEG	1	RECIPE PLAIN PASTRY
1	TABLESPOON BUTTER OR MARGARINE		

Blend sugar, flour, nutmeg, and butter. Add eggs and beat smooth. Pour over rhubarb in 9-inch pastry lined pie pan. Top with pastry cut in fancy shapes. Bake in a 450 degree oven for 10 minutes. Reduce heat to 350 degrees, and bake, about 30 minutes. Yield: 8 servings.

Janice Maben—First Presbyterian Church
Jewett, New York

Fresh Strawberry Pie

1 BAKED 9-INCH PIE CRUST	3 CUPS WHOLE FRESH STRAWBERRIES
1/2 CUP HEAVY CREAM, WHIPPED	

Glaze:

1 CUP SUGAR	3 TABLESPOONS STRAWBERRY JELLO
3 TABLESPOONS CORNSTARCH	1 CUP WATER

Mix all ingredients for glaze in saucepan. Cook over medium heat until thick and clear. Arrange berries (reserving a few for garnish) in cooked pie crust. Pour glaze over berries. Top with whipped cream. Garnish with reserved berries and sprig of mint, if available.

Betty Graham—First Presbyterian Church
Medina, New York

Southern Heavenly Pie

15 ZWIEBACK CRACKERS (CAN USE GRAHAM)	1 EGG
1/2 STICK MARGARINE, MELTED	1/2 CUP CRUSHED PINEAPPLE, DRAINED
1/2 CUP BUTTER OR MARGARINE	1/2 PINT WHIPPING CREAM
3/4 CUP SUGAR	1/2 CUP NUTS, CHOPPED (PECANS OR WALNUTS)

Crush crackers and add 1/2 stick melted margarine. Press into pie pan. Cream 1/2 cup butter with sugar. Add beaten egg, nuts and pineapple. Fold in whipped cream and pour into crust. Chill for 3 or more hours. Does not freeze well.

Charlotte Vedeler—Old Presbyterian Meeting House
Alexandria, Virginia

Chapter Six

Eggs and Cheese—Grits

EGGS AND CHEESE

Mary Jackson's Cheese Fondue

6	SLICES BREAD (CRUST TRIMMED).	1/4	TEASPOON DRY MUSTARD
1	POUND GRATED SHARP CHEDDAR CHEESE		PINCH OF CAYENNE PEPPER
2	CUPS MILK		SALT TO TASTE, IF DESIRED
1/8	POUND (1/2 STICK) OF MARGARINE	4	EGGS, SEPARATED

Mix cubed bread with cheese. Heat milk (do not boil) and stir in bread, cheese, and seasonings. Add beaten egg yolks. Beat egg whites until stiff and fold in, lightly. Bake for 50-60 minutes in a 350 degree oven. Yield: 6 servings

[Cheese Fondue For Two]

2	SLICES OF BREAD	1	TABLESPOON BUTTER
2	INCH SQUARE OF CHEDDAR CHEESE	1/16	TEASPOON DRY MUSTARD
1	CUP OF MILK		DASH OF CAYENNE PEPPER AND SALT
2	EGGS		

Follow same instructions. Yield: 2 servings.
   Mary Jackson (the beloved cook at Westminster for many years)—Westminster Presbyterian Church
   St. Louis, Missouri

Cheese And Onion Pudding

2	TABLESPOONS BUTTER	3	LARGE EGGS
2	MEDIUM ONIONS, PEELED AND SLICED	2	CUPS MILK
1	CUP SOFT WHITE BREAD CRUMBS		SALT AND PEPPER
1	CUP CHEDDAR CHEESE, GRATED		

Sauté onions gently in butter until golden. Add milk and bring to boil. Pour over the bread crumbs, stir well. Fold in cheese, seasoning and beaten eggs. Turn into a greased pie dish and bake in a 375 degree oven for 30 minutes or until well risen and golden brown. Serve immediately.

Sybil Chandler—Ash United Reformed Church
Kent, England

RED APPLE INN CREAM CHEESE SOUFFLÉ

8	EGGS, SEPARATED	12	OUNCES CREAM CHEESE
1/2	TEASPOON SALT	2	CUPS SOUR CREAM
2	TABLESPOONS FLOUR	1/2	CUP HONEY

Beat yolks of eggs until thick and creamy. Add salt and flour. Combine sour cream and cream cheese, blending until smooth. Add to egg yolk mixture and beat with electric beater until smooth, adding honey gradually. Beat egg whites until stiff but not dry, and fold in yolk mixture. Pour into ungreased 3 quart baking dish. Place in pan of water and bake in preheated 300 degree oven for 1 hour. Serves 10-12. This is to be served as a side dish, and is good with ham, or any kind of meat. Should freeze well, but would need to be cooked first.

Elsie Dunklin—Highland Park Presbyterian Church
Dallas, Texas

SUPPER CHEESE SPREAD

1	CUP CHEESE, GRATED	1	TEASPOON VINEGAR
1	MEDIUM TOMATO		PINCH SALT
1	EGG, BEATEN		PINCH DRY MUSTARD

Peel tomato and chop. Add all other ingredients and mix together. Pour into a heat proof bowl, cover with foil and put bowl in a saucepan with 2 or 3 inches of water, cover saucepan and steam for 20 minutes. Serve cold.

M.B.S.—Isle of Cumbrae Parish Church
Isle of Cumbrae, Scotland

Chili Relleno Casserole

1	CAN (4 OUNCE) GREEN CHILIES	1	TEASPOON SALT
1	CUP CHEDDAR CHEESE, GRATED	1/4	TEASPOON CHILI POWDER
1	CUP MONTEREY JACK CHEESE, GRATED	1 1/2	CUPS MILK
1	EGG, BEATEN	1/2	CUP FLOUR

Split chilies, remove seed and place in bottom of 8 inch square dish. Mix together remaining ingredients and pour carefully over chilies. Bake in a 350 degree oven until casserole just solidifies and top crust forms, about 45 minutes. If you desire, chop the chilies and mix with all other ingredients. Freezes well. Yield: 4-5 servings.

Helen Brooks (Mrs. William D., Jr.)—Sea Island Presbyterian Church
Beaufort, South Carolina

Delicate Egg and Cheese Bake

8	EGGS (EGG SUBSTITUTES MAY BE USED)	12	OUNCES SMALL CURD COTTAGE CHEESE
1	ENVELOPE GOOD SEASON'S ITALIAN SALAD DRESSING MIX, DRY	1/2	RED OR GREEN PEPPER, CHOPPED
		1/3	CUP FLOUR
12	OUNCES MONTEREY JACK CHEESE, SHREDDED	1	TEASPOON BAKING POWDER
		1/3	BUTTER OR MARGARINE, MELTED.

Beat eggs and salad dressing mix in a large bowl. Stir in cheeses and pepper. Mix flour with baking powder. Add flour and melted butter into cheese mixture. Pour into a greased 8 inch square pan. Bake in a 375 degree oven for 35 minutes until golden. Yield: 8 or 9 servings.

Ann Rogers—Providence Presbyterian Church
Fairfax, Virginia

Easter Brunch Casserole

2/3-1	POUND CUBED HAM	1	RECIPE OF CHEESE SAUCE (SEE BELOW)
1/2	CUP CHOPPED GREEN ONION	8	TEASPOONS BUTTER
6	TABLESPOONS BUTTER	4 1/2	CUPS BREAD CRUMBS
24	EGGS, BEATEN	1/4	TABLESPOON PAPRIKA
2	CANS MUSHROOMS (3 OUNCES, EACH)		

Cook ham and onion in butter until tender but not brown. Add eggs and scramble until just barely set. Add mushrooms, eggs, ham, and onions to the cheese sauce. Place combination into a casserole dish. Combine 8 teaspoons butter, crumbs, and paprika and sprinkle over eggs. Cover and chill. May be made ahead and frozen until ready for use. Thaw and bake in a 350 degree oven for 30 minutes. Yield: 24 servings.

Cheese Sauce:

4	TABLESPOONS BUTTER	1	TEASPOON PEPPER
4	TABLESPOONS FLOUR	2	CUPS AMERICAN CHEESE
1	TEASPOON SALT		

Melt butter. Blend in flour, salt and pepper. Add milk cook and stir until bubbly. Stir in cheese until melted. Freezes well.

Board of Deacons—First Presbyterian Church
New Vernon, New Jersey

EGGS BETTINA

8   EGGS, HARD BOILED AND COOLED

Make sauce of:

5	TABLESPOONS BUTTER	3	CUPS MILK
7	TABLESPOONS FLOUR		

Add to sauce:

1 1/2	TABLESPOONS PIMENTO	1 1/3	CUPS CHEDDAR CHEESE, GRATED
1 1/2	TABLESPOONS PARSLEY, CHOPPED	1/2	TEASPOON PAPRIKA
1	TEASPOON SALT	1	TEASPOON ONION, GRATED
3/4	CUP CELERY, FINELY CHOPPED	1/2	CUP STUFFED OLIVES, SLICED

Put some sauce in the bottom of a 7 1/2 x 11 1/2 flat pyrex casserole. Cut eggs lengthwise into fourths and lay on top of the sauce. Cover with balance of sauce. Crush 1 cup of corn flakes and place on top. Then add 6 slices of uncooked bacon which has been cut into small pieces, spreading the bacon pieces around. Bake in a 350 degree oven for 30 minutes. Yield: 8 servings.

Fran Barnard—First Presbyterian Church
Beaufort, South Carolina

Ortega Eggs

2	4 OUNCE CANS DICED GREEN CHILES	4	CUPS CHEDDAR OR JACK CHEESE, GRATED
	DASH OF LAWRY'S SEASONED SALT	10	EGGS
	FLOUR	3/4	CUP PLUS 1 TABLESPOON EVAPORATED MILK
	DASH OF PAPRIKA		(1 SMALL CAN)

Grease a 9 x 13" pan and dust with flour. Spread green chilies in the pan evenly. Sprinkle with Seasoned Salt, a little flour, and paprika. Add cheese (may use a mixture of both). Beat together eggs and milk. Pour eggs/milk mixture over cheese. Bake in a 325 degree oven for 30 minutes. Allow to set before serving.

Margaret Botsford—First Presbyterian Church
Casa Grande, Arizona

Presbyterian Eggs (Breakfast Casserole)

Note: Mrs. McIntire notes that this dish is served yearly at the Easter Brunch held by her church in the fellowship hall between services. Her young children named the dish, Presbyterian Eggs, since it was an annual tradition along with coffee cake.

1 1/2	POUNDS OF SAUSAGE MEAT	1 1/2	TEASPOONS DRY MUSTARD
9	EGGS, BEATEN	3	SLICES OF BREAD, CUBED 1/4 INCHES
3	CUPS OF MILK	1 1/2	CUPS CHEDDAR CHEESE, GRATED

Brown sausage and drain well. Mix eggs, milk, and mustard. Stir in bread, sausage, and cheese. Pour into a 9 x 13 x 2 inch dish. Refrigerate overnight, covered. Bake uncovered in a 350 degree oven 1 hour.

Suzan E. McIntire—First Presbyterian Church, Paola, Kansas
Mickey Nordin—Highland Presbyterian Church, Winston-Salem, North Carolina
Diane Peebles—Guilford Park Presbyterian Church, Greensboro, North Carolina

Overnight Breakfast Casserole

6	EGGS	6	SLICES BREAD, CRUST REMOVED AND CUBED
1	TEASPOON PEPPER	1	POUND OF SAUSAGE, COOKED AND DRAINED
1	TEASPOON SALT	1/2	CUP DICED GREEN PEPPER
2	CUPS MILK	4	OUNCE CAN MUSHROOMS, DRAINED

Note: Ham or bacon may be used also. In a 13 x 9 x 2 inch dish, layer ingredients: Bread cubes; sausage; green pepper, mushrooms, and finally cheese. Beat together the eggs, milk, salt and pepper. Pour over layers. Cover and refrigerate overnight. Bake uncovered in a 350 degree oven for 35 minutes.

Youth Group—St. Andrews Presbyterian Church
Jacksonville, Florida

EASY QUICHE LORRAINE

Crust:

1	CUP FINELY CRUMBLED CHEESE CRACKERS	3	SLICES COOKED, CRISP BACON, CRUMBLED
1	TABLESPOON POPPY SEED	1/4	CUP MARGARINE, MELTED

Combine all ingredients and press into 9 inch pie pan. Bake in a 350 degree oven for 8-10 minutes. Allow to cool.

Filling:

3	CUPS THINLY SLICED ONIONS	1/2	TEASPOON SALT
2	TABLESPOONS MARGARINE		DASH OF BLACK PEPPER
1	CUP GRATED, SHARP CHEESE		DASH OF THYME
1	CUP SCALDED MILK	6	SLICES CRISPLY FRIED BACON
3	EGGS, SLIGHTLY BEATEN		

Sauté onion in margarine until golden. Spoon over crust. Sprinkle cheese over onions. Combine milk, eggs, salt, pepper and thyme. Pour into crust. Bake in a 350 degree oven for 20-25 minutes until a knife comes out clean. Top with the six slices of bacon arranged like spokes in a wheel. Yield: 6 servings.

Harriet Inscoe—First Presbyterian Church
Morganton, North Carolina

BREAKFAST BEFORE

1	POUND BULK SAUSAGE	1	TEASPOON DRY MUSTARD
6	EGGS	2	SLICES BREAD, CUBED
2	CUPS MILK	1	CUP GRATED SHARP CHEESE
1	TEASPOON SALT		

Brown sausage and drain well. Put bread in a 2 quart casserole. Add a layer of sausage and then a layer of cheese. Repeat layers. Mix eggs, milk, salt, and mustard and pour over cheese-sausage layers. Refrigerate overnight. Bake in a 350 degree oven for 45 minutes. Yield: 8 servings.

Emily Macey—Trinity Presbyterian Church
Charlotte, North Carolina

SAUSAGE BREAKFAST CUPS

1	CAN BUTTER-ME-NOT BISCUITS	1	TABLESPOON CHIVES OR ONION
1	CUP COTTAGE CHEESE	1/4	CUP PARMESAN CHEESE
2	EGGS	1/2	POUND SAUSAGE

Brown sausage; drain and crumble. Set aside. Press biscuit dough into greased muffin tins. Put sausage in cups and add liquid mixture to about 3/4 full. Bake in a 350 degree oven for 15-17 minutes. This recipe may be frozen, and doubled if you like. Reheat in a 375 degree oven for 10-12 minutes. Do not microwave.

Margarett C. Tiddy—John Knox Presbyterian Church
Shelby, North Carolina

SAUSAGE AND CHEESE CASSEROLE

1	POUND HOT SAUSAGE	1/4	TEASPOON PAPRIKA
1	POUND MILD SAUSAGE	1	GREEN ONION, MINCED
8	SLICES STALE WHITE BREAD	1/2	TEASPOON DRY MUSTARD
1 1/2	POUNDS SHARP, GRATED CHEESE	1/2	TEASPOON SALT
6	EGGS, SLIGHTLY BEATEN	1/8	TEASPOON PEPPER
2 1/2-3	CUPS LIGHT CREAM	1/8	TEASPOON CAYENNE PEPPER
1	TEASPOON BROWN SUGAR	1/2	TEASPOON WORCESTERSHIRE SAUCE

Cook and drain sausage. Remove crusts from bread, butter well and cut into 1/4 inch cubes. Arrange half the bread cubes on bottom of greased 2 quart baking dish. Cover with half the cheese, then half the sausage. Repeat layers as listed above. Add rest of ingredients to eggs, blending lightly. Pour over sausage mixture. Cover with plastic wrap. Refrigerate for 24 hours. Before cooking, allow to stand at room temperature for 1/2 hour. Set the dish into a shallow pan with brown paper on bottom. Add 1/2 inch of cold water. Bake in a 300 degree oven for 1 hour. Turn off oven. Let casserole remain in oven for 20 minutes or longer. Yield: 12 to 14 servings. Great for brunch or Sunday night supper. Keep one in your freezer. Then add eggs and milk for a delicious late breakfast treat for your next weekend guests!

Maryann C. Abbott—First Presbyterian Church
Greenville, South Carolina

GRITS

Domino Grits Casserole

1	CUP GRITS	1/8	TEASPOON PEPPER
1	QUART MILK	1/3	CUP MELTED BUTTER
1/2	CUP BUTTER	1	CUP GRUYERE CHEESE
1	TEASPOON SALT	1/2	CUP PARMESAN CHEESE

Bring milk just to boil and add butter, gradually. Stir in grits very slowly. Cook, stirring constantly until done. Add salt and pepper. Beat with an electric beater for five minutes. Pour into 13x9x2" flat casserole. Cover and refrigerate overnight. Next day, cut grits into 1x1 1/2" pieces the size of dominoes. Place in greased casserole (same size), like fallen dominoes. Sprinkle with melted butter and cheeses. Bake in a 400 degree oven for 30 minutes. Yield: 8-10 servings.

Fran Barnard—First Presbyterian Church
Beaufort, South Carolina

Grits and Sausage Casserole

1	POUND BULK PORK SAUSAGE	2	TABLESPOONS BUTTER
3	CUPS HOT, COOKED GRITS	3	EGGS, BEATEN
2 1/2	CUPS CHEDDAR CHEESE, SHREDDED	1 1/2	CUPS MILK

Place cooked, drained sausage in a lightly greased 9x13" pan. Mix grits, cheese, and butter together. Set aside. Combine eggs and milk. Add mixture to grits and pour over sausage. Bake in a 350 degree oven, uncovered, for 1 hour or until firm.

Jerry Harper—Estill Presbyterian Church
Estill, South Carolina

Grits Soufflé with Cheese

1	CUP QUICK GRITS, COOKED	2	EGGS, WELL BEATEN
4	CUPS BOILING WATER	1	SMALL CLOVE GARLIC, MINCED (OPTIONAL)
1	TEASPOON SALT	1	TEASPOON TABASCO SAUCE
1 1/2	CUPS SHREDDED, SHARP CHEDDAR	1	TEASPOON WORCESTERSHIRE SAUCE
1/4	POUND BUTTER OR MARGARINE		PAPRIKA
1/2	CUP MILK		

Mix all ingredients. Cook on low until cheese is melted. Pour into a 2 quart greased casserole dish or an 8x8" pan. Sprinkle with paprika. Bake uncovered in a 350 degree oven for 1 hour, or until golden brown. Serve hot. Yield: 8 servings.

Jeanne Kuebler—First Presbyterian Church
Easton, Pennsylvania

Chapter Seven

Fish — Shellfish

FISH

Grouper Mediterranean

3	POUNDS FILET OF FIRM, WHITE FISH	8	LARGE TOMATOES (NOT TOO RIPE)
	JAR OF CAPERS		OLIVE OIL
	WHITE WINE OR OUZO (GREEK LIQUEUR)		GREEK OLIVES
1/2	POUND FETA CHEESE		SALT AND PEPPER TO TASTE
4	TABLESPOONS BUTTER		

Core the tomatoes and dice. Put olive oil and wine in a saucepan and lightly saute the tomatoes. Slice olives into ringlets, add to pan with capers, salt and pepper. Steam until done through (check with fork). Do not overcook. Drain liquid from pan. Pour sauce over fish and crumble feta cheese on top. Put lid back on and put over heat until cheese begins to bubble. Remove from heat and serve at once.

Box Alex—First Presbyterian Church
Dunedin, Florida

Kedgeree

1	CUP LONG GRAIN RICE	4	HARD-BOILED EGGS
1	CUP HADDOCK POACHED IN	1/4 TO 1/2	CUP BUTTER
	MILK (OR OTHER COOKED FISH)	1	TABLESPOONS CHOPPED PARSLEY
2-3	SPRING ONIONS (CHOPPED)	1/2	PINT SINGLE CREAM
	SALT AND PEPPER TO TASTE		

Boil rice until tender. Drain. Drain fish and flake (remove bone). Shell eggs and keep 2 yolks for garnish. Finely chop remainder. Toss rice, fish, and eggs together then mix in cream and onions. Season. Spread Kedgeree in ovenproof dish and dot with butter. Cover with foil and bake in a 350 degree oven for 20-30 minutes until heated through. Garnish with parsley and egg yolks.

Sheila Munro—Ervie-Kirkcolm with Leswalt
Stranraes, Scotland

Oven-Fried Fish

- 1 POUND FISH FILLETS
- 1 TABLESPOON OIL
- 7 TABLESPOONS FINE DRY BREAD CRUMBS
- 3 TABLESPOONS MINCED FRESH PARSLEY
- 1 TEASPOON PAPRIKA
- VEGETABLE COOKING SPRAY

Coat fillets with oil. Combine bread crumbs, parsley, and paprika. Dredge coated fillets in bread crumb mixture. Arrange fillets on a baking sheet coated with cooking spray. Bake in a 450 degree oven for 10-12 minutes, or until fillets flake easily with a fork. Note: The fish turns out brown and crispy.

Anne Lindsay—Hampton Presbyterian Church
Hampton, South Carolina

Salmon Loaf with Mustard Lemon Sauce

Salmon loaf:

- 1 (16 OUNCE) CAN SALMON
- 1 1/2 CUP FRESH BREAD CRUMBS
- 1/2 CUP DAIRY SOUR CREAM
- 1/2 CUP CHOPPED ONION
- 1/2 CUP CHOPPED CELERY
- 1/4 CUP CHICKEN STOCK
- 2 EGGS
- 1 TABLESPOON LEMON JUICE
- 1 TEASPOON WORCESTERSHIRE SAUCE
- 3/4 TEASPOON SALT
- 1/4 TEASPOON MARJORAM
- 1/8 TEASPOON PEPPER

Combine loaf ingredients. Mix and place into greased 9x5 inch loaf pan. Place pan in water bath (water 1 1/2 inches deep). Bake in a 350 degree oven one hour or until knife comes out clean. Remove loaf pan from water bath and let rest for 10 minutes before unmolding. Yield: 6 to 8 servings.

Mustard lemon sauce:

- 2 TABLESPOONS BUTTER OR MARGARINE
- 2 TABLESPOONS FLOUR
- 1/2 TEASPOON SALT
- 1/8 TEASPOON PEPPER
- 1 CUP MILK
- 1 TABLESPOON LEMON JUICE
- 1 TEASPOON GRATED LEMON RIND
- 1 TEASPOON PREPARED MUSTARD

2. In saucepan, melt butter; blend in flour, salt, and pepper. Add milk, lemon juice, lemon rind, and mustard. Cook, stirring constantly until thickened and smooth. Serve over salmon loaf. Serve, eat, and enjoy.

Eleanor Yocum—Faith Presbyterian Church
Harrisburg, Pennsylvania

Salmon Quiche

Flan Base:

- 2 OUNCES PLAIN CRACKERS, CRUSHED (SUCH AS SALTINES OR RITZ)
- 2 OUNCES BUTTER
- 1 OUNCE CHEESE, GRATED

Filling:

- 1/2 OUNCE BUTTER
- 1/2 OUNCE FLOUR
- 1 OUNCE FINELY CHOPPED ONION
- 1 CAN SALMON (3 1/2 OUNCE)
- 2 TABLESPOONS MILK
- 1 TEASPOON LEMON JUICE

To make flan base, melt butter and add crushed crackers. Mix in grated cheese and press into a seven-inch ovenproof plate.

To make filling, melt butter. Cook onion, add flour and cook for a few minutes. Add milk, juice from can of salmon and lemon juice. Cook for several minutes. Add flaked salmon to this mixture, pour into flan base and heat through in a 350 degree oven for 10 minutes. May be served chilled with a green salad. Yield: 3 servings.

Hamish and Christine Cameron—Portmoak Church
Milnathort, Scotland

Spinach and Salmon Terrine

- 1 POUND FRESH SALMON
- 1 POUND SPINACH LEAVES
- 3 EGGS
- 1 TEASPOON SALT
- 1 TEASPOON NUTMEG
- 2/3 CUP LIGHT CREAM

Tarragon dressing

- 4 TABLESPOONS OLIVE OIL
- 1 JUICED LEMON
- PINCH OF SUGAR
- 1 TABLESPOON FRESH TARRAGON, CHOPPED

Put the eggs, spinach, roughly chopped, half of salmon, seasonings and cream in blender and blend until smooth. Cut remaining salmon into small cubes and stir into spinach mixture. Pour into a buttered heat proof bowl. Cover with foil and place in a pan of hot water, bake in a pre-heated 350 degree oven for 30 minutes, until firm to the touch. Cool before turning out. Shake the dressing ingredients in a covered jar until well-blended. Cut the terrine into slices and serve with the tarragon dressing.

Mrs. Margaret Keay—Auchtergaven & Moneydie Parish Church
Perth, Scotland

Filet of Sole Casserole

2	POUNDS SOLE		BREAD CRUMBS
2	CUPS MILK	4	TABLESPOONS BUTTER
1/4	CUP BUTTER	3/4	POUND MUSHROOMS, SLICED
4	TABLESPOONS FLOUR	2	CUPS SEEDLESS GRAPES (GREEN)
1	TEASPOON SALT	1/3	POUND VELVEETA CHEESE
1/4	TEASPOON PEPPER	2	OUNCES WHITE WINE

Cover sole with milk. Cook over low heat for 5 minutes. Drain, reserving milk. Melt 4 tablespoons butter, blend in flour. Add remaining milk gradually, stirring constantly. Continue stirring, and cook over low heat until thick. Melt 1/3 pound cheese in sauce. Add two ounces white wine. Melt 1/4 cup butter and add mushrooms and cook 5 minutes. Flake fish and place mushrooms, grapes and fish in layers in a 2 quart, buttered casserole. Pour sauce over top with bread crumbs. Heat through in a 350 degree oven for 25 minutes.

Winkie Keith—First Presbyterian Church
New Vernon, New Jersey

Tuna Chow Mein Casserole

1	SMALL CAN CHOW MEIN NOODLES	1/2	CUP CASHEW NUTS
1	CAN UNDILUTED MUSHROOM SOUP	1	CUP FINELY DICED CELERY
1/4	CUP WATER	1/2	CUP MINCED ONION
1	CAN CHUNK-STYLE TUNA		SALT AND PEPPER TO TASTE IF DESIRED

Set aside 1/2 cup of noodles for the topping. Mix all the ingredients and put into casserole. Sprinkle noodles over top. Cook for 40 minutes in a 325 degree oven. Yield: 4 servings.

Mickey Nordin—Highland Presbyterian Church
Winston-Salem, North Carolina

Tuna-Potato Supreme

6	LARGE BAKING POTATOES	4	OUNCES SHARP CHEDDAR CHEESE, GRATED
2	CANS TUNA	1	SMALL ONION, CHOPPED
1	(8 OUNCE) SOUR CREAM		SALT AND PEPPER TO TASTE
1	STICK MARGARINE		

Wash potatoes thoroughly. Rub potato skins with margarine. Wrap in foil and bake in a 350 degree oven for 45 to 60 minutes until done. Remove from oven and partially unwrap foil. Cut oval slice lengthwise on 1 side of potato. Scoop out potato and mix with next 4 ingredients. Return mixture to the potato skins; top with cheese. Place side-by-side in baking dish. Bake in 325 degree oven 30 minutes or until lightly brown on top. Served with salad, rolls, dessert, and beverage it makes a wonderful meal. Yield: 6 servings.

Celeste Wiggins—Bryson City Presbyterian Church
Bryson City, North Carolina

SHELLFISH

Clam Casserole

30	SALTINES, CRUSHED	2	EGGS, BEATEN
1	CAN MINCED CLAMS	1	CUP MILK
1	CAN MUSHROOM SOUP	1/4	CUP MELTED MARGARINE

Mix ingredients in above order. Place in casserole and bake in a 350 degree oven for 1 hour. Yield: 4 servings.

Faye K. Traugh—First Presbyterian Church
Fort Lauderdale, Florida

CRAB A LA LORRAINE

1	CAN WHITE CRAB MEAT	1/2	TEASPOON SALT
1	JAR OLD ENGLISH CHEDDAR CHEESE	1/2	TEASPOON GARLIC POWDER
1	STICK BUTTER	6	ENGLISH MUFFINS
2	TEASPOONS MAYONNAISE		

Blend all ingredients well. Spoon mixture onto muffin halves. Freeze slightly for easier cutting. Cut each muffin half into 6 wedges. Bake immediately or freeze and bake as needed. Bake in a 350 degree oven for 10 minutes. Yield: 72 wedges.

Marianne G. Moody—Ray Memorial Presbyterian Church
Monroe, Georgia

DEVILED CRAB CASSEROLE

1	POUND CRAB MEAT	1	TABLESPOON MAYONNAISE
15	SALTINES	1	TEASPOON WORCESTERSHIRE SAUCE
1/2	STICK BUTTER	2	TABLESPOONS SHERRY
3 TO 4	EGGS (BEATEN)		SALT AND PEPPER TO TASTE
	MILK (TO MAKE CONSISTENCY OF GRITS)		DASH NUTMEG

Crush saltines and mix with crab, reserving some for top. Mix all ingredients together and top with remaining crushed saltines. Bake in a 350 degree oven for 45 minutes.

Suedell Hills Read—New Wappetaw Presbyterian Church
McClellanville, South Carolina

HEALTH-WISE CRAB CURRY QUICHE

1	UNCOOKED PIE SHELL	1/2	CAN MUSHROOM SOUP
1/2	POUND ALASKAN CRAB (WHITEFISH)	1	CUP EVAPORATED MILK
1	CUP GRATED MOZZARELLA CHEESE	1/2	TEASPOON CURRY POWDER
2	EGG-BEATER EGGS	1/4	TEASPOON SALT

Cut up crab into small pieces and place in bottom of unbaked pie shell. Put cheese on top. Mix Egg-beaters with mushroom soup and add milk. Beat. Pour mixture over crab and cheese. Bake in a 350 degree oven for 45 minutes. Yield: 6 servings.

Joanne Folger—Fairview Presbyterian Church
North Augusta, South Carolina

SEAFOOD CASSEROLE III

8	OUNCES MACARONI	1/2	TEASPOON DRY MUSTARD
2	CUPS CUBED CHEDDAR CHEESE	1/4	TEASPOON PEPPER
2 1/2	CUPS MILK	1	CUP SLICED FRESH MUSHROOMS
2	TABLESPOONS OLEO	1	POUND COOKED SHRIMP, LOBSTER, OR CRAB
1/4	CUP FLOUR		WHITE WINE TO TASTE (OPTIONAL)
1/2	TEASPOON SALT		

Cook macaroni for 6 minutes; rinse in cold water and drain. Heat oleo over low heat; stir in flour, salt, pepper, and mustard until smooth. Remove from heat and gradually stir in milk until smooth. Return to heat and cook until thickened, stirring constantly. Remove from heat. Layer macaroni, cheese, mushrooms, and seafood in buttered baking dish. Sprinkle with 1/4 cup white wine if desired. Pour in milk mixture and bake for 25 minutes in a 375 degree oven. Yield: 6-8 servings.

Ellen Abramson—The Presbyterian Church of Bloomingdale
Brandon, Florida

SEAFOOD CASSEROLE IV

1/2	POUND IMITATION CRAB MEAT	1	CAN WHITE CRAB MEAT
1/2	POUND COOKED SHRIMP	1	PACKAGE KRAFT OLD ENGLISH CHEESE SLICES (8)
3	EGGS		
1	TEASPOON DRY MUSTARD	1/4	CUP MELTED BUTTER
6	SLICES WHITE BREAD, REMOVE CRUST	2	CUPS WHOLE MILK

In a casserole dish, layer first 5 items. Drizzle melted butter over top. Beat eggs until fluffy. Add mustard and milk. Blend together and pour over casserole. Cover and allow to stand overnight. Bake covered, for 1 hour in a 350 degree oven. Let stand for 10 minutes before serving.

Mrs. William H. Pohler, Jr.—First Presbyterian Church
Naples, Florida

Drain oysters reserving 1/4 cup liquor. Combine crumbs and butter. Spread 1/3 of crumbs in greased 8x1 1/4 inch round pan. Cover with half oysters. Sprinkle with pepper. Using another third of crumbs, spread a second layer; cover with remaining oysters. Sprinkle with pepper. Combine cream, oyster liquor, Worcestershire, and salt. Pour over the oysters. Top with remaining crumbs. Bake in a 350 degree oven for 40 minutes.

Paula Gottlieb—Faith Presbyterian Church
Harrisburg, Pennsylvania

OYSTER PIE

1	PINT OYSTERS	1/2	CUP OLEO OR BUTTER
2	CUPS COARSELY BROKEN SALTINES		PEPPER TO TASTE
2	CUPS MILK		

Spray 1 quart casserole with Pam or grease with butter. Cover bottom of casserole with 1/2 of the saltines. Heat oysters in own juice but do not boil. Pour oysters and juice over saltines. Add 1/2 butter cut into small pats. Cover with remaining crackers. Heat milk and pour over crackers. Must be very juicy. Allow to sit about five minutes. If not juicy, add more milk. Add pepper to taste. Bake uncovered until browned lightly and bubbly in a 375 degree oven for 20 to 30 minutes. Does not freeze well.

Mrs. Richard Elliott—Estill Presbyterian Church
Estill, South Carolina

SCALLOPED SCALLOPS

1 1/2	POUNDS FROZEN SCALLOPS	1/4	TEASPOON DRY MUSTARD
1	POUND MEDIUM SHRIMP, COOKED		SALT AND PEPPER TO TASTE
2	CUPS MEDIUM-THICK CREAM SAUCE	2	TABLESPOONS SHERRY
1	CUP GRATED CHEDDAR CHEESE	1/2	CUP BUTTERED BREAD CRUMBS

Thaw and cook scallops in salted water for apporximately three minutes. Drain. Toss shrimp into drained scallops. Set aside. Mix together, cream sauce, cheese, mustard, salt, pepper, and sherry. Add scallops and shrimp. Pour into a greased, shallow casserole dish. Sprinkle the top with 1/2 cup buttered bread crumbs. Bake in a preheated 350 degree oven for about 30 minutes, or until mixture is boiling hot and crumbs are golden.

Joan Roberts—First Presbyterian Church
Medina, New York

Bob Shepard's Shrimp Pie

1 TO 2 POUNDS PEELED, RAW SHRIMP	TABASCO TO TASTE
1/2 TO 1 POUND BACON	SALT AND PEPPER TO TASTE
2 CANS STEWED TOMATOES	2 TABLESPOONS SUGAR
1 CUP SHARP CHEDDAR CHEESE	5 SLICES OF BREAD TORN INTO SMALL PIECES
1 TABLESPOON WORCESTERSHIRE SAUCE	LOTS OF GARLIC
1 ONION, DICED	2 BELL PEPPERS, DICED

Cut bacon in small pieces and cook until crisp. Drain. Add shrimp, garlic, onion, bell pepper. Sauté until shrimp are pink. Pour all ingredients into flat casserole dish. Bake in a 350 degree oven for 30 minutes. Serve over rice.

Roberta Shepard—Westminster Presbyterian Church
Charleston, South Carolina

Curried Shrimp Casserole

- 4 CUPS COOKED SALTED RICE (INSTANT RICE MAY BE USED)
- 1 1/2 POUNDS COOKED AND CLEANED SHRIMP
  (IF FRESH SHRIMP ARE NOT AVAILABLE, USE FROZEN OR 4 SMALL CANS)
- 3/4 STICK MELTED MARGARINE
- 1 CAN TOMATOES
- 1 1/2 TEASPOON CURRY POWDER
  BREAD CRUMBS

Mix together in a casserole dish, the rice and shrimp. In saucepan, combine the melted margarine, tomatoes, and curry powder. Pour this liquid mix over rice and shrimp. Stir. Top with buttered bread crumbs. Heat in a 350 degree oven until brown on top.

Lucie Barnes—Ray Memorial Presbyterian Church
Monroe, Georgia

Fresh Shrimp and Crab Meat Au Gratin

1 POUND LUMP CRAB MEAT	3 CUPS MEDIUM CREAM SAUCE
1 POUND SHRIMP, BOILED	SALT AND PEPPER, TO TASTE
3 TABLESPOONS BUTTER	1/2 CUP CRUSHED CRACKER CRUMBS
2 TEASPOONS SHERRY	1/2 CUP ROMANO CHEESE
3 OUNCES SHARP AMERICAN CHEESE	1 TABLESPOON PAPRIKA

Sauté shrimp and crabmeat in butter. Add sherry, American cheese and hot cream sauce. Season with salt and pepper. Cook thoroughly, pour into casserole. Sprinkle top with cracker crumbs, Romano cheese and paprika. Dot with butter and put in a 350 degree oven until golden brown. Yield: 4-6 servings. Wonderful!

Susie Neal—Fort Hill Presbyterian Church
Clemson, South Carolina

NEPTUNE CASSEROLE

1	CUP CHOPPED ONION	1	SMALL JAR PIMIENTO, SLICED
1	CUP CHOPPED CELERY	1	4 OUNCE JAR MUSHROOMS, DRAINED
1	TABLESPOON MARGARINE	1	POUND COOKED SHRIMP
1	CAN CREAM OF SHRIMP SOUP	3	CUPS COOKED RICE
1	8 OUNCE CONTAINER SOUR CREAM	1	CUP GRATED SHARP CHEESE
1	TEASPOON SALT	1/2	TEASPOON PEPPER

Sauté onions and celery in margarine until crisp. Stir in all other ingredients except cheese. Pour into a greased, shallow 2 quart casserole. Bake in a 350 degree oven for 25 minutes. Add sharp cheese to top and bake 5 minutes more. Yield: 8 servings.

Marian Guill—North Augusta Presbyterian Church
North Augusta, South Carolina

OVERSEER'S SHRIMP

2	POUNDS PEELED SHRIMP	6	TABLESPOONS BUTTER
1	TABLESPOON BACON DRIPPINGS	1/2	PINT SOUR CREAM
6	SLICES CRISP BACON	1	CUP RICE
1	TEASPOON SALT	1/2	TEASPOON GARLIC POWDER
12	WHOLE MARJORAM LEAVES		

Add bacon drippings, garlic powder, salt, and marjoram to 3 cups water. Simmer for 5 minutes, then boil shrimp in this mixture for 2 minutes. Drain shrimp and save broth. Cook rice in 2 1/2 cups broth for 25 minutes. Remove from heat and stir in butter and sour cream until thoroughly mixed. Crumble bacon, add to rice then stir in shrimp. Place into casserole, cover and warm in a 250 degree oven just before serving. Yield: 4 servings.

John W. Myers, Trustee
Stoney Creek Foundation

Pickled Shrimp Appetizer

12 pounds medium-size shrimp, cooked in seasoned water (use shrimp boil). Allow to simmer for 12-15 minutes. Cool and peel shrimp and devein. In large pan, arrange shrimp in layers with 16 medium onions thinly sliced; 4 boxes of bay leaves and 2 large cans of black olives.

Combine the following ingredients and pour over each layer of shrimp.

5	CUPS SALAD OIL	9	TABLESPOONS CAPERS AND JUICE
3	CUPS WARMED WHITE VINEGAR	1	CUP WORCESTERSHIRE SAUCE
5	TEASPOONS SALT	4	TABLESPOONS YELLOW MUSTARD
9	TEASPOONS CELERY SEED		DASH OF HOT SAUCE

Cover pan and store in refrigerator for at least 24 hours. Will keep a week or more. To serve, drain but save some sauce for leftovers. Arrange on platter with cocktail picks.

Dorothy Calkins—Memorial Drive Presbyterian Church
Houston, Texas

Pierre's Shrimp and Crab Gravy

This gravy will make you forget steak!

2	POUNDS RAW, PEELED SHRIMP		SALT AND PEPPER TO TASTE
1/2	POUND CRAB MEAT, CLAW OR WHITE		FLOUR, PLAIN
1	LARGE ONION, CHOPPED SMALL	4	DROPS TABASCO
1/4	POUND GOOD QUALITY BACON	1/2	POUND BUTTER
2	GARLIC PODS, SLICED	2	CUPS WATER
1/2	BELL PEPPER, CHOPPED (OPTIONAL)		

Dice and brown bacon in a large skillet. Drain. When bacon is nearly cooked, add onions and garlic. Mix with bacon and cook 3-4 minutes. Set aside for adding later. Place butter in same skillet and heat to 300 degrees. Add shrimp which have been salted, peppered and liberally rolled in flour. Shake in bag. Do not add excess flour when frying shrimp. Brown the shrimp in butter approximately three minutes, turning only once. Add bacon, onions stirring constantly. Add water, crab, bell pepper and Tabasco. Continue stirring for 5 minutes. Serve over rice. May require a little more water, depending upon desired consistency. Yield: 6 servings. Freezes well.

Pierre McGowan—First Presbyterian Church
Beaufort, South Carolina

SHRIMP AND RICE CASSEROLE

- 1 CAN MUSHROOM SOUP
- 1 CUP MILK
- 1/2 CUP MAYONNAISE
- 1 CUP DICED ONION
- 1 CUP DICED CELERY
- 1/2 TEASPOON PARSLEY FLAKES
- 1 CAN WATER CHESTNUTS, SLICED
- 4 OR 5 SHAKES TABASCO
- 2 POUNDS COOKED AND CLEANED SHRIMP
- 3 CUPS COOKED RICE

Sauté onions and celery in butter until tender. Mix all ingredients together and pour in greased casserole. Bake uncovered in a 350 degree oven for 35 minutes. Makes one large or two small casseroles. May be frozen.

Julia Randel—First Presbyterian Church
Beaufort, South Carolina

SHRIMP CURRY

- 1/4 CUP FLOUR
- 1/4 CUP MARGARINE
- 1 TEASPOON CURRY POWDER
- 1 MILK
- 1 CUP WATER
- 1 CHICKEN BOUILLON CUBE
- 2 EGG YOLKS
- 3 CUPS COOKED SHRIMP
- SALT AND PEPPER TO TASTE

Melt margarine in heavy saucepan. Add flour and curry powder; stir well. Add milk, water and bouillon cube and cook, stirring constantly until thickened. Add a little sauce to well-beaten egg yolks; mix well and stir into the sauce. Cook two minutes. Add cooked shrimp, salt and pepper. Serve over hot, cooked rice. Serve toasted coconut or toasted slivered almonds sprinkled over each serving.

Betty L. Waskiewicz—First Presbyterian Church
Beaufort, South Carolina

SHRIMP GRAVY

- 2 POUNDS OF SMALL SHRIMP, PEELED
- 8 SLICES OF BACON
- 2 TABLESPOONS CATSUP

Prepare shrimp by flouring them. Cook bacon in pan on medium heat. When bacon is crisp, remove from grease and set aside. Add extra oil to bacon grease. Sauté shrimp to a light brown. Add water gradually until a gravy is formed by stirring water and shrimp. Break up bacon into small pieces and add to gravy. To give the gravy some *zest*, add 2 tablespoons of catsup then salt to taste. Serve over grits or rice.

Annie Frampton—Harmony Presbyterian Church
Crocketville, South Carolina

Shrimp Harpin

2	POUNDS LARGE RAW SHRIMP	1	TEASPOON SALT
1	TABLESPOON LEMON JUICE	1/8	TEASPOON PEPPER
3	TABLESPOONS SALAD OIL	1/8	TEASPOON MACE
3/4	CUP RAW RICE		DASH OF RED PEPPER
2	TABLESPOONS BUTTER OR OLEO	1	CAN TOMATO SOUP
1/4	CUP MINCED ONION	1/2	CUP SHERRY
1/4	CUP MINCED GREEN PEPPER	1/2	CUP ALMONDS

Peel raw shrimp and cook in boiling salt water for 5 minutes. Place in casserole and sprinkle with lemon juice and oil. Marinate overnight. Cook rice and drain. Sauté pepper and onion in butter. Add to rice, shrimp, seasonings, soup, and sherry. Place in 2 quart casserole. Sprinkle top with almonds and paprika. Bake in a 350 degree oven for 55 minutes, or until bubbly. Yield: 6-8 servings.

Mrs. Harry Hilton—Oakland Avenue Presbyterian Church
Rock Hill, South Carolina

Shrimp or Crawfish Fettucine

1 1/2	CUP MARGARINE	1	PINT HALF-AND-HALF
3	MEDIUM ONIONS, FINELY CHOPPED	1	POUND VELVEETA CHEESE, CUT INTO PIECES
1/4	CUP ALL-PURPOSE FLOUR		SALT TO TASTE
4	TABLESPOONS DRIED PARSLEY		BLACK PEPPER TO TASTE
3	POUNDS CRAWFISH TAILS OR SHRIMP	1	POUND FINE FETTUCINE NOODLES
	RED PEPPER TO TASTE		GARLIC TO TASTE
3	MEDIUM BELL PEPPERS, FINELY CHOPPED		

Melt margarine in large saucepan. Add onions and bell peppers. Cool, covered, 15-20 minutes. Add flour. Cook crawfish or shrimp. Cook for 15 minutes. Add cream, cheese, garlic, salt, and pepper. Cover and cook on low heat for 30 minutes, stirring occasionally. Cook fettucine according to package directions. Mix crawfish mixture and fettucine thoroughly. Pour mixture into two 3 quart casseroles. Sprinkle top with Parmesan cheese. Bake in a 350 degree oven for 15 to 20 minutes. Yield: 16 servings.

Marcia Picard—Grace Presbyterian Church
Lafayette, Louisiana

SHRIMP AND WILD RICE CASSEROLE

1	BELL PEPPER	1/2	TEASPOON DRY MUSTARD
1	SMALL ONION	1	TABLESPOON LEMON JUICE
2	TABLESPOONS BUTTER OR MARGARINE	1/2	TEASPOON BLACK PEPPER
3	POUNDS SHRIMP, PEELED & DEVEINED	1	CUP GRATED CHEDDAR CHEESE
1	BOX UNCLE BEN'S LONG GRAIN AND WILD RICE MIX, COOKED	1	CAN CREAM OF MUSHROOM SOUP
		1	TABLESPOON WORCESTERSHIRE SAUCE

Sauté bell pepper and onion in margarine or butter. Add shrimp. Sauté until shrimp are pink in color. Pour off most of the juice. Add cooked rice. Mix all ingredients together and put into large casserole. Sprinkle more cheese on top and bake in a 375 degree oven for 30 minutes. Yield: 8 servings.

(This recipe was borrowed from Frances Ann Corey Andrzejczyk)
Pat Von Harten—First Presbyterian Church, Beaufort, South Carolina
Similar recipe submitted by: Macie T. Bowers—Estill Presbyterian Church, Estill, South Carolina

CIOPPINA
(Italian Fish Stew)

1/4	CUP OLIVE OIL	1	POUND RAW, CLEANED SHRIMP OR LOBSTER TAIL
1/2	CUP PARSLEY LEAVES	2	CUPS WATER
1	MEDIUM ONION	1	TABLESPOON SUGAR
1/2	MEDIUM GREEN PEPPER	2	TEASPOONS SALT
2-3	CLOVES PEELED GARLIC	1/4	TEASPOON PEPPER
1/4	TEASPOON MARJORAM	1	28 OUNCE CAN TOMATOES, UNDRAINED
1	DOZEN FRESH CLAMS (OR 6 OUNCE CAN CLAMS UNDRAINED)	1	8 OUNCE CAN TOMATO SAUCE
2	POUNDS MILD FISH FILETS, CUT IN PIECES (I LIKE CATFISH)		ADDITIONAL SEAFOOD SUCH AS SCALLOPS, CRAB OR IMITATION CRAB CAN BE ADDED

Sauté chopped parsley, garlic, onion, and pepper in olive oil for about 10 minutes. Add tomatoes, sauce, water, sugar, salt, marjoram, and pepper. Cover and simmer for about 30 minutes. Add seafood and cook slowly for about 5 minutes or until done. Yield: 8 servings (1 1/2 cup each). Freezes well.

Eunice M. Rogers—Christ Presbyterian Church
Camp Hill, Pennsylvania

Seafood Casserole I

1/2	POUND SHRIMP, COOKED AND SHELLED	1/2	POUND LUMP CRAB MEAT
1/2	POUND SLICED MUSHROOMS	6	OUNCES LOBSTER OR SCALLOPS
1	CUP SOUR CREAM	4	TABLESPOONS BUTTER (DIVIDED)
1	TABLESPOON CHOPPED GREEN PEPPER	2	CUPS COOKED RICE
	DASH CAYENNE PEPPER	1	CUP RICOTTA CHEESE
1/4	CUP BREAD CRUMBS	1	TABLESPOON WORCESTERSHIRE SAUCE
2	TABLESPOONS WHITE WINE	1/2	CUP GRATED PARMESAN CHEESE
2	TABLESPOONS CHOPPED SCALLIONS		SALT TO TASTE

Note: Crab meat and shrimp may be fresh or canned. Heat 2 tablespoons butter and sauté mushrooms for 5 minutes. Add seafood. Fold in rice and all other ingredients except bread crumbs. Place in buttered casserole. Mix 2 tablespoons melted butter with bread crumbs and sprinkle over top. Bake for 20 minutes in a 350 degree oven. Yield: serves 8.

Joanne Strickland—Bryn Mawr Presbyterian Church
Bryn Mawr, Pennsylvania

Seafood Casserole II

1	POUND RAW SHRIMP	1	SMALL ONION, CHOPPED
1	POUND BAY SCALLOPS	1	SMALL CAN STEMS AND PIECES MUSHROOMS
1	CAN CRAB MEAT		SALT AND PEPPER TO TASTE
1	CAN MINCED CLAMS, DRAINED, SAVE BROTH	1	CAN CREAM OF CELERY SOUP
		8-10	CUPS COOKED HOT RICE
1/4	CUP COOKED BACON, CRUMBLED	1/4-1/2	CUP SHREDDED SWISS CHEESE
1	CUP CHICKEN STOCK	1/2	CUP PEPPERIDGE FARM HERBED DRESSING
1/2	PINT CREAM		

Clean and devein shrimp. Fry bacon, drain and crumble. In crock pot, on highest setting, cook chopped onion and bacon pieces in broth reserved from clams. When onions are transparent, add chicken stock. When stock is thoroughly heated, add raw shrimp and scallops. Cover and cook until done. Add drained clams, drained crabmeat, salt and pepper, and cream of celery soup. Heat thoroughly. Slowly stir in cream. Cook ten minutes. Add mushrooms. Lower heat to low setting. Cook for 15 minutes. In large, shallow casserole dish, spread hot, cooked rice evenly and pour seafood mixture, including all broth, over rice. Top with Swiss cheese. Sprinkle stuffing mix over casserole. Cover and bake for 45 minutes in a 350 degree oven, or until heated thoroughly. Yield: 12-15 servings. Freezes well, but never lasts long enough to be frozen.

Deborah Baker Covington—First Presbyterian Church
Beaufort, South Carolina

Low Country Deviled Crab

1/2	STICK MARGARINE	1	DASH TABASCO SAUCE
1/2	SMALL ONION, CHOPPED	1/2	TEASPOON SALT
1/2	BELL PEPPER, CHOPPED	1	DASH BLACK PEPPER
1	STEM CELERY, CHOPPED	1/4	CUP MILK
3	EGGS, BEATEN	1	POUND CLAW CRAB MEAT
12	RITZ CRACKERS, CRUMBLED	1	HEAPING TABLESPOON MAYONNAISE
1	TEASPOON PREPARED MUSTARD	1	TABLESPOON WORCESTERSHIRE

Melt margarine in heavy saucepan. Sauté onion, celery and pepper until tender but not browned. Beat eggs and add all other ingredients. Toss together lightly until well-mixed. Turn into 1 quart casserole, sprinkle with additional cracker crumbs and paprika. Bake in a 325 degree oven for 25-30 minutes, or until firm and browned.

Betty L. Waskiewicz—First Presbyterian Church
Beaufort, South Carolina

Very Best Crab Casserole

4	TABLESPOONS BUTTER	1/2	POUND MUSHROOMS
4	TABLESPOONS FLOUR		BUTTER
2	CUPS HALF-AND-HALF	1	POUND LUMP CRAB
2	EGG YOLKS, BEATEN	3	TABLESPOONS CHOPPED PARSLEY
1/2	TEASPOON SALT	1/4	CUP WHITE WINE
1	TEASPOON WORCESTERSHIRE SAUCE		BUTTERED BREAD CRUMBS

Make cream sauce with butter, flour and cream. Remove from heat; add egg yolks, salt and Worcestershire sauce. Broil or sauté mushrooms in butter and combine all ingredients. Pour in casserole and top with bread crumbs. Bake in a 350 degree oven for 20 to 30 minutes, until lightly browned and bubbly. Yield: 6 servings.

Ann Bruce Faircloth—Oakland Avenue Presbyterian Church
Rock Hill, South Carolina

Scalloped Oysters

Excellent side dish at Thanksgiving.

1	PINT OYSTERS	1/4	CUP OYSTER LIQUOR
2	CUPS COARSE CRACKER CRUMBS	1/4	TEASPOON WORCESTERSHIRE SAUCE
1/2	CUP BUTTER OR MARGARINE, MELTED	1/2	TEASPOON SALT
3/4	CUP LIGHT CREAM		PEPPER TO TASTE (WHITE)

Seafood Supreme

4	TINS SHRIMP (5-6 OUNCE SIZE) OR 20 BIG FRESH SHRIMP COOKED AND CUT INTO PIECES
4	TINS CRAB MEAT (6 1/2-TO 7-OUNCE SIZE)
3	CUPS SHREDDED WHITE BREAD ("DAY OLD" IS FINE)
1	CUP SLICED CELERY
2	TABLESPOONS CAPERS
1	TABLESPOON CAPERS' LIQUID
1	TABLESPOON LEMON JUICE
1/2	TEASPOON CURRY POWDER
1	TABLESPOON WORCESTERSHIRE SAUCE
1	TEASPOON DRY MUSTARD
1	CUP MAYONNAISE

Mix all ingredients. Put into 3 quart casserole dish. Refrigerate several hours, or, overnight. Bake in a 350 degree oven for one hour. Mixture should be moist. Liquid from canned shrimp, water, or mayonnaise can be used if needed.

Caroline Wright—Highland Presbyterian Church
Winston-Salem, North Carolina

"Under the Sea"

2	POUNDS RED SNAPPER OR FLOUNDER
1	POUND MEDIUM-LARGE SHRIMP
3/4	POUND SCALLOPS
1/2	POUND OF CRAB MEAT)
1/4	CUP BUTTER OR MARGARINE
2	TABLESPOONS WORCESTERSHIRE SAUCE
4	CLOVES GARLIC, CRUSHED
1/4	CUP CHABLIS OR COOKING WINE
3	CANS CAMPBELL'S CREAM OF SHRIMP SOUP
1/4	POUND SALTINE CRACKERS, CRUSHED
	PAPRIKA

Note: Imitation crab meat may be used. Spray baking dish with vegetable oil and place snapper in center of dish. Spread scallops and crab meat around fish. Place a few shrimp on top, saving the remaining shrimp. Set aside.

In a saucepan, cook cream of shrimp soup, add butter and Worcestershire sauce, wine and garlic. Stir until blended. Pour sauce over fish. Sprinkle crushed crackers over top and sprinkle paprika over crackers for color. Bake in a 350 degree oven for 30 minutes. Add remaining shrimp on top and bake an additional 15 minutes.

Edith B. Moore—Westminster Presbyterian Church
Burlington, North Carolina

Chapter Eight

Meats—Entrées and Casseroles

BEEF

BARBECUPS

3/4	POUND GROUND BEEF	1	CAN (8 OUNCES) REFRIGERATOR BISCUITS
1/2	CUP BARBECUE SAUCE	3/4	CUP SHREDDED CHEESE
1	TABLESPOON INSTANT MINCED ONION	2	TABLESPOONS BROWN SUGAR

Brown beef in a skillet and drain. Add barbecue sauce, onion and brown sugar. Separate biscuit dough into 12 biscuits. Place in ungreased muffin cups, pressing dough up the sides. Spoon beef mixture into cups. Sprinkle with cheese. Bake in a 400 degree oven for 10-12 minutes.

Robbie Knox—First Presbyterian Church
Aiken, South Carolina

CRANBERRY BEEF BRISKET

1	5-POUND BRISKET	3/4	CUP DRY RED WINE
1	PACKAGE DRY LIPTON ONION SOUP MIX	1/2	CUP WATER
1	CAN JELLIED CRANBERRY SAUCE		

Sprinkle package of onion soup mix on bottom of pyrex pan. Place meat, fat side down. Spread cranberry sauce on top. Add water and wine. Cover tightly with heavy-duty foil. Bake in a 350 degree oven for 3 hours. Yield: 8 servings.

Brenda Kepley—Providence Presbyterian Church
Fairfax, Virginia

Westminster Brisket

1	BEEF BRISKET, 4 1/2-5 1/2 POUNDS	2	CUPS WATER
	SEASONED SALT (SEE BELOW)	1	CUP KETCHUP
1	LEMON, SLICED	1/2	CUP WORCESTERSHIRE SAUCE
1	ONION, SLICED	2	TABLESPOONS FLOUR

Sprinkle with onion salt, garlic salt, celery salt, Lawry's Seasoned Salt. Wrap in heavy foil and put in pan. Bake in 300 degree oven for 4 1/2 hours. Pour off liquid. Put lemon slices and onion slices or flakes over top. Put under broiler for 10 minutes. Mix water, ketchup, and Worcestershire sauce and baste. Rewrap and put in oven for 45 minutes. Baste again. Cool and refrigerate. Next day, slice. Before serving, put back into 300 degree oven (in foil) until reheated. Thicken basting sauce with flour. Heat and serve with meat.

Irene Bleckschmidt—Westminster Presbyterian Church
St. Louis, Missouri

Corned Beef Hash

2	CUPS CHOPPED CORNED BEEF	1/4	CUP CHOPPED TURNIPS
1/2	CUP CHOPPED CARROTS	2	CUPS CHOPPED POTATOES
1/2	CUP CHOPPED CABBAGE	2	TEASPOONS SALT
1/4	CUP CHOPPED ONIONS	1/8	TEASPOON BLACK PEPPER

Mix all ingredients in a large bowl. Put them into a well-greased baking pan. Bake in a preheated 300 degree oven for 40 minutes. Serve with poached eggs as with roast beef hash. Note: This can be made with leftovers.

Dorothy King—The Plymouth Church
Framingham Centre, Massachusetts

Nannie's Plantation Hash

3	CUPS LEFTOVER ROAST OR SOUP MEAT	2	TABLESPOONS FLOUR (LEVEL)
4 OR 5	MEDIUM POTATOES (WHITE BEST)	2 OR 3	BEEF BOUILLON CUBES
1	LARGE ONION, CHOPPED	1	PINCH BASIL LEAVES
4	TABLESPOONS COOKING OIL		GARLIC POWDER

Chop meat into small pieces. Let soak in bouillon cubes dissolved in 2 cups of boiling water, for a few minutes. Make a medium shade roux with oil and flour. To roux, add chopped onion and potatoes. Let fry a few minutes. Add meat and stir well. Cook over low heat, about 2 minutes. Add sufficient water to cook potatoes, which will make a medium to thin gravy. Add a pinch of basil leaves and shake or two of garlic powder. Add more water if necessary. Serve over rice.

Bonnie Mahaffey—First Presbyterian Church
Baton Rouge, Louisiana

RAPID ROAST

1-3 POUNDS EYE-OF-ROUND ROAST LEMON-PEPPER SEASONING
SALT OR GARLIC SALT

Salt to taste by using either plain salt or garlic salt, mixed with lemon-pepper seasoning. Rub well with your bare hands (because they will be warm and will cause the ingredients to cling to the roast.) Place roast in a shallow roasting pan in a preheated 500 degree oven. Cook uncovered 4 minutes per pound for rare, 5 minutes per pound for medium and 6 minutes per pound for well-done. Turn oven off and do not open for at least 2 hours. Freezes well. Yield: 6 servings.

Mary Cook—First Presbyterian Church
Demopolis, Alabama

TWENTY-FOUR HOUR ROAST BEEF

15 POUNDS BEEF, BONELESS GARLIC SALT OR SALT TO TASTE

Sprinkle beef with seasoning. Place in open pan. Do not add water. Bake 18-24 hours in a 150 degree oven. Beef will be pink and very tender. An excellent way to cook beef for a large crowd. Do not overcook. Yield: 10-15 servings.

Gloria Schmidt—Pacific Palisades Presbyterian Church
Pacific Palisades, California

Pepper Steak (Lot Ju Kair Ngow)

1	POUND ROUND STEAK	1	CUP SLICED CELERY
1/4	CUP COOKING OIL	1	CUP BEEF BOUILLON
1	TEASPOON SALT, DASH PEPPER	2	TABLESPOONS CORNSTARCH
1/4	CUP DICED ONION	1/4	CUP WATER
1	CLOVE GARLIC	1	TEASPOON SOY SAUCE
4	GREEN PEPPERS, CUT IN 1" PIECES		

Cut steak diagonally into thin slices, then into 2" pieces. Heat oil with salt and pepper in medium skillet. Add meat, cook over high heat until brown, stirring frequently. Add next 5 ingredients. Cover and cook over moderate heat until vegetables are crisply tender, about 10 minutes. Blend cornstarch, water and soy sauce. Add to meat, cook and stir until thickened, about 5 minutes. Serve with hot cooked rice.

Doris Ryba—First Presbyterian Church
Rutherford, New Jersey

GROUND BEEF

Hamburger Stroganoff

1/2	CUP MINCED ONIONS	1/4	TEASPOON ACCENT
1/4	CUP BUTTER OR MARGARINE	1/2	TEASPOON PEPPER
1	POUND GROUND BEEF	1/4	TEASPOON PAPRIKA
1	GARLIC CLOVE, MINCED	1	CAN CONDENSED CREAM OF MUSHROOM SOUP
2	TABLESPOONS FLOUR	1	PINT SOUR CREAM
2	TEASPOONS SALT		PARSLEY, CHIVES OR FRESH DILL

Sauté onion in butter until golden. Stir in beef and next 7 ingredients. Saute' 5 minutes. Add soup. Simmer uncovered for 10 minutes. Stir in sour cream; sprinkle with parsley, dill and/or chives. Serve on hot mashed potatoes, fluffy rice, toast, noodles or a bun. Garnish with parsley, chives or fresh dill. Yield: 4-6 servings.

Phyllis Berggreen—Pacific Palisades Presbyterian Church
Pacific Palisades, California

Marilyn's Smothered Burritos

1	POUND STEW MEAT	1	CAN REFRIED BEANS
1	CAN (16 OUNCES) WHOLE TOMATOES		SALT & PEPPER
1	CAN (4 OUNCES) GREEN CHILIES		FLOUR TORTILLAS

Condiments:

CHOPPED LETTUCE	CHOPPED ONION
GRATED CHEDDAR CHEESE	SLICED AVOCADO
CHOPPED TOMATO	SOUR CREAM

Cut meat into bite size pieces and brown in medium saucepan. Add chopped tomatoes, diced chilies; salt and pepper to taste. Simmer until thick. Heat refried beans. Warm tortillas. Place small amount of beans on each tortilla and roll up. Place meat mixture over top. Add whatever condiments you like on top. Yield: 5-6 servings.

Susan Leyden—Providence Presbyterian Church
Fairfax, Virginia

MEAT LOAF I

1 1/2	POUNDS GROUND STEAK	1	EGG, BEATEN
1/2	POUND SMOKED HAM, GROUND		SALT AND PEPPER TO TASTE
3	SLICES BREAD (IN CRUMBS)		

Mix all ingredients together thoroughly. Place in ovenproof loaf pan. Place pan in sauce pan and add boiling water. Cover saucepan and steam for 2 hours. (Do not let the pan boil dry.) Remove half of the liquid from the top of the loaf, pierce the loaf to allow remainder of liquid to penetrate the loaf. Serve hot with vegetables or cold with a green salad.

A. Duncans—Isle of Cumbrae Parish Church
Isle of Cumbrae, Scotland

MEAT LOAF II

3/4	CUP KETCHUP	1	TEASPOON SALT
1/2	CUP MUSHROOMS	1	POUND GROUND BEEF
1/2	CUP MILK	1	TABLESPOON CHOPPED GREEN PEPPER
1/4	CUP CHOPPED ONIONS	1	EGG
1/4	TEASPOON PEPPER	3/4	CUP BREAD CRUMBS OR OATMEAL

Spread some ketchup over bottom of loaf pan. Mix all ingredients thoroughly and pack lightly in loaf pan. Bake in a 375 degree oven for 1 1/2 to 1 1/2 hours.

Kathleen Allen—Paint Gap Presbyterian Church
Burnsville, North Carolina

World's Greatest Meatloaf

Luscious leftovers for sandwiches!

2	POUNDS LEAN GROUND BEEF	1/2	CUP CHOPPED ONION
1	POUND GROUND PORK	1	EGG
2	CUPS PLAIN BREAD CRUMBS	1	TEASPOON MUSTARD
1	CUP MILK	1/2	TEASPOON PEPPER
1	CUP GRATED CARROTS		

Place all ingredients in a large bowl and mix by hand. Pack tightly into 1 1/2 quart loaf tin. Bake in preheated a 350 degree oven for 1 hour. Remove from oven and drain. Return to oven for 1/2 hour more. Slice and serve.

Dr. John H. Niles, Minister—Fallston Presbyterian Church
Fallston, Maryland

Wonderful Meat Loaf

2	SLICES OF BREAD	1	TEASPOON SALT
1	CUP MILK	1/2	TEASPOON SAGE
1 1/2	POUNDS GROUND BEEF	1/8	TEASPOON PEPPER
2	EGGS, BEATEN	1	SMALL CAN MUSHROOM SAUCE
1/4	CUP MINCED ONION		

Glaze (mix together):

3	TABLESPOONS BROWN SUGAR	1/2	TEASPOON NUTMEG
1/4	CUP KETCHUP	1	TEASPOON DRY MUSTARD

Soak bread in milk (mix to break bread into small particles). Add other ingredients and mix thoroughly. Shape into loaf and spread with glaze mixture. Bake in a 350 degree oven. Yield: 6-8 servings.

Monica McGregor—Fort Hill Presbyterian Church
Clemson, South Carolina

MOTHER'S BEST MEATLOAF

1	POUND GROUND BEEF	1	ONION, DICED
1	POUND GROUND TURKEY	2	EGGS
1	POUND GROUND PORK OR PORK SAUSAGE	1	TABLESPOON SUGAR
4	LARGE SLICES WHOLE WHEAT BREAD	1	TEASPOON NUTMEG
2	SMALL CANS TOMATO JUICE		SALT AND PEPPER TO TASTE

Sauté diced onion in oil in a covered frying pan. Break bread into small pieces in a large bowl; add tomato juice. Mix well. Beat eggs and mix in sugar, nutmeg, salt, and pepper. (If using pork sausage use less salt and pepper.) Mix all and shape into a loaf. Place in large baking dish and bake in a 325 degree oven for about an hour. Pour off drippings before serving. Yield: 18 servings.

Vivien Skinner Grant—First Presbyterian Church
Dunedin, Florida

RICE AND MEATBALLS

1	CUP MINUTE RICE, UNCOOKED	2	TEASPOONS SALT
1	POUND GROUND BEEF		DASH PEPPER
1	EGG	2 1/2	CUPS TOMATO JUICE
2	TABLESPOONS GRATED ONION	1/2	TEASPOON SUGAR

Combine rice, beef, egg, onion, salt, pepper and 1/2 cup tomato juice; mix well. Shape into 18 balls and place in skillet. Add sugar to remaining tomato juice; pour over meatballs in skillet. Bring to boil; then simmer, covered, for 15 minutes. Yield: 12 servings.

Lola Rolen—Bryson City Presbyterian Church
Bryson City, North Carolina

"SOUPER" SUPPER

1/2	POUND GROUND BEEF	1	CAN VEGETABLE SOUP
1	ONION, CHOPPED	2	CUPS COOKED RICE
1	TABLESPOON OIL		SALT AND PEPPER TO TASTE

Brown ground beef and onion in oil. Drain well. Add undiluted soup and simmer 15 minutes. Season to taste and serve over rice. Yield: 4 servings.

Mary Bray Wheeler—Glencliff Presbyterian Church
Nashville, Tennessee

PORK

HAM BALLS AND GREEN RICE

Edna Hinman was the long-time cook at this church. Green rice and ham balls (her recipes) are still among the top favorites for church-related meals. She now resides in a Helena nursing facility. We hope that she will be pleased that her recipes will be used by people from all over!

Ham Balls

1	POUND SMOKED HAM	1	CUP MILK
1 1/2	POUND LEAN PORK	2	BEATEN EGGS
1	CUP BREAD CRUMBS		SALT AND PEPPER TO TASTE

Sauce

1/2	CUP VINEGAR	1 1/2	CUPS BROWN SUGAR
1/2	CUP WATER	1	TEASPOON MUSTARD (DRY)

Mix the ground meat well with the beaten eggs, bread crumbs, milk and salt and pepper. Form into balls and place in casserole. Mix together vinegar, water, brown sugar, and mustard and bring to a boil. Pour this mixture over meatballs. Bake in a 350 degree oven for 1 hour. Turn meatballs once during cooking. Yield: 8 servings.

Green Rice

2	CUPS COOKED RICE (3/4 CUP UNCOOKED)	1/4	CUP SALAD OIL
1/2	CUP CHOPPED PARSLEY	2	CUPS MILK
1	SMALL ONION, CHOPPED	2	WELL BEATEN EGGS
1	CUP CHEDDAR CHEESE, CUBED OR GRATED		

Mix above ingredients thoroughly; pour into a well-buttered flat pan. Bake in a 350 degree oven for 45 minutes.

Edna Hinman—First Presbyterian Church
Helena, Montana

HAM LOAF I

2 POUNDS PORK GROUND WITH	3/4 CUP MILK
1 POUND HAM	2 CUPS CRACKER CRUMBS
2 EGGS	

Syrup:

1 CUP BROWN SUGAR	1/4 CUP VINEGAR
1 CUP WATER	

Mix together first four ingredients in a large bowl. Shape as desired and place in baking pan. Cover with syrup. Bake for 1 hour in a 300 degree oven, rotating pan. Yield: 1 large loaf (or 27 balls).

Philathea Sunday School Class—Rocky Grove Avenue Presbyterian Church
Franklin, Pennsylvania

HAM LOAF II

1 POUND GROUND PORK	1 CUP MILK
1 POUND GROUND HAM	2 TABLESPOONS CHILI SAUCE
2 EGGS	1 CUP BREAD CRUMBS

Sauce (simmer together 5 minutes):

1/2 CUP BROWN SUGAR	1/4 CUP VINEGAR
1/2 TEASPOON DRY MUSTARD	1/4 CUP WATER

Mix pork and ground ham well. Add eggs, milk, chili sauce, and bread crumbs and blend. Shape into a loaf, cover with sauce, and bake in a 350 degree oven for 1 1/2 hours. Yield: 1 loaf (10 slices).

Central Presbyterian Church, Fort Smith, Arkansas

Ham Loaf with Mustard Sauce

- 1 POUND HAM (GROUND AND UNCOOKED)
- 1 POUND VEAL (GROUND AND UNCOOKED)
- 1 POUND PORK (GROUND AND UNCOOKED)
- 1 CUP CRACKER CRUMBS
- 1 CUP MILK
- 1 CUP CATSUP
- 2 EGGS, UNBEATEN

Note: If veal is not available use 2 pounds of ham or 1 pound of pork. Form into loaf and bake in moderate oven at 350 degrees for 1 1/2 to 2 hours. Yield: 12 servings.

Sauce:

- 1 1/2 CUPS WATER
- 1/2 CUP VINEGAR
- 1 CUP SUGAR
- 1/2 TEASPOON SALT
- 1/4 CUP BUTTER
- 2 TABLESPOONS FLOUR
- 1 EGG
- 1/3 BOTTLE FRENCH'S PREPARED MUSTARD

Put all ingredients in top of double boiler, beat with egg beater. Cook until thickens. Pour over sliced ham loaf.

Peachtree Presbyterian Church, Atlanta, Georgia

Baked Ham Loaf

- 1 POUND GROUND HAM
- 1 POUND GROUND PORK
- 2 EGGS, BEATEN
- 2 CUPS CORNFLAKES, CRUSHED
- 3/4 CUP MILK
- 1-2 TABLESPOONS GRATED ONION
- 2 TABLESPOONS FRESH PARSLEY
- SALT AND PEPPER TO TASTE

Glaze:

- 1/4 CUP BROWN SUGAR
- 1 TEASPOON PREPARED MUSTARD

Soak crushed cornflakes in milk and eggs for 10 minutes. Mix ham, pork, onion, parsley, salt, and pepper. Add cornflake mixture to meat, and blend all ingredients lightly. Place in greased loaf pan, approximately 6x12. Bake in a 325 degree oven 1 hour. Remove from oven. Cover with glaze (paste of brown sugar and mustard). Return to oven and continue baking 30 minutes. Watch closely; if necessary cover lightly with foil sprayed with Pam. Do not let glaze burn. Remove from oven and let sit 5 minutes before slicing. Yield: 8-10 servings.

Mary Lou Francisco—First Presbyterian Church
Medina, New York

BAKED PORK CHOPS

- 6 PORK CHOPS
- 4 TABLESPOONS BROWN SUGAR
- 6 TABLESPOONS KETCHUP
- DASH OF WORCESTERSHIRE SAUCE
- DASH OF HOT SAUCE (OPTIONAL)

Salt and pepper pork chops and place in baking dish (do not stack). Combine remaining ingredients. Moisten brown sugar and drizzle over chops. Cover with foil. Bake for 1 hour in a 400 degree oven. Yield: 6 servings.

Ruby J. Campen—Highland Presbyterian Church
Fayetteville, North Carolina

BARBEQUED PORK RIBS

"I serve this at the National Presbyterian Church real often, and it is a real favorite with most everyone."

Brown 10 pounds of country-cut pork ribs in a small amount of oil. Place in a large roasting pan. Drain, setting aside a small amount of the drippings. Brown 2 sliced onions and 1 cup of chopped celery. Spread this over the ribs. Add sauce and bake until tender in a 350 degree oven. Serves about 25.

Sauce:

- 2 CUPS CATSUP
- 2 CUPS WATER
- 6 TABLESPOONS WORCESTERSHIRE SAUCE
- 2 TEASPOONS HORSERADISH
- 1 TEASPOON RED PEPPER
- 4 TABLESPOONS BROWN SUGAR
- 8 TABLESPOONS LEMON JUICE
- 4 TABLESPOONS VINEGAR
- 4 TEASPOONS DRY MUSTARD
- 2 TEASPOONS PAPRIKA
- 1 CUP COOKING SHERRY

Mix and pour over browned ribs and bake.

Arlie O. Holcomb—National Presbyterian Church
Washington, D.C.

Pork Chops and Stuffing

6-8	PORK LOIN CHOPS	1/4	CUP ONIONS (CHOPPED)
1	PACKAGE PREPARED STUFFING MIX	2	BOUILLON CUBES
1	CUP RAISINS (CHOPPED)	1-1 1/2	CUPS HOT WATER
1	CUP CELERY (CHOPPED)	6-8	APPLES (CORED, HALVED)

Brown pork chops in heavy skillet. Remove and place in baking pan. Use a large bowl to mix the stuffing, raisins, apples, celery, and onion. Dissolve the bouillon cubes in the hot water. Add the dissolved cubes to the dressing mixture and stir. Pour mixture from bowl over the pork chops, spread evenly. Place apple halves with the skin side up on top of dressing. Cover with foil and bake in a 350 degree oven for 50 minutes or until brown.

First Presbyterian Church, Coalinga, California

Pork with Apricots and Prunes

1	POUND PORK, CUBED	1	CHICKEN STOCK CUBE
2	TABLESPOONS OIL	1	TABLESPOON SHERRY
1	CARROT, SLICED	1	TABLESPOON CORNSTARCH
1	ONION, CUT IN RINGS		SALT AND PEPPER
1	SMALL CAN APRICOTS OR 10 DRIED		
1	SMALL CAN PRUNES OR 10 DRIED (PITTED)		

If using dried apricots and prunes, these can be soaked in water or sherry overnight. The liquid is used in the sauce. Heat oil and gently saute' onions and carrots. Add pork and brown lightly. Season with salt and pepper. Strain juice from apricots and prunes into measuring cup. Add stock, cube and make up to 1 pint with boiling water. Add to rest of mixture. Add half of apricots and prunes. Add to rest of mixture. Heat gently and transfer to casserole. Bake in a 350 degree oven for 1-1 1/2 hours. Blend cornstarch with a little water and stir into casserole. Return to oven 5-10 minutes. Add remaining prunes and apricots. Serve with rice. Yield: 3-4 servings.

Barbara Dick—Isle of Cumbrae Parish Church
Isle of Cumbrae, Scotland

LAMB

BRAISED LAMB SHANKS

2	TABLESPOONS BUTTER	1/2	TEASPOON THYME
4	LAMB SHANKS	1	TEASPOON SALT
1	MEDIUM ONION SLICED	1/4	TEASPOON BLACK PEPPER
1	MEDIUM GREEN PEPPER, CHOPPED	1/2	CUP STOCK
1/4	CUP FLOUR	1	CUP RED WINE
1/2	TEASPOON BASIL		

Brown shanks in butter on all sides. Add onions and green pepper, and brown slightly. Combine flour, basil, thyme, salt, and pepper, and mix well. Gradually add stock, stirring constantly until well blended. Add wine. Pour this mixture into skillet with shanks and mix with butter. Cover and cook over low heat for a minimum of one and one half hours, stirring occasionally. Lamb should be tender. Additional liquid may be added if it gets too thick. Serve over rice. Yield: 4 servings.

Fran Olsen—First Presbyterian Church
Beaufort, South Carolina

LAMB CUTLETS IN OATMEAL/HERB CRUST

8	LAMB CUTLETS, TRIMMED	4	TABLESPOONS FRESH PARSLEY, TARRAGON OR ROSEMARY, CHOPPED
1	LARGE ONION, CHOPPED		
1/2	STICK BUTTER, MELTED	1/2	STICK BUTTER
1/2	CUP OATMEAL	1 1/4	CUPS GOOD BEEF OR LAMB STOCK
1	CLOVE GARLIC, CRUSHED	1/2	TEASPOON ENGLISH MUSTARD
	GRATED RIND OF A LEMON	1	CUP STEWED TOMATOES
2	TABLESPOONS RAISINS		SALT AND PEPPER TO TASTE
2	TABLESPOONS WHISKY		SPRIG OF ROSEMARY TO GARNISH

Mix together the crumb ingredients and season to taste. Dip the cutlets in melted butter. Coat with the oatmeal mixture. Place on a greased baking pan and bake in a 350 degree oven for about 15 minutes until cooked through. Meanwhile, saute' onion in butter until soft. Add tomatoes, stock, and mustard. Reduce by half, until the consistency of sauce is reached. Liquify in a blender. Soak raisins in whisky and boil for one minute. Stir raisins into mixture. Taste for seasoning. Serve the sauce with cutlets and garnish with a sprig of fresh rosemary.

Mrs. Margaret Keay—Auchtergaven & Moneydie Parish Church
Letchworth, England

STAY-A-BED STEW

"Put casserole in oven and go back to bed!"

2	POUNDS LEAN BEEF (STEW MEAT OF CHUCK ROAST)	1	CAN TOMATO OR CREAM OF CELERY SOUP
1	LARGE POTATO, SLICED	1/4	CUP A-1 SAUCE
1	CUP CARROTS, SLICED	1	ONION, SLICED
1/2	CUP WATER		SALT AND PEPPER TO TASTE
		1	CAN LESEUR PEAS, PARTIALLY DRAINED

Beef may be browned slightly before putting all ingredients together in a covered 3-quart casserole. Bake in a 275 degree oven for 4 1/2-5 hours.

Lyda Graham—New Wappetaw Presbyterian Church
McClellanville, South Carolina

AARDVARK TOOTH CASSEROLE

"So named because it has everything in it except the tooth of an aardvark!"

2	POUNDS GROUND BEEF	1	MEDIUM JAR WHOLE STUFFED GREEN OLIVES (DRAINED)
3	LARGE ONIONS, SLICED		
2	CLOVES GARLIC, MINCED	1	MEDIUM JAR WHOLE PITTED RIPE OLIVES (DRAINED)
8	OUNCES WIDE NOODLES, COOKED		
1 1/2	CUPS COOKED CUBED CHICKEN	1	CUP CHICKEN BROTH
1	#2 CAN TOMATOES	1	TEASPOON CHILI POWDER
1	#2 CAN WHITE CREAMSTYLE CORN	1	6 OUNCE CAN MUSHROOMS, SLICED
1	#2 CAN HOT TAMALES	1	TEASPOON TABASCO
1	#2 CAN CREAM OF MUSHROOM SOUP	1	TEASPOON SALT

Sauté ground beef, onions, and garlic. Drain. Combine meat and cooked noodles. Drain both jars of olives and add along with other ingredients straight from the can. Mix well and place in a large greased casserole (4 quart oblong). Grate 1/2 pound Mozzarella cheese and sprinkle on top. Bake in a 325 degree oven for 1 hour. Yield: 16 servings. Freezes beautifully.

Anne N. Thomas—First Presbyterian Church
New Vernon, New Jersey

Applesauce Meatballs

1 1/2	CUPS HERB-SEASONED BREAD CRUMBS	1/8	TEASPOON BLACK PEPPER
1/2	CUP SKIM OR LOW FAT MILK	1 1/2	POUNDS LOW FAT GROUND BEEF
1	EGG	1	(10 3/4 OUNCE) CAN CREAM OF CELERY SOUP
3/4	CUP UNSWEETENED APPLESAUCE	1/2	CUP WATER
3	TABLESPOONS FINELY CHOPPED ONION		

In a large bowl, add bread crumbs, milk, applesauce, onion, pepper, and let stand 5 minutes, then mix. Add meat and mix thoroughly. Form 18 meatballs, about 2" in diameter, and place in a 7x11" (2 quart) baking pan. Mix soup and water and pour mixture over the meatballs. Bake, uncovered, in a 350 degree oven for 1 hour or more, until the liquid is bubbly. Yield: 18 meatballs.

Nancy Nelson—The Presbyterian Church
Basking Ridge, New Jersey

Beef and Macaroni Casserole

1	POUND BOX LARGE ELBOW MACARONI	2	CUPS GRATED CHEDDAR CHEESE
2	POUNDS GROUND BEEF	1/4	TEASPOON BLACK PEPPER
1	GREEN PEPPER, CHOPPED	1/2	TEASPOON SALT
1	ONION, CHOPPED	1	TEASPOON GARLIC (SALT OR MINCED)
2	CANS CREAM OF MUSHROOM SOUP	1	SOUP CAN OF WATER OR MILK
1	CAN CHEDDAR CHEESE SOUP		

Cook macaroni. Brown meat, onion, and green pepper; add to macaroni with seasonings. Put in casserole dish. Top with grated cheese. Bake in a 350 degree oven for 45 minutes. Yield: 12 servings.

Committee Who Feed the Homeless—Trinity Presbyterian Church
Charlotte, North Carolina

Beef Noodle Casserole

1	POUND GROUND BEEF, BROWNED		DASH OF PEPPER AND GARLIC POWDER
3	8 OUNCE CANS TOMATO SAUCE	1	8 OUNCE PACKAGE NOODLES (COOKED)
1	TEASPOON SALT	1/2	PINT SOUR CREAM
1	TEASPOON SUGAR	6 OR 8	CHOPPED GREEN ONIONS

Simmer beef, tomato sauce, salt sugar, pepper and garlic powder for 20 minutes, until meat is browned. Combine with noodles, sour cream and green onions. Bake in 350 degree oven for 30 minutes.

Emily G. Lytle—East Ridge Presbyterian Church
Chattanooga, Tennessee

Beef-n-Noodles in Sour Cream

"My children and grandchildren love it!"

1	CUP CHOPPED ONION	2	TEASPOONS SALT (OR LESS)
2	TABLESPOONS OIL	2	TEASPOONS CELERY SALT
1	POUND GROUND CHUCK		DASH PEPPER
3	CUPS NOODLES (UNCOOKED)	2	TEASPOONS WORCESTERSHIRE SAUCE.
3	CUPS V8 JUICE	1	CUP SOUR CREAM

Cook onion in oil until tender but not brown. Add meat and brown lightly. Place uncooked noodles in layer over meat. Combine remaining ingredients except sour cream and pour over noodles to moisten mixture, bring to boil. Cover and simmer over low heat 30 minutes or until noodles are tender. Stir in sour cream and heat just to boiling. Yield: 6 servings.

Mary Barber—Fripp Island Chapel
Fripp Island, South Carolina

Burns Burgers

"Created by my mother, Gladys Burns, over thirty years ago, to feed a Westminster Youth Fellowship group at Camp Hill Presbyterian Church; this recipe has become a family favorite, and has been requested and enjoyed by a multitude of youth over the years."

1	POUND GROUND BEEF*	1	TEASPOON MINCED ONION
1/3	CUP CHILI SAUCE	1/2	TEASPOON LITE SALT
1 1/2	TEASPOON WORCESTERSHIRE SAUCE	1/8	TEASPOON PEPPER
1 1/2	TEASPOON PREPARED MUSTARD	4	HAMBURGER BUNS, SPLIT
1 1/2	TEASPOON HORSERADISH		

*Ground turkey may be substituted for ground beef—just add 1/2 teaspoon cumin for flavor!

Combine all ingredients and spread on 1/2 of a hamburger bun. Broil 5-7 inches from heat for 6-8 minutes. Edges should be sizzling, and center done. Yield: 8 servings.

Pam Thompson—Faith Presbyterian Church
Harrisburg, Pennsylvania

Cheese and Pasta in a Pot

2	POUNDS GROUND BEEF	1	3 OUNCE CAN SLICED MUSHROOMS, UNDRAINED
2	MEDIUM ONIONS, CHOPPED	8	OUNCE SHELL MACARONI
1	GARLIC CLOVE, CRUSHED	3	CUPS SOUR CREAM
1	14 OUNCE JAR SPAGHETTI SAUCE	1	8 OUNCE PACKAGE PROVOLONE CHEESE
1	16 OUNCE CAN STEWED TOMATOES	1	8 OUNCE PACKAGE MOZZARELLA CHEESE

Brown beef; drain off fat. Add onions, garlic, spaghetti sauce, tomatoes and mushrooms. Simmer 20 minutes. Cook macaroni, drain, and rinse with cold water. Pour 1/2 of shells into deep casserole. Cover with half of tomato-meat sauce. Spread 1/2 sour cream over sauce. Top with slices of provolone. Repeat layers, ending with slices of mozzarella. Cover and bake in a 350 degree oven, until mozzarella melts, for about 40 minutes. Uncover briefly to brown. This can be baked and served immediately, or frozen for later use. Yield: 8-10 servings.

Mrs. Roger Smith—South Salem Presbyterian Church
South Salem, New York

Chili

2	TABLESPOONS COOKING OIL	1-2	TABLESPOONS CHILI POWDER
1	POUND GROUND BEEF	2	TABLESPOONS COLD WATER
1/2	POUND GROUND PORK	2	CUPS CANNED TOMATOES
	(OR HOT ITALIAN SAUSAGE)	2	TEASPOONS SALT
1 1/2	CUPS THINLY SLICED ONION	1	TEASPOON SUGAR
1	CUP FINELY DICED CELERY	1	TEASPOON WORCESTERSHIRE SAUCE
2	GARLIC CLOVES, CUT FINE	4	CUPS CANNED RED KIDNEY BEANS
1/2	CUP GREEN PEPPER, DICED		

In deep skillet, brown beef and pork in oil. Add onions, celery, garlic, and green pepper. Cook 10 minutes. Add balance of ingredients (except beans). Bring to a boil, lower heat, cover and simmer 1 hour. Add drained beans. Cook, uncovered, until well-heated and chili is desired thickness.

Mary Lou Zimmerman—First Presbyterian Church
Medina, New York

Chili Relleno Bake

1/2	POUND SAUSAGE	4	EGGS
1/2	POUND GROUND BEEF	1/4	CUP FLOUR
1	ONION, CHOPPED	1 1/2	CUP MILK
1	GARLIC CLOVE, CRUSHED		SALT, TABASCO TO TASTE
2	4 OUNCE CANS WHOLE GREEN CHILIES	2	CUPS SHREDDED CHEDDAR CHEESE

Seed and drain chiles. Set aside. Brown the meat. Add onion and garlic. Layer in 8" square pan, 1 1/2 cups cheese, meat mixture, chilies. Mix eggs, flour, milk, salt, and Tabasco to taste. Pour in pan. Top with remaining 1/2 cup cheese. Bake in a 350 degree oven for 45 minutes.

Nancy Kay—Fairfax Presbyterian Church
Fairfax, Virginia

Company Casserole

4	POUNDS LEAN GROUND BEEF	2	POUNDS CREAM CHEESE
4	CANS (15 OUNCE) TOMATO SAUCE	1	CUP SOUR CREAM
1	TABLESPOON SALT	1 1/2	CUPS (2-5 BUNCHES) GREEN ONIONS, CHOPPED
2	POUNDS NOODLES	1/4	CUP GREEN PEPPER, CHOPPED
2 1/2	POUNDS COTTAGE CHEESE		

Brown beef in skillet. Add tomato sauce and salt. Remove from heat. Cook noodles 10 minutes. Drain and rinse. Combine cottage cheese and cream cheese, sour cream, onion and green pepper. Place in layers in 2 13x9" pans, noodles, cheese, noodles. top with meat sauce. Bake in a 350 degree oven for 1 hour. Yield: 25 servings.

Dianne Stumbaugh—First Presbyterian Church
Aiken, South Carolina

Delicious Hamburger Casserole

2-2 1/2	POUNDS HAMBURGER	1	CAN TOMATO SOUP
1	LARGE DICED ONION	1	(8 OUNCE) BOX WIDE NOODLES
1	MEDIUM GREEN PEPPER, DICED	1	CUP GRATED SHARP CHEESE
2	STALKS CELERY, CHOPPED		SALT AND PEPPER TO TASTE
1	CAN MUSHROOM SOUP		

Brown onion, pepper, and celery in oil. Add hamburger. Brown, season to taste, drain. Add undiluted soups and simmer for 20 minutes. Cook noodles and drain. Pour sauce and noodles into buttered casserole dish. Top with grated cheese. Bake in a 350 degree oven for 20-25 minutes. May be frozen. Yield: 8 servings.

Pauline Ledford—Paint Gap Presbyterian Church
Burnsville, North Carolina

Enchilada Casserole

2	POUNDS GROUND BEEF	1	CUP SOUR CREAM
1	LARGE ONION	1/4	CUP MILK
1	CAN CHOPPED RO*TEL TOMATOES	1/4	TEASPOON GARLIC POWDER
1	PACKAGE CHOPPED FROZEN SPINACH	12-16	CORN TORTILLAS
	SALT AND PEPPER (FRESH-GROUND)	1/2	CUP BUTTER, MELTED
1	CAN CREAM OF MUSHROOM SOUP	2	CANS CHOPPED GREEN CHILIES (4 OUNCES)
1	CAN GOLDEN MUSHROOM SOUP	1/2	POUND CHEDDAR CHEESE, GRATED

Brown meat. Drain. Stir in onion, tomatoes, and salt and pepper to taste. Cook spinach according to package directions, squeeze dry when cooked. Add to meat mixture. Combine the soups, chilies, sour cream, milk, and garlic powder in a bowl. Mix well. Dip half the tortillas in melted butter. Arrange on bottom and around sides of a large, shallow casserole. Spoon in the meat mixture, taking care not to disarrange the tortillas. Add all but about 1/2 cup of the cheese. Dip the remaining tortillas and place on top. Pour in the sauce. Smooth the sauce with a spatula and sprinkle the reserved cheese on top. Bake in a 325 degree oven for 35-40 minutes, or until bubbling. Yield: 12 servings. Should freeze well. Keeps in refrigerator for a week.

Jane Peterson—Highland Park Presbyterian Church
Dallas, Texas

German Meat Casserole

3	LARGE POTATOES, SLICED	1	POUND GROUND BEEF OR TURKEY
5	CARROTS, QUARTERED	2	TABLESPOONS MARGARINE
1	SMALL ONION, DICED		SALT AND PEPPER TO TASTE
1	TABLESPOON CATSUP	1	3 1/2 OUNCE CAN FRENCH FRIED ONION RINGS
1	CAN CREAM OF MUSHROOM SOUP		
1/2	CAN WATER		

Parboil potatoes and carrots just until tender. Sauté onion in margarine. Add ground meat and cook until it turns gray. Butter a 2 1/2 quart casserole dish. Add soup, water and catsup to sautéed meat. Layer in casserole, potatoes and carrots, then meat mixture. Top with onion rings. Bake in a 350 degree oven for 20 minutes or until onion rings are brown and crisp. Yield: 6 servings.

Beryl Bland—West Baton Rouge Presbyterian Church
Port Allen, Louisiana

Kathleen's Aunt Sharon's Beans

5	LARGE CANS BUSH'S BAKED BEANS	3	CLOVES MINCED GARLIC
2	POUNDS BACON, FRIED VERY CRISP	1 1/2	CUPS KETCHUP
2	POUNDS GROUND BEEF, WELL DONE	2	TABLESPOONS MUSTARD
2	CUPS MINCED ONIONS	3/4	CUPS STRONG BEEF BOUILLON OR BROTH
2	CUPS MINCED CELERY		

Brown bacon separately; drain and break up in small pieces. Cook ground beef with celery, onions, and garlic; drain. Combine bacon, beef mixture, beans, ketchup, mustard, and beef broth. Bake in a 325 degree oven for 1 hour. Yield: 20 servings.

Kathleen Moore—St. Andrews Presbyterian Church
Jacksonville, Florida

Lumberjack

3	CUPS SLICED RAW POTATOES	2	CUPS THINLY SLICED CARROTS
2	CUPS SLICED CELERY	2	POUNDS LEAN GROUND BEEF
2	CUPS SLICED ONIONS	28	OUNCE CAN TOMATOES
1 1/2	CUPS CHOPPED GREEN PEPPER		SALT & PEPPER TO SPRINKLE LAYERS

In a 4 quart casserole, place ingredients in layers; start with potatoes. Break up the meat to cover the top. Chop the tomatoes if whole, and put on top of meat. (If desired, drain off the juice after cooking. Remove fat and make a gravy with remaining juice. Return gravy to casserole.) Bake in a 350 degree oven for 2 hours. Yield: 12 servings.

Gwen Brain—St. Columba Presbyterian Church
Belleville, Ontario, Canada

One-dish Dinner

3-4	ONIONS (CHOPPED)	2	CUPS COOKED MACARONI
2-3	POUNDS GROUND BEEF	1	CAN WHOLE KERNEL CORN
1	CUP DICED CELERY	1	CAN TOMATO SOUP
1	CUP DICED GREEN PEPPER	1	CAN MUSHROOM SOUP

Brown onions lightly in a little oil. Add ground beef and brown, stirring often. Add celery, pepper, and simmer until soft, stirring often. Add mushroom soup, corn, and 1/2 cup water, and simmer. Add macaroni. Put in a large casserole, cover with tomato soup. Sprinkle grated cheese to cover the soup. Bake in a 350 degree oven, until mixture bubbles. Yield: 8-10 servings. This casserole freezes well.

Edmee Boyd—Hampton Presbyterian Church
Hampton, South Carolina

MARZETTI

1	POUND GROUND BEEF OR TURKEY	1	CAN TOMATO SOUP
1	CHOPPED GREEN PEPPER	1	PACKAGE NOODLES
1	CHOPPED ONION		SALT AND PEPPER TO TASTE
1/2	POUND EXTRA SHARP CHEESE, GRATED		

Cook noodles. Brown ground meat. Combine all ingredients, with exception of 1/2 of cheese, mixing well. Sprinkle remaining cheese on top of casserole. Bake in a 350 degree oven for 30-45 minutes. Yield: 6-8 servings.

Margee Daniels Kooistra—Market Square Presbyterian Church
Harrisburg, Pennsylvania

MEXICAN CASSEROLE

1 1/2	POUNDS LEAN GROUND CHUCK	1	CAN CREAM OF MUSHROOM SOUP
1/2	CHOPPED ONION	1	CAN RO★TEL WITH CHILIES
2	TABLESPOONS CHILI POWDER	6-8	CORN TORTILLAS
1	CAN CREAM OF CHICKEN SOUP	1	CUP SHARP CHEDDAR CHEESE, GRATED

Line casserole with tortillas. Brown meat and onion. Add chili powder. Spoon over tortillas, reserving a portion of mixture. Combine soups with can of Rotel and heat. Pour portion of soup mixture over meat. Layer more tortillas with remaining meat and soup mixture. Cover with grated cheese. Bake in a 350 degree oven for 25 minutes. Yield: 6 servings.

Mrs. S.R. Jackson, Jr.—First Central Presbyterian Church
Abilene, Texas

PICADILLO (SPANISH-STYLE GROUND BEEF)

1 1/2	POUNDS GROUND BEEF	1/4	CUP OLIVE OIL
1	MEDIUM ONION, CHOPPED	2	TABLESPOONS CAPERS
2	CLOVES GARLIC, MINCED		GREEN OLIVES TO TASTE
1	SMALL GREEN BELL PEPPER, CHOPPED	1	BAY LEAF
1/4	TEASPOON CUMIN		SALT & PEPPER TO TASTE
1	SMALL CAN TOMATO SAUCE		

Combine all ingredients except capers, olives, and tomato sauce. Brown meat, onion, garlic, pepper, and cumin in olive oil over medium heat until done, approximately 10 minutes. Add rinsed capers and olives, and tomato sauce. Simmer for 30 minutes. Serve over white or yellow rice. Yield: 4 servings.

Violet Costello—First Presbyterian Church
Tampa, Florida

SOUTHWEST CASSEROLE

1	LARGE ONION, CHOPPED	1	TEASPOON GARLIC POWDER
2	TABLESPOONS OIL	1	CAN (1 POUND) KIDNEY BEANS, DRAINED
1	POUND GROUND BEEF	1	CAN (29 OUNCE) TOMATOES
2	TABLESPOONS CHILI POWDER	1	CAN (6 OUNCE) TOMATO PASTE
2	TEASPOONS SALT, DIVIDED	4 1/2	CUPS WATER, DIVIDED
1/2	TEASPOON OREGANO, CRUSHED	1	CUP YELLOW CORNMEAL
1/2	TEASPOON GROUND CUMIN	1/2	CUP SHREDDED CHEDDAR CHEESE

Sauté onion in oil until tender. Add ground beef and brown, breaking apart with fork. Add chili powder, 1 teaspoon salt, oregano, garlic powder and cumin. Mix well. Add drained beans, tomatoes, tomato paste and 1/2 cup water; simmer 1 hour. Combine cornmeal with 1/2 cup water. Bring remaining water to boil. Add 1 teaspoon salt and cornmeal. Cook 10 minutes or until thickened. Spread half of cornmeal mixture in bottom of a deep 2 1/2 - 3 quart baking dish. Add bean and meat mixture; spread remaining cornmeal mixture over all. Bake in a 350 degree oven for 30 minutes or until thoroughly heated. Sprinkle with cheese and bake 5 minutes longer. Yield: 8 servings.

Myrtie Dunn—First Presbyterian Church
Cuero, Texas

SPAGHETTI AND BEEF CASSEROLE

3	TABLESPOONS VEGETABLE OIL	1	TEASPOON GARLIC POWDER
2	POUNDS GROUND BEEF	16	OUNCES SPAGHETTI, COOKED
2	MEDIUM ONIONS, CHOPPED	8	OUNCES CREAM CHEESE, SOFTENED
2	CANS (4 OUNCES) MUSHROOMS	2	CUPS COTTAGE CHEESE
2	CANS TOMATO SAUCE (8 OUNCES)	1/2	CUP CHOPPED CHIVES
1	CAN (6 OUNCES) TOMATO PASTE	1/2	CUP COMMERCIAL SOUR CREAM
1	TEASPOON GROUND OREGANO	1/2	CUP BUTTERED FINE DRY BREAD CRUMBS

Heat oil in heavy skillet. Add ground beef and onions; sauté until meat is browned, stirring to crumble. Drain off drippings. Combine mushrooms, tomato sauce, tomato paste, oregano and garlic powder; add to meat mixture, mixing well. Simmer 15 minutes, uncovered. Place half of spaghetti in a buttered 13x9x2" baking dish. Combine cream cheese, cottage cheese, chives, and sour cream; mix well. Spoon cream cheese mixture over spaghetti layer, spreading evenly. Place remaining spaghetti over cream cheese mixture. Pour meat sauce over spaghetti and sprinkle with bread crumbs. Bake in a 350 degree oven for 30-40 minutes, until bubbly. Yield: 12 servings.

Margaret S. Hayward—Sea Island Presbyterian Church
Beaufort, South Carolina

Spaghetti Pie

1	POUND SPAGHETTI (I USE VERMICELLI)	2	8 OUNCE CANS TOMATO PASTE
4	TABLESPOONS BUTTER	1	TEASPOON GARLIC SALT
2/3	CUP PARMESAN CHEESE	2	TEASPOONS SUGAR
3	EGGS	2	TEASPOONS OREGANO
2	POUNDS GROUND BEEF	2	CUPS COTTAGE CHEESE
1	CUP CHOPPED ONION		MOZZARELLA CHEESE (GRATED) FOR TOPPING
1/2	CUP CHOPPED GREEN PEPPER		

Cook spaghetti and drain. Add butter, beaten eggs, and parmesan; mix together and spread in 3 pie plates or 9x13" casserole. Brown ground beef. Saute' onion and pepper. Combine beef, onion, pepper, oregano, sugar, and garlic salt. Simmer 15-20 minutes. Spread cottage cheese over spaghetti in casserole dish. Top with sauce and bake in a350 degree oven for 20 minutes. Sprinkle with mozzarella and bake 5 minutes. Yield: 3 pies or 1 casserole.

Peggy Ashley—Bryson City Presbyterian Church
Bryson City, North Carolina

Taty Pot

3	LARGE POTATOES	2	BEEF BOUILLON CUBES
1	LARGE ONION	2	CUPS WATER, BOILING
6	OUNCES CORNED BEEF		SALT AND PEPPER TO TASTE

Place a layer of sliced raw potatoes in a large saucepan, then a layer of chopped onion, a layer of corned beef, continue layers until all ingredients are used. The top layer should be potatoes Melt bouillon cubes in the boiling water and add salt and pepper, add to saucepan, stir gently as you bring to a boil, reduce heat and simmer for about 30 minutes. Stir occasionally. You may have to add more water. Serve with crusty bread.

Elsie Ridley—The Bethel Reformed Church
Chester-le-Street, England

Texas Hash

- 1 POUND GROUND BEEF
- 3 LARGE ONIONS, CHOPPED
- 1 LARGE GREEN PEPPER, CHOPPED
- PAPRIKA
- 1 16 OUNCE CAN TOMATOES
- 1 SMALL CAN TOMATO PASTE
- 1/2 CUP UNCOOKED RICE
- CHILI POWDER
- SALT AND PEPPER TO TASTE

Brown beef with pepper and onion. Drain well. Add all other ingredients to skillet and mix well. Simmer approximately 1 hour or until rice is tender.

Judy Cannon—First Presbyterian Church
Beaufort, South Carolina

Togliarini

- 1 LARGE ONION, CHOPPED
- 1 LARGE GREEN PEPPER, CHOPPED
- 1 CLOVE GARLIC, CHOPPED FINE
- 2 POUNDS GROUND BEEF
- 8 OUNCES VERY FINE NOODLES, COOKED
- 1 CAN TOMATO PASTE
- 1 #2 CAN CREAM-STYLE CORN
- 1 #2 CAN TOMATOES
- 1 CAN RIPE OLIVES WITH SOME JUICE
- SEASON WITH SALT, PEPPER, CAYENNE
- 2 TABLESPOONS CHILI POWDER
- 1 TABLESPOON WORCESTERSHIRE SAUCE

Brown ground beef, onion, green pepper and garlic. Add tomato paste, corn, tomatoes, ripe olives with some liquid, and seasonings. Add cooked noodles and combine well. Sprinkle with grated cheese. Bake in a 350 degree oven for 1 1/2 hours. This casserole should be made a day ahead and refrigerated.

Frances J. Huhn—First Presbyterian Church
Beaufort, South Carolina

PORK CASSEROLES

Chinese Pork Casserole

- 1 CAN CONDENSED CREAM OF CHICKEN SOUP
- 1/2 CUP WATER
- 1 TEASPOON SOY SAUCE
- 1/2 CUP THINLY SLICED CELERY
- 1/2 CUP COOKED PEAS
- 2 TABLESPOONS THINLY SLICED GREEN ONIONS
- 1 CUP DICED, COOKED PORK
- 4 CUPS FINELY SHREDDED CABBAGE
- 1/2 CUP CHINESE NOODLES

Blend soup, water, and soy suace in a 1 1/2 quart casserole. Stir in remaining ingredients except noodles. Bake in a 350 degree oven for 20 minutes. Sprinkle noodles around edge of casserole. Bake 10 minutes more. Yield: 4 servings. Does not freeze. *(Recipe originally from* The Washington Post.*)*

Florence May—Fairfax Presbyterian Church
Fairfax, Virginia

FARMER'S CASSEROLE

1/2	CUP UNCOOKED RICE	1 1/2	CUP CHOPPED ONIONS
1	CUP BOILING WATER	1/2	CUP GREEN PEPPER, CHOPPED
1	TEASPOON SALT	1/2	CUP CHOPPED PIMENTO
1/2	POUND EACH, PORK AND VEAL OR BEEF	1	CAN CREAM OF MUSHROOM SOUP
1 1/2	CUP CHOPPED CELERY	2	TABLESPOONS SOY SAUCE

Cut meat into 1" cubes. Put rice into 2 quart casserole. Add boiling water and salt. Set aside. Brown meat in heavy skillet in 2 tablespoons oil. Add onions, celery, and green pepper and cook until onion is golden. Mix in pimento, soup, and soy sauce. Put into casserole with rice. Blend gently. Cover and bake in a 350 degree oven, about 1 1/4 hours or until meat and rice are tender. Remove cover the last 15 minutes to brown. *Delicious!*

Mickey Nordin—Highland Presbyterian Church
Winston-Salem, North Carolina

PARTY HAM CASSEROLE

4	OUNCES NOODLES	1	CUP SOUR CREAM
1	CAN CREAM OF MUSHROOM SOUP	2	CUPS COOKED HAM IN 1" SLIVERS
1/2	CUP MILK	1/4	CUP PACKAGED DRY BREAD CRUMBS
1	TEASPOON INSTANT MINCED ONION	1	TABLESPOON GRATED PARMESAN CHEESE
2	TEASPOONS PREPARED MUSTARD		

Grease 1 1/2 quart casserole. Cook noodles as directed on package. In small saucepan, combine soup and milk, stirring until smooth. Add onions, mustard, and sour cream, combine well. In casserole, layer 1/2 noodles, ham and sauce. Repeat layer. Toss crumbs with butter, sprinkle over casserole and top with cheese. Bake uncovered in a 325 degree oven for 25 minutes or until golden brown. Yield: 6 servings.

Amy Mather—Pittsgrove Presbyterian Church
Daretown, New Jersey

Pork and Hamburger Dish

1	POUND PORK, CUT INTO BITE SIZE PIECES	1	CUP CHOPPED ONION
1	POUND GROUND BEEF	1	CUP CHOPPED CELERY
1	SMALL HEAD OF CABBAGE, SHREDDED	1	BELL PEPPER, CHOPPED
1	GARLIC BUD	3	DROPS HOT SAUCE
3	DROPS WORCESTERSHIRE SAUCE		

Cook pork and garlic in pan on top of stove for 15 minutes. Add beef and cook 15 minutes more. Add celery, onion, green pepper, hot sauce, and Worcestershire, and cook 15 minutes more. Add drained cabbage and cook 10 minutes. Good served with baked sweet potatoes. Yield: 6 servings. This dish does not freeze.

Charlotte Vedeler—Old Presbyterian Meeting House
Alexandria, Virginia

Fidget Pie

2	MEDIUM ONIONS		PEPPER TO TASTE
1	LARGE COOKING APPLE	2	TEASPOONS SUGAR
1/2	POUND PORK SAUSAGE	1 1/4	CUPS CHICKEN OR HAM STOCK
4	SLICES OF BACON, CUT UP	1	POUND POTATOES
1	TEASPOON SALT		

Peel and thinly slice onions, potatoes, and apple. Spread 1/3 of mixture in a layer in a large pie plate. Roll sausage into 12 balls. Place six on top of potatoes, spread 1/2 the bacon over the top, repeat the layers ending with the potatoes, onion, and apple. Mix seasonings in stock and pour over the layers. Top with crust.

Crust:

1 1/2	CUPS FLOUR		COLD WATER TO MIX
	PINCH OF SALT	1	EGG, BEATEN FOR GLAZE
3/4	STICK MARGARINE		

Cut margarine into the flour and salt until mixture resembles bread crumbs. Add about 2 tablespoons cold water and mix with a fork to form a stiff dough. Roll out on floured surface. Cover the pie with the crust. Use the trimmings to form leaves, brush pie with beaten egg. Place leaves on top and brush with egg. Bake in a 350 degree oven for 1 1/4 to 1 1/2 hours. Serve hot with a green vegetable.

Esther Goater—Letchworth Free Church
Letchworth, England

BAKED SAUSAGE AND RICE

- 1 POUND BULK SAUSAGE
- 1 SMALL ONION, CHOPPED
- 2 STALKS CELERY, CHOPPED
- 1 PACKAGE DRY CHICKEN NOODLE SOUP
- 3 CUPS WATER
- 2 OUNCES SLIVERED OR CHOPPED ALMONDS
- 1/2 CUP SLICED MUSHROMS (OPTIONAL)
- 2/3 CUP UNCOOKED LONG GRAIN RICE

Brown sausage, onion, and celery for 30 minutes. Drain. Place sausage into greased baking dish. Add mixed dried noodle soup, rice, water, and mushrooms. Sprinkle with almonds and bake, covered, for 1 hour in a 350 degree oven. Remove cover and bake for another 15 minutes. Yield: 4-6 servings. (Turkey sausage may be substituted for pork sausage—just reduce browning time to 15-20 minutes.)

Sara Abramson Heap—The Presbyterian Church of Bloomingdale
Brandon, Florida

SAUSAGE CASSEROLE

- 1 POUND HOT SAUSAGE
- 1 PACKAGE DRY CHICKEN NOODLE SOUP
- 1 CUP RAW RICE (REGULAR)
- 1 MEDIUM BELL PEPPER

Cook sausage, breaking up into small pieces, and drain, Mix with rice and chopped pepper. Spread soup mix in casserole, add 4 cups water and spoon rice mixture into casserole. Do not stir. Cover, place in a 350 degree oven and bake 1 hour.

Ruby J. Campen—Highland Presbyterian Church
Fayetteville, North Carolina

DR. MARTIN'S SAUSAGE CASSEROLE MIX

- 1 1/2 POUNDS SAUSAGE (HOT OR MILD)
- 1 BELL PEPPER, CHOPPED
- 2 GREEN ONIONS OR 1 MEDIUM ONION
- 2 CUPS CHICKEN OR BEEF BROTH
- 3 STALKS CELERY, SLICED
- 1 CUP UNCOOKED RICE
- 1 TABLESPOON WORCESTERSHIRE SAUCE
- 1/4 TEASPOON SALT

Crumble sausage and brown in large skillet. Drain well. Add all other ingredients and mix well. Simmer on low heat for 1 hour (or longer if necessary for rice).

Gary Cannon—First Presbyterian Church
Beaufort, South Carolina

Sausage Casserole with a Snap

2	POUNDS HOT SAUSAGE	4	EGGS, BEATEN
2	SMALL ONIONS, CHOPPED	1	CAN CREAM OF CELERY SOUP
2	CUPS COOKED RICE	1/4	CUP MILK
20	OUNCES SHARP CHEDDAR CHEESE	4-6	CUPS RICE KRISPIES CEREAL

Brown sausage and onions. Drain off grease. In a separate bowl, mix eggs, soup and milk. In a greased (I use Pam) glass, 13" casserole dish, layer sausage mixture, rice, Rice Krispies, cheese, ending with soup, egg and milk mixture poured over top. Bake in a 350 degree oven for 40 minutes. This dish freezes well either before or after it is baked. Serves many, depending on size of squares you cut!

Meredith Bradley—Bethesda Presbyterian Church
Camden, South Carolina

Tourtiere

6	SLICES BACON	1/4	TEASPOON BLACK PEPPER
1	POUND MINCED PORK	1/4	TEASPOON CELERY SALT
1/2	POUND LEAN MINCED VEAL	1/4	TEASPOON SAGE
1	SMALL ONION, FINELY CHOPPED		PINCH OF GROUND CLOVES
1/2	CUP BOILING WATER	1	CUP MASHED POTATOES
1	CLOVE GARLIC, MINCED (OPTIONAL)		PASTRY FOR DOUBLE CRUST
1 1/2	TEASPOON SALT		

Cut bacon into small pieces and fry over moderate heat until cooked but not crisp. Add pork, veal, and onion; cook until meat is lightly browned. Add water and spices; reduce heat to simmer. Cover pan and simmer 45 minutes more. Combine meat with mashed potatoes; cool slightly. Meanwhile, line a 9" pie plate with pastry; fill with meat mixture, place top crust in position, seal and flute edges. Slash top several times to release steam. Bake in a 450 degree oven 10 minutes, reduce heat to 350 degrees and bake 30 minutes longer. Yield: 5-6 servings.

Verla Fiveash—St. Stephens Presbyterian Church
Scarborough, Ontario, Canada

Chapter Nine

Poultry—Entrées and Casseroles

CHICKEN

Another Chicken Casserole

2 CUPS COOKED, CUBED CHICKEN	1 TEASPOON MRS. DASH SEASONING MIX
1 CAN CREAM OF MUSHROOM SOUP	1/4 TEASPOON GARLIC POWDER
1 4 OUNCE CAN OF MUSHROOM STEMS & PIECES WITH LIQUID	1 8-OUNCE CAN OF SLICED WATER CHESTNUTS
2 CUPS COOKED RICE	1 TABLESPOON DRIED PARSLEY FLAKES
1 MEDIUM ONION, CHOPPED	1 CUP PEPPERIDGE FARM SEASONED STUFFING MIX
LITE SALT TO TASTE	1/4 CUP OF MELTED MARGARINE

In a two quart casserole, combine all but the seasoned stuffing mix and melted margarine. Toss together the seasoned stuffing mix and melted margarine. Spread evenly over the casserole. Bake in a 350 degree oven for 30 minutes or until heated through and bubbly. Yield: 4-6 servings.

Pam Thompson—Faith Presbyterian Church
Harrisburg, Pennsylvania

Aunt Kitty's Chicken and Corn Flakes

2 CUPS CUBED CHICKEN	1/4 TEASPOON PEPPER
2 CUPS SLICED CELERY	2 TEASPOONS GRATED ONION
1/2 POUND FRESH MUSHROOMS	3 TABLESPOONS MARGARINE
1/2 CUP BLANCHED ALMONDS OR PECANS	2 TABLESPOONS LEMON JUICE
1/2 TEASPOON SALT	1 CUP MAYONNAISE

Sauteé mushrooms in margarine. Combine all ingredients and place in greased baking dish. Over top, sprinkle 1/2 cup shredded cheddar or colby cheese and 1 cup corn flakes. Bake in microwave oven, medium heat for 10-12 minutes, or bake in a 350 degree conventional oven for 25 minutes. (Can substitute potato chips for corn flakes).

Betsy Brooks Woodford—First Presbyterian Church
Paris, Kentucky

BAKED ONION CHICKEN

24-30 CHICKEN WINGS
1 PACKAGE LIPTON ONION SOUP MIX
1/2 CUP WATER

Remove tips of the chicken wings, then separate each section of the wings by cutting between the connecting joint. Place wing sections in large baking pan, keeping them in a single layer. Combine soup mix and water, and mix thoroughly. Pour over wing sections and bake in a 400 degree oven for at least 1 hour until most of liquid is absorbed. If you want a pan gravy, you can discontinue baking at the hour mark, mix cornstarch and water, and combine with pan juices while stirring. Yield: 12 to 15 servings.

Renee Raines—United Presbyterian Church
Paterson, New Jersey

BARBECUED CHICKEN

1 3 POUND FRYER, CUT UP
1/2 CUP SALAD OIL
3/4 CUP CHOPPED ONION
3/4 CUP KETCHUP
3/4 CUP WATER
1/3 CUP LEMON JUICE
3 TABLESPOONS SUGAR
3 TABLESPOONS WORCHESTERSHIRE SAUCE
2 TABLESPOONS PREPARED MUSTARD
2 TEASPOONS SALT
1/2 TEASPOONS PEPPER

Put oil in skillet. Brown chicken pieces slowly. Remove chicken. Cook onions in salad oil until tender. Add remaining ingredients and simmer 15 minutes. Skim off excess fat. Place chicken in 11x7x1 1/2" baking dish. Pour sauce over chicken. Bake uncovered in a 325 degree oven 1 1/4 hours or until done. Baste occasionally with sauce. Yield: 6 servings.

Genon Neblett—Glencliff Presbyterian Church
Nashville, Tennessee

Broccoli Chicken Casserole

1	10 OUNCE PACKAGE FROZEN BROCCOLI (OR 2 MEDIUM HEADS FRESH)	2	STALKS CELERY, CHOPPED
2	TABLESPOONS BUTTER	2 1/2	CUPS COOKED RICE
1	POUND BONELESS, SKINNED CHICKEN BREASTS	2	CANS CREAM OF MUSHROOM SOUP
1	SMALL OR MEDIUM ONION, CHOPPED	2	CUPS MONTEREY JACK CHEESE, GRATED
			SALT AND PEPPER TO TASTE

Thaw and drain frozen broccoli. If you are using fresh, separate the stems from head. Peel the stem if necessary, and then blanch or steam stems and head for 3 to 5 minutes until crisp tender. When cool, cut head into small flowerettes and slice the stem into 1/4" pieces. Set aside. Saute´ the onions and celery in the butter or margarine until limp and translucent, but not browned. Cut the chicken breasts into 1/2" cubes, add to the onions and celery and stir fry until done. Remove from heat and mix in the reserved broccoli, cooked rice, mushroom soup, and cheese. Taste for seasoning and add salt and pepper to taste. Turn into a 13x9 baking pan. Bake in a preheated 350 degree oven for 15 to 20 minutes or until heated through.

Mickey Nordin—Highland Presbyterian Church
Winston Salem, North Carolina

Chicken a la Marsala

2	WHOLE LARGE CHICKEN BREASTS, BONE SPLIT (4 PIECES, SKIN NOT REMOVED)		SALT
	FLOUR FOR COATING		FRESHLY GROUND PEPPER TO TASTE
1/2	POUND MUSHROOMS, SLICED	1	CLOVE GARLIC, CRUSHED
1/2	CUP (GOOD QUALITY) MARSALA WINE	4	TABLESPOONS BUTTER, DIVIDED

Coat chicken with flour, salt, and pepper. Melt 3 tablespoons butter in skillet. Saute´ garlic until golden brown. Add chicken, and brown well on both sides. Transfer to heavy shallow baking pan. Add 1 tablespoon butter to skillet, add mushrooms, cook, stirring 2 to 3 minutes. Add Marsala, simmer 2 minutes. Pour over chicken in baking pan. Bake covered in a preheated 350 degree oven for 20 minutes or until done, but still moist.

Grace Moore—Westminster Presbyterian Church
St. Louis, Missouri

Chicken Almond Supreme

- 2 CUPS CHICKEN (FAIRLY LARGE PIECES)
- 1 CUP SAUTEED MUSHROOMS (OR SMALL JAR CAPS)
- 1 CUP WATER CHESTNUTS
- 1 CUP SLIVERED ALMONDS

Supreme Sauce:

- 2 TABLESPOONS BUTTER, MELTED
- 3 TABLESPOONS FLOUR
- 1 CUP CHICKEN STOCK
- 1/3 CUP CREAM

Spread mushrooms over chicken. Make another layer of water chestnuts, sliced paper thin. Set aside. To melted butter, add flour—blend well. Add slowly (stirring) chicken stock. Boil 2 minutes and add cream. Pour on top of chicken dish and cover with almonds. Bake in a 375 degree oven until thoroughly heated and almonds are brown. Yield: 4-5 servings.

Mrs. Henry A. Matoon—Norfield Congregational Church
Weston, Connecticut

Chicken and Corn Casserole

- 4 BROILER-FRYER CHICKEN BREASTS, HALVED
- 2 (17 OUNCE) CANS CREAMED CORN
- 1 CUP MILK
- 2 EGGS, BEATEN
- 1 1/2 TABLESPOON FLOUR
- 6 GREEN ONIONS, CHOPPED (GREEN AND WHITE PARTS INCLUDED)
- 1 TEASPOON SALT
- 1 TEASPOON PAPRIKA
- 18 SALTINE CRACKERS, CRUSHED
- 2 TABLESPOONS MARGARINE, CUT IN SMALL PIECES
- 1 CAN (3 OUNCES) MUSHROOMS, DRAINED

In large shallow baking dish, mix together corn, milk, eggs, and flour. Stir in onion. Sprinkle chicken with salt and paprika. Place, skin side up, on top of corn mixture. Sprinkle crackers over chicken and corn mixture; dot with margarine. Bake in a 350 degree oven for 1 hour, or until fork can be inserted in chicken with ease. Remove from oven; place mushrooms in center of casserole. Return to oven and bake about 10 minutes longer. Yield: 4 servings.

Pat Perkins—First Presbyterian Church
Beaufort, South Carolina

CHICKEN OR HAM SUPPER CASSEROLE

2	CUPS COOKED CHICKEN OR HAM, DICED BUT NOT TOO SMALL	1/2	TEASPOON SALT
		1	TABLESPOON FRESH LEMON JUICE
1/4	CUP WATER		DASH PEPPER
1	CUP RAW CELERY SLICED DIAGONALLY IN 1/2 INCH PIECES	3/4	CUP MAYONNAISE
		1/2	CUP CHOPPED ALMONDS OR PECANS
1	MEDIUM ONION, CHOPPED VERY FINE	3	HARD BOILED EGGS
1 1/2	CUPS COOKED RICE, NOT CONVERTED	2	CUPS FRESH BREAD CRUMBS
1	CAN CREAM OF MUSHROOM SOUP, UNDILUTED		MELTED BUTTER

Prepare the night before; refrigerate overnight. ESSENTIAL. Mix all ingredients except eggs. Put a layer of half the mixture on the bottom of a 14x9x2 inch casserole. Cover with sliced hard boiled eggs. Add the rest of rice mixture. Top with bread crumbs which have been tossed in melted butter. Sprinkle chopped nuts over the crumbs. Bake in a 400 degree oven for about 45 minutes. DOES NOT FREEZE WELL.

Barbara Lehr—First Presbyterian Church
Easton, Pennsylvania

CHICKEN AND SPINACH CASSEROLE

4	BONELESS, SKINLESS BREASTS, HALVED	1	CUP MILK
3/4	CUP ITALIAN BREAD CRUMBS	2	TABLESPOONS BUTTER OR MARGARINE
1/2	CUP PARMESAN CHEESE	4	OUNCE BOILED HAM, SLICED AND DICED
1/2	CUP GREEN ONION SLICED	10	OUNCE PACKAGE SPINACH, THAWED
2	TABLESPOONS FLOUR		

Bread cutlets in crumbs and cheese. Lay in baking dish. (Save leftover crumbs). Melt butter and saute' onion until tender. Mix in flour, pour milk in all at once. Cook, stirring, until bubbly, cook 1 minute longer. Add drained spinach and ham to sauce. Spread on top of cutlets. Cover with crumbs and bake in a 350 degree oven for 40-45 minutes. Yield: 6-8 servings.

Edyth Mitchell—Ashland Evangelical Presbyterian Church
Voorhees Township, New Jersey

Chicken and Wild Rice Casserole I

- 4 CUPS DICED CHICKEN
- 4 CUPS UNCLE BEN'S WHITE AND WILD RICE COOKED
- 2 CANS CREAM OF MUSHROOM SOUP
- 1 SOUP CAN MILK
- 1/2 CUP CHOPPED GREEN PEPPER

Mix together all of the above and put in a flat casserole.

- 1 PACKAGE PEPPERIDGE FARM HERB STUFFING
- 2 STICKS BUTTER

Brown stuffing in butter. Cover casserole with browned dressing. Bake in 350 degree oven for 30 minutes. Yield: Serves 12.

Frances Parker—Hampton Presbyterian Church, Hampton, South Carolina
Third Presbyterian Church, Birmingham, Alabama

Chicken and Wild Rice Casserole II

- 1 CUP WILD RICE
- 1/2 CUP CHOPPED ONION
- 1/2 CUP OLEO OR BUTTER
- 1/4 CUP FLOUR
- 6 OUNCE CAN SLICED MUSHROOMS
- 1 1/2 CUPS HALF-AND-HALF
- 2 CUPS CHICKEN, COOKED AND DICED
- 1 1/2 CUPS CHICKEN BROTH
- 1/4 CUP DICED PIMENTO
- 2 TABLESPOONS MINCED PARSLEY
- 1 1/2 TEASPOONS SALT
- 1/4 TEASPOON PEPPER
- 1/2 CUP SLIVERED BLANCHED ALMONDS

Prepare wild rice. Saute´ onion in butter or oleo. Stir chicken broth into flour gradually; add cream. Cook and stir until mixture thickens. Add rice, mushrooms, chicken, pimento, parsley, salt, and pepper. Place in 2 quart casserole. Sprinkle with almonds. Bake in a 350 degree oven for 25-30 minutes.

Diane Schroeder—Memorial Drive Presbyterian Church, Houston, Texas
Covington United Presbyterian Church, Pavilion, New York

Chicken Breast

- 6 DEBONED CHICKEN BREASTS
- 1 CAN WHOLE CRANBERRY SAUCE
- 1 PACKAGE ONION SOUP MIX
- 1 SMALL BOTTLE RUSSIAN DRESSING

Put cranberry sauce and soup mix over breasts, wrap in foil. Bake 1 1/2 hours in a 250 degree oven. Uncover. Pour Russian dressing over top. Bake 1 hour.

Virginia Pipe—West Side Presbyterian Church
Ridgewood, New Jersey

CHICKEN ARTICHOKE CASSEROLE

"Micronote: Assemble as directed. Cook in microwave oven on HIGH 10-12 minutes, turning dish twice during cooking."

2	(14 OUNCE) CANS ARTICHOKE HEARTS, DRAINED AND QUARTERED	1	TEASPOON LEMON JUICE
		1/4	TEASPOON CURRY POWDER
3	CUPS COOKED DICED CHICKEN	1-1 1/2	CUPS GRATED SHARP CHEDDAR CHEESE
2	(10 1/2 OUNCE) CANS CREAM OF CHICKEN SOUP	1/3	CUP WHITE WINE (OPTIONAL)
		1 1/4	CUPS BREAD CUBES OR CRUMBS
1	CUP MAYONNAISE	2	TABLESPOONS BUTTER, MELTED

Arrange artichokes over bottom of greased 12x9x2 baking dish. Layer chicken over artichokes. Blend soup, mayonnaise, lemon juice, curry powder, and wine; pour over chicken. Sprinkle with cheese. Toss bread cubes with butter; arrange over cheese (May be covered at this point and refrigerated for later use. Allow to return to room temperature before baking). Bake in a 350 degree oven for 25 minutes.

Variation: Chicken-broccoli-rice—instead of artichokes, layer casserole with 2 boxes, slightly cooked chopped broccoli, then 3 cups cooked rice, and cooked chicken. Cover with sauce and proceed as directed.

Vivian Carstens—Dahlonega Presbyterian Church
Dahlonega, Georgia

CHICKEN BROCCOLI FETTUCCINE

1	TABLESPOON MARGARINE	1/4	CUP GRATED PARMESAN CHEESE
1	CLOVE GARLIC, MINCED	1 1/2	CUPS COOKED CHICKEN CUT IN STRIPS
1	CAN CAMPBELL'S BROCCOLI CHEESE SOUP	3	CUPS HOT COOKED FETTUCCINE (8 OUNCES DRY)
1	CUP MILK		

In skillet, in hot margarine, cook garlic 2 minutes stirring constantly. Stir in soup, milk, and cheese. Heat to boiling. Add chicken. Cook over low heat 5 minutes, stirring often. Toss with fettuccine. Garnish with cherry tomatoes and fresh parsley if desired. Yield: 4 servings.

Tip: For cooked chicken, cook 3 skinless, boneless chicken breast halves and cut in strips.

Jancie Maben—Presbyterian Church
Jewett, New Jersey

Chicken Casserole

3	CUPS COOKED CHICKEN	1	1 OUNCE JAR CHOPPED PIMENTO
8	OUNCES RAW MACARONI	1	TEASPOON CHOPPED ONION
2	CANS CREAM OF MUSHROOM SOUP	1/4	CUP CHOPPED GREEN PEPPER
2	CUPS MILK	1	TEASPOON SALT
1/2	POUND SHARP CHEDDAR CHEESE, GRATED	1	TEASPOON DRIED ROSEMARY

Mix all ingredients together. Place in 2 quart casserole which has been lightly greased. Refrigerate overnight or for 6-8 hours. Bake in a 350 degree oven for 1 1/4- 1 1/2 hours. Yield: 10 servings.

Doris Hjortsberg—Trinity Presbyterian Church
Arlington, Virginia

Chicken Divan

3	WHOLE CHICKEN BREASTS	1	TABLESPOON LEMON JUICE
2	PACKAGES FROZEN BROCCOLI	1	TEASPOON CURRY POWDER
2	CANS CREAM OF CHICKEN SOUP		SALT AND PEPPER TO TASTE
1	CUP MAYONNAISE		PARMESAN CHEESE
1	CARTON SOUR CREAM		PAPRIKA
1	CUP GRATED SHARP CHEESE		

Cook chicken breasts. Cook broccoli. Mix soup, sour cream, mayonnaise, grated cheese, and seasonings. Drain broccoli and arrange in bottom of flat greased casserole (3 quart). Sprinkle generously with Parmesan cheese. Remove skin from chicken and take chicken from bone, pulling apart into pieces and spread over broccoli. Sprinkle again with Parmesan cheese. Pour sauce over all. Sprinkle with Parmesan and paprika. Dot with butter. Cook 30 to 40 minutes in a 350 degree oven or until bubbly and hot through. Yield: 6 to 8 servings.

Elizabeth B. Wyman—The Estill Presbyterian Church
Estill, South Carolina

Chicken Enchiladas

24	TORTILLAS (HEATED IN SKILLET)	2	CUPS CHICKEN, DICED
1	(12 OUNCE) PACKAGE MONTERREY CHEESE	1	ONION, CHOPPED AND SAUTÉED
1	(12 OUNCE) PACKAGE CHEDDAR CHEESE		

Heat tortillas and spread with cheese, chicken and onion; roll up and place in large casserole dish.

Sauce:

1	STICK MARGARINE	1	CAN CHICKEN BROTH
5	TABLESPOONS FLOUR	1	TABLESPOON HOT SAUCE
1/4	CUP MILK	1	PINT SOUR CREAM

Mix sauce ingredients adding sour cream last. Heat 1/2 minute and pour over enchiladas. Sprinkle with additional cheese if desired. Bake uncovered in a 350 degree oven for 25 minutes or until bubbly. Yield: 8-12 servings.

Kathleen Garvin—First Presbyterian Church
Rogers, Arkansas

CHICKEN LASAGNA

8	OUNCES LASAGNA NOODLES (COOKED)	2	CUPS SHREDDED CHEDDAR CHEESE
1	RECIPE MUSHROOM SAUCE	3/4	CUP GRATED PARMESAN
1 1/2	CUPS SMALL CURD COTTAGE CHEESE	3	CUPS DICED COOKED CHICKEN

Mushroom sauce:

3	TABLESPOONS BUTTER	1	CAN CREAM OF CHICKEN SOUP (PLUS 1/2 CAN MILK)
1	6 OUNCE CAN MUSHROOMS		
1/2	CUP CHOPPED ONION	1/2	TEASPOON BASIL
1/2	CUP CHOPPED GREEN PEPPER		

In a large skillet sauté onion, green pepper, and mushrooms in butter. Add soup, milk, and basil. In buttered 9x13" pan or glass baking dish, layer cooked noodles, sauce, cottage cheese, chicken, cheddar cheese and Parmesan; repeat layer. Bake in a 350 degree oven for 45 minutes (cover first 30 minutes). Freezes well.

Nancy Winters—First Presbyterian Church
Findlay, Ohio

CHICKEN MUSHROOM CASSEROLE

6	CHICKEN BREASTS, BONED AND HALVED	1	PACKAGE DRIED BEEF
1	CAN CREAM OF MUSHROOM SOUP	6	STRIPS BACON
1	CARTON SOUR CREAM OR HALF-AND-HALF		

Place dried beef in layer on bottom of casserole dish. Wrap each half chicken breast in a strip of bacon. Combine soup and sour cream and pour over chicken. Salt and pepper are not needed. Bake in a 275 degree oven for 3 hours. Yield: 6 servings.

Margaret Corbin Vail—Church of The Holy Spirit
Lake Forest, Illinois

Chicken of the North

2	CUPS UNCOOKED RICE	1/2	TEASPOON SALT
2	10 OUNCE CANS CREAM OF CHICKEN SOUP	1/4	TEASPOON PEPPER
1 1/2	CUPS MILK	1/2	CUP CELERY, CHOPPED
1	8 OUNCE CHEESE WHIZ OR	1/2	CUP ONION, CHOPPED
1	CUP AGED CHEESE, GRATED	6	BONELESS CHICKEN BREAST, COOKED AND CUT IN BITE SIZE PIECES
1	CAN WATER CHESTNUTS, CHOPPED		
1	LARGE BUNCH BROCCOLI		

Steam broccoli until just crisp. Mix all ingredients, pour into 8"x12" baking dish. Bake in a 350 degree oven for 1 hour. Yield: 8 servings.

St. Columba Presbyterian Church
Belleville, Ontario, Canada

Chicken Parmigiana

4	BONELESS SKINLESS CHICKEN BREASTS	1/2	CUP GRATED PARMESAN CHEESE
2	EGGS, BEATEN	1	JAR (15 1/2 OUNCE) MEAT FLAVORED SPAGHETTI SAUCE*
1	CUP PROGRESSO* ITALIAN STYLE BREAD CRUMBS	1	CUP SHREDDED MOZZARELLA CHEESE
1/4	CUP PROGRESSO* OLIVE OIL		*Use brand of your choice

Dip chicken into egg and then into bread crumbs, coating thoroughly. In a medium skillet, heat olive oil. Cook chicken in oil until done and well-browned on both sides. Pour spaghetti sauce into an 11x7 inch baking dish. Place chicken on sauce and top with Parmesan and mozzarella cheese. Bake in a 400 degree oven for 15 minutes or until cheese is melted and lightly browned. Yield: 4 servings.

Bernetta Winfrey—Covenant Presbyterian Church
San Antonio, Texas

Chicken Rice Casserole

6	RAW CHICKEN BREASTS	1/2	CUP CELERY
2	CUPS UNCOOKED RICE	1	SMALL ONION
2	CANS CREAM SOUP (CHICKEN OR MUSHROOM)	2	CANS OF MILK
			SALT AND PEPPER
1/4	CUP GREEN PEPPER		

Combine everything but chicken. Put in a 9x13" baking dish. Add chicken breasts and cook uncovered in a 350 degree oven for 1 hour. Yield: 6 servings.

Kirk of the Hills Presbyterian Church
Fairfield Bay, Arkansas

Chicken Sopa with Swiss Cheese

- 1 CUP COOKED CHICKEN, DICED
- 1 CAN CREAM OF CHICKEN SOUP
- 2 SMALL CANS GREEN CHILI PEPPERS
- 1 8 OUNCE PACKAGE SLICED SWISS CHEESE
- 1 DOZEN CORN TORTILLAS

Combine chicken, soup and chopped chili peppers in sauce pan and heat. Break tortillas in pieces. Butter 1 1/2 quart casserole and alternate layers of tortillas and cheese and soup mixture. Sprinkle cheese on top. Bake in a 350 degree oven for 30 minutes. Serve with picante sauce. Freezes well. Yield: 8 servings.

Mrs. Robert White—First Central Presbyterian Church
Abilene, Texas

Chicken Spaghetti

- 1 8 OUNCE PACKAGE SPAGHETTI
- 2 1/2 CUPS COOKED CHICKEN, CHOPPED
- 1/2 CUP DICED CELERY
- 1 SLICED MEDIUM ONION
- 1/2 CUP DICED GREEN PEPPER
- 1 CAN CONDENSED MUSHROOM SOUP
- 1 CAN TOMATO SOUP
- 1/4 CUP WATER
- 1/4 CUP COOKING SHERRY
- 1/4 CUP SLICED STUFFED OLIVES
- GRATED CHEESE (SHARP)

Cook spaghetti in boiling salted water until tender. Place spaghetti and chicken in alternate layers in a 3 quart casserole. Brown celery, onion, and pepper in a little butter for 10 minutes. Add soups and water. Cook 5 minutes. Add sherry and olives. Pour sauce over chicken and spaghetti and bake in a 350 degree oven for 30 minutes. When ready to serve, sprinkle with cheese and heat 5 minutes. Can be made a day ahead and is sometimes better that way. May be divided into small casseroles, frozen and used as needed. Yield: 8 servings.

Ruth Dowdle—First Presbyterian Church
York, South Carolina

Chicken Spectacular

Ever played the game "Telephone" in which a nugget of information is whispered from person to person? The final player announces the saying only to find out how astonishingly far from the original his words really are. Versions of this recipe remind me of "Telephone" so if anyone is interested in what I believe to be the original version, here it is:

1	LARGE CHICKEN, DICED	1	CAN SLICED WATER CHESTNUTS, DRAINED
1	6 OUNCE PACKAGE UNCLE BEN'S CURRIED RICE	1	CAN CREAM OF CELERY SOUP
1	SMALL ONION, CHOPPED	1	CUP MAYONNAISE (I USE MIRACLE WHIP)
1	CAN DEL MONTE SEASONED GREEN BEANS, DRAINED	1	SMALL JAR CHOPPED PIMENTO

Cook rice in chicken broth (from cooking chicken) for 25 minutes. Add onion and cook 5 more minutes. Combine all ingredients. Salt if needed. Bake in casserole in a 350 degree oven for 40 minutes or heat until bubbly in microwave.

Anne Kilpatrick—Westminster Presbyterian Church
St. Louis, Missouri

Chicken Tettrazini

1/2	CUP MARGARINE	2	(8 OUNCE) CANS MUSHROOMS
2 TO 3	CUPS CUBED CHICKEN	1	(7 OUNCE) PACKAGE THIN SPAGHETTI
2	CANS CREAM OF CHICKEN SOUP	1 1/2	CUPS PARMESAN CHEESE

Break spaghetti in 1 inch pieces. Cook, drain. Melt margarine; add and mix all remaining ingredients except cheese. Bake in large Pyrex casserole (lasagne type) in a 350 degree oven for about 45 minutes. The trick of this recipe is to generously top with parmesan cheese over all before cooking. Yield: 8 servings.

Marty Shoemaker—First Presbyterian Church
Fort Lauderdale, Florida

Easy Chicken Pie

1	FRYER, COOKED, DEBONED	1	CUP MILK
1	SMALL CAN ENGLISH PEAS	1 1/2	CUPS CHICKEN BROTH
3	HARD BOILED EGGS, SLICED	1	CAN CREAM OF CHICKEN SOUP
1	STICK OLEO, MELTED	1	CUP SELF-RISING FLOUR

Cut chicken into bite-sized pieces and place in greased casserole dish. Layer egg slices and then peas. Pour mixed chicken soup and broth over all. Mix milk, self-rising flour, and oleo. Pour over chicken mixture. Bake in a 425 degree oven for 30 minutes. (Crust rises to top as it cooks.) Yield: 6-8 servings.

Karen Lashley—First Presbyterian Church
Demopolis, Alabama

EASY CHICKEN PIE CASSEROLE

3	CUPS DICED COOKED CHICKEN	1/4	TEASPOON PEPPER (BLACK)
1	PACKAGE (10 OUNCE) FROZEN MIXED VEGETABLES	1	CUP CHICKEN BROTH
		1	CUP SELF RISING FLOUR
1	CAN CREAM OF CELERY SOUP	1/2	CUP (1 STICK) BUTTER OR MARGARINE, MELTED
1	CUP MILK		

Grease a shallow 2 quart baking dish. Place chicken and vegetables in baking dish. Stir together soup, chicken broth, and pepper. Pour over chicken mixture. Combine flour, milk and melted butter, stir until smooth. Pour over mixture in baking dish. Bake in a 400 degree oven until lightly browned. Yield: 5 servings. NOTE: If using all purpose, add 1 1/2 teaspoons baking powder and 1/2 teaspoon salt to flour.

Emma Lou Holcombe—Paint Gap Presbyterian Church
Burnsville, North Carolina

CREAMY BAKED CHICKEN BREASTS

5	WHOLE CHICKEN BREASTS, SPLIT, SKINNED AND BONED	10	SLICES (4X4) SWISS CHEESE (LORRAINE/ALPINE LACE)

Poulet Sauce:

1	CAN CREAM OF CHICKEN SOUP	2	TEASPOONS LEMON JUICE
1 1/2	CUPS MILK (2%) SKIM MAY BE USED	2	TABLESPOONS CHOPPED FRESH PARSLEY
2	TABLESPOONS DRIED CHOPPED ONION	1 1/2	CUPS HERB STUFFING MIX, CRUSHED

Arrange chicken in lightly greased (Pam) baking dish. Top with cheese slices. Mix soup, milk, onion, lemon juice, and parsley, spoon sauce evenly over chicken, and sprinkle with stuffing mix. Bake uncovered in a 350 degree oven for 45-55 minutes. Check after 30 minutes. If crumbs are dark, place a piece of foil lightly over top. Do not seal. Continue to bake until chicken is cooked through. Yield: 10 servings.

Mary Lou Francisco—First Presbyterian Church
Medina, New York

GLORIA'S CHICKEN

This is a great company dish—everyone loves it.

4	BONED CHICKEN BREASTS (8 HALVES)	2	CUPS PEPPERIDGE FARM STUFFING MIX
8	SLICES SWISS CHEESE	1	CAN WATER CHESTNUTS, SLICED
1	4 OUNCE CAN MUSHROOMS, DRAINED	1/2	STICK MARGARINE, MELTED
2	CANS CREAM OF CHICKEN SOUP		

Grease 9x13" pan. Place chicken in pan (do not crowd pieces) and cover each with a slice of cheese. Spoon mushrooms over this, then cover with soup. Cover with foil and bake for 45 minutes in a 350 degree oven. While chicken is baking, combine melted margarine, chestnuts, and stuffing mix. Remove from oven. Take foil from chicken and sprinkle with stuffing mixture. Bake uncovered for 15 minutes more.

Barbara Pennington—Fairfax Presbyterian Church
Fairfax, Virginia

HAWAIIAN CHICKEN

2	CUT UP FRYERS (3-3 1/2 POUND)	1	CUP CELERY
1/3	CUP CORNSTARCH	1/4	CUP SOY SAUCE
1/2	CUP SALAD OIL	1/4	CUP BROWN SUGAR
3	GREEN PEPPERS, SEEDED AND CUBED	1/2	CUP WHITE WINE
3	LARGE WHITE ONIONS, THICK SLICES	1	CAN (#2 1/2) PINEAPPLE CHUNKS, DRAINED

Shake chicken pieces in bag with cornstarch until coated. Cook chicken in oil until medium brown. Remove chicken from pan. Saute´ onions, celery, and green peppers. Drain off excess oil and add pineapple, soy sauce, brown sugar, wine and enough cornstarch to thicken mixture. Replace chicken in frying pan. Simmer for about 30 minutes so that the chicken will absorb the flavor.

First Presbyterian Church, Coalinga, California

HAWAIIAN CHICKEN CASSEROLE

4	CUPS TURKEY OR CHICKEN, COOKED AND CUBED	1	CUP CHEDDAR CHEESE, SHREDDED
		4	TABLESPOONS LEMON JUICE
4	CUPS CHOPPED CELERY	1	TEASPOON SALT
1	CUP SLIVERED ALMONDS, TOASTED	1/2	TEASPOON PEPPER
4	GREEN ONIONS, CHOPPED	1	CUP MAYONNAISE
1	CAN WATER CHESTNUTS, SLICED	1	CUP SOUR CREAM
1	CAN CHOW MEIN NOODLES		

Mix mayonnaise, sour cream, lemon juice, salt, pepper. Combine celery, chicken, almonds, onions, and water chestnuts. Add to liquid mixture. Place in shallow 3 quart casserole. Top with cheese and chow mein noodles. Bake in a 425 degree oven for 10-15 minutes. Yield: 8-10 servings.

Esther Bletcher—Pacific Palisades Presbyterian Church
Pacific Palisades, California

HOT CHICKEN SALAD I

4	CUPS DICED COOKED CHICKEN	4	TABLESPOONS LEMON JUICE
2	CANS CREAM OF CHICKEN SOUP	5	HARD COOKED EGGS, CHOPPED
3/4	CUP SLIVERED ALMONDS	2	CUPS DICED CELERY
3/4	CUP MAYONNAISE	4	TABLESPOONS DICED ONIONS
1	TABLESPOON SALT	3/4	CUP CHICKEN BROTH
1/2	TEASPOON PEPPER	1	CUP CRACKER CRUMBS OR STUFFING

Combine all ingredients except cracker crumbs. Put in 3-4 quart casserole. Top with crumbs. Bake in a 350 degree oven for 40 minutes. Yield: 10-12 servings.

Janie Correll—The United Presbyterian Church
Lenoir, North Carolina

HOT CHICKEN SALAD II

3	CUPS COOKED CHICKEN	3	CUPS DICED CELERY
1	CUP CHOPPED TOASTED ALMONDS	1 1/2	TEASPOON SALT
4	TABLESPOONS GRATED ONION	1	CUP CHOPPED GREEN PEPPER
4	TABLESPOONS PIMENTO	4	TABLESPOONS LEMON JUICE
1	CUP GRATED AMERICAN CHEESE	1	CUP MAYONNAISE
1	CAN CREAM OF CHICKEN SOUP	6	CUPS CRUSHED POTATO CHIPS

Reserve 1/2 cup grated cheese and 2/3 cup potato chips. Mix all other ingredients together and pour into casserole dishes. Top with reserved cheese and chips. Bake in a 350 degree oven for 25 minutes. Yield: 18-20 servings.

Elizabeth Murray—Mount Hermon Presbyterian Church
Ila, Georgia

Hot Chicken Soufflé

13	SLICES WHITE BREAD	1/2	CUP WATER CHESTNUTS
5	CUPS COOKED CUBED CHICKEN BREASTS	1	CUP MAYONNAISE
1	CUP CHOPPED GREEN PEPPER		SALT AND PEPPER TO TASTE
1/2	CUP GREEN PEPPER	5	EGGS, BEATEN
1/2	CUP ONION	4	CUPS MILK
1/2	CUP PIMENTO	2	CANS MUSHROOM SOUP
1/2	CUP CELERY	2	CUPS GRATED CHEESE

Trim and cube 4 slices of bread. Place on bottom of 3 quart casserole. Combine next five ingredients and spoon over bread. Trim remaining bread, and crumble or place cubes over chicken mixture. Combine eggs and milk and pour over above. Cover and chill or freeze overnight. When ready to bake, spoon soup over top. Cook in a 325 degree oven for 1 hour, or until set. Top with grated cheese during the last few minutes of baking. Yield: 14 servings.

Elizabeth C. Robertson—Greenville Presbyterian Church
Donalds, South Carolina

King Ranch Chicken

1	FRYING CHICKEN (2 1/2 POUNDS)	1	CAN CREAM OF CHICKEN SOUP
1	PACKAGE TORTILLA CHIPS (6 1/4 OUNCE)	1	CAN CREAM OF MUSHROOM SOUP
3/4	CUP CHOPPED ONION	1	CAN RO★TEL TOMATOES AND GREEN CHILIES, MINCED
1	CUP MILK		
1/2	CUP CHOPPED GREEN PEPPER	1/2	POUND FRESH MUSHROOMS, DICED
1	TEASPOON CHILI POWDER	1/2	POUND SHARP CHEDDAR CHEESE GRATED

Cook chicken until tender in 5 to 6 cups water; drain. Remove meat from bones and cube. Crush tortilla chips and spread in 2 quart casserole. Add chicken. Blend remaining ingredients except cheese, and pour over chicken. Top with cheese. Bake in a 350 degree oven for 40 minutes. Yield: 8 servings.

Sue Neuhs—Highland Presbyterian Church
Fayetteville, North Carolina

Overnight Chicken Casserole

2-3	CUPS DICED COOKED CHICKEN	3	OUNCES SLIVERED ALMONDS
4	EGGS, COOKED AND CHOPPED	1	CUP MAYONNAISE
2	CUPS COOKED RICE	1	TEASPOON SALT
1 1/2	CUPS CELERY, CHOPPED	2	TABLESPOONS LEMON JUICE
1	SMALL ONION, CHOPPED	1	CUP BREAD CRUMBS
2	CANS MUSHROOM SOUP	2	TABLESPOONS BUTTER OR MARGARINE

Mix all ingredients except bread crumbs and margarine. Place mixture in buttered dish (13x9). Brown bread lightly in margarine and sprinkle on top. Refrigerate overnight. Bake in a 350 degree oven for 40-45 minutes. Yield: 8-12 servings.

Carol C. Ackerson—East Ridge Presbyterian Church
Chattanooga, Tennessee

POPPYSEED CHICKEN

2	LARGE FRYERS	1	STICK MARGARINE
8	OUNCES SOUR CREAM	2	TABLESPOONS POPPY SEED
1	CAN CREAM OF CHICKEN OR MUSHROOM SOUP	1 1/2	CUPS CRUSHED RITZ CRACKERS

Boil chicken until tender. Cool and debone. Place pieces into greased casserole. Mix sour cream and soup. Spread on top of chicken. Top with cracker crumbs. Place chunks of margarine on top. Sprinkle poppy seeds over crumbs. Bake in a 350 degree oven for 30-40 minutes or until bubbly and slightly brown. Yield: 8-10 servings.

Cindy Taylor—First Presbyterian Church
Alexandria, Louisiana

ROBERTA SHEPARD'S CHICKEN

3	POUNDS CHICKEN PARTS	1 1/2	CUP CELERY, CHOPPED
1/2	STICK MARGARINE	1	CUP ONION, CHOPPED
1	CAN CREAM OF CHICKEN OR MUSHROOM SOUP	2	TABLESPOONS FLOUR
1/2	CUP THIN CREAM (CANNED)	1	CUP DICED CHEDDAR CHEESE
2	TABLESPOONS PIMENTO CHOPPED		SALT, PEPPER, AND, PAPRIKA TO TASTE
			PEPPERIDGE FARM HERB STUFFING MIX

Remove excess skin from chicken parts. Sprinkle with salt, pepper, and paprika. Lightly brown in margarine in large frying pan. Remove chicken to casserole dish. Add 2 tablespoons flour to remaining margarine in pan. Add a cup of water to make a gravy Add chicken, cover and simmer until done, about 20-30 minutes. Add celery and onions and cook a few minutes. Add cream of chicken soup, cream, pimento, cheese. Pour over chicken in casserole, sprinkle with more pepper and paprika. Top with Pepperidge Farm Herb Stuffing Mix. Bake in a 350 degree oven.

Roberta Shepard—Westminster Presbyterian Church
Charleston, South Carolina

South Carolina Chicken Pie

1	3 POUND CHICKEN	1	STICK MELTED MARGARINE
3	CUPS BROTH	1	CUP SELF RISING FLOUR
1	CAN CREAM OF CHICKEN SOUP	1	CUP MILK
1	TEASPOON ONION SALT		

Cook chicken, debone, and cut into strips. Reserve broth. Combine broth, soup, onion, and onion salt. Place chicken in greased 8x12x2" casserole dish or 2 quart size. Pour mixture over chicken. Make a batter of margarine, flour, and milk. Pour over top. Bake in a 400 degree oven until crust is golden brown. Yield: 6-8 servings.

Caroline Wright—Highland Presbyterian Church
Winston Salem, North Carolina

Cheddar Chicken Casserole

5	OUNCES BROAD EGG NOODLES, COOKED	2	TEASPOONS GRATED ONION
2 1/2	CUPS DICED COOKED CHICKEN	1/4	TEASPOON SALT
1	JAR (4 1/2 OUNCES) SLICED MUSHROOMS		DASH CAYENNE PEPPER
1	CUP MILK	1	CUP COARSELY CRUMBLED CHEESE CRACKERS
1	CAN CONDENSED CHEDDAR CHEESE SOUP	3	TABLESPOONS BUTTER, MELTED

Combine cooked chicken, noodles, and drained mushrooms. Put in casserole. Blend together milk, undiluted soup, onion, salt, and cayenne pepper and pour over mixture in casserole. Combine crackers and butter and sprinkle over top of casserole. Bake uncovered in a 350 degree oven, for 35 minutes or until bubbly. Yield: 4-6 servings.

Ede Powell—Northminster Presbyterian Church
Cuyahoga Falls, Ohio

Country Style Chicken Kiev

2/3	CUP BUTTER	1/2	TEASPOON GARLIC SALT
1/2	CUP BREAD CRUMBS (ITALIAN STYLE)	2	CHICKEN BREASTS, SPLIT
2	TABLESPOONS PARMESAN CHEESE	1/4	CUP DRY WHITE WINE
1	TEASPOON BASIL LEAVES	1/4	CUP CHOPPED ONION
1	TEASPOON OREGANO LEAVES	1/4	CUP CHOPPED PARSLEY

Melt butter in a saucepan. On waxed paper, combine bread crumbs, parmesan cheese, basil, oregano, and garlic salt. Dip chicken breasts in melted butter, then roll in crumbs. Place in ungreased baking pan. Bake for 50-60 minutes in a 375 degree oven, or until golden brown. Meanwhile, add wine, onion and parsley to remaining melted butter. Pour over chicken the last 5 minutes of baking time.

Mrs. David Stedman—First Presbyterian Church
Haddonfield, New Jersey

CRESCENT CHICKEN ROLLS

1	PACKAGE CRESCENT ROLLS		PEPPER
3	OUNCES CREAM CHEESE	1	TABLESPOON CHIVES
1	TABLESPOON BUTTER	1	TABLESPOON PIMENTO CUT UP
2	CUPS CHICKEN, CUT UP	1	TABLESPOON MELTED BUTTER
2	TABLESPOONS MILK	3/4	CUP BREAD CRUMBS
1/2	TEASPOON SALT		

Separate crescent rolls, using 4 rectangles. Blend cream cheese and butter. Add all other ingredients. Put 1/4 of mixture into center of each rectangle. Fold up corners and twist together. Dip in 1 tablespoon melted butter and the bread crumbs. Bake on ungreased baking sheet for 20-25 minutes in a 350 degree oven. Yield: 4 servings.

Mary C. Rhody—First Presbyterian Church
Haddonfield, New Jersey

CURRIED CHICKEN/RICE/BROCCOLI CASSEROLE

4	CUPS COOKED RICE	1	CUP MAYONNAISE
4	CUPS DICED COOKED CHICKEN	2	CANS CREAM OF CHICKEN SOUP
2	PACKAGES BROCCOLI PIECES, THAWED, UNCOOKED	4	TABLESPOONS LEMON JUICE
		1/2 TO 1	TEASPOON CURRY POWDER
2	CUPS SHARP CHEESE, GRATED		BUTTERED BREAD CRUMBS

Layer rice, chicken, broccoli, and cheese in 9x13 buttered dish. Combine mayonnaise, soup, lemon juice, and curry powder and spread over cheese. Cover with buttered bread crumbs. Bake in a 350 degree oven for 30 minutes. Yield: serves 10.

Jane Shaffer—First Presbyterian Church
Waynesboro, Virginia

Chinese Chicken

12	OUNCE JAR APRICOT PRESERVES	8	OUNCE BOTTLE RUSSIAN SALAD DRESSING
1	PACKAGE ONION SOUP MIX	8 OR 10	PIECES OF CHICKEN

Mix preserves, onion soup mix, and Russian dressing. Pour mixture over chicken pieces in a shallow baking dish. Cover baking dish with top or foil. Bake in a 350 degree oven for one hour. Mixture can be used over again.

Irene Grant—East Ridge Presbyterian Church
Chattanooga, Tennessee

Chinese Chicken Casserole

8	POUNDS FRESH, WHOLE CHICKEN	2	8 OUNCE CANS SLICED MUSHROOMS
6	MEDIUM ONIONS	2	8 OUNCE CANS SLICED WATER CHESTNUTS
6	STALKS CELERY	4	CANS CREAM OF MUSHROOM SOUP
	SALT AND PEPPER TO TASTE	2	CUPS MILK
	BUTTER	4	5 OUNCE CANS CHINESE NOODLES
1	SMALL JAR PIMENTO	2	8 OUNCE CANS SLICED BAMBOO SHOOTS
2	CUPS CASHEW NUTS (RAW, UNSALTED)		

Boil chicken with 2 onions, 2 stalks celery, salt and pepper. Cool. Cut meat in bite-sized pieces. Discard onion and celery. Dice remaining celery. Slice remaining onions. Saute' celery, onions, green pepper in butter, until soft. Add pimento, mushrooms, bamboo shoots, water chestnuts, soup, milk, salt, pepper, and chicken. Mix well. Place one can noodles in bottom of each of two 9x13x2 casseroles. Pour 1/2 of chicken mixture into each casserole. Cover with remaining noodles. Sprinkle with nuts. Bake in a 350 degree oven for 20-30 minutes. Yield: 20-24 servings.

Mrs. William A. Wildhack, Jr. (Marty)—Little Falls Presbyterian Church
Arlington, Virginia

TURKEY

MAXINE'S GRILLED TURKEY BREAST

1	TURKEY BREAST (6 POUNDS) BONED, POUNDED FLAT	2	TABLESPOONS WORCESTERSHIRE SAUCE
1	CUP LEMON JUICE	1	ONION, SLICED IN RINGS
4	TABLESPOONS SOY SAUCE	1	STICK MARGARINE, MELTED
	GARLIC POWDER	1	PACKAGE ITALIAN DRESSING
			PEPPER, TO TASTE

Melt butter in saucepan. Add all other ingredients and mix well. Pour over turkey breast. Place in Ziploc bag and marinate in refrigerator up to 3 days. Cook on grill.

Kathy Emerson—Oakland Avenue Presbyterian Church
Rock Hill, South Carolina

PAM'S *PHAKE* CHILI

(This is a crock pot, low cholesterol recipe.)

1 1/2-2	POUNDS GROUND TURKEY, BROWNED AND DRAINED	1	16 OUNCE CAN OF SLICED, STEWED TOMATOES
1/2	5-OUNCE PACKAGE OF CHILI SEASONING MIX	1	MEDIUM ONION, CHOPPED
		1/2	GREEN PEPPER, DICED
1	16 OUNCE CAN OF BAKED BEANS AND SAUCE	1	8 OUNCE CAN OF TOMATO SAUCE

Combine all ingredients in a crock pot and stir well. Cook 8-10 hours at low setting. Skim any fat from surface. Serve in bowls, topped with shredded mozzarella cheese. Yield: 6-8 servings.

Pam Thompson—Faith Presbyterian Church
Harrisburg, Pennsylvania

Low Country Fried Turkey

WARNING: THIS IS NOT A RECIPE FOR AN INEXPERIENCED COOK—COOK OUTDOORS ONLY.

- 1 12 TO 14 POUND TURKEY
- TONY CHACHERES CREOLE SEASONING
- 5 GALLONS PEANUT OIL
- OLIVE OIL
- SALT AND PEPPER
- 60 QUART COOKING CONTAINER
- JAR RACK FROM A COLD PACK CANNER

Wash and dry turkey, rub inside and out with salt and pepper and refrigerate overnight. Remove turkey from refrigerator and pat dry, rub thoroughly inside and out with olive oil, then coat with Creole seasonings, inside and out (the more seasoning the better). Tie the turkey securely to the rack from a cold pack canner (this will keep the turkey from floating in the hot oil.) Using a gas cooker, heat the oil to 375 degrees (this takes about 30 minutes). **Very carefully lower the turkey into the hot oil, making sure the cavity fills with oil.** It is almost impossible, at this point, to keep the hot oil from splattering so be sure to wear hot pad gloves, long sleeves and long pants to prevent burns. Allow 3 minutes per pound plus 8 to 10 minutes. When the turkey is done, use the handles of the cold pack rack to lift the turkey from the oil. Place the rack and the turkey over a container to catch the dripping oil. Let cool about an hour before carving. Enjoy your low country bird. This is delicious, the meat is moist and contrary to expectations it is not greasy! (You should use heavy wire to make extensions for the handles on the canner rack.)

W. Thomas Logan, Trustee
Stoney Creek Foundation

Turkey Royale

Stuffing (mix well):

- 2 (8 OUNCE) PACKAGES PEPPERIDGE FARM SEASONED BREAD CRUMB DRESSING
- 3/4 CUP OLEO
- 1 1/2 CUPS WARM WATER

Turkey (mix well):

- 4 CUPS TURKEY (COOKED AND CUBED)
- 1 CUP CHOPPED CELERY
- 1 CUP CHOPPED ONION
- 1 CUP HELLMAN'S MAYO

Egg mixture:

- 2 EGGS
- 1 CUP MILK

Topping:

1	CAN CREAM OF MUSHROOM SOUP	1/2	CAN EVAPORATED MILK

Put half of stuffing mixture in bottom of a 9x13 pan. Top with all of turkey mixture, pressing it into corners. Place remaining stuffing mixture on top of turkey mixture. Drizzle egg mixture over top. Refrigerate overnight (covered). One hour before baking, mix soup and milk. Pour over pan mixture. Bake uncovered in a 350 degree oven for 50 minutes. Yield: serves 12.

Presbyterian Women—First Presbyterian Church
Oil City, Pennsylvania

TURKEY CHUNK CHILI TACOS

2	CUPS CHICKEN BROTH SAUCE	1	CAN DRAINED KIDNEY BEANS (OPTIONAL)
3	TABLESPOONS CHILI POWDER	1/2	CUP EACH DICED GREEN PEPPER, ONION, CELERY
1	TEASPOON MINCED GARLIC	2	CUPS LEFT OVER TURKEY OR CHICKEN
2	CUPS CANNED TOMATOES DRAINED, CHOPPED		LETTUCE, AVOCADO, CHEESE TACO SHELLS

Combine ingredients. Heat and serve in taco shells with shredded lettuce, diced avocado, and grated cheddar cheese.

Chicken broth sauce:

1/4	CUP BUTTER OR MARGARINE	2	CUPS CHICKEN BROTH
1/4	CUP PRE-SIFTED FLOUR		

Melt butter in saucepan over low heat. Add flour and stir smooth and cook about 3 minutes. Add broth and stir and cook until sauce is thick and smooth. Makes more than 2 cups.

Ruth Sheldon—University Presbyterian Church
San Antonio, Texas

Smoked Turkey

Equipment: Smoker

- 10 POUND BAG MATCH LIGHT CHARCOAL
- 1 SMALL BAG HICKORY WOOD CHIPS

- 1 (10-15 POUNDS) HEN TURKEY
- ALL PURPOSE GREEK SEASONING
- PEPPER
- SALT

Soak wood chips in water for 15 minutes. After soaking period, completely drain in colander until all excess water removed. Chips that are too wet will put out fire.

Prepare turkey that has been completely thawed, if frozen. Wash well. Season generously according to taste with salt, pepper, and Greek seasoning.

Be sure charcoal is well lit and that there is a good strong fire in smoker. When fire is going well, place well drained soaked chips over charcoal. Next, replace water pan to smoker. Fill completely with water. Place well-seasoned bird on rack in smoker. Cover with lid and DO NOT OPEN for 12 hours. At the end of cooking time, you will have brown, delicious bird with wonderful smoked flavor.

Neil W. Trask, Trustee
Stoney Creek Foundation

Turkey Burgers with Salsa

- 1 1/2 POUNDS GROUND FRESH TURKEY
- 2 TABLESPOONS CORNMEAL
- 1 TABLESPOON LIME JUICE
- 1 EGG WHITE
- 2 TEASPOONS CHILI POWDER
- 1/2 TEASPOON SALT (OPTIONAL)
- 1/4 TEASPOON PEPPER
- 2 TABLESPOONS CHOPPED GREEN CHILIES
- 1 TABLESPOON VEGETABLE OIL
- 1 CUP FROZEN CORN
- 2/3 CUP PICANTE' SAUCE

In bowl combine turkey, cornmeal, lime juice, egg white, green chilies, and seasonings. Mix and shape in 6 patties. Heat oil in heavy skillet. Cook patties 3 to 5 minutes on both sides or until no longer pink inside. Meanwhile, in saucepan cook corn and salsa together. Serve over patties. Serve with cornbread on the side. Yield: 6 servings. Calories 255, protein 26 g., carbohydrate 11 g., fat 13 g., cholesterol 76 mg.

Virginia Kanaga—First Presbyterian Church
Chandler, Arizona

Chapter Ten

Rice — Beans — Pasta

RICE

CRUNCHY RICE

- 1 CUP LONG GRAIN RICE, UNCOOKED
- 1/2 CUP CELERY, CHOPPED
- 1/2 CUP ONION, CHOPPED
- 1/2 CUP GREEN PEPPER, CHOPPED
- SALT AND PEPPER, TO TASTE
- 1 PACKAGE FROZEN SMALL GREEN PEAS (10 OUNCE SIZE)
- 1 CUP FRESH MUSHROOMS, SLICED
- 1 CUP MAYONNAISE

Cook rice according to directions. Mix all ingredients together. Place in deep casserole dish. Bake uncovered in a 350 degree oven for 45 minutes.

Bonnie Plyler—Oakland Avenue Presbyterian Church
Rock Hill, North Carolina

LOUISIANA RED BEANS AND RICE

- 2 POUNDS DRY RED KIDNEY BEANS
- 16 CUPS WATER (TO COOK BEANS)
- 6 CUPS RICE
- 2 ONIONS, CHOPPED
- 1 RIB CELERY, DICED
- 2 CLOVES GARLIC, MINCED
- 1 SMALL BELL PEPPER, CHOPPED
- 1 POUND PICKLED PORK OR 4 OUNCES HAM OR 1 LARGE HAM BONE
- 1 BAY LEAF
- 1 TEASPOON TABASCO SAUCE OR TO TASTE
- SALT AND PEPPER, TO TASTE

If possible soak beans overnight. Drain. Place beans in large pot. Add 16 cups water, onions, celery, garlic, bell pepper, meat, bay leaf, Tabasco, salt, and pepper. Bring to a boil. Simmer for 3 hours until beans are very tender and creamy. Stir frequently during the first 20 minutes to keep beans from sticking. Steam rice (6 cups) and set aside. Yield: 12 servings.

Gretna Presbyterian Church, Gretna, Louisiana

Red Rice

1	CUP ONIONS, CHOPPED	2	CUPS INSTANT RICE
1/2	CUP GREEN PEPPER, CHOPPED	1/4	CUP COOKING OIL AND 1 TABLESPOON OLEO OR
1	CAN TOMATO SAUCE OR FRESH TOMATOES		5 PIECES BACON
1	TEASPOON SALT		RED OR BLACK PEPPER TO TASTE
3	TEASPOONS SUGAR		

Saute´ onions and green pepper in the oil and oleo (if preferred, fry enough bacon to use instead and add some for crisp crumbled bacon topping). Add tomato, salt, sugar, and rice. Cover and bake in a 350 degree oven. Add pepper last.

Sara B. MacDonald—Oakland Avenue Presbyterian Church
Rock Hill, South Carolina

Rice-a-Roni

1	BOX CHICKEN RICE-A-RONI, COOKED AND COOLED	6	GREEN ONIONS, CHOPPED
1/2	GREEN BELL PEPPER, DICED	1/4	CUP MAYONNAISE
1	CAN MARINATED, CHOPPED ARTICHOKES (RESERVE JUICE)	1/4	TEASPOON CURRY POWDER

Cook Rice-a-Roni and allow to cool. Add chopped pepper, green onion, and artichokes. Mix juice from artichokes, mayonnaise, and curry powder. Add to rice mixture. Refrigerate and serve chilled. Yield: 8 to 10 servings.

Barbara Dark—First Presbyterian Church
Marion, North Carolina

Rice and Cheese Casserole

1	CUP RICE, COOKED AND DRAINED	1/2	POUND KRAFT OLD ENGLISH CHEDDAR CHEESE, GRATED
4	TABLESPOONS BUTTER	1	EGG, BEATEN
4	TABLESPOONS FLOUR	1 1/8	TEASPOONS DRY MUSTARD
4	CUPS MILK		
	SALT TO TASTE (OPTIONAL)		

In a double boiler, melt the butter and stir the flour into it, making a paste. Add the milk gradually to make a white sauce. Add cheese. Stir in cheese until melted. Add the egg and mustard. Mix the sauce and rice in a large casserole dish. Bake in a 325 degree oven for about 1 hour until the consistency of custard. Freezes well. Yield: 8 servings.

Carolyn Lowe (Mrs. S. Arthur)—United Church of Ellicottville
Ellicottville, New York

Rice and Vegetable Casserole

1 1/2	CUPS RAW RICE	3/4	CUP FINELY CHOPPED CARROTS
1/8	POUND OF BUTTER	1/2	CUP FINELY CHOPPED GREEN ONION
3	CUPS BOILING HOT BROTH (CANNED OR CUBES)	3/4	CUP FINELY CHOPPED PARSLEY
		3/4	CUP PINE NUTS OR BLANCHED ALMONDS

Place and empty casserole with lid in a 350 degree oven. In a large skillet, place the butter and rice. Stir until brown, about 5 minutes. Remove casserole from oven and combine broth and rice. Cook for 45 minutes in oven. After 30 minutes, add the vegetables and nuts.

Carolyn Lowe—First Presbyterian Church
Beaufort, South Carolina

Wild Rice Casserole

3/4	CUP UNCOOKED WILD RICE	1	CAN CREAM OF CHICKEN SOUP
1 1/2	POUNDS, GROUND BEEF	1	CAN CREAM OF MUSHROOM SOUP
1	CUP CELERY, CHOPPED	1	CAN (4 OUNCES) MUSHROOMS
1	SMALL ONION, CHOPPED	1 TO 2	CUPS WATER
1/2	GREEN PEPPER, CHOPPED		

Cook wild rice according to directions on container. Brown beef. Drain. Mix all ingredients with 1 cup of water. Place in a 9x13 inch casserole. Bake in a 300 degree oven for 1 1/2 hours. Stir several times for the first 1/2 hour. Add the second cup of water as needed to keep moist. Yield: 6 servings.

Helen Karinen—North Como Presbyterian Church
St. Paul, Minnesota

BEANS

Ann's Baked Beans

4	1 POUND CANS PORK AND BEANS	1	CUP CHOPPED ONION
1	POUND, COOKED DICED BACON	1	CUP CHOPPED GREEN PEPPER
1	CUP BROWN SUGAR	3	TABLESPOONS OREGANO
1	CUP CATSUP		

Mix all ingredients and bake in a 300 degree oven for 3 hours. Yield: 16 servings.

Mrs. Ann Welk—First Presbyterian Church
Dunedin, Florida

Baked Beans

- 1 16 OUNCE CAN OF PORK AND BEANS
- 1/2 MEDIUM SIZE, GREEN PEPPER, CHOPPED
- 1 ONION, CHOPPED
- 1/4 POUND GROUND CHUCK
- 1/4 TEASPOON GARLIC POWDER
- 1 TABLESPOON WORCESTERSHIRE SAUCE
- 2 TABLESPOONS CATSUP
- 3-4 TABLESPOONS SOY SAUCE (MAY USE LIGHT)
- 1 TABLESPOON PREPARED MUSTARD

Brown meat, pepper and onions. Drain. Add beans and seasonings. Bake in a 425 degree oven for 30 minutes.

Ruth Saunders—United Presbyterian Church
Lenoir, North Carolina

Dr. Pepper Baked Beans

Editor's note: We became acquainted with Mrs. Amann through her writings for our daily meditations in "These Days" and appreciate her donations of recipes and funds for our project.

- 3 (#2 1/4) CANS PORK AND BEANS
- 1 CUP DR. PEPPER
- 1/2 CUP CATSUP OR CHILI SAUCE
- 2 TABLESPOON PREPARED MUSTARD
- 1 LARGE ONION, CHOPPED FINE
- 5 SLICES BACON

Drain beans and combine with Dr. Pepper, catsup, mustard, and onion. Pour into greased 2 1/2 quart casserole. Cut bacon in 1/2 inch lengths and arrange on top. Bake, uncovered, in a 350 degree oven for 1 1/2- 2 hours. Yield: 12 servings.

Peg Bohner Amann—First Presbyterian Church
Kerrville, Texas

Fancy Baked Beans

- 1 LARGE ONION, CHOPPED
- 1/2 POUND BACON, COOK AND CRUMBLE
- 1 CAN DARK RED KIDNEY BEANS, DRAINED
- 1 CAN LIMA BEANS, DRAINED
- 1 TEASPOON DRY MUSTARD
- 1 CAN PORK AND BEANS, PARTIALLY DRAINED
- 1/2 CUP TOMATO KETCHUP
- 1/2 CUP BROWN SUGAR
- 1/4 CUP VINEGAR
- 1/2 TEASPOON SALT
- DASH OF PEPPER

Cook bacon until crisp. Reserve 2 tablespoons drippings. Saute' onion in drippings until clear. Mix with all other ingredients. Pour into 9x13 casserole dish. Bake in 350 degree oven for 30-40 minutes.

Judy Cannon—First Presbyterian Church
Beaufort, South Carolina

Frijoles con Chilies y Queso

1 1/2	CUPS RICH VEGETABLE OR MEAT STOCK	1/8	TEASPOON OREGANO
2	CANS (4 OUNCES EACH) WHOLE OR DICED GREEN CHILIES	3/4	CUP SOUR CREAM
		1/2	TEASPOON BASIL OR THYME
6	6 1/2 CUPS DRAINED, COOKED OR CANNED LARGE OR BABY LIMA BEANS	1/2	POUND MONTEREY JACK CHEESE

Spread 1/3 of beans in shallow 2-3 quart casserole dish. Sprinkle with 1/2 of each herb. Cut whole chilies lengthwise and crosswise in 1/2 inch squares or use diced chilies from can. Cut cheese in 1/2 inch strips or grate. Scatter 1/2 of the chilies and 1/3 of the cheese over the layer of beans. Top with remaining beans and sprinkle with cheese and chilies. Mix stock and sour cream until smooth. Liquid should almost cover beans. Bake uncovered in a 325 degree oven for 30 to 45 minutes, or until bubbling. Yield: 8-10 servings.

United Presbyterian Church, Paterson, New Jersey

After Tennis Chili with Beans

4	LARGE CANS (3 POUND, 3 OUNCE) KIDNEY BEANS, DRAIN BUT RESERVE LIQUID	4	TABLESPOONS CHILI POWDER (OR MORE)
5-7	POUNDS GROUND BEEF, SAUTÉED AND DRAINED	1	TABLESPOON HOT TACO SAUCE
			WORCESTERSHIRE SAUCE TO TASTE
2	CUPS ONIONS, CHOPPED AND SAUTÉED	2	PACKAGES CHILI SEASONING MIX
2	LARGE JARS SPAGHETTI SAUCE	2	TABLESPOONS CRUSHED OR MINCED PARSLEY
2	CANS TOMATO SAUCE WITH PIECES	2	CANS CHOPPED, PITTED BLACK OLIVES
		1	PACKAGE CHOPPED FINE, ALMONDS

To prepare: Mix all ingredients except beans. Add beans and heat gently, stirring well. Taste for seasoning. Add bean liquid to achieve desired consistency. Can be made a day ahead. Check seasonings again on 2nd day. Yield: 30 or more servings.

Gini Marquess—Brown Memorial Woodbrook Presbyterian Church
Baltimore, Maryland

Lentil Roll

Emily Reid of Millport, Scotland tells us that the following recipe was introduced to her family during the First World War of 1914-18, and is reputed to be like the "Mess of Pottage" for which Esau sold his birthright.

8	TABLESPOONS LENTILS	1	LARGE ONION, CHOPPED FINE
4	TABLESPOONS UNCOOKED RICE	4	BRIMMING TEACUPS, WATER
2	OUNCES BUTTER OR MARGARINE		SALT AND PEPPER TO TASTE

Place all ingredients into a large saucepan and bring to a boil, stir constantly. Reduce heat, cover, and simmer for about 30 minutes, stirring occasionally, until all liquid is absorbed. Pour the mixture into a casserole dish and allow to cool. Refrigerate. When ready to serve, slice and fry with bacon, serve with tomato on side. Yield: 4 servings.

Emily Reid—Parkhead Congregational Church
Glasgow, Scotland

Baked Lima Beans

2	(10 OUNCE) PACKAGES FROZEN LIMAS	1/2	TEASPOON SALT
1/2	CUP CHOPPED ONION	1/4	CUP BROWN SUGAR
2	TABLESPOONS BUTTER	1/4	CUP KETCHUP
1	CUP DAIRY SOUR CREAM	1/8	TEASPOON PEPPER

Cook lima beans in boiling salted water until tender. Drain. Cook onion in butter until soft. Stir in remaining ingredients and blend. Stir in limas. Place in 1 1/2 quart casserole dish and bake in a 350 degree oven for 25 minutes. Yield: 6 servings.

Flo Phillips—Westminster Presbyterian Church
St. Louis, Missouri

Limas Supreme

4	SLICES BACON, BROILED CRISP	1	PACKAGE FROZEN BABY OR FORDHOOK
4	TABLESPOONS BUTTER		LIMA BEANS
1	SMALL CAN MUSHROOM PIECES	1/2	CUP BOILING WATER
3/4	TEASPOONS SALT		

Use a pot with a tight fitting lid. Sauté mushrooms in butter. Add salt and water. Bring to a boil; add limas. Cover and cook for 10-15 minutes until tender. Sprinkle broken bacon over top.

Kathryn Summers Powell—Oakland Avenue Presbyterian Church
Rock Hill, South Carolina

STRETCH OR SHRINK BEAN DISH

This is a good dish to have or take anywhere when you don't know how many people to prepare for. Just add another can of beans.

2	CANS CAMPBELL'S PORK AND BEANS	1	MEDIUM SIZE ONION, CHOPPED FINE
1	POUND GROUND BEEF OR TURKEY	2	TABLESPOONS BROWN SUGAR
1	BOTTLE CHILI SAUCE	2	TABLESPOONS PREPARED MUSTARD

Saute´ meat and onions in large skillet. Add pork and beans, Del Monte or Heinz chili sauce, mustard, sugar, and pinch of salt. Simmer 20 minutes. Serve!

Mildred Neil—Shandon Presbyterian Church
Columbia, South Carolina

THREE BEAN CASSEROLE

1/4	POUND OF BACON	1	POUND, GROUND BEEF
1/2	CUP CHOPPED ONION	1/2	CUP BROWN SUGAR
1	CAN PORK AND BEANS	1/2	CUP CATSUP
1	CAN KIDNEY BEANS, DRAINED	1	TEASPOON MUSTARD (DRY)
1	CAN CHICK PEAS, DRAINED	2	TABLESPOONS VINEGAR

Cook and crumble bacon and brown and drain ground beef. Mix all ingredients together and place in casserole. Bake covered in a 350 degree oven for 30 minutes. Then uncover and bake for 30 minutes more. Yield: 8 servings.

Ruth A. Wiley—The National Presbyterian Church
Washington, D.C.

PASTA

CROCK POT MACARONI AND CHEESE

8	OUNCES MACARONI (1 3/4 CUP RAW)	1	LARGE CAN PET MILK (EVAPORATED MILK)
1	STICK OF MARGARINE	1 1/2	CUPS MILK
2	EGGS, BEATEN	3-4	CUPS SHARP OR MEDIUM SHARP CHEESE
	SALT AND PEPPER TO TASTE		

Cook and drain macaroni. Place all ingredients in a crock pot at low temperature and cook for 2 to 3 hours.

Anne Lindsay—Hampton Presbyterian Church
Hampton, South Carolina

Macaroni and Cheese

- 2 POUNDS OF MACARONI, COOKED
- 2 POUNDS OF CHEESE, GRATED
- 2 QUARTS MILK
- 1 CUP FLOUR
- 1/4 POUND OF MARGARINE
- SALT TO TASTE

Melt margarine, add flour, milk, salt, and cheese. Stir over heat until thickened. Add macaroni and stir. Place into casserole dishes and bake in a 350 degree oven for 20 minutes. Yield: 40 servings.

Mrs. Marian Davis—First Presbyterian Church
Dunedin, Florida

Macaroni Topkapi

- 4 OUNCES MACARONI
- 3 TABLESPOONS BUTTER
- 1 ONION, PEELED AND SLICED
- 1/4 CUP PLAIN FLOUR
- SALT AND PEPPER TO TASTE
- 1/2 CUP MUSHROOMS, SLICED
- 1 1/4 CUPS MILK
- 1/2 TEASPOON MIXED HERBS
- 3/4 CUP GRATED CHEDDAR CHEESE
- 2 EGGS, BOILED AND SLICED
- 1 TOMATO, SLICED

Cook macaroni until tender. Drain well. Melt butter in a saucepan and fry the onion until soft, add mushrooms and continue cooking for a minute. Stir in the flour. Cook for 1 minute. Gradually, stir in the milk. Bring to a boil and simmer for 2 minutes, season well. Stir in the herbs and 1/2 cup of the cheese, then mix in the cooked macaroni. Pour half the mixture into a greased ovenproof dish, cover with most of the sliced eggs, then the remaining macaroni mixture. Sprinkle with the remaining cheese and bake in a 400 degree oven for 25 to 30 minutes, or until the top is slightly browned. Garnish with the remaining slices of egg and tomato, serve hot.

Bessie McLeish—The Bethel Reformed Church
Chester-le-Street, England

Newberry Macaroni Casserole Specialty

Julia Randel, (Mrs. Morgan), submitted this recipe in memory of her mother, Mrs. Smith. Aveleigh Church was founded in 1835 and named by a prominent member/founder for his parents' church in Ireland. Mrs. Randel's great, great grandfather was the church's minister in the 1800's. Her great grandfather, grandfather, and father all served as elders. She was married in the church fifty years ago.

- 1 1/2 CUPS RAW, ELBOW MACARONI, COOKED AND DRAINED
- 2 16-OUNCE CANS TOMATOES MASHED
- 3/4 POUND CHEDDAR CHEESE, GRATED
- 4 TABLESPOONS MARGARINE
- 4 LARGE ONIONS, CHOPPED AND COOKED IN 3 CUPS WATER
- SALT AND PEPPER TO TASTE

Cook onion in water until tender. Add mashed tomatoes to onion in the water. Boil about 10 minutes. Mix macaroni, cheese, tomatoes, onions, onion water, margarine, salt and pepper. Place into a casserole and cook in a 350 degree oven for 30-40 minutes, until lightly browned and bubbly. Ground beef may be added to make a one-dish meal. Yield: 10-12 servings.

Mrs. Derrill Smith—Aveleigh Presbyterian Church
Newberry, South Carolina

SUPER MACARONI 'N CHEESE

7 TO 8	OUNCES ELBOW MACARONI		DASH OF PEPPER
1	CAN CREAM OF MUSHROOM SOUP	6 TO 8	OUNCES MEDIUM CHEDDAR, CUBED
2/3	CUP MILK	3 TO 4	OUNCES SHREDDED MOZZARELLA
1/2	TEASPOON SALT	1/2	CUP BUTTERED BREAD CRUMBS

Cook macaroni as directed on package. Drain. Combine soup, milk, salt, and pepper. Alternate layers into greased 2 quart baking dish as follows, macaroni, soup, cheddar cheese, macaroni, soup, mozzarella cheese, and repeat. Top with buttered bread crumbs. Bake in a 350 degree oven for 45 minutes. Yield: 6-8 servings. Freezes well.

Jo Ann C. Leist—Ray Memorial Presbyterian Church
Monroe, Georgia

MANICOTTI FLORENTINE

1	10 OUNCE PACKAGE FROZEN SPINACH	2	CUPS RICOTTA OR LOW FAT COTTAGE CHEESE
1/2	TEASPOON SALT	1	8 OUNCE PACKAGE MANICOTTI PASTA SHELLS
2	CUPS SHREDDED MOZZARELLA CHEESE	1/4	TEASPOON PEPPER
2	EGGS WHITES	3 1/2	CUPS SPAGHETTI SAUCE
1/4	CUP GRATED PARMESAN CHEESE		

Thaw and drain spinach. Combine spinach, ricotta and mozzarella cheeses, salt, pepper, and egg whites. Fill cooked shells with heaping spoons of mixture. Place in a 9x13" baking dish. Pour spaghetti sauce over top. Cover with foil and bake in a 350 degree oven for 35-40 minutes. Remove foil and sprinkle Parmesan cheese on top. Return to oven and bake for 10-15 minutes longer. Yield: 8 servings.

Mrs. Robert White—First Central Presbyterian Church
Abilene, Texas

Lasagna

1	POUND GROUND BEEF	1/2	TEASPOON PEPPER
1/2	POUND SAUSAGE	1	TEASPOON SALT
1	CLOVE GARLIC, MINCED OR	1	TEASPOON OREGANO
1/2	TEASPOON GARLIC POWDER	3	HARD COOKED EGGS, CUT UP
1	MEDIUM ONION, CHOPPED	1	SMALL CAN MUSHROOMS, DRAINED
2	CANS TOMATO PASTE	1	8 OUNCE PACKAGE, MOZZARELLA CHEESE
12	OUNCES WATER	1	12 OUNCE CONTAINER COTTAGE CHEESE
1	LARGE CAN TOMATOES, CHOPPED	1	TABLESPOON PARSLEY

Brown meats with onion and garlic. Drain off excess fat. Add remaining ingredients, except eggs. Simmer for 45 minutes. Add egg. Combine mozzarella cheese, cottage cheese and parsley. Cook 1/2 package lasagne noodles as directed on box. Alternate in layers: cooked noodles, sauce, and cheeses. Top with cheese layer. Bake uncovered in a 325 degree oven for 20-25 minutes until bubbly. Let stand for 20 minutes before serving.

Mary Ann Shaw—Westminster Presbyterian Church
St. Louis, Missouri

Presbytery Lasagna

This recipe was prepared by ladies of Highland Church to serve to a meeting of former Concord Presbytery.

1	POUND GROUND BEEF	1	POUND SHREDDED MOZZARELLA CHEESE
1	TEASPOON OIL	1/4	POUND SHREDDED ROMANO CHEESE
	SALT AND PEPPER TO TASTE	1	TABLESPOON CHOPPED PARSLEY
2	6 OUNCE CANS TOMATO PASTE	1	PACKAGE LASAGNA NOODLES, COOKED
4	TOMATO PASTE CANS WATER	1/2	CUP GRATED PARMESAN
2	ENVELOPES SPAGHETTI SAUCE MIX		
2	12 OUNCE PACKAGES COTTAGE CHEESE		

Brown ground beef in large skillet in oil. Use next 4 ingredients to prepare a spaghetti-like sauce, simmering about 15-20 minutes. Meanwhile, combine cheese and parsley. Grease bottom of large baking dish or lasagna pan with oleo (or spread a thin layer of the meat sauce juices). Layer the ingredients in this order, using 1/2 or each, lasagna noodles; cottage cheese; then, meat sauce. Repeat the layers. Top with 1/2 cup grated Parmesan cheese. Cover with foil. Bake in 350 degree oven for at least 30 minutes. Let cool, about 10 minutes. Cut into squares to serve. Can be made ahead of time, baked and frozen, then reheated. (In fact, it's easier to serve following this plan because it "sets up" and is not so juicy.) Yield: 10-15 servings.

Caroline Wright—Highland Presbyterian Church
Winston-Salem, North Carolina

Super Easy Lasagna

- 1 QUART, SPAGHETTI SAUCE
- 9 UNCOOKED, LASAGNA NOODLES
- 1 CARTON RICOTTA CHEESE (15-16 OUNCES)
- 8 OUNCES SHREDDED MOZZARELLA CHEESE
- 1 EGG, BEATEN
- 1 PACKAGE FROZEN CHOPPED SPINACH
- 1 TEASPOON OREGANO
- 1/2 TEASPOON GARLIC SALT OR POWDER
- 4 TABLESPOONS PARMESAN CHEESE

Thaw spinach and squeeze dry. Mix together both cheeses, egg, spinach, seasonings and 2 tablespoons Parmesan. Spread the bottom of a 9x13 pan with 1/2 cup spaghetti sauce. Layer 3 uncooked noodles over it. Spread half the cheese mixture. Top the cheese with 3 more noodles, then the rest of the cheese mixture. Add the last 3 noodles. Pour the rest of the spaghetti sauce over all. Top with the last 2 tablespoons Parmesan. Pour 1/2 cup water around the edges. Cover tightly with foil. Bake in a 350 degree oven for 1 hour and 15 minutes. Remove from oven and allow to stand for 15 minutes with foil on.

Susan Boutwell—Fairfax Presbyterian Church
Fairfax, Virginia

Inside-Out Ravioli

Ms. Webster says that this is the Church's all-time favorite and the recipe is requested each time it is served. She hopes that it is as well-liked elsewhere.

- 5 POUNDS GROUND BEEF OR TURKEY
- 2 1/2 CUPS CHOPPED ONION
- 50 OUNCES OF SPAGHETTI SAUCE WITH MUSHROOMS
- 40 OUNCE CAN OF TOMATO SAUCE
- 30 OUNCE CAN TOMATO PASTE
- 5-10 PACKAGES FROZEN, CHOPPED SPINACH
- 10 CUPS (5-7 OUNCE BOXES) ELBOW MACARONI
- 5 CUPS CHEDDAR CHEESE, SHREDDED
- 2 1/2 CUPS ITALIAN FLAVORED BREAD CRUMBS
- 10 WELL-BEATEN EGGS
- 1 CUP WATER
- SALT, PEPPER AND GARLIC TO TASTE

Thaw spinach and squeeze dry. Cook and drain macaroni. Brown meat and onion. Add water, tomato sauce, tomato paste, and spaghetti sauce to meat mixture and stir well. Simmer 10 minutes. Combine spinach, macaroni, eggs, bread crumbs, and cheese. Mix well. Spread into greased pans. Season meat mixture and spoon over macaroni. Bake in a 350 degree oven for 30-40 minutes. Cook through making certain that eggs are done. Allow to stand for 10 minutes before serving. Yield: 50 servings.

Patricia Webster, Hostess—First Presbyterian Church
Spartanburg, South Carolina

Betty Kirk's Turketti

1/2	POUND SPAGHETTI, BROKEN, COOKED	1/2	CUP CHOPPED GREEN PEPPER
3 1/2 OR 4	CUPS TURKEY, CUBED	1	MEDIUM ONION CHOPPED
1/2	CUP CHOPPED PIMENTO	1	TEASPOON SALT
2	CANS MUSHROOM SOUP	1/2	TEASPOON PEPPER
1/2	CUP SOUR CREAM	1/2	TEASPOON MSG (OPTIONAL)
4	CUPS SHREDDED SHARP CHEESE (1 POUND)		

Cook and drain spaghetti. Mix all together, saving 1 cup cheese. Place in greased 9x13 pan. Sprinkle remaining cup of cheese over top.

Topping:

1	CUP LIGHTLY CRUSHED CORN FLAKES	1	TABLESPOON MELTED BUTTER

Mix corn flakes and butter and spread evenly over top. Bake for 50 or 60 minutes in a 350 degree oven until brown and bubbly. (This is a good recipe for leftover turkey even if it's been frozen) Serves 10.

Betty Kirk—Grosse Pointe Woods Presbyterian Church
Grosse Pointe, Michigan

Turketti Spaghetti

1	PACKAGE (16 OUNCE) SPAGHETTI, BROKEN UP	3	CUPS CHICKEN BROTH
		2	CANS CREAM OF MUSHROOM SOUP
2	CUPS COOKED DICED TURKEY OR CHICKEN		(MAY USE CREAM OF CELERY OR CHICKEN)
1	CUP GREEN PEPPER, SLICED THIN	1	TEASPOON SALT
1	LARGE ONION, CHOPPED FINE		PEPPER TO TASTE
1	JAR DICED PIMENTOS (4 OUNCES)	1	CUP CHEDDAR CHEESE, GRATED

Blend all ingredients except cheese. Place into a greased 9x13 casserole. Sprinkle top with the grated cheese. Bake in a preheated, 350 degree oven uncovered, for 45-60 minutes. Yield: 8-10 servings. Freezes like a dream!

Marge Canham—First Presbyterian Church
Medina, New York

Vegetable Lasagna

1/3	CUP OLIVE OR SALAD OIL	1/2	CUP DRY RED WINE, SUCH AS BURGUNDY
1	LARGE ONION, CHOPPED	1	MEDIUM CARROT, SHREDDED
2	CLOVES GARLIC, MINCED	1/4	CUP PARSLEY, CHOPPED
2	TEASPOONS OREGANO LEAVES	1	MEDIUM EGGPLANT, UNPEELED AND DICED
1/4	POUND MUSHROOMS, SLICED	1	TEASPOON BASIL
1	LARGE CAN ITALIAN TOMATOES	1	TEASPOON SALT, IF DESIRED
1	CAN TOMATO SAUCE (8 OUNCES)	1/4	TEASPOON PEPPER

Sauté onion and garlic in oil, add eggplant and mushrooms. Add all other ingredients and simmer briefly to make thick sauce.

Make filling out of:

2	CUPS RICOTTA CHEESE	1 1/2	CUPS GRATED PARMESAN CHEESE
2	CUPS SHREDDED MOZZARELLA CHEESE		

Cook per package instructions 1 box whole wheat or regular lasagna noodles. Layer noodles, filling and sauce until noodles and filling are used up. Place remainder of sauce on top and bake at 350 degrees for 40-50 minutes. This amount fills a 9x13" pan. Yield: 8 servings.

Jeanne Soule—Jewett Presbyterian Church
Jewett, New York

Baked Ziti

1	POUND GROUND ROUND BEEF	8	OUNCE RICOTTA CHEESE
1	26-30 OUNCE JAR SPAGHETTI SAUCE	8	OUNCES SHREDDED MOZZARELLA CHEESE
1	POUND ZITI OR MOSTACCIOLA PASTA	8	OUNCES GRATED ROMANO CHEESE

Loosely brown meat in large skillet. Drain any excess fat. Add spaghetti sauce. Stir and heat (simmer) for about 35-40 minutes. Cook pasta according to directions and drain. (Pasta should be slightly undercooked). Put small amount of sauce in bottom of lasagna pan. Add 1/3 cooked ziti in an even layer. Dot with spoonfuls of ricotta, sprinkle with mozzarella and Romano and cover with sauce. Repeat procedure until all ziti is used up, ending with cheeses and sauce. Bake in a 350 degree oven for 1 1/2-2 hours, until top is bubbling and heated through. Yield: 12-15 servings.

W. Hugh Mortonson—Sea Island Presbyterian Church
Beaufort, South Carolina

Chapter Eleven

Salads

CHICKEN / TURKEY SALADS

Cabbage, Chicken, and Ramen Noodle Salad

- 1 PACKAGE CHICKEN RAMEN NOODLES
- 1 VERY SMALL HEAD OF CABBAGE, CHOPPED
- 4 GREEN ONIONS, CHOPPED
- 1 CUP SLIVERED ALMONDS, TOASTED
- 2 TABLESPOONS SESAME SEEDS, TOASTED
- 2 CUPS COOKED CHICKEN (CHILL AND SHRED)

Crush dry Ramen noodles into 1/2" pieces. Set aside. Toss cabbage, onions, almonds, sesame seeds, and chicken. Add noodles and toss again.

Dressing:

- 1 FLAVOR PACKAGE (RAMEN NOODLES)
- 1/2 CUP OIL
- 2 TABLESPOONS VINEGAR
- 2 TABLESPOONS SUGAR

Mix and toss with the salad and toss just before ready to serve. Do not add dressing ahead or noodles will not be crunchy. Yield: 10 servings.

Marion Baskin—Providence Presbyterian Church
Fairfax, Virginia

Chicken Delight Salad

- 4 CUPS COOKED CHICKEN
- 2 CUPS CELERY, DICED
- 1 CUP GREEN ONION, CHOPPED
- 1 CUP SLIVERED ALMONDS
- 1 CAN SLICED WATER CHESTNUTS
- 2 (13 OUNCE) CANS PINEAPPLE CHUNKS
- 1 LARGE CAN CHOW MEIN NOODLES

Dressing:

- 1 CUP MAYONNAISE
- 1/3 CUP SOUR CREAM
- 4 TABLESPOONS MAJOR GREY CHUTNEY
- 1 TABLESPOON LIME JUICE
- 1 TEASPOON CURRY
- 1/2 TEASPOON SALT

(Prepare dressing a day ahead to allow ingredients to mellow.) Drain pineapple. Mix all ingredients except pineapple and noodles. Add them at the last moment.

Lyn Greene—Hodges Presbyterian Church
Hodges, South Carolina

Chicken Salad

- 1 1/2 QUARTS MAYONNAISE
- 1 CUP CHICKEN BROTH (FROM CHICKEN STOCK)
- 4 TABLESPOONS LEMON JUICE
- 4 CHICKENS, BOILED, BONED AND DICED
- 4 PACKAGES (7 OUNCES EACH) LARGE MACARONI RINGS OR SMALL SHELLS
- 4 BOXES FROZEN PEAS
- 2 ONIONS, DICED
- 1 PINT SWEET PICKLES, DICED
- 1 SMALL JAR PIMENTOS, DICED
- 6-8 HARD BOILED EGGS, CHOPPED COARSELY
- 1 BUNCH CELERY, DICED
- 4 CUPS GREEN SEEDLESS GRAPES
- SALT AND PEPPER TO TASTE

Mix together mayonnaise and chicken broth. Add lemon juice to mixture. Combine all other ingredients and mix well. Spoon mayonnaise mixture over all ingredients and mix to cover total contents. Yield: 50 servings.

Marilyn Johnson—First Presbyterian Church
Belle Plain, Minnesota

Cool Chicken Salad

A good picnic dish.

Dressing:

- 1 TEASPOON GINGER JUICE (OR 2 TEASPOONS FRESH PULP, GRATED FINELY)
- 2 TEASPOONS DRY MUSTARD
- 2-3 TABLESPOONS SOY SAUCE
- 2-3 TABLESPOONS PEANUT OIL
- 1-2 TABLESPOONS VINEGAR
- 2 CLOVES GARLIC, CHOPPED FINE
- 3-4 TEASPOONS SUGAR (GRANULATED)
- 1 TEASPOON SALT, OPTIONAL
- 2-3 TEASPOONS SESAME OIL
- 1/4 CUP CHOPPED GREEN ONION

Combine all ingredients, mix well and set aside.

- 3 LARGE CHICKEN BREASTS
- 1/2 POUND BEAN SPROUTS
- 2-4 SCALLIONS
- 1/2 CUP SESAME SEEDS
- 2 TEASPOONS CORIANDER SEED OR
- 1/2 BUNCH FRESH CORIANDER
- 1/2 POUND SHREDDED LETTUCE

Boil chicken until done, about 15 minutes. Bone, skin, and chop meat into 1/2" cubes. Place meat into a bowl and add dressing. Mix well and coat entire amount. Refrigerate for 1 hour to cool. Dip bean sprouts in boiling water for 1 minute. Remove and place into cool water. Drain well. Chop coriander in food grinder, mix with green onions and sesame seeds and add to bean sprouts. Combine with chicken. Add lettuce just before serving and toss thoroughly. Yield: 5-6 servings.

Bob Holmes— Clairmont Presbyterian Church
Decatur, Georgia

Chicken Soup Salad

1 ENVELOPE UNFLAVORED GELATIN	1 CARROT, GRATED
1 CAN CREAM OF CHICKEN SOUP	2 HARD-COOKED EGGS
1/2 CUP MAYONNAISE	1/2 CUP DICED CELERY
1/4 TEASPOON SALT	1 LEMON, JUICED
1/2 TEASPOON GRATED ONION	1 CUP COOKED, DICED CHICKEN
1 PACKAGE CREAM CHEESE (3 OUNCES)	

Soften gelatin in 1/4 cup water. Bring soup to a boil and pour over gelatin. Stir constantly, until gelatin is dissolved. Cool. Combine cream cheese, mayonnaise and lemon juice and mix well. Add to the gelatin mixture. Add remaining ingredients and chill in refrigerator until firm, or overnight.

Evelyn Rogers—Covenant Presbyterian Church
San Antonio, Texas

Festive Turkey Salad

2 1/2 CUPS CUBED TURKEY	1/2 CUP MANDARIN ORANGES
3/4 CUP THINLY SLICED CELERY	1 1/2 CUPS COOKED RICE
3/4 CUP SEEDLESS GRAPES, HALVED	1 CUP (OR LESS) BOTTLED RANCH DRESSING
1/2 CUP SLIVERED ALMONDS	1/2 CUP MAYONNAISE
1/2 CUP PINEAPPLE TIDBITS	

Toss all ingredients together and serve on a bed of greens. Yield: 8 servings.

Pat Perkins (with thanks to Marge Chavers)—First Presbyterian Church
Beaufort, South Carolina

Minnesota Chicken Salad

3 CUPS WILD RICE (ABOUT 2/3 CUP, RAW)	1 CUP CASHEW OR PECAN NUTS
1 CUP COOKED CHICKEN, CUT IN CHUNKS	1 CUP WATER CHESTNUTS, SLICED OR CHOPPED
1 1/2 CUPS GREEN SEEDLESS GRAPES, HALVED	1 CUP MAYONNAISE
1 TEASPOON SALT	

Cook rice and cool. Mix with other ingredients. Chill and serve. Yield: 6 servings.

Pauline Bringen (Social Committee/Bazaar Bake Sale Chair)—National Presbyterian Church
Washington, D.C.

Party Chicken Salad

3	CUPS COOKED WHITE MEAT CHICKEN	2	TABLESPOONS FRESH PARSLEY, MINCED
1/3	CUP SLICED GREEN ONION	3/4	CUP MAYONNAISE
2/3	CUP SLICED CELERY	1/4	CUP PLAIN YOGURT
1 1/2	CUPS SEEDLESS RED GRAPES	2/3	CUP TOASTED, SLICED ALMONDS
1/2	TEASPOON DILL WEED		

Cook and dice chicken. Place chicken, green onion, celery, and grapes in a large bowl. Mix mayonnaise and yogurt and pour over chicken mixture. Sprinkle with dill and parsley. Gently blend all ingredients. Garnish with toasted almonds. Chill. Serve on a bed of greens. Yield: 5 one cup servings.

Mary Lou Francisco—First Presbyterian Church
Medina, New York

Salad by Committee

This salad yields enough for a Wednesday Night Supper group or ladies luncheon.

- 2 POUNDS COOKED CHICKEN OR TURKEY BREAST, DICED
- 2 POUNDS COOKED HAM, DICED
- 2 POUNDS CHEDDAR CHEESE, GRATED
- 2 POUNDS BACON, FRIED AND CRUMBLED
- 1 DOZEN HARD-BOILED EGGS, GRATED
- 3-4 RIPE AVOCADOS, DICED
- 1 POUND FRESH MUSHROOMS, THINLY SLICED
- 1 (7 3/4 OUNCE) CAN PITTED RIPE OLIVES, SLICED
- 2 BUNCHES RADISHES, THINLY SLICED
- 2 BUNCHES GREEN ONIONS, THINLY SLICED
- 1 1/2 PINTS, CHERRY TOMATOES, HALVED
- 3 (6 OUNCE) JARS MARINATED ARTICHOKE HEARTS, DICED (RESERVE JUICE)
- 5-6 HEADS OF LETTUCE, PREFERABLY MIXED VARIETY

Dressing:

1	CUP SALAD OIL	1	TEASPOON SUGAR (GRANULATED)
1/3	CUP WINE VINEGAR	1/2	TEASPOON SALAD HERBS
	RESERVED ARTICHOKE JUICE FROM JARS		SALT AND PEPPER TO TASTE
1/2	TEASPOON GARLIC POWDER		

Mix oil, vinegar, artichoke juice, and seasonings. Marinate mushrooms and artichoke hearts in dressing for 3-4 hours. When ready to serve, mix remaining ingredients in a very large wooden bowl. Toss with dressing, mushrooms, and artichoke hearts.

Eve Renfroe—First Presbyterian Church
Valdosta, Georgia

CONGEALED FRUIT SALADS

APRICOT CONGEALED SALAD

1	SMALL CAN CRUSHED PINEAPPLE	1	(8-OUNCES) PACKAGE COOL WHIP
1	(3 OUNCES) PACKAGE APRICOT JELLO	2	CUPS BUTTERMILK

Mix pineapple and Jello together in a saucepan and bring to a full boil. Cool. Add 2 cups buttermilk to above mixture and refrigerate until it begins to set. Stir in Cool Whip. Chill. Serve with a topping of equal parts of sour cream and mayonnaise.

First Presbyterian Church
Marion, North Carolina

ARIZONA SALAD

2	(3 OUNCE) PACKAGES OF ORANGE JELLO	1	MEDIUM CAN OF CRUSHED PINEAPPLE (SWEET OR UNSWEETENED)
2 1/2	CUPS BOILING WATER		
1	(6 OUNCE) CAN OF FROZEN ORANGE JUICE	2	APPLES (1 GREEN, 1 RED) PEELED AND GRATED

Pour boiling water over Jello. After Jello is dissolved, melt frozen orange juice in Jello mixture. Add pineapple and apples. Congeal in a 9x13" dish. Yield: 12-14 servings.

Elizabeth Patrick—Trinity Presbyterian Church
Charlotte, North Carolina

BLUEBERRY JELLO SALAD

Mrs. Sparks is a writer whom we have appreciated reading in our Presbyterian daily meditation booklet, THESE DAYS.

2	CUPS BOILING WATER	1	CUP SOUR CREAM
1	LARGE BLUEBERRY OR GRAPE JELLO	1/2	CUP SUGAR
1	LARGE CAN CRUSHED PINEAPPLE, UNDRAINED	1	TEASPOON VANILLA
1	CAN BLUEBERRY PIE FILLING CHOPPED NUTS	1	CREAM CHEESE BRICK (8 OUNCES) AT ROOM TEMPERATURE

Dissolve Jello in water. Add pineapple and pie filling. Chill 7 hours in a 9x13 pan. Cream the cheese and add the remaining ingredients as a topping. Spread onto the solid, chilled Jello. Sprinkle the nuts over all.

Martha Evans Sparks—Trinity Avenue Presbyterian Church
Durham, North Carolina

Cherry Pie Salad

- 1 LARGE BOX OF CHERRY JELLO
- 1 CAN OF CHERRY PIE FILLING
- 1 CUP CELERY, DICED
- 1 CUP OF DAIRY SOUR CREAM
- 1/2 CUP WALNUTS, CHOPPED
- 1 LARGE CAN CRUSHED PINEAPPLE, WELL-DRAINED

Dissolve Jello in 2 cups of boiling water. Add 1 cup cold water, the pie filling, celery, and nuts. Pour evenly into a 9x13" pan. Chill until set. Spread mixed sour cream and pineapple over the set Jello mixture. Chill until firm. Yield: 12-15 servings.

Pam Thompson—Faith Presbyterian Church
Harrisburg, Pennsylvania

Cottage Cheese Fruit-Jello Salad

May be used as a dessert also.

Servings:	10	50	100
FRUIT COCKTAIL	1 LARGE CAN	5 CANS	10 CANS
COTTAGE CHEESE	12 OUNCES	60 OUNCES	120 OUNCES (7 1/2 POUNDS)
COOL WHIP	1 SMALL	2 1/2 LARGE	5 LARGE
LIME JELLO	3 OUNCES	15 OUNCES	30 OUNCES
MARSHMALLOW MINIATURES	1 CUP	5 CUPS	10 CUPS

Drain fruit cocktail well. Mix Jello and cottage cheese and allow to sit until dissolved. Fold in the Cool Whip and marshmallows. Carefully fold in the drained fruit. Allow to set for several hours in the refrigerator or overnight. Yield: 10, 50, or 100 servings.

Presbyterian Women (Eleanor Campbell)—First Presbyterian Church
Athens, Georgia

Lemon Salad

- 2 (3 OUNCES) PACKAGES LEMON JELLO
- 2 CUPS WATER (1 HOT, 1 COLD)

Mix above and set aside.

- 2 (3 OUNCES) PACKAGES CREAM CHEESE
- 4 TABLESPOONS MAYONNAISE
- 2 CUPS CELERY
- 1 CUP NUTS, CHOPPED
- 1 LARGE CAN PINEAPPLE, CRUSHED WITH JUICE

Cream the mayonnaise and cream cheese and then add all the rest of the ingredients. Mix thoroughly. Pour into mold and place in refrigerator. When congealed, turn from mold onto your favorite greens.

Sarah Harley—First Presbyterian Church
Beaufort, South Carolina

Pineapple Congealed Salad

1	(12 OUNCES) CARTON COTTAGE CHEESE	1/2	CUP PECANS, CHOPPED
1/2	CUP MAYONNAISE	2	SMALL PACKAGES LEMON JELLO (SUGAR FREE)
2	TABLESPOONS LEMON JUICE	2/3	CUP HOT WATER
1	CAN CRUSHED PINEAPPLE, PACKED IN JUICE (15 1/4 OUNCES)	1/2	CUP SHREDDED CHEESE (OPTIONAL)
1	(9 OUNCE) PACKAGE COOL WHIP	1/2	CUP CHERRIES, CHOPPED RED OR GREEN (OPTIONAL)

Mix first 5 ingredients. Dissolve Jello in hot water and add to mixture. Place in a large casserole dish so that depth of mixture will be 1 1/2 to 2 inches deep. Refrigerate. For a different color and taste, you may top with shredded cheese or 1/2 cup of red or green cherries. Yield: 16 servings.

Kitty Harley—First Presbyterian Church
Beaufort, South Carolina

Pretzel Salad

1 1/2	CUP CRUSHED PRETZELS	1/2	CUP POWDERED SUGAR
1/2	CUP SUGAR (GRANULATED)	2	SMALL PACKAGES STRAWBERRY GELATIN
1/2	CUP MELTED MARGARINE	1	CUP CRUSHED PINEAPPLE
1	(8 OUNCES) SOFTENED CREAM CHEESE	1	PACKAGE (1 POUND) FROZEN STRAWBERRIES (1 QUART)
1	(9 OUNCES) PACKAGE COOL WHIP		

Combine crushed pretzels, sugar, and margarine and spread in a 9x13" pan. Bake for 10 minutes in a 325 degree oven. Set aside to cool. Blend cream cheese, Cool Whip, powdered sugar and spread on pretzel layer. Dissolve gelatin in 2 cups hot water. Drain pineapple. Stir pineapple and frozen strawberries into gelatin. When thickened slightly, pour over mixture. Keep refrigerated. Can be made a day ahead.

Val Manley—Preston Hills Presbyterian Church
Kingsport, Tennessee

Reception Salad

1	(3 OUNCES) PACKAGE LEMON JELLO	1	LARGE CAN CRUSHED PINEAPPLE
3/4	CUP CHOPPED NUTS	1	SMALL JAR OF MARASCHINO CHERRIES
1	CARTON COOL WHIP	8	OUNCES CREAM CHEESE

Drain pineapple and reserve juice. Finely chop cherries. Mix cream cheese, cherries, and pineapple together. Heat pineapple juice and dissolve Jello in it. Add to cream cheese mixture. After Jello has cooled, stir in nuts and fold in Cool Whip last. Chill thoroughly before serving. Serve on greens as a salad or as a dessert. Yield: 12 servings.

Imogene Holmes—Lillington Presbyterian Church
Lillington, North Carolina

RED, WHITE, AND BLUE JELLO MOLD

- 1 SMALL PACKAGE RASPBERRY JELLO
- 1 ENVELOPE KNOX GELATINE
- 1/2 CUP SUGAR (GRANULATED)
- 1 TEASPOON VANILLA
- 2 SMALL PACKAGES LEMON JELLO
- 1 CAN BLUEBERRIES IN LIGHT SYRUP
- 1 CUP LIGHT CREAM
- 1 CUP SOUR CREAM

Use a large mold. Prepare raspberry Jello as usual. Pour into mold and chill until firm. Dissolve Knox Gelatine in 1/2 cup cold water. Scald the sugar in light cream. Add the gelatin and cool in a separate dish for about 1/2 an hour. Add the sour cream and vanilla and mix well until smooth. Pour over the raspberry Jello. Chill until firm. Dissolve the lemon Jello in 2 cups of boiling water. Add the blueberries and their syrup. Stir well and add as a 3rd layer. Chill until firm. To remove from mold, loosen edges with a sharp knife. Hold the mold in hot water for a few seconds. Do not grease mold before filling. For a special occasion, you might place tiny flags in it.

Jean Nevius—Hampton Presbyterian Church
Hampton, South Carolina

FROZEN FRUIT SALADS

FROZEN FRUIT SALAD

- 3/4 CUP SUGAR (GRANULATED)
- 1 LARGE CAN CRUSHED PINEAPPLE
- 8 OUNCES CREAM CHEESE
- 2 BANANAS, CRUSHED
- 1 (10 OUNCE) PACKAGE FROZEN STRAWBERRIES, THAWED
- 1/2 CUP PECANS, CHOPPED
- 1 PINT COOL WHIP

Drain pineapple. Cream the cheese, add the sugar and juice from strawberries. Add fruits and nuts. Mix well. Add Cool Whip. Pour into freezer-proof dish. Cover and freeze until ready to serve. Yield: 8 servings.

Jean Blackwell Mulcay (1914-77, Beloved wife of our Pastor)
First Presbyterian Church
Frostproof, Florida

Frozen Peach Salad

1	CAN PEACH PIE FILLING	1/2	CUP LEMON JUICE
1	(8 OUNCE) CAN CRUSHED PINEAPPLE	1/4	TEASPOON ALMOND EXTRACT
1	CAN EAGLE BRAND CONDENSED MILK	1/2	CUP PECANS

Drain pineapple. Mix all ingredients well and pour into an 8x8" Pyrex dish. Cover and freeze. When ready to serve, remove from freezer about 30 minutes before. Cut into small squares. May be refrozen.

Note: We are indebted to individual members of this church for their support and for requests for our book by others. We thank Dr. Ronald Botsford (Pastor) who graciously gave us many of the contacts in England, Scotland, and Ireland, with whom he has exchanged summer pulpits.

Jane Lewis—First Presbyterian Church
Highlands, North Carolina

Pink Frozen Salad

1	CAN (16 OUNCES) CHERRY PIE FILLING	2	CUPS MINIATURE MARSHMALLOWS
1	CAN (13 1/2 OUNCES) CRUSHED PINEAPPLE	1	CUP PECANS
1	CARTON (13 1/2 OUNCES) WHIPPED TOPPING		
1	CAN (14 OUNCES) SWEETENED CONDENSED MILK (EAGLE BRAND)		

Mix all ingredients in order listed. May use muffin tins with liners or 8 cup molds. Freeze. Yield: 14-16 servings.

First Presbyterian Church, Marion, North Carolina

FRUIT SALADS

Fruit Salad

1	CAN FRUIT COCKTAIL (#2), DRAINED	1	PACKAGE BANANA CREAM INSTANT PUDDING
1	CAN PINEAPPLE CHUNKS (#2), DRAINED	3	TABLESPOONS TANG (ORANGE DRINK)
3/4	CUP PINEAPPLE JUICE (RESERVED)	3	SMALL OR 2 LARGE BANANAS

Mix dry instant pudding with Tang powdered drink mix and add the pineapple juice. Stir well. Add the two cans of drained fruit. Just before serving, add the sliced bananas. Mix and serve.

Jerri Boyd—Hampton Presbyterian Church
Hampton, South Carolina

SUMMER FRUIT BOWL

1	CANTALOUPE, CUBED	2	PEACHES, PEELED AND CUBED
1	CAN PINEAPPLE CHUNKS AND LIQUID (20 OUNCES)	2	BANANAS, SLICED
		1	CUP STRAWBERRIES
2	UNPEELED APPLES, CUBED	1	6 OUNCE CAN OF FROZEN ORANGE JUICE

Place all fruit in a bowl in the order given. Pour thawed, undiluted orange juice over all. Cover and refrigerate for about 6 hours. Serve in glass bowl.

Diane Hutchins—Providence Presbyterian Church
Fairfax, Virginia

❖ PASTA / RICE SALADS ❖

LIGHT GARDEN PASTA SALAD

8-10	OUNCES ROTINI PASTA	1/2	CUP FRESH TOMATO, CHOPPED
3	CARROTS, SLICED AND QUARTERED	2	PACKAGES GOOD SEASONS DRY LOW-CAL ITALIAN DRESSING
1	CUCUMBER, PEELED AND DICED	1/2	CUP VINEGAR
6-8	RADISHES, SLICED	1/4	CUP WATER
1	CUP BROCCOLI, CHOPPED		PARMESAN CHEESE, GRATED

Cook Rotini noodles according to package directions. Rinse under cold running water and drain. Place in a large bowl. Add cut vegetables and mix well. Pour dressing over salad. Allow to stand in refrigerator for about 2 hours. Mix prior to serving. Garnish with Parmesan cheese. Yield: 12 servings. (Per serving: Calories: 111, Fat: 0.6 gm., Cholesterol: 1 mg., Sodium: 195 mg.)

Patricia T. Kirkpatrick, R.D., L.D.—Alamo Heights Presbyterian Church
San Antonio, Texas

Very Easy Pasta Salad

2	BOXES SMALL SHELL PASTA	1/2	LARGE BELL PEPPER, CHOPPED
	REDUCED CALORIE MAYONNAISE		CELERY SEED
2	STALKS CELERY, SLICED THIN		DILL
1/2	ONION, CHOPPED		SALT AND PEPPER TO TASTE

Cook pasta until just barely done. Add all other ingredients except mayonnaise. Mix well. Coat salad lightly with mayonnaise and mix again. Serve on lettuce leaves.

Terri Laws—First Presbyterian Church
Marion, North Carolina

Fruited Rice Salad

1	CAN PINEAPPLE CHUNKS (8 OUNCES)	1/2	CUP CELERY, SLICED
1	CAN TENDER CHUNK HAM, CHICKEN OR TURKEY, FLAKED WITH FORK	2	CUPS COOKED RICE, COOLED
		1/4	CUP NUTS, CHOPPED
1/2	CUP GRAPES OR APPLES	1/2	CUP MAYONNAISE

Drain pineapple, reserving 3 tablespoons juice. Combine all ingredients except mayonnaise. Mix well and chill. Just before serving add the mayonnaise which has been combined with the reserved pineapple juice. Toss well and serve on salad greens if desired. Yield: 4 servings.

Irene Grant—East Ridge Presbyterian Church
Chattanooga, Tennessee

Pizza Rice Salad

2	CUPS COOKED RICE	1	CUP ITALIAN SALAD DRESSING
1	CUP MOZZARELLA CHEESE, SHREDDED		GRATED PARMESAN CHEESE
2	CUPS TOTAL SLICED OR CHOPPED VEGETABLES (GREEN PEPPERS, FRESH MUSHROOMS, BLACK OLIVES OR GREEN ONIONS)	1	CUP TOMATO, CHOPPED
		3/4	CUP SLICED PEPPERONI, HALVED

Cook rice, chill and crumble apart. Combine all ingredients except the dressing and cheese. Lightly toss with 1/2 cup of dressing and chill. Before serving, toss in remaining dressing and sprinkle with Parmesan cheese. Yield: 8-10 servings.

Pam Thompson—Faith Presbyterian Church
Harrisburg, Pennsylvania

SEAFOOD SALADS

Pasta and Shrimp Salad

1	POUND PASTA WHEELS, COOKED	2-2 1/2	CUPS MAYONNAISE OR MIRACLE WHIP
9	HARD-BOILED EGGS, SLICED/CUBED	2	TABLESPOONS SWEET RELISH
1	POUND SALAD SHRIMP	1	TEASPOON SALT
1 1/2	CUPS, SLICED CELERY	1/4	TEASPOON PEPPER
1/3	CUP CHOPPED ONION		

Cook and drain pasta wheels. Clean and cook shrimp. In a large bowl, lightly toss all ingredients. Chill immediately. Serve on lettuce leaf bed. Garnish with parsley and paprika. Yield: 25 servings.

Virginia Roberts—First Presbyterian Church
Medina, New York

Shrimp and Rice Salad

1	BOX RICE-A-RONI	1 1/2	POUNDS SHRIMP, COOKED, SHELLED, AND DEVEINED
1/2	GREEN PEPPER, CHOPPED		
1	ONION, FINELY CHOPPED	1/4	CUP MAYONNAISE
1	CAN SLICED WATER CHESTNUTS	1/4	TEASPOON CURRY POWDER
1	CAN ARTICHOKE HEARTS, DRAIN & SAVE LIQUID (OR 2 JARS, 6 OUNCES EACH)		BEAU MONDE SEASONING

Cook Rice-a-Roni according to directions (use chicken or almond fried). Sauté onion and pepper in 1 tablespoon butter. Mix with Rice-a-Roni. Mix mayonnaise and curry powder in 1/2 of the liquid from artichokes. Mix with the Rice-a-Roni. Toss in the shrimp, drained water chestnuts and artichoke hearts. Chill and serve with avocado, tomatoes, hard-boiled eggs and black olives. Yield: 6 servings.

Helen Harvey Laffitte—First Presbyterian Church
Columbia, South Carolina

Shrimp Salad (from Connie Trask)

1	POUND HILLSHIRE FARM SMOKED SAUSAGE	2	FRESH TOMATOES, DICED
1	POUND SHRIMP, COOKED/CLEANED	1	BUNCH RAW BROCCOLI (IN SMALL PIECES)
1	CAN BLACK OLIVES	1 1/2	CUPS SPAGHETTI OR MACARONI
			RANCH AND ITALIAN DRESSING (EQUAL MIX)

Cook sausage and pour off grease. Cut into small pieces. Mix everything and serve cold. This is one of those recipes where amounts do not have to be exact.

Pat Von Harten—First Presbyterian Church
Beaufort, South Carolina

Tuna Salad

1	CUP MAYONNAISE	1	3 OUNCE JAR OF COCKTAIL ONIONS
1	TEASPOON LEMON JUICE	1	CUP CELERY, CHOPPED
1	TEASPOON SOY SAUCE	1	PACKAGE FROZEN PEAS (10 OUNCES), THAWED
1/8	TEASPOON CURRY POWDER	1	CAN CHOW MEIN NOODLES (3 OUNCES)
2	CANS TUNA (6 1/2 OUNCES EACH)		

Drain and halve cocktail onions. Mix first 4 items for dressing. Stir well. Add all salad ingredients except Chow Mein noodles. Mix until all ingredients are coated well. When ready to serve add the noodles and toss again. Serve on salad greens.

June Shaw—Hodges Presbyterian Church
Hodges, South Carolina

SLAWS

Apple Slaw

8	OUNCES SOUR CREAM	3/4	TEASPOON PEPPER
3	TABLESPOONS LEMON JUICE	4 1/2	CUPS APPLES, UNPEELED AND CUBED
1	TABLESPOON SUGAR (GRANULATED)	4	CUPS CABBAGE, CHOPPED OR SHREDDED
1	TABLESPOON POPPY SEED		

Mix the first 6 ingredients. Toss with the apples and cabbage. Refrigerate. Takes about 30 minutes to prepare.

Gladys Gray Sullivan—Westminster Presbyterian Church
Greenville, South Carolina

BLUE LAKE SLAW

1	MEDIUM CABBAGE	2	CUPS SUGAR
1	LARGE ONION	1	TEASPOON SALT
1	BELL PEPPER	1	TEASPOON CELERY SEED
1 1/2	CUPS WHITE VINEGAR	1	TEASPOON MUSTARD SEED

Chop cabbage. Pour boiling water over cabbage. Let stand for 1 minute. Drain immediately. Rinse in ice water. Add other ingredients and mix well. Keeps for weeks in refrigerator and freezes well.

Ethel Styles—Paint Gap Presbyterian Church
Burnsville, North Carolina

NORWEGIAN SLAW

1	MEDIUM HEAD CABBAGE, SLICED	1	GREEN PEPPER, DICED
1	TABLESPOON SALT	2	CUPS CELERY, DICED
1 1/2	CUPS SUGAR	1	TEASPOON MUSTARD SEED
1	CUP WHITE VINEGAR	1	TEASPOON CELERY SEED
1	SMALL ONION, DICED		

Combine cabbage and salt. Allow to stand for 2 hours. Boil sugar and vinegar. Cool. Add remaining ingredients to the cooled syrup. Pour the cooled vinegar syrup over the cabbage. Mix well and freeze.

To serve: Thaw slightly and break up frozen slaw with a fork. Place in refrigerator for 3-4 hours before serving. Serve ice-cold. Crisp and delicious.

Eunice Morde Doty—Trinity Presbyterian Church
Arlington, Virginia

SUPERB SLAW

4	HEADS OF CABBAGE, SHREDDED	4	CUPS SUGAR, GRANULATED
4	ONIONS, CHOPPED OR SLICED		

Dressing:

4	CUPS VINEGAR	4	TEASPOONS DRY MUSTARD
3	CUPS OIL	4	TABLESPOONS CELERY SEED
8	TEASPOONS SALT		

Mix cabbage, onion, and sugar. Combine dressing ingredients and heat. Make layers of cabbage mixture alternating with dressing. Top with dressing. Cover and store 4-6 hours. Will keep for 2-3 weeks. Yield: 32 servings.

Eleanor Hook—Fort Hill Presbyterian Church
Clemson, South Carolina

PEA / BEAN SALADS

Blackeyed Pea (Soul Food) Salad

This recipe has two secrets: Flavor of blackeyed peas and the savory method in which they are cooked.

1	POUND BLACKEYED PEAS	1/4	CUP WHITE PEPPER
6	CUPS HOT WATER	2	JARS MARINATED ARTICHOKE HEARTS
2	TABLESPOONS SHORTENING OR OIL	1	CUP RADISHES OR CARROTS, SLICED
2	TEASPOONS ONION SALT	1	CUP CELERY, THINLY SLICED
	1/4 TEASPOON GARLIC SALT	1/2	CUP SLICED GREEN ONIONS
1	TABLESPOON CHICKEN STOCK BASE		

Soak peas overnight, rince and drain. Place peas in hot water. Add shortening or oil, onion salt, and garlic salt. Add chicken stock and white pepper. Simmer gently until barely tender. Drain while hot. Cool quickly, uncovered. Place peas in bowl and drizzle marinade from artichoke hearts over them. Cut artichokes in bite sized pieces. Add artichokes, radishes, carrots, celery, onions, and peas. Add your favorite French or Italian dressing to cover and pepper to taste. Chill before serving and spoon onto lettuce leaves. Yield: 8 servings.

United Presbyterian Church, Paterson, New Jersey

Kidney Bean Salad

1	PACKAGE (7 OUNCE) FROZEN RICE AND PEAS WITH MUSHROOMS	1/2	TEASPOON SALT
1	ENVELOPE FRENCH DRESSING, (MIX AS DIRECTED ON PACKAGE)	1/2	CUP GREEN PEPPER, SLIVERED
		3-4	DROPS HOT PEPPER SAUCE
		1/4	CUP ONIONS, RINGED THINLY
1	CAN (16 OUNCE) KIDNEY BEANS, WASHED AND DRAINED	1/4	TEASPOON CHILI POWDER
		1	MEDIUM DILL PICKLE, DICED
1/2	CUP SLICED CELERY		

Prepare rice, peas, and mushrooms as directed on package. Combine 3/4 cup French dressing with rice mixture. Add remaining ingredients. Toss well and chill for several hours. Serve on crisp greens, garnishing with additional dill pickle and parsley. Yield: 8-10 servings.

Lois Campbell—Trinity Presbyterian Church
Baton Rouge, Louisiana

LeSeur Pea Relish Salad

1	CAN LESEUR PEAS, DRAINED	1	CUP GREEN PEPPER, DICED
1	CAN LESEUR WHITE CORN, DRAINED	1	CUP ONION, DICED
1	CAN FRENCH CUT GREEN BEANS, DRAINED	1	CUP CELERY, DICED
1	SMALL JAR DICED PIMENTO, DRAINED		

Marinade:

1/2	CUP SUGAR, (GRANULATED)	3/4	CUP VINEGAR
1/2	CUP COOKING OIL	1	TEASPOON PEPPER
3/4	TEASPOON SALT		

Combine the ingredients thoroughly. Add the marinade and mix well. Chill at least 24 hours before serving. Will keep in refrigerator up to 3 weeks. Makes 2 quarts.

Kathleen Garvin—First Presbyterian Church
Rogers, Arkansas

Marinated Vegetable Salad

1	(10 OUNCE) PACKAGE FROZEN GREEN BEANS	1	(15 OUNCES)CAN KIDNEY BEANS
1	(10 OUNCES)PACKAGE FROZEN PEAS	3/4	CUP WATER
1/2	GREEN PEPPER, CHOPPED	1/2	CUP WHITE VINEGAR
3	ONIONS, MINCED	1/4	CUP OIL
1	CUP CELERY, SLICED	1/2	CUP SUGAR, GRANULATED
1	CAN WATER CHESTNUTS, SLICED	1/2	TEASPOON SALT
1	(11 OUNCE) CAN MANDARIN ORANGES, DRAINED		PEPPER TO TASTE

Cook and drain beans and peas. In a large bowl, toss beans, peas, green pepper, onions, celery with drained water chestnuts, oranges, and kidney beans. Set aside. Mix water, vinegar, oil, sugar, salt and pepper. Pour over vegetables. Cover and chill overnight. Yield: 12 servings.

Mary Hall—St. Luke's Presbyterian Church
Dunwoody, Georgia

Mustard Marinated Beans

1/2	CUP SUGAR (GRANULATED)	3	TEASPOONS INSTANT, MINCED ONION
1/2	CUP CIDER VINEGAR	1/2	TABLESPOON DILL WEED
3	TABLESPOON PREPARED MUSTARD	2	CUPS CANNED GREEN BEANS

Mix the above ingredients except beans and bring to a boil. Simmer and then pour over beans and refrigerate until ready to serve.

Mrs. A. Dial Gray, Jr.–First Presbyterian Church
Whiteville, North Carolina

Pea Salad

This dish is quick and easy to prepare and excellent with beef or any main course. Use amount of mayonnaise/horseradish according to the taste and texture desired.

2-3	TABLESPOONS MAYONNAISE OR SALAD DRESSING	1	BAG FROZEN GREEN PEAS (16 OUNCES)
1	CAN WATER CHESTNUTS, SLICED	2-3	TEASPOONS HORSERADISH (PREPARED TYPE)

Prepare peas according to directions. Allow to cool slightly. Mix mayonnaise with horseradish and drained water chestnuts. Fold in peas last. Chill before serving.

Ann S. Ritter-Holmes—Clairmont Presbyterian Church
Decatur, Georgia

Note: Of special interest, Ann Ritter-Holmes' great-great grandparents, Elizabeth Martin Blount and James Cornwell Searson were married in Stoney Creek Chapel.

Pennsylvania Dutch Salad

1	CAN GREEN BEANS (16 OUNCES)	1	JAR PIMENTOS (4 OUNCES)
1	CAN LIMA BEANS (8 1/2 OUNCES)	1/2	CUP SLICED RIPE OLIVES
1	CAN SLICED MUSHROOMS (4 OUNCES)	1/2	CUP RED ONION, CHOPPED
1	CAN SLICED CARROTS (16 OUNCES)		

Marinade:

3/4	CUP BROWN SUGAR	1/3	CUP CIDER VINEGAR
2/3	CUP SALAD OIL	1/2	TEASPOON WORCESTERSHIRE SAUCE

Combine all vegetables in a large bowl. Mix marinade in blender and pour over the vegetables. Marinate at least 24 hours. Delicious and colorful, keeps for weeks in refrigerator. Drain marinade off before serving.

Virginia Roberts—First Presbyterian Church
Medina, New York

Summer Salad

1	CAN BABY PEAS	1	SMALL JAR, PIMENTO, CHOPPED
1	CAN SHOEPEG CORN	1	CUP CELERY, CHOPPED
1	CAN FRENCH STYLE GREEN BEANS	1	MEDIUM ONION, CHOPPED

Marinade:

- 3/4 CUP VINEGAR
- 1/2 CUP OIL
- 1 TABLESPOON WATER
- 1 TEASPOON SALT
- 1 TEASPOON PEPPER
- 2/3 CUP SUGAR

Drain vegtables and mix altogether. Boil marinade. Pour over the vegetables and marinate for at least 12 hours.

Mary Runkle—Kings Grant Presbyterian Church
Virginia Beach, Virginia

Pepperoni/Garbanzo Salad

The combination of pepperoni and garbanzo beans makes this salad good with any Italian fare.

- 1 HEAD LETTUCE
- 2 TOMATOES, CUT IN WEDGES
- 1 CUP MOZZARELLA CHEESE, CUBED
- 1 CUP DRAINED GARBANZO BEANS
- 1/2 CUP THINLY SLICED PEPPERONI
- 6 SLICED GREEN ONIONS
- 1/2 CUP ITALIAN STYLE SALAD DRESSING

Tear lettuce into serving pieces, add the remaining condiments and toss with an Italian dressing of your choice. Yield: 6-8 servings.

Teri Knight—First Presbyterian Church
Beaufort, South Carolina

❖ POTATO SALADS ❖

Potato Salad

- 5 POUNDS POTATOES, PARED AND DICED
- 1 MEDIUM ONION, GRATED
- 2 GREEN PEPPERS, GRATED
- 4 HARD-BOILED EGGS, CHOPPED
- 5 STALKS CELERY, CHOPPED
- 3/4 CUP PICKLE RELISH
- 1 PINT HELLMAN'S MAYONNAISE
- SALT AND PEPPER TO TASTE

Cook potatoes in boiling water with salt until tender. Drain. Mix together onion, green pepper, eggs, celery, and relish. Add mayonnaise, salt and pepper to taste. Toss mixture with cooled potatoes. Refrigerate immediately and chill thoroughly. Yield: 4 quarts, 25-30 servings.

Joan Murden—Harmony Presbyterian Church
Crocketville, South Carolina

The Potato Salad

If you only make one potato salad this year, try this one.

1	TEASPOON SUGAR	4	CUPS COOKED, CUBED POTATOES
1	CUP MAYONNAISE	1	CUP SLICED CELERY
2	TABLESPOONS WHITE VINEGAR	1/2	CUP CHOPPED ONION
1 1/2	TEASPOONS SALT	2	HARD BOILED EGGS, CHOPPED
1/4	TEASPOON PEPPER		

Mix sugar, mayonnaise, vinegar, salt, and pepper in a large bowl. Add rest of ingredients and toss to coat well. Chill and serve.

Irene Grant—East Ridge Presbyterian Church
Chattanooga, Tennessee

Potato Salad

10	POUNDS POTATOES	SWEET PICKLE RELISH
1 1/2-2	DOZEN HARD BOILED EGGS	MIRACLE WHIP SALAD DRESSING
1	VERY LARGE ONION	

Cook the potatoes with the skins on. When the potatoes are done, peel and cut into small pieces and cool. Boil the eggs and run cool water over them as soon as they are boiled and they will peel easier. Cool. Chop the eggs and onion and mix with the cooled potatoes. Add enough salad dressing and pickle relish to make the salad the consistency that you desire. This recipe can be reduced or enlarged easily.

Sandra Stoehr—Ray Memorial Presbyterian Church
Monroe, Georgia

❖ CONGEALED VEGETABLE SALADS ❖

Beet Gelatin

1	PACKAGE LEMON GELATIN	2	TEASPOONS ONION JUICE OR GRATED ONION
1	CUP BOILING WATER	1	TABLESPOON HORSERADISH
3/4	CUP BEET JUICE	3/4	CUP CELERY, DICED
3	TABLESPOONS VINEGAR	1	CUP COOKED BEETS, DICED
1/2	TEASPOON SALT		

Dissolve gelatin in boiling water. Add beet juice, vinegar, salt, onion juice, and horseradish. Chill. When slightly thickened, fold in celery and beets. Turn into mold. Chill until firm. Remove from mold onto crisp lettuce.

Inez V. Chalmers—First Presbyterian Church
Fort Lauderdale, Florida

RED BEET JELLO SALAD

1 1/2	CUPS BOILING WATER	3/4	CUP SUGAR
2/3	CUP VINEGAR	10	WHOLE CLOVES
2	CANS SHOESTRING BEETS	1	(6 OUNCES) CHERRY JELLO

Simmer water, vinegar, sugar, and cloves for 10 minutes. Strain out cloves. Measure liquid and add to Jello. Stir until dissolved. Strain liquid from beets and save. Add enough beet liquid to make 3 1/2 cups with Jello mixture and chill. When Jello starts to congeal, add the beets. When ready to serve, you may top with sour cream, mayonnaise, or plain yogurt. The tart-and-sweet flavor combination always encourages recipe requests.

Hazel Murray—First Presbyterian Church
Beaufort, South Carolina

CORNED BEEF JELLIED SALAD

Soften:

1 ENVELOPE OF KNOX UNFLAVORED GELATIN IN 1/4 CUP COLD WATER.

Add:

1 1/2 CUPS TOMATO JUICE, HEATED

Toss:

1	TABLESPOON MINCED ONION	1	CAN CORNED BEEF, IN SMALL CUBES (EASIER TO DICE WHEN CHILLED)
1	CUP MAYONNAISE		
1	TABLESPOON LEMON JUICE	2	CUPS CELERY, FINELY CHOPPED
1	TEASPOON SALT	4	HARD-BOILED EGGS, DICED

Allow gelatin to set slightly and then stir in the mixture above. Yield: 8 servings.

Mrs. Norman S. Fitzhugh—First Presbyterian Church
Charleston, West Virginia

CREAMY CUCUMBER SALAD RING

1	PACKAGE LIME JELLO	1/4	TEASPOON SALT
3/4	CUP HOT WATER	2	TABLESPOONS LEMON JUICE
2	(3 OUNCES) PACKAGES CREAM CHEESE	2	CUCUMBERS, PEELED AND SEEDED AND FINELY CHOPPED OR GRATED, EQUAL TO 3/4 CUP
1	TEASPOON HORSERADISH		
1	CUP MAYONNAISE	1/2	CUP ONIONS, FINELY SLICED

Dissolve Jello in hot water. Add cream cheese, mayonnaise, horseradish, and salt. Beat with mixer until smooth. Add lemon juice. Chill until partially set about 30 minutes. Stir in cucumbers and onions. Pour into a 1 quart ring mold and chill until firm. Top with mayonnaise when served. Yield: 6 servings.

Mrs. Gale Oliver, Jr.—First Presbyterian Church
Cuero, Texas

CUCUMBER MOUSSE

5	MEDIUM CUCUMBERS	1/4	TEASPOON PEPPER
2 1/4	CUPS WATER		DASH OF ACCENT
2	TABLESPOONS LEMON JUICE		DASH OF TABASCO
4	GREEN ONIONS AND TOPS	1	CUP MAYONNAISE
1/2	CUP PARSLEY LEAVES, NO STEMS	3	ENVELOPES UNFLAVORED GELATIN
4	TEASPOONS WORCESTERSHIRE SAUCE	1	CUP HEAVY CREAM
1 1/2-2	TEASPOONS SALT		

Peel cucumbers, slice in half lengthwise. Slide spoon down middle to remove seeds. Cook cucumbers in 2 cups of water with lemon juice until tender, about 20 minutes. Drain well. Purée in a blender with onions and parsley. Not too long so that green specks show. Add Worcestershire, salt, pepper, Accent, Tabasco and mayonnaise. Blend. Heat gelatin in 1/4 cup of water until dissolved. Stir into cucumber mixture and chill until mixture mounds in a spoon. Whip cream, and fold into mixture. Check for seasoning. Pour into a 6 cup ring mold and chill overnight. Fill center with seafood, tomato wedges or cucumber slices which have been marinated in Italian or French dressing. Offers many potentials. Yield: 8 servings.

Mrs. Gale Oliver, Jr.—First Presbyterian Church
Cuero, Texas

Horseradish Mold

1/2 CUP BOILING WATER	5 OUNCES PREPARED HORSERADISH
1 PACKAGE LEMON JELLO	1 CUP SOUR CREAM
1 ENVELOPE, KNOX GELATIN	1 SCANT CUP MAYONNAISE
3 TABLESPOONS COLD WATER	

Dissolve Jello in boiling water. Dissolve the gelatin in cold water. Mix together. Blend the remaining ingredients and pour into a mold. Refrigerate for several hours or overnight. (Note: Keeps well in the refrigerator. This recipe doubles nicely.)

A. Arlene Hershey—Pine Street Presbyterian Church
Harrisburg, Pennsylvania

Spinach Salad

1 SMALL PACKAGE LEMON JELLO	1/2 CUP CELERY
3/4 CUP BOILING WATER	1/3 CUP CHOPPED ONION
1 TABLESPOON VINEGAR	1 CUP COTTAGE CHEESE
1 CUP MAYONNAISE	1 PACKAGE CHOPPED SPINACH

Dissolve Jello in boiling water and add vinegar. Add mayonnaise and cool. Cook spinach and drain well. Beat spinach slightly with electric beater until fluffy. Add celery, onion, and cottage cheese. Mix well. Pour into a mold and chill.

Doris W. Baker—First Presbyterian Church
Fort Lauderdale, Florida

Easy Tomato Aspic

4 CUPS OF V 8 JUICE	SPRINKLE OF ONION POWDER
2 (4 OUNCES) BOXES LEMON JELLO	

Bring 2 cups juice to boil. Add onion powder and stir in Jello to dissolve. Cool a bit and add remaining juice. Chill in molds or glass dish until firm. Serve on lettuce with garnish of olives, shrimp, pepper rings, or mayonnaise. Aspic can be chilled in a fancier mold and garnished—use asparagus spears held with lemon twist, or make a broccoli "Christmas Tree" with bits of cauliflower for ornaments.

Caroline Wright—Highland Presbyterian Church
Winston-Salem, North Carolina

MIXED VEGETABLE SALADS

Eight Layer Salad

ROMAINE AND RED LEAF LETTUCE	CANNED TINY PEAS, WELL DRAINED
CARROTS	1 SMALL JAR MAYONNAISE
CELERY	1 SMALL JAR MIRACLE WHIP
PURPLE ONIONS	2 TABLESPOONS LEMON JUICE

Chop all the vegetables and layer in a glass bowl. Mix mayonnaise and Miracle Whip with lemon juice. Spread over the entire top of vegetables to seal. (This is the secret to a crisp salad.) On top of mayonnaise mixture, sprinkle bacon bits. Sprinkle well with Parmesan cheese. Make a 1/4-1/2 inch topping of the cheese. Chill 8 hours. Yield: 10-12 servings.

Meredith Bradley—Bethesda Presbyterian Church
Camden, South Carolina

Layered Salad

2 PACKAGES FROZEN SPINACH, COOKED	1/2 POUND BACON, CRUMBLED (COOKED)
1 PACKAGE FROZEN PEAS, UNCOOKED	4-6 HARD-BOILED EGGS, CHOPPED COARSELY
THINLY SLICED RED ONION	1-2 CUPS MAYONNAISE
CHOPPED LETTUCE TO COVER	

Thaw and drain peas. Drain cooked spinach very well. Layer with other ingredients in a 13x9" pan or dish. Cover entire top with mayonnaise. Cover with plastic wrap and refrigerate for several hours. Cut into squares.

Bet Girardeau—First Presbyterian Church
Aiken, South Carolina

Taco Salad

1 1/2 POUNDS GROUND BEEF	1 BOX PASTEURIZED CHEESE SPREAD (1 POUND)
1 CUP GREEN PEPPER, CHOPPED	1 SMALL CAN TOMATOES & GREEN CHILIES
1 1/2 CUPS ONION, CHOPPED	1 HEAD OF LETTUCE
1 TABLESPOON CHILI POWDER	2 MEDIUM TOMATOES, CHOPPED
6-8 DASHES CUMIN POWDER	1 (6 OUNCE) BAG OF CORN CHIPS
SALT AND PEPPER TO TASTE	

Brown meat well in a large skillet. Drain. Add the green pepper and onion. Season to taste with salt and pepper. Brown a few more minutes. Add the chili and cumin powders. Meanwhile, melt cheese over very low heat. Stir in tomatoes and green chilies. In large bowl place ingredients in this order, lettuce torn into bite sized pieces, chopped tomatoes, crumbled corn chips, hot meat mixture and then, hot cheese mixture. Serve immediately. Yield: 8-10 servings.

Dorothy H. Hammond—Alamo Heights Presbyterian Church
San Antonio, Texas

TOSSED SALAD

1	HEAD LETTUCE	1	ONION, CHOPPED FINE
1	HEAD CAULIFLOWER, BROKEN IN BITS	1	CAN BACON BITS

Dressing:

1 1/2	OUNCES PARMESAN CHEESE	1 1/2	CUPS MIRACLE WHIP SALAD DRESSING
1/4	CUP SUGAR, GRANULATED		

Wash, thououghly dry, and tear lettuce into bites. Place all ingredients in glass or plastic container. Cover tightly and refrigerate. Mix dressing ingredients together and pour over salad just before serving.

Thelma Howe—Olney Presbyterian Church
Gastonia, North Carolina

BROCCOLI SALAD

A wonderful, healthy salad and you can see how popular it is by the number of persons submitting it. Use broccoli florets, nuts, or any onion for variety.

4	STALKS BROCCOLI, RAW AND CHOPPED	3/4-1	CUP MAYONNAISE
1	CUP SUNFLOWER SEEDS	2	TABLESPOONS VINEGAR
1/2	CUP ONION, CHOPPED OR SLICED THINLY	1/2	CUP SUGAR (OR 3 PACKS EQUAL
3/4-1	POUND BACON, COOKED CRISP AND CRUMBLED		OR 3 TABLESPOONS HONEY)
1/4-1 1/2	CUPS RAISINS		

Combine first five ingredients. Mix mayonnaise, vinegar (wine, white, or cider), and sugar dressing. After the dressing has been tossed with salad, refrigerate and allow to stand at least 2 1/2 hours or overnight before serving.

Dorothy Cronk—Chevy Chase Presbyterian Church, Washington, D.C.
Mary Danielson—First Presbyterian Church, Beaufort, South Carolina
Mary Lou Huske— Highland Presbyterian Church, Fayetteville, North Carolina
Annette Dowdle—Ray Memorial Church, Monroe, Georgia
Helen Stambaugh—Maximo Presbyterian Church, St. Petersburg, Florida

Cold Broccoli Casserole

2	BUNCHES BROCCOLI, CHOPPED FINE	2/3-3/4	CUP MAYONNAISE
1	ONION, CHOPPED FINE	1/4	CUP SUGAR OR 4-5 ENVELOPES SWEET AND LOW
2/3	CUP CHEDDAR CHEESE, GRATED	2	TABLESPOONS VINEGAR
5-6	PIECES BACON, COOKED AND CRUMBLED		SALT AND PEPPER

Mix altogether and refrigerate.

Marcia B. Love—Olney Presbyterian Church
Gastonia, North Carolina

Cornbread Salad

1	BOX JIFFY CORNBREAD MIX	2	TOMATOES, CHOPPED
1	CUP MAYONNAISE	1/2	CUP BELL PEPPER, CHOPPED
1/2	CUP PICKLE JUICE	1/2	CUP ONION, CHOPPED
1/2	CUP PICKLE RELISH/CHOPPED PICKLES	10	SLICES BACON

Cook drain, and crumble bacon. Bake cornbread. Cool, and crumble. Layer starting with cornbread, then bell pepper, onion, bacon. Make a dressing out of the mayonnaise, pickle and pickle juice. Layer over the top. Yield: 12 servings.

Luncheon Circle—Church of the Way, Presbyterian
Baton Rouge, Louisiana

Marvelous Mess

Faye notes that this recipe is the most requested of any at their church suppers.

1	TEASPOON DRY MUSTARD	1/4	CUP HORSERADISH, PREPARED CREAM STYLE
1	TEASPOON LEMON JUICE	1/4	CUP KETCHUP
1/4	TEASPOON SALT	1/4	CUP PLAIN YOGURT
1	CUP HELLMAN'S MAYONNAISE		

Put into a large glass bowl a full cup (or more) of each of the following:

FRESH CAULIFLOWER FLORETS	WATER CHESTNUTS, SLICED
PITTED RIPE OLIVES	FRESH BROCCOLI FLORETS
COOKED SHRIMP (I USE 1 POUND)	FRESH MUSHROOMS, SLICED
CHERRY TOMATOES, HALVED	

Add the blended seasonings to the vegetables and shrimp. Mix well and chill.

Faye McDonald Bain—Lillington Presbyterian Church
Lillington, North Carolina

OVERNIGHT VEGETABLE SALAD

- 1 (10 OUNCE) PACKAGE FROZEN GREEN PEAS, THAWED
- 1 CAN RED KIDNEY BEANS (15-16 OUNCES) DRAINED
- 1 CAN CUT GREEN BEANS (16 OUNCES)
- 1 (12 OUNCE) CAN WHITE KERNEL CORN, DRAINED
- 1 CUP CELERY, DICED
- 1 MEDIUM ONION, DICED
- 1/2 CUP GREEN PEPPER, DICED
- 1 JAR PIMENTOS, DRAINED AND DICED

2	TABLESPOONS SALAD OIL	3/4	CUP WHITE VINEGAR
1/2	TEASPOON PAPRIKA	2	TEASPOONS WATER
1/2	CUP SUGAR (GRANULATED)	1 1/2	TEASPOONS SALT

Combine first 8 ingredients in a 3 quart serving dish. Combine remaining ingredients and stir until sugar is dissolved. Pour over vegetables and refrigerate for 24 hours. Yield: 12 servings.

Nancy Camise—Deerfield Presbyterian Church
Deerfield Street, New Jersey

STAY CRISP SALAD

10	POUNDS CABBAGE, SHREDDED	2	LARGE ONIONS, CHOPPED
2	POUNDS CARROTS, SHREDDED	4	GREEN PEPPERS, CUT IN THIN STRIPS

Combine all vegetables and mix well. Set aside.

Dressing:

1 3/4	CUPS SALAD OIL	1	TEASPOON PEPPER
2	CUPS VINEGAR	8	TEASPOONS CELERY SEED
1/2	CUP WATER	2	TABLESPOONS SALT
3	CUPS SUGAR (GRANULATED)	3	ENVELOPES UNFLAVORED GELATIN
1	CUP WATER		

Soften gelatin in 1 cup of water. Place the 1/2 cup of water, sugar, pepper, celery seed, and salt in a saucepan and bring to a boil. Remove from heat and stir in the softened gelatin. Cool until slightly thickened; beat well with hand or electric mixer. Beat in the salad oil. Pour dressing over the vegetables and mix. May be served at once or will keep several days in the refrigerator. Yield: 100 servings.

Elvira Brodie—Stone Church Presbyterian Church
Bergen, New York

Mrs. Yoder's Spinach Salad

This recipe is submitted in memory of our beloved church cook, Mrs. Yoder.

- 1 POUND FRESH SPINACH, TORN UP
- 3 HARD-BOILED EGGS, CUT IN CHUNKS
- 8 SLICES BACON, FRIED CRISP AND CRUMBLED

Dressing:

- 1 CUP SALAD OIL
- 1/2 CUP VINEGAR
- 1/3 CUP CATSUP
- 1/2 CUP SUGAR
- 1 TEASPOON ONION SALT
- 1 TEASPOON GARLIC SALT

Combine salad ingredients. Add dressing just before serving. Yield: 10-12 servings.

Presbyterian Women (Virginia Rosemeyer, Moderator)—First Presbyterian Church
South Bend, Indiana

Sweet and Sour Spinach Salad

This recipe was given by a dear friend of Mrs. Brown's, Gwen Boyette, who visited her in St. Louis several times.

- 1 PACKAGE SPINACH
- 1 CAN BEAN SPROUTS, DRAINED
- 4 SLICES BACON, FRIED AND CRUMBLED
- 4 HARD-BOILED EGGS, CHOPPED

Dressing: Blend in electric blender.

- 1 CUP OIL
- 1/4 CUP VINEGAR
- 2/3 CUP SUGAR
- 1/3 CUP CATSUP
- 1 TEASPOON WORCESTERSHIRE SAUCE
- 1 ONION

Combine all ingredients and chill, if desired. Just before serving, dress with the blended dressing.

Catherine Brown—Westminster Presbyterian Church
St. Louis, Missouri

MARYL'S SPINACH SALAD

1	POUND FRESH SPINACH	1	CUP PECAN HALVES, TOASTED
1	CUP STRAWBERRIES, HALVED		

Dressing:

1/3	CUP CIDER VINEGAR	1	TEASPOON SALT
1/3	CUP VEGETABLE OIL	1/2	TEASPOON PEPPER
1/4	CUP SUGAR	1	SMALL ONION, CHOPPED
1	TEASPOON DIJON MUSTARD		

Blend all dressing ingredients in food processor or blender, and then stir in 2 teaspoons poppy seeds. Dress salad just before serving.

Teri Knight—First Presbyterian Church
Beaufort, South Carolina

TART CARROTS

5	CUPS SLICED, COOKED CARROTS	1	CUP SUGAR
1	SWEET ONION, SLICED	1/2	CUP SALAD OIL
1	GREEN PEPPER, CHOPPED	3/4	CUP CIDER VINEGAR
1	LARGE STALK CELERY, CHOPPED	1	TEASPOON PREPARED MUSTARD
1	CAN TOMATO BISQUE SOUP, UNDILUTED	1	TEASPOON WORCESTERSHIRE SAUCE

Bring all the liquids to a boil and simmer for 5 minutes. Pour over the vegetables and refrigerate. This will keep for several days in the refrigerator. Yield: 10 servings.

Anne Johnson—Wayside Presbyterian Church
Erie, Pennsylvania

BROCCOLI SALAD, EASY TO CARRY

Julie is tha daughter of Frances and Sam Huhn, First Presbyterian Church, Beaufort, South Carolina. She states that every Sunday, her church in Zimbabwe offers prayers for the USA to once again allow school prayer daily.

1	HEAD OF CAULIFLOWER, BROKEN OR CUT INTO BITE-SIZED PIECES
1	BUNCH OF BROCCOLI, FLORETS ONLY, BITE-SIZE
	GREEN ONIONS TO TASTE, CUT IN 1/2" LENGTHS

Plenty of homemade or good quality mayonnaise to mix generously. Season to personal taste. Green or ripe olives may be added for additional enhancement, but aren't necessary. Keep well-refrigerated. Easy to carry.

Julie Huhn Niehau—Christ Church Borrowdale
Harare, Zimbabwe

Chapter Twelve

Sauces—Fruit Dishes—Pickles

SAUCES

Basic White Sauces

WHITE SAUCE	LIQUID	THICKENING	DRIPPINGS/FAT	SALT
#1 THIN	1 CUP MILK	1 TABLESPOON FLOUR	1 TABLESPOON	1/2 TEASPOON
#2 MEDIUM	1 CUP MILK	2 TABLESPOONS FLOUR	1 1/2 TABLESPOON	1/2 TEASPOON
#3	1 CUP MILK	3 TABLESPOONS FLOUR	1 TABLESPOON	1 TEASPOON
#4 THICK	1 CUP MILK	4 TABLESPOONS FLOUR	2 1/2 TABLESPOON	1 TEASPOON

Use #1 sauce for cream soups.
Use #2 sauce for creamed/scalloped dishes or gravy.
Use #3 sauce for soufflés.
Use #4 sauce for croquettes.
Add 1 cup grated cheese for cheese sauce.

Mederia Rivers Stanley—Harmony Presbyterian Church
Crocketville, South Carolina

Cheddar Curry Sauce

1/2	POUND CHEDDAR CHEESE, CUBED		1	TEASPOON CURRY POWDER
1	MEDIUM ONION		1	PINT MILK (2 CUPS)
1/4	STICK MARGARINE		1/4	CUP SULTANAS (GOLDEN RAISINS)
1/4	CUP FLOUR		1	TABLESPOON FRUIT PICKLES

Chop onion, fry in margarine until soft. Add flour and curry powder, cook for 1 minute. Gradually, add milk stirring until mixture thickens, then add sultanas and pickle. Stir well. Add the cubed cheese, stir and cook for 2 minutes. Serve immediately. Can be served with brown rice.

Esther Goater—Letchworth Free Church
Letchworth, England

Harold Gooding's Clemson Sauce for Barbecuing Chicken

For 5 chickens (10 halves):

1/2	CUP VINEGAR	1	TEASPOON TABASCO SAUCE
1/2	CUP WATER	1/2	TEASPOON PEPPER
1	CUP CATSUP	1	FINELY CHOPPED MEDIUM ONION, OPTIONAL
1/4	POUND BUTTER OR OLEO	2	TABLESPOONS SALT
1	TABLESPOON SUGAR	1	TABLESPOON WORCESTERSHIRE SAUCE

Bring sauce to a boil and let stand overnight to blend flavors. Keep sauce warm while basting chickens.

Marion Vaughan—Hampton Presbyterian Church
Hampton, South Carolina

Dressing for Baked Potatoes

2	CUPS MAYONNAISE	DASH OF CHIVES
1 1/2	CUPS BUTTERMILK	DASH OF GARLIC

Mix together well and refrigerate until ready for use. Yield: Enough for 6-8 potatoes.

Edmee Boyd—Hampton Presbyterian Church
Hampton, South Carolina

Kentucky Sauce (Bowl Lickin' Good)

1	CUP GRANULATED SUGAR	1	ORANGE (USE RIND)
1	CUP BROWN SUGAR	1	LEMON (USE RIND)
1	CUP WATER	1	CUP BOURBON WISKEY
1	CUP STRAWBERRY PRESERVES	1	CUP BROKEN PECANS

Mix sugar and water and cook until it almost spins a thread. Cool. Cut orange and lemon into sections and remove seeds. Grind or mince in food processor. Mix this with the sugar water mixture. Add good quality, strawberry preserves and broken pecans (or walnuts). Add 1 "running over" cup of bourbon whiskey. Mix well and refrigerate. May add additional nuts as long as sauce lasts. It will keep for weeks. Serve over ice cream, pound cake, sponge cake or whatever!

Tillie Edwards—Peachtree Presbyterian Church
Atlanta, Georgia

Mother Mather's Fudge Sauce

1 1/2 CUPS SUGAR	BUTTER THE SIZE OF AN EGG (ABOUT 1/2 CUP)
2 SQUARES MELTED BAKING CHOCOLATE	1/2 CUP MILK

Melt butter in chocolate. Add sugar and milk alternately. Boil for 3 minutes, stirring constantly.

Amy Mather—Pittsgrove Presbyterian Church
Daretown, New Jersey

FRUIT DISHES

Apple Chutney

3 POUNDS COOKING APPLES	1 TEASPOON GROUND GINGER
1/2 POUND ONIONS	1 TEASPOON SALT
3/4 CUP SULTANAS (GOLDEN RAISINS)	1 ROUNDED TABLESPOON CORNSTARCH
1 POUND BROWN SUGAR	2 1/2 CUPS VINEGAR
1 TABLESPOON CURRY POWDER	

Peel, core and slice apples and onions. Add the other ingredients except cornstarch. Bring to a boil and simmer until tender. Mix cornstarch with a little extra vinegar and add to contents of pan. Cook until thickened. Place in warm jars while hot.

Neil Robertson—Letchworth Free Church
Letchworth, England

Cranberry Stewed Apples

"This is how it came to me (not how I adapted it). You can serve half a batch as a meat accompaniment at one meal, then stir an additional tablespoon or 2 of sugar into remainder and serve another day as a dessert with cream cheese and crackers."

6 MEDIUM APPLES	1/4 TEASPOON SALT
2 CUPS FRESH CRANBERRIES	1/2 TEASPOON GROUND CINNAMON
1 CUP GRANULATED SUGAR	1/4 TEASPOON GROUND GINGER
1/2 CUP WATER	1/2 TEASPOON GROUND CLOVES

Select apples that hold shape when cooked. Peel, quarter, and remove cores. Place in saucepan with cranberries, sugar, water, and salt. Add spices, (optional). Serve with poultry, ham, pork, or veal. For a dessert, add 1/4 cup sugar and serve with cream cheese and crackers.

Dallas Beauchamp—Westminster Presbyterian Church
St. Louis, Missouri

BAKED CURRIED FRUIT

- 16 OUNCE CAN PEACH SLICES
- 16 OUNCE CAN PEAR HALVES, SLICED
- 16 OUNCE CAN APRICOT HALVES
- 20 OUNCE CAN PINEAPPLE CHUNKS
- 11 OUNCE CAN MANDARIN ORANGES
- 1 CUP BROWN SUGAR
- 2 TABLESPOONS CURRY POWDER

Drain first 5 ingredients and place in a casserole dish. Mix brown sugar and curry powder and pour over fruit. Dot well with butter. Bake in a 350 degree oven for 45 minutes. Yield: Serves large crowd.

Mary Kleinecke—First Presbyterian Church
Cuero, Texas

BRANDIED PEACHES

- 1 LARGE CAN PEACH HALVES (24 OUNCE)
- 1 BOX OF MINCEMEAT (12 OUNCE)
- 4 TABLESPOONS BRANDY

Drain peaches, saving 3/4 cup juice. Crumble mincemeat and add the juice. Boil for 3-4 minutes. Spoon mixture over peaches. Bake for about 15 minutes in 350 degree oven.

Libby Neale—First Presbyterian Church
Homestead, Florida

FRUIT CUP

- 1 (44 OUNCE) CAN PEACHES IN LIGHT SYRUP, DRAINED AND CHOPPED
- 36 OUNCE CAN PINEAPPLE TIDBITS IN OWN JUICE, UNDRAINED
- 9 CUPS SLICED STRAWBERRIES OR GRAPES OR 4 1/2 CUPS EACH (IF WHOLE BERRIES USED, SLICE)
- 7 CUPS SLICED BANANA, APPLE OR PEARS
- 1 TABLESPOON INSTANT LEMONADE POWDER OR POWDERED ORANGE BREAKFAST DRINK
- 4 PACKAGES (9 OUNCE) INSTANT VANILLA PUDDING

Stir all ingredients together and chill. When using bananas, wait until ready to serve, then slice and stir in at last moment. You may experiment with different fruit and pudding combinations to find your favorite.

Patricia Webster—First Presbyterian Church
Spartanburg, South Carolina

Hot Sherried Fruit

1	LARGE CAN PINEAPPLE CHUNKS	1/4	POUND OF BUTTER
1	LARGE CAN APRICOTS	1/2	CUP SUGAR
1	MEDIUM CAN PEARS	2	TABLESPOONS FLOUR
1	MEDIUM CAN PEACHES	1	CUP SHERRY
1	MEDIUM JAR SPICED APPLE RINGS		

Drain fruit well. Place fruit in casserole dish with red apple rings on top. In a double boiler, place butter, sugar, flour, and sherry. Cook until thick sauce. Pour sauce over fruit in casserole. Bake in a 350 degree oven for 40 minutes. May be prepared ahead and refrigerated until ready to cook. Yield: 12 servings.

St. John's Presbyterian Church, Reno, Nevada

Pineapple Au Gratin

2	CANS PINEAPPLE CHUNKS, DRAINED	6	TABLESPOONS FLOUR
2	CUPS SHARP, GRATED CHEESE		SALTINE CRACKER CRUMBS
2/3	CUPS SUGAR	1	STICK MARGARINE

Melt margarine and mix with enough cracker crumbs to cover top. Combine pineapple and cheese. Mix flour and sugar. Stir together. Place in casserole, cover with cracker crumbs, and bake in a 350 degree oven for 30-40 minutes, until slightly brown. Yield: 8-10 servings.

Julie LaGrone—First Presbyterian Church
Beaufort, South Carolina

Pineapple Bread Pudding

1/2	CUP BUTTER OR MARGARINE	1	CAN CRUSHED PINEAPPLE (20 OUNCES)
1	CUP SUGAR	6	SLICES WHITE BREAD, CUBED
4	EGGS		

Cream butter and sugar. Beat in the eggs, one at a time. Add the pineapple. Fold in bread cubes. Put into a greased 1 1/2 quart casserole. Bake uncovered in 350 degree oven for 1 hour. Very good served warm with ham. If crusts are removed from bread, add 2 more slices. Yield: 10 servings. (Recipe may be doubled to serve 20.)

Fairfax Presbyterian Church, Fairfax, Virginia

Pineapple Casserole

1	CAN PINEAPPLE CHUNKS (20 OUNCES)	1	CUP SHREDDED CHEDDAR CHEESE
1/3	CUP SUGAR	3/4	STICK OF BUTTER, MELTED
3	TABLESPOONS FLOUR	1	CUP CRACKER CRUMBS

Drain pineapple, reserving 3 tablespoons juice. Combine sugar, flour and juice. Add cheese and pineapple chunks. Spoon into buttered 1 1/2 quart casserole. Combine butter and cracker crumbs. Sprinkle over pineapple. Bake uncovered in 350 degree oven for 20-30 minutes or until lightly browned.

Marty Neale—First Presbyterian Church
Homestead, Florida

PICKLES

Fresh Kosher Dill Pickles

5	MEDIUM CUCUMBERS	1/2	CUP VINEGAR
1	CLOVE GARLIC	1	TABLESPOON ROCK SALT
1	ONION, SLICED	1/4	TEASPOON TUMERIC
1	HEAD OF FRESH DILL		

Wash cucumbers and quarter. Place into clean quart jar, layering with dill and onion. Add salt, vinegar, and tumeric. Fill to top with water. Place garlic into jar. Cover tightly and refrigerate for 2-3 days. Makes 1 quart and will keep for about 2 weeks under refrigeration.

Faye McGowan—First Presbyterian Church
Beaufort, South Carolina

Frozen, Sliced, Sweet Dill Pickles

1	POUND (3 INCH) CUCUMBERS, SLICED	3/4	CUP SUGAR
3/4	POUND YELLOW ONIONS, SLICED THIN	2	TABLESPOONS WATER
	(2 CUPS PACKED)	1/2	CUP CIDER VINEGAR
4	TEASPOONS SALT	1	TEASPOON DRIED DILLWEED

Mix cucumbers, onions, salt, and water. Allow to stand about 2 hours. Drain but do not rinse. Add sugar, vinegar, and dill. Allow to stand until sugar has dissolved. Stir occasionally so that liquid covers the vegetables. Pack into freezer containers. Seal tightly and freeze. Defrost before serving.

Esther Rusmisel—Highland Presbyterian Church
Fayetteville, North Carolina

Frozen Pickles

7	CUPS CUCUMBERS, SLICED	2	TABLESPOONS CELERY SEED
1	CUP ONION, CHOPPED	1	TABLESPOON SALT
1	CUP GREEN PEPPER, CHOPPED	1	CUP WHITE VINEGAR
1 1/2	CUPS SUGAR, GRANULATED		

Mix all ingredients together and allow to set overnight. Pack into freezer containers, dividing liquid equally. Freeze. To serve, allow to thaw overnight in the refrigerator.

Julia O. Ramsey—Highland Presbyterian Church
Fayetteville, North Carolina

Crispy Hot Pickles

Everyone loves these!

1	GALLON SOUR PICKLES, SLICED THIN	6	CLOVES OF GARLIC, CHOPPED
5	POUND SUGAR	1	BOTTLE TABASCO SAUCE

Drain pickles, slice thin. Repack jar with alternating layers of pickles, sugar and garlic until all used. Pour Tabasco over all. Allow to sit for 5-6 days, turning the jar upside down then turning it up right daily. Refrigerate before serving.

First Presbyterian Church, Cuero, Texas

Mama's Peach Pickles

7	POUNDS CLING PEACHES, PEELED	4 OR 5	STICKS OF CINNAMON
3 1/2	POUNDS GRANULATED SUGAR		CLOVES
1	PINT VINEGAR		

(Use only early Cling peaches-not quite ripe: Beware of split pits.)

Stick 2 whole cloves into each peach. Make a syrup of sugar, vinegar, cinnamon and cook for 20 minutes. Add a few peaches at a time. Cook until tender. Place peaches into hot, sterile jars. After all peaches are cooked, boil the syrup down, about 20 or more minutes. Pour over the peaches to cover. Seal. Don't use for at least 1 month. Do not double recipe or the syrup will be too thin!

Grace B. Coggeshall, "Mama" of Helen C. Harvey—First Presbyterian Church
Beaufort, South Carolina

Uncooked Pickles

7	POUNDS RIPE TOMATOES	2	OUNCES MUSTARD SEED
7	MEDIUM-SIZE ONIONS	2 1/2	POUNDS SUGAR
	FEW STALKS CELERY	2	CUPS VINEGAR
2	GREEN PEPPERS		

Chop tomatoes, onions, celery, green peppers. Add mustard seed and place in a large bowl for 24 hours. Place in muslin bag and strain for 24 hours. Discard drippings. In a saucepan, dissolve the sugar in heated vinegar. Cool. Combine strained ingredients with cooled sugar/vinegar mixture. Place into jars, seal and store. Will keep for twelve months.

Hamish and Christine Cameron—Portmoak Church
Milnathort, Scotland

Zucchini Relish

6-7	LARGE ZUCCHINI, SHREDDED TO MAKE 12 CUPS	2	TABLESPOONS SALT
		4	ONIONS, CHOPPED FINE

Mix together and allow to stand overnight. Rinse in cold water and drain. In a large kettle combine:

2 1/2	CUPS VINEGAR	3/4	TEASPOON CORNSTARCH
4	CUPS SUGAR (GRANULATED)	3/4	TEASPOON TUMERIC
1	TABLESPOON DRY MUSTARD	1/2	TEASPOON BLACK PEPPER
3/4	TEASPOON NUTMEG		

Cook until mixture begins to thicken. Add zucchini mixture and cook slowly for 30 minutes. Pack into jars and seal. Yield: 5 pints. Good on hamburgers, hot dogs, greens or your choice.

Imogene Holmes—Lillington Presbyterian Church
Lillington, North Carolina

Chapter Thirteen

Soups — Stews

SOUPS

BEAN SOUP I

6	(15 OUNCE) CANS WHITE BEANS	3	TABLESPOONS BACON DRIPPINGS
3	ONIONS, CHOPPED	1	QUART TOMATO JUICE
1 1/2	CUPS DICED HAM	1 1/2	CUPS SPAGHETTI, BROKEN
6	MEDIUM POTATOES, PEELED AND DICED		SALT AND PEPPER TO TASTE

Cook potatoes, onions, ham (or large ham bone), and bacon drippings in lightly salted water to cover until potatoes are thoroughly cooked. Do Not Drain. Cook spaghetti until tender. Drain and rinse in cold water. Place beans into a large kettle. Add tomato juice, potato mixture, including water. Season to taste. Cook for 10 minutes and when soup comes to a boil, add spaghetti. If soup is sour, add a small amount of sugar. Yield: 2 gallons.

The Glock Family, submitted by Deneice Hall—Fallston Presbyterian Church
Fallston, Maryland

BEAN SOUP II

5	CUPS HAM STOCK, NOT TOO SALTY	1	ONION CHOPPED
1/2	CUP RED LENTILS	1/2	LEEK, SLICED OR 1/2 MILD ONION
1	MEDIUM POTATO, CUT INTO CUBES		

Bring to a boil and simmer for 30 minutes. Serve with a sprig of parsley. Yield: 2 servings.

Isle of Cumbrae Parish Church, Isle of Cumbrae, Scotland

Cold Weather Bean Soup

1/2	CUP ONION, FINELY CHOPPED	1/2	TEASPOON DRIED BASIL
2	CLOVES GARLIC, MINCED	1/2	TEASPOON CELERY FLAKES
1	TABLESPOON OLIVE OIL	1/2	TEASPOON DRIED OREGANO
1	MEDIUM TOMATO, FINELY CHOPPED	3	CANS GREAT NORTHERN BEANS (16 OUNCES EACH) RINSED AND DRAINED
2	(14 1/2 OUNCE) CANS CHICKEN BROTH		
	GRATED PARMESAN CHEESE	1	CUP ELBOW MACARONI, UNCOOKED
1 3/4	CUPS WATER	1/4	TEASPOON PEPPER

Cook onion and garlic in oil in a dutch oven over medium high heat, until tender. Stir constantly. Add tomato and simmer 5 minutes. Add chicken broth, water, basil, oregano, and celery flakes. Bring to a boil. Reduce heat and simmer for 5 minutes, uncovered. Add beans, macaroni, and pepper; return to boil. Cover and reduce heat, simmer for 15 minutes or until macaroni is tender. Stir once. Spoon into bowls and sprinkle with Parmesan cheese. Freezes well. Yield: 8 cups.

Irene Grant—East Ridge Presbyterian Church
Chattanooga, Tennessee

Mission Bean Soup for 100

Use a total of 6 pounds of dried beans and peas in approximately the following weights:

1	POUND LIMA BEANS	6	CUPS CHOPPED ONION
1	POUND PINTO BEANS	6	20 OUNCE CANS TOMATOES
1	POUND BLACK BEANS		GARLIC
1	POUND KIDNEY BEANS		SALT AND PEPPER TO TASTE
1	POUND NAVY BEANS	2	TABLESPOONS CHILI POWDER
1	POUND TOTAL OF THE FOLLOWING:		JUICE OF 3 LEMONS
	LENTILS		
	SPLIT PEAS		
	HULLED BARLEY		
	BLACK EYED PEAS		

Wash beans thoroughly and place in large kettles. Cover with water and soak overnight. Drain. Add 20 quarts of water, ham and ham hocks (6 ham hocks and scraps—more is better). Bring to a boil and simmer 3 hours or more. Add onion and tomatoes, chili powder, lemon juice, garlic, salt, and pepper. Simmer another hour, add water if needed to thin. Yield: 6-7 gallons.

Dorothy Pray Wilson—National Presbyterian Church
Washington, D.C.

SAVORY BEAN SOUP

1	SMALL ONION, CHOPPED	2	TEASPOONS CHILI POWDER
1	CELERY STALK, CHOPPED	3	(15 1/4-19 OUNCE) CANS WHITE BEANS
2	OUNCES COOKED SMOKED HAM OR TURKEY, CHOPPED	1	TABLESPOON OLIVE OIL
		1	CHICKEN FLAVORED BOUILLON ENVELOPE

Heat oil in a 3 quart saucepan or Dutch oven, and add onion, celery, ham or turkey, and chili powder. Cover and cook at a high temperature setting for 6-10 minutes. Stir once. Add the beans and their liquids, bouillon and 1 cup water. Cook covered at medium to high setting for 10-15 minutes. Stirring occasionally. Yield: 8 cups.

Irene Grant—East Ridge Presbyterian Church
Chattanooga, Tennessee

BROCCOLI-CORN CHOWDER

1	CAN CREAM OF BROCCOLI SOUP	2	TABLESPOONS ONION FLAKES
1/2	CUP HALF-AND-HALF	1/4	TEASPOON CELERY SEEDS
1	CAN (16 OUNCE) CORN	1/4	TEASPOON PEPPER

Blend undiluted soup with half-and-half in a saucepan. Stir in corn, undrained and remaining ingredients. Bring to a boil, then simmer, stirring until heated thoroughly. Yield: 4 servings.

Irene Grant—East Ridge Presbyterian Church
Chattanooga, Tennessee

CREAM OF BROCCOLI SOUP

5-7	POUNDS PICNIC SHOULDER (MAY USE BAKED HAM IF DESIRED)	1	GALLON HOMOGENIZED MILK
5	PACKAGES FRESH BROCCOLI	1	LARGE JAR, COFFEE MATE
6	BUNCHES GREEN ONIONS, CHOPPED		SALT AND PEPPER
1	BUNCH, CELERY		WORCESTERSHIRE SAUCE (5 SHAKES)
10	CANS, CREAM OF ASPARAGUS SOUP		CHEDDAR SHARP CHEESE, GRATED

Remove skin and fat from ham. Cut in chunks and boil in water for 1 hour. Chop broccoli, trim celery, and discard heavy white parts and stringy areas. Chop celery. Sauté broccoli, onion, and celery in butter until tender. Put all ingredients in large pot and simmer until well-blended; at least 1 hour. When serving, sprinkle cheese on top of each cup of hot soup. Can also be served cold. Yield: 45-50 servings.

Clel Shore—Bryson City Presbyterian Church
Bryson City, North Carolina

Cream of Broccoli Soup II

1	WHOLE HEAD OF BROCCOLI	6	CUPS OF MILK
1/2	CUP ONION, CHOPPED	4	CHICKEN BOUILLON CUBES
1/2	CUP BUTTER, MELTED	1	TEASPOON WHITE PEPPER
1/2	CUP FLOUR		

Cook broccoli and chop. Sauté onion in butter in Dutch oven, about 10 minutes. Mix in flour and stir until smooth, then gradually add milk. Add the bouillon cubes and cook until mixture thickens. Add broccoli and pepper. Simmer about 20 minutes. Freezes well. Yield: 10 servings.

Marjorie M. Hiers—Harmony Presbyterian Church
Crocketville, South Carolina

Ann's Cauliflower Soup

1	HEAD OF CAULIFLOWER, SEPARATED	1/2	CUP FLOUR
1/2	CUP MARGARINE	3	CANS CHICKEN BROTH
1	LARGE ONION, CHOPPED	2	CUPS HALF-AND-HALF (OR SKIM MILK)
2	CLOVES GARLIC, CHOPPED		SALT AND PEPPER TO TASTE

Sauté onion and garlic in margarine. Add the flour and stir until almost smooth. Gradually stir in broth. Add the cauliflower. Simmer for 50 minutes. Put into a blender or food processor in half amounts for a few seconds or until well blended. Return to the pot and add the milk, salt, and white pepper. Heat until well warmed.

Bonnie Mahaffery—First Presbyterian Church
Baton Rouge, Louisiana

Cheesy Chicken Vegetable Soup

6	CUPS CHICKEN BROTH	1	(20 OUNCE) PACKAGE FROZEN BROCCOLI
2 1/2	CUPS POTATOES, DICED	1	(20 OUNCE) PACKAGE FROZEN CAULIFLOWER
1	CUP ONIONS, DICED	1	POUND VELVEETA CHEESE, CUBED
1	CUP CELERY, DICED	2	CANS CREAM OF CHICKEN SOUP
1	CUP CARROTS, DICED		

Cut broccoli and cauliflower into samll pieces and place with potatoes, onions, celery, and carrots in a large pot. Add chicken broth. Bring to a boil. Cook for 5 minutes or until vegetables are done. Add cheese and cream of chicken soup. Add the desired amount of diced chicken or turkey (at least 2-3 cups). Heat thoroughly. This reheats well. Yield: 4 quarts.

Ruth A. Wiley—The National Presbyterian Church
Washington, D.C.

Corn Chowder

This recipe is a popular feature of our Autumn Bazaar and luncheon each October and is our big fund raiser for our projects.

1	POUND LEAN BACON	1/2	POUND BUTTER
1	LARGE ONION, CHOPPED	1/4	TEASPOON SAGE (OPTIONAL)
4	PACKAGES FROZEN CORN	1/2	TEASPOON GROUND PEPPER
3	QUARTS, CUBED COOKED POTATOES	1	TEASPOON PAPRIKA (OPTIONAL)
3 1/2	QUARTS MILK		

Brown bacon, and drain, reserving drippings. Sauté onion gently. Thaw, cook, and drain corn. In a large pot; place corn and potatoes. Add onions and remaining bacon drippings. Mix in milk and butter. Add any seasonings. Heat until just under boiling point. Top with crumbled bacon. Yield: 20-25 servings.

First Presbyterian Church, Wyoming, New York

New England Clam Chowder

This soup is very popular at our Lenten Lunches.

1	CAN CHOPPED CLAMS (51 OUNCES)	1 1/2	QUARTS DAIRY HALF-AND-HALF
1 1/2	CUPS ONION, FINELY CHOPPED	1/2	CUP INSTANT POTATO FLAKES
1 1/2	CUPS CELERY, FINELY DICED	1/4	CUP RED WINE VINEGAR
3	CUPS POTATOES, DICED		SALT AND WHITE PEPPER TO TASTE
1 1/2	STICKS BUTTER OR MARGARINE		CHOPPED CHIVES
1/2	CUP FLOUR		OYSTER CRACKERS

Drain juice from clams and reserve. Check clams for shell fragments. In a 6 quart sauce pan add clam juice, onions, celery, potatoes. Should juice not cover vegetables, add enough water to cover. Simmer covered until tender but still firm. To prepare roux: melt butter and add flour, blending with a wire whisk. Cook at low heat, stirring for 2-3 minutes. Heat half-and-half and add the potato flakes. Stir until blended. Combine melted butter with potato, and milk mixture. Cook gently until thickened. Stir often. Add the roux to undrained vegetables. Add clams. Heat through. Do not boil (clams will toughen). Season with salt, pepper, and wine vinegar. Garnish with chives and oyster crackers. Yield: 4 quarts.

Mary Lou Francisco—First Presbyterian Church
Medina, New York

San Francisco Crab Soup

2	CUPS COOKED CRAB MEAT	1/2	CUP UNCOOKED RICE
1/4	CUP BUTTER	3	RIPE TOMATOES, PEELED AND DICED
1	MEDIUM ONION, FINELY CHOPPED	1	TEASPOON WORCESTERSHIRE SAUCE
1	GREEN PEPPER, FINELY CHOPPED		SALT AND PEPPER TO TASTE
2	QUARTS CLAM JUICE		

Melt butter in 3 quart saucepan. Add vegetables and simmer until tender. Add clam juice and rice. Bring to a boil. Simmer covered for 20 minutes. Add tomatoes, Worcestershire sauce, and crab meat. Bring back to a boil then simmer for 20 minutes.

Mayestelle Phelan—Faith Presbyterian Church
Harrisburg, Pennsylvania

Fish Soup

1/4	CUP MARGARINE	2	CUPS TOMATO JUICE
2	CUPS ONION, CHOPPED	1	CUP TOMATOES, CHOPPED
1	CUP GREEN PEPPER, CHOPPED	2	TEASPOONS THYME
1/2	CUP CELERY, CHOPPED	1/2	CUP CHOPPED PARSLEY
4	CLOVES GARLIC, MINCED	1	TEASPOON BASIL
2	POUNDS WHITE FISH FILLETS	2	BAY LEAVES
10	CUPS CHICKEN BROTH	1	TEASPOON SALT, PEPPER TO TASTE

Combine all ingredients except fish. Simmer for 30 minutes. Add fish and cook 15 minutes more. If desired, add frozen shrimp or other shellfish.

Diane McCunn—Valley Community Presbyterian Church
Golden Valley, Minnesota

La Souppa

This was a favorite of early Waldensian settlers to Valdese and was the basis for a simple Waldensian meal, served with a glass of wine and cheese.

1	PACKAGE OF BREAD STICKS (OR 1 LOAF FRENCH BREAD, TOASTED)		GRATED CHEESE
		2-4	TABLESPOONS BUTTER
1-2	QUARTS, CHICKEN BROTH, SEASONED		DASH OF CINNAMON (OPTIONAL)

Break bread sticks or bread in moderately shallow baking dish. Saturate with the broth. Sprinkle with cheese and cinnamon. Dot with butter. Bake in moderately hot oven until brown. Serve while hot.

Waldensian Cookbook—Waldensian Presbyterian Church
Valdese, North Carolina

London Particular

This soup is so-called after the dense London fogs of the last century, known as "pea-soupers." One such fog was referred to by a character in Charles Dickens' Bleak House as 'a London Particular.'

1	POUND GREEN SPLIT PEAS, SOAKED		FRESHLY GROUND BLACK PEPPER
4	SLICES OF BACON, DICED	2	TEASPOONS WORCESTERSHIRE SAUCE
1	LARGE ONION, SLICED	3	TABLESPOONS LIGHT CREAM
4	PINTS WATER OR HAM STOCK (NOT TOO SALTY)		

Soak the split peas in cold water and cover overnight. Cook the bacon in a large saucepan until the fat runs out, then just soften the onion in the fat. Add the peas, the soaking liquid and the water of ham stock. Cover and bring to a boil. Lower heat and simmer about 2 hours. Stir from time to time to prevent sticking. Stir well and adjust the seasoning. Add the Worcestershire sauce. Before serving, stir in the cream. Serve garnished with small croutons. Yield: 6-8 servings.

Mrs. A. G. Fox—Letchworth Free Church
Letchworth, Scotland

Minestrone Soup I

1/2	CUP SALAD OIL	1	CUP CABBAGE, CHOPPED
1	CLOVE GARLIC, MINCED	2	CARROTS, SLICED THIN
2	CUPS ONION, CHOPPED	2	TEASPOONS SALT
1	CUP CELERY, CHOPPED		DASH SAGE
4	TEASPOONS PARSLEY, CHOPPED	1/4	TEASPOON PEPPER
1	CAN TOMATO PASTE	1	CAN KIDNEY BEANS (16 OUNCES)
1	CAN (10 1/2 OUNCES) BEEF BOUILLON	1	CUP GREEN BEANS OR PEAS
9	CUPS WATER	1	CUP ELBOW MACARONI

Heat oil in large pot. Add garlic, onions, celery, and parsley. Cook until soft. Stir in tomato paste, undiluted bouillon, water, cabbage, carrots, salt, sage, and pepper. Mix well. Bring to a boil. Lower heat. Cover and simmer slowly for 1 hour. Add remaining ingredients. Cook 10-15 minutes more or until macaroni is tender. Do not overcook macaroni. Yield: 18 servings.

Laverne Ginn—Dahlonega Presbyterian Church
Dahlonega, Georgia

Minestrone Soup II

1/2	CUP ONION, COARSELY CHOPPED	1	TEASPOON BASIL
1	TABLESPOON OLIVE OIL	1	TEASPOON OREGANO
2	POTATOES, DICED	1/2-1	TEASPOON SALT
4	CARROTS, SLICED	1	CAN KIDNEY BEANS (15 OUNCES)
2	CELERY STALKS, SLICED	1	CAN TOMATOES (16 OUNCES)
1/4	CUP LONG-GRAIN RICE		

In saucepan, sauté onion in olive oil until tender. Mix in potatoes, carrots, and celery. Add water to cover. Add rice, basil, oregano, salt, kidney beans, and tomatoes. Bring to a boil. Reduce heat, cover and simmer until rice is cooked and vegetables are tender, about 25-30 minutes. Yield: 8-1 cup servings.

Jean Waldron—Providence Presbyterian Church
Fairfax, Virginia

Cream of Peanut Soup

2	STALKS, CELERY, CHOPPED FINE	2	QUARTS CHICKEN STOCK (MAY USE BOUILLON)
1/2	ONION, CHOPPED FINE	8	OUNCES CREAMY PEANUT BUTTER
1/2	STICK BUTTER OR MARGARINE	2	CUPS HALF-AND-HALF
1	TABLESPOON FLOUR		

Sauté celery and onion in butter and cook until soft. Add flour and cook until well-blended. Add stock. Bring to a boil. Stir in peanut butter, until well-blended. Add half-and-half just until warm and serve. Yield: 6 servings.

Charlotte Vedeler—The Old Presbyterian Meeting House
Alexandria, Virginia

PICCADILLO

(A favorite of Everett's.)

2	MEDIUM ONION, DICED	4	FULL TABLESPOONS OLIVE OIL
2	LARGE GREEN PEPPERS, DICED	2	FULL TABLESPOONS WORCESTERSHIRE SAUCE
	MEDIUM JAR STUFFED OLIVES, DRAINED	1/2	TEASPOON ACCENT
	RESERVE 1/2 OF OLIVE JUICE	1/4	TEASPOON OREGANO
	SMALL JAR OF CAPERS	1/2	TEASPOON GARLIC POWDER
1/2	PACKAGE SEEDLESS RAISINS	1/4	TEASPOON PAPRIKA
1 1/2	POUNDS GROUND BEEF	1/4	TEASPOON FRESHLY GROUND PEPPER
	LARGE CAN, HUNTS TOMATO SAUCE	1/2	TEASPOON CELERY SALT

Saute' onions and peppers in 2 tablespoons olive oil. Set aside. Saute' meat in 2 remaining tablespoons olive oil, stir in seasonings. Add Worcestershire and tomato sauces. Stir well. Add rest of ingredients and cook for about 40 minutes over slow heat, covered. Serve over yellow rice with black beans as a side dish. Yield: 8 servings.

Catherine Brown—Westminster Presbyterian Church
St. Louis, Missouri

BAKED POTATO SOUP

3	LARGE BAKING POTATOES, BAKED	2	TABLESPOONS OLIVE OIL
1/2	CUP CELERY, DICED	1	PINT WATER
3/4	CUP CARROTS, DICED	2	TEASPOONS CHICKEN SEASONED STOCK BASE
3/4	CUP ONIONS, DICED	2 2/3	CUPS WHIPPING CREAM OR MILK
1/3	CUP GREEN ONION, DICED	12	OUNCES SWISS CHEESE, GRATED
1	TEASPOON PEPPER,	1/2	CUP FLOUR
1	MINCED GARLIC	1 1/2	OUNCE BUTTER
1	TEASPOON SEASONED SALT	4	SLICES BACON, COOKED AND CRUMBLED

Peel potatoes. Cut into 1/2 inch chunks; set aside. If desired, add some peel. In large bowl, mix celery, carrots, onion, green onions, pepper, salt and garlic. Set aside. In a Dutch oven, heat the olive oil and add the cooked bacon and vegetable mixture. Saute' until tender. Add the potato chunks and cook a bit longer. Add water, chicken base, cream or milk. Stir constantly for 5 minutes. Fold in the cheese and allow to melt and blend. Heat butter over low heat and whisk in the flour. Add to soup and stir until thoroughly blended. Reduce heat and simmer for 30 minutes, stirring occasionally. If desired, garnish with more green onions, bacon, and cheese. Yield: 2 quarts.

Dorothy Calkins—Memorial Drive Presbyterian Church
Houston, Texas

Red Riding Hood Soup

1	POUND GROUND BEEF	1	PACKAGE DRY ONION SOUP MIX
2	CANS TOMATO SAUCE (8 OUNCES EACH)	4	BEEF BOUILLON CUBES
2	CANS STEWED TOMATOES (1 POUND, EACH)	3	TABLESPOONS SUGAR
2	PACKAGES BROWN GRAVY MIX	2	PACKAGES FROZEN MIXED VEGETABLES
4	CUPS WATER	1/2	CUP PEARL BARLEY

Brown meat and drain. Add tomato sauce, stewed tomatoes and brown gravy mix. Stir. Add water, dry onion soup mix, beef bouillon, sugar, vegetables, and pearl barley. Simmer for 45 minutes. Yields: 8 servings. (This is a very thick soup. You may water it down to serve a few more.)

Donor Unnamed—First Presbyterian Church
Morristown, New Jersey

Hearty Tomato Soup

1	MEDIUM ONION, FINELY CHOPPED	1	SOUP CAN, MILK
2	TABLESPOONS MARGARINE	1/2	TEASPOON PAPRIKA
3	OUNCES CREAM CHEESE, SOFTENED	1/2	TEASPOON BASIL
2	CANS (10 3/4 OUNCES) TOMATO SOUP	1/8	TEASPOON GARLIC POWDER

In medium saucepan, cook and stir onions in the margarine until tender. Stir in cream cheese. Gradually stir in soup and milk. Stir until smooth. Add the seasonings. Do not boil.

Anne Schofield—Providence Presbyterian Church
Fairfax, Virginia

Tortilla Soup

1/2	LARGE ONION, CHOPPED	2	CANS STEWED TOMATOES, UNDRAINED
2	CLOVES GARLIC, MINCED	1/2	CUP PICANTÉ SAUCE
2	TABLESPOONS MARGARINE	8	OUNCES MONTEREY JACK CHEESE, GRATED
2	TEASPOONS GROUND CUMIN		CORN TORTILLA CHIPS
2	CANS CHICKEN BROTH		

Saute' garlic and onion in margarine in large saucepan or Dutch oven for 2 minutes. Add cumin, cook and stir for 1 minute. Add broth, coarsely chopped tomatoes, and picanté sauce; bring to a boil. Reduce heat; cover and simmer for 30 minutes. Place 1/4 cup of cheese in bottom of each soup bowl. Ladle 1 cup of soup over cheese; serve with tortilla chips. Yield: 8 servings.

Peg Bohner Amann—First Presbyterian Church
Kerrville, Texas

Turkey Vegetable Soup

"Today, Ellicottville remains a small village in the Allegheny Highlands of western New York. Every winter, skiers flock to the area's skiing resorts. When trees are brilliantly colored in Autumn, the village holds a festival which attracts over twenty-five thousand people from New York, Ohio, Pennsylvania, and Ontario. A favorite stop of these visitors is our church where they may purchase this hot soup to ward off the Autumn chill."

25	POUNDS OF POTATOES	JAR OF CHICKEN BASE
20	POUNDS CARROTS	SALT AND PEPPER
5	POUNDS ONIONS	CELERY SALT
2	TURKEYS, COOKED WITH STOCK	

Dice the potatoes, slice the carrots, and chop the onions. Remove turkey meat from bones and chop. Heat the stock from turkeys, add the jar of chicken base. At the same time cook the vegetables in water until just tender. Add vegetables to the stock along with the chopped turkey. Season to taste. Yield: 16 gallons.

United Church of Ellicottville, Presbyterian Church, USA
Ellicottville, New York

Vegetable Soup

10	POUNDS BEEF, CUBED		FROZEN VEGETABLES:
16	POUNDS BEEF BONES	3	PACKAGES CORN (20 OUNCES EACH)
4	POUNDS CARROTS, DICED	3	PACKAGES PEAS (20 OUNCES EACH)
3	POUNDS ONIONS, DICED	3	STRING BEANS (20 OUNCES EACH)
5	POUNDS POTATOES, DICED	3	LIMA BEANS (20 OUNCES EACH)
6	LARGE CANS TOMATOES	1	POUND BOX, ALPHABET NOODLES
8	TOMATO SAUCE CANS (15 OUNCES)		WATER TO MAKE UP 13 GALLONS
4	LARGE CANS V 8 JUICE		BEEF BOUILLON AS NEEDED
3	HEADS, CABBAGE, CHOPPED		
3	BUNCHES, CELERY, DICED		

Cook meat and bones the day before soup is to be served. When tender, remove bones, cool meat and cut into small pieces. Chop the fresh vegetables and place into bags in refrigerator overnight. If soup is to be served at lunch, start heating the stock at 7:30 a.m.

Divide stock into 3 large pots. Divide tomatoes, sauce, juice, also. When liquid comes to a boil, add remaining ingredients except the noodles. Divide equally among the 3 pots. Simmer about 1 hour. Add noodles and beef broth (takes about 1 large jar for all 3 pots). Cook until noon. Yield: 13 gallons.

Everyone among the United Presbyterian Women—Pittsgrove Presbyterian Church
Daretown, New Jersey

STEWS

CHOWNING'S BRUNSWICK STEW

1	STEWING HEN (6 POUND) OR	3	MEDIUM POTATOES, DICED
2	FRYERS (3 POUNDS EACH)	4	CUPS CORN (FRESH, FROZEN, OR CANNED)
2	LARGE ONIONS	3	TEASPOONS SALT
2	CUPS OKRA	1	TABLESPOON SUGAR
2	CANS TOMATOES (1 POUND EACH) OR	1	TEASPOON PEPPER
4	CUPS FRESH TOMATOES	2-3	QUARTS WATER (3 FOR THINNER STEW)
2	CUPS LIMA BEANS		

Cut chicken in pieces. Simmer in water until tender, about 2 1/2 hours. Remove chicken and set aside. Add vegetables and simmer uncovered until beans and potatoes are tender. Stir occasionally, to avoid scorching. Bone and cube chicken and add it to mixture. Season and simmer. Allow to season overnight.

Margaret Rose Kilgore—Shandon Presbyterian Church
Columbia, South Carolina

FIVE HOUR STEW

(Or—How To Make 100 People Happy at a Lenten Dinner)

"When Westminster cooks Lenten dinners for the Union Avenue Association, we are famous for our adaption of this recipe for 100-120 people. We have removed the sherry, added green beans, sometimes used canned potatoes, but always succeeded in "wowing" the eaters!"

2	LARGE CANS TOMATOES (WHOLE)	1	PACKAGE FROZEN BRUSSELS SPROUTS
4	POUNDS STEWING BEEF	2	LARGE GREEN PEPPERS, CHUNKED
10	LARGE CARROTS, CUT IN CHUNKS	1/2-3/4	CUP SHERRY, IF DESIRED
10	STALKS CELERY, CUT IN CHUNKS		WORCESTERSHIRE SAUCE (3 SHAKES)
8	ONIONS, HALVED OR QUARTERED		TAPIOCA (SMALL AMOUNT TO THICKEN)
6	LARGE POTATOES, HALVED/QUARTERED		GARLIC POWDER

Place all ingredients in a large pot. Cover and cook for 5 hours, stirring occasionally. Yield: 10-12 servings. Serve with french bread and a nice salad. Rice goes well with this also.

Sheila Cawns—Westminster Presbyterian Church
St. Louis, Missouri

HARRIET'S TOMATO BEEF GOULASH

5	POUNDS GROUND BEEF	2	ONIONS, SLICED
2-3	LARGE (NO.10) CANS SAUERKRAUT	2	APPLES, CHOPPED
1	POUND BROWN SUGAR	2	POUNDS NOODLES
2	LARGE (NO.10) CANS TOMATOES		

Note: You may substitute chuck roast (ground beef does not require as much simmering as the chuck roast does—so it goes faster). If using ground beef brown the meat. Combine all the ingredients except noodles in a large pot—cover and simmer. If using chuck roast simmer for about 8-10 hours so that the meat falls apart. If using ground beef simmer long enough for vegetables to cook and flavors to mingle. After mixture simmers cook noodles and add to the above mixture. Yield: 50 servings.

Church of the Pilgrims, Washington, D.C.

ST. PHILLIP'S ISLAND VENISON STEW

3	POUNDS VENISON (CUBED FOR STEW)		SALT
1	POUND BACON, THICK SLICED		PEPPER
2	MEDIUM ONIONS, CHOPPED		FLOUR (PLAIN)
3	GARLIC CLOVES, SLICED	6	DROPS TABASCO SAUCE
1	CAN TOMATOES (15 OUNCES, WHOLE)	3	CUPS WATER

Dice and cook bacon in skillet. Drain and place in a 3 1/2 quart crock pot or Dutch oven. Thoroughly brown all of the venison in same skillet after liberally sprinkling salt, pepper and rolling in flour. Brown venison in vegetable oil. Add venison to crock pot. Stir well and mix with other ingredients. Add chopped tomatoes. Pour water over venison. Add Tabasco, salt and pepper. Cover. Cook at low temperature setting for 12-15 hours. (May place all ingredients in crock pot the evening before you plan on serving and cook overnight.) Serve over rice or spaghetti. Yield: 8 servings.

Pierre McGowan—First Presbyterian Church
Beaufort, South Carolina

Chapter Fourteen

Vegetables

VEGETABLE DISHES

Asparagus Casserole

2	CANS CREAM OF CELERY SOUP, UNDILUTED	4	CANS ASPARAGUS, DRAINED
4	TEASPOONS ONION, MINCED	4	HARD BOILED EGGS, CHOPPED
2	DASHES TABASCO SAUCE	2	CUPS CHEESE, GRATED
1/2	TEASPOONS SEASONING SALT		

Layer asparagus in a well-buttered casserole. Mix all other ingredients except cheese and spread over asparagus. Sprinkle cheese on top. Bake in a 350 degree oven for 30-40 minutes or, until hot and bubbly. Yield: 8-12 servings.

Jessie Greyer—Bryson City Presbyterian Church
Bryson City, North Carolina

Sweet and Sour Asparagus

2/3	CUP VINEGAR	1	TEASPOON WHOLE CLOVES
1/2	CUP WATER	1	TEASPOON CELERY SEED
1/2	CUP SUGAR	3	STICKS CINNAMON
1/2	TEASPOON SALT	2	(15 OUNCE) CANS ASPARAGUS SPEARS

Drain asparagus, or if using fresh asparagus, steam and allow to cool. Boil together all ingredients except asparagus. Pour mixture over the asparagus. Refrigerate and serve chilled, or at room temperature. Keeps well for a long time.

Mrs. Norman Olsen—First Central Presbyterian Church
Abilene, Texas

Broccoli Casserole

- 2 PACKAGES FROZEN, CHOPPED BROCCOLI
- 2 EGGS, BEATEN
- 1 CUP MAYONNAISE
- 1/2 CUP MILK
- 1 CUP SHARP CHEDDAR CHEESE, GRATED
- 1 CAN CONDENSED CELERY SOUP
- 1 TEASPOON WORCESTERSHIRE SAUCE
- 1 SMALL ONION, MINCED
- SALT AND PEPPER TO TASTE
- 1 STACK OF RITZ CRACKERS, CRUMBLED
- BUTTER

Cook broccoli until tender and drain. Combine remaining ingredients except crackers and butter. Mix with broccoli. Place in buttered or sprayed with Pam, casserole. Sprinkle with cracker crumbs and dot with butter. Bake in 350 degree oven for 40-50 minutes. Yield: 10-12 servings.

Susie Neal—Fort Hill Presbyterian Church, Clemson, South Carolina
Arlene Fawns—First Presbyterian Church, Blackwood, New Jersey
Marjorie Hill—Olney Presbyterian Church, Gastonia, North Carolina

Broccoli and Cauliflower Duet

- 2 PACKAGES FROZEN BROCCOLI / CAULIFLOWER MIX (16 OUNCES)
- 1 CUP MAYONNAISE
- 1 CAN CREAM OF MUSHROOM SOUP
- 1 EGG
- 1 1/2 CUPS CRACKER CRUMBS
- 12 OUNCES CHEDDAR CHEESE, SHREDDED

In a large bowl, mix mayonnaise, undiluted soup, and egg. Add the cheese. Stir in uncooked vegetables. Pour into large ungreased casserole dish and cover with cracker crumbs. Bake uncovered, in a 350 degree oven for 45 minutes. Check after 25 minutes. If top is getting too brown, cover for remaining cooking time. Yield: 12 servings.

Karen Larson—First Presbyterian Church
Medina, New York

Cauliflower

- 1 WHOLE CAULIFLOWER
- 1/2 CUP MAYONNAISE
- 2 TEASPOONS DIJON MUSTARD
- 1/2 CUP CHEESE, GRATED

Cook or steam whole cauliflower by your favorite method. Mix mayonnaise and mustard well and spread over entire top of cooked cauliflower. Sprinkle cheese over all. Bake in a 350 degree oven until thoroughly melted. Serve warm.

Janice Kitchens—Hodges Presbyterian Church
Hodges, South Carolina

COMPANY CARROTS

2 1/2	POUNDS WHOLE CARROTS		SALT AND PEPPER TO TASTE
1/2	CUP MAYONNAISE	1/2	CUP SALTINE CRACKERS, FINELY CRUSHED
1	TABLESPOON MINCED ONION		PARSLEY, CHOPPED
1	TABLESPOON PREPARED HORSERADISH		PAPRIKA

Cook carrots in boiling salted water until tender. Reserve 1/4 cup cooking liquid. Cut carrots in narrow strips, lengthwise. Arrange in a 9" square baking dish and set aside. Combine reserved liquid with mayonnaise, onion, horseradish, salt and pepper. Pour sauce over the carrots. Sprinkle cracker crumbs over top. Dot with butter or margarine. Sprinkle with parsley and paprika. Bake in a 375 degree oven for 20 minutes. Yield: 8 servings.   Refrigerate and add sauce and crumbs just before baking.

Dixie Hopple—Fairfax Presbyterian Church
Fairfax, Virginia

MANDARIN CARROTS

2	(11 OUNCE) CANS MANDARIN ORANGES	1 1/2	CUPS SUGAR
2	(16 OUNCE) CANS CUT CARROTS	1	(6 OUNCE) CAN FROZEN ORANGE JUICE,
1/2	CUP BUTTER		THAWED BUT UNDILUTED

Mix drained carrots and oranges in large bowl. In saucepan, combine sugar, orange juice, and butter. Simmer 20 minutes, stirring constantly. Pour hot mixture over carrots and oranges. Cover tightly and place in refrigerator overnight. Before serving, turn into a 1 1/2 quart casserole and heat in a 350 degree oven for 15 minutes or until heated thoroughly. You may prefer to heat it in a microwave oven.

Susie Neal—Fort Hill Presbyterian Church
Clemson, South Carolina

PARSLEYED CARROTS

1/4	CUP BUTTER OR MARGARINE	2	TEASPOON SUGAR
3/4	CUP CHICKEN BROTH	5	CUPS CARROTS (DIAGONAL SLICES)
1	TEASPOON SALT	2	TEASPOONS LEMON JUICE
1/8	TEASPOON WHITE PEPPER	1/4	CUP PARSLEY, CHOPPED

Boil chicken broth. Add butter, salt, pepper, sugar, and carrots. Simmer covered until tender and crisp. Remove from heat. Add the lemon juice and parsley, serve immediately. Yield: 6 servings.

Helen Krog—First Presbyterian Church
Medina, New York

Pineapple Carrots

Mrs. Smith says that her children just love these!

2	POUNDS CARROTS, SLICED	4	TEASPOONS CORNSTARCH
1	TEASPOON SALT	1	(6 OUNCE) CAN PINEAPPLE JUICE
2	CUPS BOILING WATER	2	TABLESPOONS BUTTER
1/2	CUP SUGAR	1	TABLESPOON MINT LEAVES, CHOPPED

Combine carrots, salt, and water in saucepan. Cover and simmer 25 minutes. Drain. Combine sugar, cornstarch, and pineapple juice. Cook, stirring constantly over medium heat until sauce thickens. Boil for 1 minute. Add butter and stir until melted. Stir in carrots and mint. Prepare just before serving! Yield: 6-8 servings.

Patty Smith—Roswell Presbyterian Church
Roswell, Georgia

Marinated Carrots

2	POUNDS CARROTS, SLICED/COOKED	3/4	CUP VINEGAR
1	ONION SLICED	1	TABLESPOON PREPARED MUSTARD
1	TOMATO SOUP	1	TABLESPOON WORCESTERSHIRE SAUCE
1	CUP VEGETABLE OIL		SALT AND PEPPER TO TASTE
1	CUP SUGAR		

Cook carrots until tender. Alternate layers of carrots and onions in a bowl. Mix other ingredients and pour over carrots and onions. Marinate in refrigerator for 24 hours.

Mary Logan—First Presbyterian Church
Beaufort, South Carolina

Oriental Celery Casserole

4	CUPS CELERY, SLICED	1	CAN CREAM OF CHICKEN SOUP, UNDILUTED
1	(4 OUNCE) CAN MUSHROOMS		PEPPERIDGE FARM DRESSING
1	CAN WATER CHESTNUTS, DRAINED AND SLICED (8 OUNCES)		BUTTER
			ALMONDS
1	SMALL JAR PIMENTOS, CHOPPED		

Cook celery for 8 minutes in salted water. Put celery, mushrooms, water chestnuts, pimentos, and soup into a greased casserole (2 quart), well-mixed. Cover with dressing, dot with butter and sprinkle with almonds. Bake for 25 minutes in a 350 degree oven.

Sarah Harley—First Presbyterian Church
Beaufort, South Carolina

Corn Pudding au Gratin

- 1 (16 OUNCE) CAN CREAM CORN
- 1 (8 OUNCE) CAN WHOLE KERNEL CORN
- 1 CUP CHEESE, DICED
- SALT TO TASTE
- 2 EGGS
- 2 TABLESPOONS FLOUR
- 1 CUP MILK
- 1 TABLESPOON SUGAR
- 2 TABLESPOONS BUTTER
- BREAD CRUMBS

Add cheese, eggs, sugar, salt, and flour to corn. Mix well. Heat the milk and add to mixture. Pour into a greased baking dish (2 quart). Top with crumbs and butter. Bake in a 375 degree oven for 30 minutes. Yield: 6 servings.

Mildred Williamson—Ray Memorial Presbyterian Church
Monroe, Georgia

Corn Pudding

- 1 PACKAGE FROZEN CORN
- 3/4 CUP SUGAR
- 1 CUP MILK
- 2 EGGS, BEATEN
- PINCH OF SALT
- 1/4 CUP BUTTER, MELTED

(You may use 5-6 ears fresh corn, cut from the cob.) Place melted butter into 10x12 baking dish. Mix all other ingredients and pour over butter. Mix again before baking. Bake in a 350 degree oven for 1 hour. Yield: 6 servings.

Mrs. Harry Athey—Stone's Chapel Church
Berryville, Virginia

Succotash

- 1 POUND BACON
- 10 ONIONS, CHOPPED
- 10 GREEN PEPPERS, CHOPPED
- 10 CANS BUTTER BEANS
- BREAD CRUMBS (TO THICKEN MIXTURE)
- 10 CANS CREAM STYLE CORN
- 10 CANS TOMATOES

Microwave bacon until crisp, crumble. Saute' onion and green pepper in bacon grease or oil. Mix with vegetables adding bread crumbs to thicken ingredients. Add the crumbled bacon and seasoning to taste. Divide into casseroles and cook in a 350 degree oven for about 45 minutes. Great with fish! Yield: 50 servings.

Martha S. Carpenter—Westminster Presbyterian Church
Greenville, South Carolina

POLENTA

Here is a corn meal mush so unusual that a holiday is celebrated in its honor. On the Friday before Lent, the people of Ponti, Italy, celebrate the feast of Polentine. The best cooks combine to create a huge dish of Polenta, said to weigh 1000 pounds. A parade and merrymaking are held to honor the Polents. At the end of the festivities, Polenta is distributed to the needy.

6 CUPS WATER	SHARP GRATED CHEESE
1 TEASPOON SALT	POLENTA SAUCE
2 CUPS UNCOOKED CORN MEAL	

Bring water and salt to a boil in large saucepan. Add corn meal slowly, stirring constantly so boiling does not stop. Using very low heat, continue cooking until thick, about 20 minutes. Stir often to ensure creamy texture. Remove from heat. Alternate in a buttered large casserole, layers of mush and about 2 cups of the Polenta sauce, topped with grated or sliced sharp cheese. Cover with a layer of cheese and bake in a 400 degree oven for about 25 minutes until hot and bubbly. Use remaining Polenta sauce as gravy for the dish when served. Yield: 8 servings.

Polenta Sauce:

2 TABLESPOONS ONION, CHOPPED	1/4 CUP PARSLEY, CHOPPED
2 TABLESPOONS BELL PEPPER, CHOPPED	2 TEASPOONS MIXED DRY HERBS (ROSEMARY, THYME, MARJORAM, ETC.)
2 EGGS, BEATEN	
1 CLOVE OF GARLIC, MINCED	1/4 CUP COOKING OIL
1/2 POUND OF GROUND BEEF	1 CUP WATER
1/2 CUP MUSHROOMS	1 TEASPOON SALT
3 1/2 CUPS CANNED TOMATOES	

Cook onion, green pepper, garlic, parsley, herbs, and beef in hot oil until lightly browned. Add remaining ingredients and simmer 1/2 hour or longer to blend and thicken. Makes 4 cups sauce.

Waldensian Presbyterian Church Cookbook—*Waldensian Presbyterian Church Valdese, North Carolina*

CREOLE EGGPLANT

1	MEDIUM EGGPLANT	2	TABLESPOONS VEGETABLE OIL
3/4	CUP ONION, CHOPPED		SALT AND PEPPER TO TASTE
1/2	CUP BELL PEPPER, CHOPPED	4	DROPS TABASCO (OPTIONAL)
3 OR 4	FRESH TOMATOES, PEELED AND CHOPPED (1 CAN MAY BE SUBSTITUTED)	1	LARGE CLOVE OF GARLIC, MINCED

Peel eggplant and cut into small squares. Sauté in the oil in large frying pan with onion and bell pepper. When eggplant is tender, add tomatoes and garlic. Season with salt, pepper and Tabasco. Cover and simmer until ingredients are well blended. Serve over rice.

Mary T. Geddings—First Presbyterian Church
Vicksburg, Mississippi

EGGPLANT CASSEROLE I

1	MEDIUM EGGPLANT	1	CUP SHARP CHEESE
2	ONIONS	1	CUP SALTINE CRACKER CRUMBS
3/4	CUP MILK	3	EGGS, WELL-BEATEN
	SALT AND PEPPER TO TASTE		

Peel and chop eggplant and onions. Drop into boiling water and cook until tender. Remove from heat and drain. Mix cracker crumbs, cheese, milk, salt and pepper together and add to eggplant. Mix well. Pour all ingredients into a buttered casserole dish. Spread beaten egg on top and bake in a 350 degree oven for 30 minutes or until firm. Yield: 8 servings.

Llewellyn Holliday—Ray Memorial Presbyterian Church
Monroe, Georgia

EGGPLANT CASSEROLE II

1	EGGPLANT, PEELED AND SLICED	1	TEASPOON ONION FLAKES
2	GREEN PEPPERS, DICED	1/4	TEASPOON PEPPER
1	TEASPOON SALT	1	CAN TOMATOES, DRAINED BUT RESERVE JUICE
1	TEASPOON OREGANO		

In a casserole dish, arrange layers of eggplant and green peppers. Season each layer with combined seasonings. Pour 1/2 of reserved juice and tomatoes over the layer. Make 2 layers in all, and finish with the juice, tomatoes and seasonings on top. Cover and bake in a 350 degree oven for 1 hour. Uncover and bake an additional 15 minutes to brown. Yield: 4-6 servings.

Margaret Botsford—First Presbyterian Church
Casa Grande, Arizona

Green Bean Casserole

2	(16 OUNCE) CANS FRENCH CUT GREEN BEANS (DRAINED)	1	CUP DICED ONION
2	CANS CREAM OF MUSHROOM SOUP	5 TO 6	RIPE OLIVES SLICED
1	CUP DICED CELERY	3/4	CUP CRUSHED POTATO CHIPS
1	CUP DICED GREEN PEPPER	1/4	CUP SLIVERED ALMONDS
		5 TO 6	PIMENTO STUFFED OLIVES SLICED

Layer half of beans, soup, celery, green pepper and onion in buttered 2 quart casserole. Repeat layers. Top with a layer of ripe olives, potato chips, almonds and stuffed olives. Bake in a 325 degree oven for 35 to 40 minutes. Yield: 8 servings.

Julia LaGrone—First Presbyterian Church
Beaufort, South Carolina

Scalloped Green Beans (for 50)

2	CANS (#10 EACH) SLICED OR FRENCH STYLE GREEN BEANS, DRAINED	1 1/2	QUARTS BUTTERED CRACKER CRUMBS
1	QUART CARROTS, GRATED	2	CUPS ONION, CHOPPED
1	CAN (50 OUNCE) CREAM OF MUSHROOM SOUP OR 5 REGULAR CANS CREAM OF MUSHROOM SOUP	2	CUPS MILK
		1	POUND CHEDDAR CHEESE, SHREDDED

Grease 2 pans (12x20"). Place vegetables into pans. Heat the soup, milk, and cheese. Stir to melt. Pour the mixture over the beans. Sprinkle with crumbs. Bake 1 hour in a 350 degree oven. Yield: 50 servings.

Marilyn Johnson—First Presbyterian Church
Belle Plaine, Minnesota

Sweet and Sour Green Beans

2-3	SLICES BACON	1	MEDIUM ONION, CHOPPED
3	TABLESPOONS SUGAR (GRANULATED)	3	TABLESPOONS VINEGAR
3	TABLESPOONS WATER		FRENCH CUT GREEN BEANS

Fry bacon until crisp and blot grease on paper towels. Sauté onion in bacon drippings until clear. Mix remaining ingredients. Bring mixture to a boil. Pour over 1 can or package frozen (cooked) beans.

Marion Vaughan—Hampton Presbyterian Church, Hampton, South Carolina
Teri Knight—First Presbyterian Church, Beaufort, South Carolina

English Pea Casserole

1	CAN ENGLISH PEAS (17 OUNCE), DRAINED	1	MEDIUM ONION, CHOPPED
1	CAN CREAM OF CHICKEN SOUP	1	CAN WATER CHESTNUTS, SLICED
1	SMALL JAR OF PIMENTOS, CHOP & DRAIN	1	PACKAGE HERB STUFFING

Mix ingredients. Place in a casserole dish. Cover with herb stuffing. Drizzle one stick of melted butter on top. Bake in a 350 degree oven for 25 minutes.

Randall K. Sullivan—Honea Path Presbyterian Church
Honea Path, South Carolina

Hominy Casserole I

1	CAN (29 OUNCE) HOMINY	1	CAN TOMATOES (15 OUNCES)
1	SMALL ONION, CHOPPED	1/4	GREEN PEPPER, CHOPPED
2	SLICES BACON, CHOPPED	4	SLICES AMERICAN CHEESE

Cook bacon, onion, green pepper, and tomatoes for 5 minutes. Meanwhile, place the hominy in a casserole dish and pour tomato mixture over it. Cover with slices of cheese or grated cheese and bake in a 350 degree oven until hot and bubbly and cheese melts. (You may want to vary this according to your taste by using some of the new stewed canned tomatoes such as, Mexican, Cajun, or Italian style and, using shredded Jalapeno or Monterey Jack cheese on top.)

Mrs. Louise Thompson—First Presbyterian Church
Cuero, Texas

Hominy Casserole II

1	LARGE CAN HOMINY	1	CAN MUSHROOMS, DRAINED
1	LARGE CAN OF TOMATOES	2	LARGE ONIONS, CHOPPED
3	CUPS GRATED, SHARP CHEESE	3	SLICES BACON, PREPARED AND CRUMBLED

Sauté mushrooms in butter. Sauté onions in bacon grease. Add remaining ingredients and cook over low heat, stirring frequently. Add 1 tablespoon chili powder, salt, and pepper to taste. For 25 persons, use 6 large cans hominy and increase other ingredients accordingly.

(Ellen Brisbin's grandmother's recipe.) Dorothy Hammond—Fort Sam Houston Chapel
San Antonio, Texas

Layered Cashew and Mushroom Roast

1	TABLESPOON OF OIL	1	TEASPOON FRESH THYME
1	SMALL ONION, FINELY CHOPPED	1	TEASPOON DRY YEAST
2	CLOVES GARLIC, CRUSHED	2/3	CUP HOT WATER OR STOCK
2	CUPS CASHEW NUTS, FINELY GROUND	2	TABLESPOONS BUTTER
1	CUP BREAD CRUMBS	1/2	POUND MUSHROOMS, CHOPPED
1	EGG, BEATEN		SALT AND FRESH PEPPER TO TASTE
3	MEDIUM PARSNIPS, COOKED AND MASHED WITH A LITTLE BUTTER	1	TEASPOON FRESH ROSEMARY

Heat oil and cook the onion and garlic until soft. Grind the cashew nuts in a nut grinder, then mix with the bread crumbs. Beat the egg and add it to the dry ingredients, then mix in the mashed parsnips and herbs. Add the fried onion, being sure to scrape the pan so that all the juices go in as nut roasts can sometimes be a little dry. Dissolve the yeast in hot water or stock and add to the other ingredients. Season well. Melt the butter in a frying pan and sauté the chopped mushrooms until soft. Grease a 2 pound loaf pan with butter. Press half the nut mixture into the pan. Cover with a layer of mushrooms and top with the rest of the nut mixture. Then cover with foil and bake for 1 hour in a 350 degree oven. When cooked, remove the loaf from the oven and let it stand for 10 minutes before turning it out. Serve hot or cold.

Miss Ella Edwards—Letchworth Free Church
Letchworth, England

Onion Pie

1	BAKED PIE CRUST	1/4	CUP SOUR CREAM
3	CUPS ONIONS, THINLY SLICED	3	TABLESPOONS FLOUR
1 1/4	CUPS SOUR CREAM	1	TEASPOON SALT
1/2	CUP MILK		

Mix 1 1/4 cups sour cream with the milk. Separately, mix the 1/4 cup sour cream with flour and salt. Saute' the onions and place in the baked crust. Beat the eggs and combine with both sour cream mixtures. Pour over the onions. Bake in a 350 degree oven for 30 minutes. Yield: 6-8 servings.

Peggy Lawton—Estill Presbyterian Church
Estill, South Carolina

SCALLOPED ONIONS AND ALMONDS

12	SMALL ONIONS, CANNED (CUT IN HALVES)	1/2	CUP SLIVERED, TOASTED ALMONDS
1	CUP CELERY, DICED AND COOKED	1	CUP MILK
4	TABLESPOONS BUTTER	1/2	CUP HALF-AND-HALF
3	TABLESPOONS FLOUR		PARMESAN CHEESE
1	TEASPOON SALT		PAPRIKA
1/8	TEASPOON PEPPER		BREAD CRUMBS

Combine butter, flour, milk, half-and-half, salt, and pepper to make the sauce. Place a layer of sauce on the bottom of a casserole dish. Place the onions over sauce. Sprinkle with celery. Top with the almonds. Pour remaining sauce over mixture, covering well. Sprinkle with paprika and Parmesan and bread crumbs. Bake in a 350 degree oven about 20-30 minutes until brown and bubbly. Yield: 6 servings.

Miriam (Mickey) Broome—First Presbyterian Church
Marion, North Carolina

VIDALIA ONION CASSEROLE

5	CUPS VIDALIA ONIONS, SLICED	1/4	CUP MILK
1	STICK BUTTER (8 OUNCE)		

Sauté the onions in the butter. Add the milk and place half of the mixture into a 9x9 casserole dish. Add 12 Ritz crackers, crumbled and 1/4 cup Parmesan cheese. Place an additional layer of onions, crackers, and cheese. Bake uncovered, in a 350 degree oven for 30 minutes. Yield: 6 servings.

Helen Harvey Laffitte—First Presbyterian Church
Columbia, South Carolina

Hash Brown Casserole

2	POUND BAG OF FROZEN HASH BROWN POTATOES
2	CANS CREAM OF POTATO SOUP
1	8 OUNCE CARTON, SOUR CREAM
1	4 OUNCE BAG OF GRATED, SHARP CHEDDAR CHEESE

SALT AND PEPPER TO TASTE
GARLIC POWDER TO TASTE
PARMESAN CHEESE
BUTTER OR MARGARINE

Allow potatoes to thaw enough to separate. Mix potatoes, soup, and sour cream together. Add seasonings and cheddar cheese. Mix well. Pour into buttered casserole dish. Sprinkle top with Parmesan cheese and dot with butter. Bake uncovered, in a 350 degree oven for 1 hour. Yield: 12 servings.

Martha J. McIntosh—First Presbyterian Church, Savannah, Georgia
Anne Smoak—Trinity Presbyterian Church, Charlotte, North Carolina

Oven-fried Hash Browns

2	POUNDS FROZEN HASH BROWNED POTATOES (THAW SLIGHTLY)	1	CAN CREAM OF CHICKEN SOUP
1	TEASPOON SALT	8	OUNCES (2 CUPS) SHREDDED CHEDDAR CHEESE
1	PINT SOUR CREAM	2	CUPS CORN FLAKES
1/2	CUP CHOPPED ONION	6	TABLESPOONS MELTED BUTTER

Combine all ingredients except cornflakes and butter. Place in slightly greased 13x9x2" dish. Cover with cornflakes. Drizzle with melted butter. Bake uncovered in a 350 degree oven for 60 minutes. Check after 30 minutes. If necessary, cover with foil to avoid over browning. Do not underbake. Yield: 8 servings. Freezes well.

Dorothy Corlis—First Presbyterian Church, Medina, New York
Nancy Partridge—Fairfax Presbyterian Church, Fairfax, Virginia
Presbyterian Women—Central Presbyterian Church, Fort Smith, Arkansas
Bobbie Farris, (Mrs. Luther, Sr.)—Trinity Presbyterian, Baton Rouge, Louisiana
Chris Rayburg—First United Presbyterian Church, Lake City, Pennsylvania

GOURMET POTATOES

6	MEDIUM POTATOES	1	TEASPOON SALT
2	CUPS, SHREDDED CHEDDAR CHEESE	1/4	TEASPOON PEPPER
1/4	CUP BUTTER	2	TABLESPOONS BUTTER
1 1/2	CUPS, SOUR CREAM		PAPRIKA
1/3	CUP CHOPPED ONION		

Cook potatoes and shred or chop coarsely. In a saucepan, over low heat, combine cheese and 1/4 cup butter; stir occasionally until almost melted. Remove from heat. Blend in sour cream, onion, and seasonings. Fold in potatoes and put into a greased 2 quart casserole. Dot with butter and sprinkle with paprika. Bake uncovered in a 350 degree oven for about 30 minutes. Or until bubbly and heated through.

Genevieve Herbst—St. Andrew Presbyterian Church, Williamsport, Maryland
Barbara M. Arnold—Paxton Presbyterian Church, Harrisburg, Pennsylvania

MICROWAVE SCALLOPED POTATOES

1 1/2	CUPS BASIC WHITE SAUCE	2	TABLESPOONS BUTTER OR MARGARINE
1/2	TEASPOON SALT	1/4	CUP DRY BREAD CRUMBS
4	MEDIUM POTATOES, PEELED AND THINLY SLICED		

Place the butter into a small glass container. Microwave about 1 minute at medium-high setting. Stir in the dry bread crumbs. Set aside. Combine all other ingredients in a 1 1/2 quart glass casserole dish. Microwave for 9 minutes at high setting. Stir well to even the cooking. Sprinkle with the buttered bread crumbs. Microwave for 9 to 11 minutes at high setting, until potatoes are tender. Allow to stand for 2 minutes. Yield: 4 servings.

Roberta Banks—Jewett Presbyterian Church
Jewett, New York

STOVED POTATOES

6 OR 8	POTATOES, PEELED AND THINLY SLICED	1/3	CUP WATER
2	ONIONS, CHOPPED		SALT AND PEPPER TO TASTE
2	TABLESPOONS COOKING OIL		

Sauté onions in oil. Add potatoes and toss together. Add seasoning and water. Cover and cook slowly for an hour. Serve very hot. Do not let the pan boil dry.

M.B.S.—Isle of Cumbrae Parish Church
Isle of Cumbrae, Scotland

POTATO PUFFS

These recipes (see also English Muffins, ch. 2), are dated 1881 and were served at the Warm Springs Hotel which was built in 1811 near the therapeutic pools. Guests visited until 1924, when the hotel closed and was razed the following year.

3	CUPS POTATOES, BOILED AND MASHED	1	TABLESPOON BUTTER
3	EGGS, SEPARATED		SALT AND PEPPER, TO TASTE
4	TABLESPOONS CREAM		

Put potatoes into a frying pan with the butter. Add the well-beaten egg yolks along with the cream, salt and pepper. Stir constantly, until quite hot. Remove from fire. Stir in carefully the egg whites, which have been beaten to a stiff, dry froth. Place mixture into greased dish. Bake in a quick oven until nicely browned.

Warm Springs Presbyterian Church
Warm Springs, Virginia

CANDIED SWEET POTATOES

2	RED SWEET POTATOES	1/3	TEASPOON VINEGAR
1	CUP SUGAR	1	TABLESPOON MARGARINE
1	CUP WATER	2	TEASPOONS VANILLA
2 1/2	TABLESPOONS LIGHT CORN SYRUP		

Place 2 large, red sweet potatoes in saucepan. Cover with water and boil about 20 minutes until skin can be pierced with knife but not too soft. Drain, peel, and slice about 1/2 inch thick. Place into a casserole dish. Combine sugar, water, and corn syrup in a saucepan. Bring to a boil. Cook covered for about 3 minutes, until steam washes down sides of pan. Uncover and continue cooking about 2 minutes longer, until the syrup begins to thicken. Remove from heat. Add the butter and vanilla. Stir well. Pour over casserole. Bake in a 350 degree oven for 45 minutes. Baste with syrup while cooking. Yield: 6-8 servings.

Mary M.L. Thompson—First Presbyterian Church
Savannah, Georgia

SWEET POTATO/BANANA CASSEROLE

2	CUPS SWEET POTATOES, COOKED AND MASHED	1/2	CUP CHOPPED NUTS
		1	TEASPOON VANILLA
4	TABLESPOONS BUTTER	2 OR 3	RIPE BANANAS, MASHED
1/2	CUP BROWN SUGAR	1	CUP CRUSHED CORNFLAKES
1/2	CUP COCONUT	1/2	CUP BROWN SUGAR

Mix first 6 ingredients. If too dry, add a small amount of milk. Place half the mixture into a buttered casserole dish. Cover with all of the bananas. Add remaining potatoes. In a separate bowl, mix cornflakes and remaining sugar. Sprinkle over potatoes as a topping. Bake in a 350 degree oven for 30 minutes.

Ruby Honeycutt—Paint Gap Presbyterian Church
Burnsville, North Carolina

SWEET POTATO CASSEROLE I

- 2 CANS (#2 1/2) SWEET POTATOES, DRAINED
- 1 CAN (#2) CRUSHED PINEAPPLE, DRAINED
- 1 TABLESPOON SUGAR, BROWN
- 1 TEASPOON CINNAMON
- 1 LEMON, JUICED

Mash potatoes. Add all other ingredients and mix well. Bake in a 350 degree oven for 45 minutes. Yield: 10 servings.

Mrs. John King—First Central Presbyterian Church
Abilene, Texas

SWEET POTATO CASSEROLE II

- 3 CUPS COOKED SWEET POTATOES
- 1 CUP SUGAR
- 2 EGGS
- 1/3 CUP MILK
- 1 TEASPOON VANILLA
- 1/2 CUP BUTTER
- 1 CUP BROWN SUGAR
- 1/3 CUP FLOUR
- 1 CUP CHOPPED NUTS
- 1/3 CUP BUTTER

Mash sweet potatoes. Add next 5 ingredients and mix well. Place into a greased casserole dish. Mix brown sugar, flour, chopped nuts, and butter and crumble on top of potatoes. Bake for 25-35 minutes in a 350 degree oven.

Cindy Keasler—First Presbyterian Church
Demopolis, Alabama

Sweet Potatoes Deluxe

2 1/4	POUNDS SWEET POTATOES, COOKED AND MASHED (ABOUT 6 POTATOES)	1/2	CUP FLAKED COCONUT
		1/2	TEASPOON VANILLA
6	TABLESPOONS MARGARINE	1/2	CUP ORANGE JUICE
3	SLIGHTLY BEATEN EGGS	1/2	TEASPOON SALT
1/2	CUP SUGAR		

Add the margarine to the mashed potatoes. Beat the eggs, sugar, coconut, orange juice, salt, and vanilla into the potatoes. Turn into a 9x13x2" inch casserole dish. Mix together the following topping and sprinkle over the casserole.

1/3	CUP MARGARINE	1	CUP CHOPPED PECANS
1/2	CUP BROWN SUGAR	1/4	TEASPOON CINNAMON
1/3	CUP FLOUR		

Bake until heated thoroughly, remove from oven and top with 10 large marshmallows. Return to oven just long enough for marshmallows to slightly brown on top.

Sally Freid—Carrollton Presbyterian Church
New Orleans, Louisiana

Yam Puff

3	CUPS YAMS, MASHED (2-16 OUNCE CANS)	2	TEASPOONS BAKING POWDER
1/4	CUP SUGAR	1	TEASPOON SALT
1/4	CUP BUTTER	3/4	CUP GRAPENUT CEREAL
2	EGGS, WELL-BEATEN	1/4	CUP SUGAR
2	TABLESPOONS ORANGE JUICE	2	TABLESPOONS BUTTER

Mix cereal, sugar, and butter. Set aside. Combine yams with all other ingredients. Place half of yam mixture into a greased, 1 quart shallow casserole dish. Top with half of the buttered cereal and sugar mix. Place remaining yam mixture on top and sprinkle the remaining cereal over all. Bake in a 350 degree oven for 30 minutes. Yield: 8 servings.

Rae Hoffecker—First Presbyterian Church
Blackwood, New Jersey

Miriam's Crunchy Sweet Potato Soufflé

2	LARGE CANS SWEET POTATOES, MASHED	1/2	CUP GRANULATED SUGAR
2/3	CUP MARGARINE	2	EGGS
1	TABLESPOON VANILLA		

Mix together all ingredients above with an electric mixer. Place into a greased baking dish. Mix the following topping ingredients:

1	CUP BROWN SUGAR	1	CAN ANGEL FLAKE COCONUT (1 CUP)
1	CUP CHOPPED NUTS	1	TABLESPOON FLOUR
2/3	CUP MELTED MARGARINE		

Place topping mixture on top of potato mixture. Bake 30 minutes in a 375 degree oven.

Margaret E. Godbold—Oakland Avenue Presbyterian Church
Rock Hill, South Carolina

LAYERED SPINACH SUPREME

1	CUP BISQUICK	1/2	CUP PARMESAN CHEESE, GRATED
1/4	CUP MILK	4	OUNCES MONTEREY JACK CHEESE, SHREDDED
2	EGGS	1	CARTON (12 OUNCE) COTTAGE CHEESE
1/4	CUP ONION, CHOPPED FINE	2	CLOVES GARLIC, MINCED OR CRUSHED
1	PACKAGE FROZEN SPINACH, CHOPPED		

Thaw and drain spinach well. Grease a rectangular baking dish (12x7 1/2x2"). Mix Bisquick, milk, eggs, and onion and beat well for 20 strokes. Spread into the dish. Add remaining ingredients and spoon evenly over batter in the dish. Bake in a 350 degree oven until set, about 30 minutes. Allow to stand for 5 minutes before serving.

Joyce Edson—National Presbyterian Church
Washington, D.C.

CRUSTLESS SPINACH QUICHE

1	(10 OUNCE) PACKAGE FROZEN CHOPPED SPINACH, THAWED AND WELL-DRAINED	2	SLICES DAY-OLD BREAD, CRUMBED
			SALT AND PEPPER TO TASTE
8	OUNCES SWISS CHEESE, GRATED	4	TEASPOONS ONION, GRATED
1/4	TEASPOON NUTMEG	1 1/2	CUPS CHOLESTEROL-FREE EGG SUBSTITUTE

Combine, spinach, cheese, crumbs, onion, egg substitute, nutmeg, salt, and pepper. Place into a greased 8" pie plate or quiche dish. Bake in a 350 degree oven for 30 minutes or until knife inserted into center comes out clean. Serve hot or cold. Calories: 204. Yield: 6-8 servings.

Patricia T. Kirkpatrick, R.D., L.D.—Alamo Heights Presbyterian Church
San Antonio, Texas

Spinach and Artichoke Casserole

2	(10 OUNCE) PACKAGE FROZEN CHOPPED SPINACH	1	CAN MUSHROOM SOUP, UNDILUTED
1	CAN ARTICHOKE HEARTS, DRAINED	1	CAN MUSHROOMS, DRAINED
2	TEASPOONS LEMON JUICE	1/2	CUP SOUR CREAM
1/2	TEASPOON GARLIC SALT	1/2	CUP MAYONNAISE
		1	CUP CHEESE, GRATED

Layer spinach in bottom of casserole dish. Top with artichokes. Cover with mushrooms, soup, and lemon juice. Mix sour cream and mayonnaise and spread over casserole contents. Bake in a 350 degree oven for 30 minutes. Top with cheese, and return to oven just long enough to melt cheese. Yield: 8 servings.

Ruth Greene—United Presbyterian Church
Lenoir, North Carolina

Spinach Soufflé

"This recipe was served at First Presbyterian Church of St. Louis for a luncheon and we begged for a copy. We have adapted this for home use as well as WOC lunches and even Lenten dinners for 100 persons. We serve it with French bread, lettuce salad, and carrot sticks."

1/2	POUND VELVEETA CHEESE, CUBED	1	PACKAGE FROZEN SPINACH
2	POUNDS COTTAGE CHEESE	1	PACKAGE CHIPPED BEEF OR DRIED BEEF
6	EGGS	1/4	POUND MARGARINE (1 STICK)
6	TABLESPOONS FLOUR		

Thaw and drain spinach. Beat eggs, add flour and remaining ingredients. Grease a 9x13" pan. Place shredded cheddar cheese on top. Bake in a 350 degree oven for 50 minutes. Cut into squares to serve. Yield: 10-12 servings.

Esther Alvis-Shiela Cawns—Westminster Presbyterian Church
St. Louis, Missouri

Spinach Casserole

1	CUP ONION, FINELY CHOPPED	2	PACKAGES FROZEN CHOPPED SPINACH, THAWED AND WELL DRAINED
1 1/2	STICKS HOT PEPPER CHEESE, GRATED		
1	CUP CELERY, FINELY CHOPPED	1	CAN MUSHROOM SOUP, UNDILUTED
1	STICK OF BUTTER (8 OUNCES)	1	CAN CREAM OF CHICKEN SOUP, UNDILUTED
2	CUPS MINUTE RICE, UNCOOKED	1	CAN CREAM OF CELERY SOUP, UNDILUTED

Sauté onion and celery in butter. Mix all ingredients in a large 9x13" casserole dish. Bake in a 350 degree oven for 20-30 minutes, until rice is done, and dish is hot and bubbly. Yield: 10 servings. Freezes well! (Broccoli may be substituted for spinach.)

Fay McGowan—First Presbyterian Church
Beaufort, South Carolina

Spinach Potato Casserole

5 TO 6	POTATOES, PEELED AND BOILED	1	TEASPOON SUGAR
3/4	CUP SOUR CREAM	1/2	CUP BUTTER
1/2	TEASPOON SALT	1	PACKAGE FROZEN CHOPPED SPINACH
1/4	TEASPOON PEPPER	1	CUP GRATED CHEDDAR CHEESE

Mash potatoes with sour cream and butter. Add sugar, salt and pepper. Stir in cooked and drained chopped spinach. Pour into casserole and sprinkle cheese on top. Bake in a 350 degree oven for about 1/2 hour or until bubbly.

Ashley Scholer (our minister's wife)—First Presbyterian Church, Beaufort, South Carolina
Similar recipe submitted: Paxton Presbyterian Church, Harrisburg, Pennsylvania

Fritatta

3	CUPS ZUCCHINI, GRATED	1/2	TEASPOON ITALIAN SEASONING
1	CUP BISQUICK	1/2	CUP OIL
1	ONION, CHOPPED	1	GREEN PEPPER, CHOPPED
1/2	CUP PARMESAN CHEESE	4	EGGS
1/2	CUP PARSLEY, CHOPPED		SALT AND PEPPER TO TASTE

Mix all ingredients. Spread into greased pan (13x9"). Bake in 350 degree oven for 25 minutes. Yield: 12 servings.

Pat Mattson—Menlo Park Presbyterian Church, Menlo Park, California
Mildred Stopyra—St. Peter's Catholic Church, Beaufort, South Carolina

Deep Dish Zucchini Pie

3	CUPS DICED ZUCCHINI	4	EGGS, BEATEN
1/2	SMALL ONION FINELY CHOPPED	1/2	CUP OIL
1	CUP BISQUICK	1/2	CUP PARMESAN CHEESE

Mix all of above ingredients until evenly coated. Pour into greased pan, 9 or 10" square or round. Bake in a 350 degree oven for 40 to 45 minutes. When it browns and is a little crusty on top, it is done.

Mildred Stopyra—St. Peter's Catholic Church
Beaufort, South Carolina

It Can't Be Squash!

2	POUNDS YELLOW SQUASH	2	TABLESPOONS SUGAR (GRANULATED)
2	POUNDS ZUCCHINI	1	TABLESPOON TABASCO SAUCE
8	MEDIUM TOMATOES	1	CUP BUTTER (2 STICKS)
2	LARGE ONIONS, CHOPPED	8	OUNCES PEPPERIDGE FARM HERB STUFFING MIX
8	OUNCES WATER CHESTNUTS, SLICED	2	CUPS SHARP CHEDDAR CHEESE, GRATED
1	CUP SOUR CREAM	1/2	CUP PARMESAN CHEESE
2	TEASPOONS MORTON'S NATURE'S SEASONING		

Cube squash and cook until barely tender, drain and coarsely chop in processor. Lightly sauté onions in butter and reserve liquid. Core, peel, and quarter tomatoes, cook until soft, and drain. Mix melted butter and stuffing. Blend 1/2 of stuffing, 1 cup cheddar cheese with first 9 ingredients, and spoon into casserole. Cover with remainder of cheddar, stuffing, and Parmesan cheese. Bake until top has lightly browned and is bubbly. Yield: 12 servings.

Elizabeth C. Harmon—First Presbyterian Church
Columbia, South Carolina

Posh Squash

2	POUNDS YELLOW SQUASH, SLICED	2	EGGS, BEATEN
1	CUP MAYONNAISE	1/2	TEASPOON SALT AND PEPPER TO TASTE
1	CUP (8 OUNCES) PARMESAN CHEESE	1/2	CUP SOFT BREAD CRUMBS
1	SMALL ONION, CHOPPED	1	TABLESPOON BUTTER OR MARGARINE

Cook squash in boiling salted water until tender, about 10-15 minutes, drain and cool slightly. Combine mayonnaise, cheese, onion, eggs, salt and pepper. Mix well. Add squash and stir gently. Pour into lightly greased 1 1/2 quart casserole. Combine bread crumbs and melted butter and spoon over squash mixture. Bake in a 350 degree oven for 30 minutes. Yield: 6 servings.

Elaine Daniel—East Ridge Presbyterian Church
Chattanooga, Tennessee

Zucchini and/or Broccoli Casserole

3	CUPS COOKED VEGETABLES	1/2	CUP SOUR CREAM
2	CARROTS, SHREDDED	1/2	PACKAGE PEPPERIDGE FARM STUFFING MIX
1	ONION, COARSELY CUT	1/2	CUP MELTED BUTTER OR MARGARINE
1	SMALL JAR DICED PIMENTOS, DRAINED		SALT AND PEPPER TO TASTE
1	CAN CREAM OF MUSHROOM SOUP		

Mix stuffing mix with butter. Blend soup and sour cream with salt and pepper. Add mixture and all other ingredients to 1/2 of the stuffing mix. Put into a 3 quart casserole after mixing well. Top with remaining stuffing. Bake in a 350 degree oven for 25 minutes. Freezes well, baked or unbaked. Also may be refrigerated a few days ahead until ready to bake. Yield: 10 servings.

Virginia Henderson—The Presbyterian Church of Cadiz, Cadiz, Ohio
Edmee Boyd—Hampton Presbyterian Church, Hampton, South Carolina

ZUCCHINI ARIZONA

1	MEDIUM ONION, SLICED	1	CAN (6 OUNCE) TOMATO JUICE
4	TABLESPOONS VEGETABLE OIL		SALT AND PEPPER TO TASTE
4-5	MEDIUM ZUCCHINI, SLICED	1/2	TEASPOON THYME
1	MEDIUM TOMATO, SLICED		MONTEREY JACK CHEESE, SLICED

In a large skillet, sauté onion in oil until clear. Add all except cheese. Cover and simmer for 30 minutes or until tender. Place cheese over zucchini mixture, cover and allow to heat until melted. May be made ahead and put into a casserole dish with the cheese on top. Reheat in oven or microwave. Yield: 4-6 servings.

Mary A. Morrison—Ray Memorial Church
Monroe, Georgia

SWEET SAUERKRAUT

| 1/2 | POUND BACON, FRIED AND CRUMBLED | 1 | CAN TOMATOES, CHOPPED COARSELY |
| 1 | CAN SAUERKRAUT, DRAINED AND RINSED | 1 | CUP SUGAR (GRANULATED) |

Mix ingredients. Place into casserole dish. Bake 1 1/2 hours in a 350 degree oven.

Alma Ward—First Presbyterian Church
Blackwood, New Jersey

MAMA'S TOMATO PUDDING

The donor relates that this recipe has been in her family for many years and is still a favorite.

2	CUPS TOMATOES, FRESH OR CANNED	1/2	TEASPOON BLACK PEPPER
	(I USE A CAN OF STEWED TOMATOES)	2	HOT DOG ROLLS (OR 4 BISCUITS) CRUMBED
1/2	CUP SUGAR		SALT TO TASTE
1/4	STICK BUTTER OR MARGARINE		

Combine all ingredients and boil until thickened. Pour into buttered casserole dish and bake in a 400 degree oven until browned and bubbly. Yield: 4 servings.

Charlotte Vedeler—Old Presbyterian Meeting House
Alexandria, Virginia

Fire and Ice Tomatoes

6	LARGE, RIPE, FIRM TOMATOES	1/2	TEASPOON BLACK PEPPER
1	LARGE GREEN PEPPER, CUT IN STRIPS	4 1/2	TEASPOON SUGAR
1	RED ONION, SLICED INTO RINGS	1 1/2	TEASPOON MUSTARD SEED
3/4	CUP VINEGAR	1/8	TEASPOON RED PEPPER
1 1/2	TEASPOON CELERY SALT	1/4	CUP COLD WATER

Skin and quarter tomatoes. Place with green pepper and onion in large bowl with tight-fitting lid. Place all other ingredients in a saucepan and bring to a boil. Immediately pour over vegetables. Chill, turning occasionally. Serve cold. Will keep for several days in refrigerator. Yield: 2 quarts.

Harriet Inscoe—First Presbyterian Church
Morganton, North Carolina

Charlotte's Tomato Casserole

We are especially pleased to include Mrs. Young's recipe since she is one of the few persons remaining who were active members of Stoney Creek until the congregation was dissolved and custodianship assigned to First Presbyterian of Beaufort.

	TOMATOES, COOKED OR CANNED	SALT TO TASTE
	ONION, CHOPPED	PEPPER TO TASTE
	GREEN PEPPER, CHOPPED	CRACKERS, SALTINE OR RITZ, COARSLEY
	CELERY, CHOPPED	CRUMBLED BY HAND
	CHEESE, SHREDDED OR SLICED	1 CAN CREAM OF MUSHROOM SOUP
	BACON, COOKED AND CRUMBLED	1/3 –1/2 SOUP CAN OF MILK

Select a casserole dish size for the number of persons you are serving. Cook as many fresh, coarsely chopped or sliced tomatoes, or warm enough canned tomatoes to fill the dish. Add to the tomato mixture: chopped onions, green pepper, and celery. Cook several slices of bacon until crisp, then crumble and add to tomatoes. Season with salt and pepper to taste. Line the bottom of the casserole with crumbled saltine or Ritz crackers. Pour half of the tomatoes into the dish. Layer additional crackers and cheese (your choice) on top. Add remaining tomato mixture. Partially dilute a can of cream of mushroom soup with milk and pour over tomatoes. Top with a layer of crackers and cheese. Bake in a 350 degree oven until bubbly and brown on top.

Note—For 6 to 8 servings suggested ingredient quantities are: 1 large (32 ounce) can of tomatoes; 1/2 cup each of the fresh chopped vegetables; 8 ounces cheese (Swiss, sharp, cheddar, or mozarella); 6 slices of bacon; approximately 2 cups of crackers.

ingredients may be halved for smaller casserole and doubled or tripled for larger amounts. When cooking the first time, measure the tomato mixture and select a casserole dish with approximately 3 inches left at the top before adding the other ingredients. This recipe is personalized by your individual taste.

Charlotte Hutson Young—Stoney Creek Independent Presbyterian Church
McPhersonville, South Carolina

MUSHROOM STUFFED TOMATOES

"My friend Jeanne Mears is a marvelous gourmet cook and invitations to Frank and Jeanne's home are accepted with alacrity, for you know that special treats always await, along with a warm welcome."—Nancy Myers, Stoney Creek Cookbook Committee

8	FIRM RIPE TOMATOES	1/4	TEASPOON GROUND OREGANO
1 1/2	POUNDS FRESH MUSHROOMS, SLICED	1	TEASPOON CHOPPED PARSLEY
1/2	CUP BUTTER OR MARGARINE, MELTED	2	TABLESPOONS DRY SHERRY
8	OUNCES SOUR CREAM		SALT AND PEPPER TO TASTE
4	TEASPOONS FLOUR		PAPRIKA
3	OUNCES ROQUEFORT OR BLUE CHEESE		

Scoop out tomatoes, leaving shells intact. Invert and drain. Sauté mushrooms in butter. Drain. Cook sour cream, flour, cheese, oregano, parsley and sherry over low heat until smooth and thickened, stirring constantly. Add mushrooms, salt and pepper. Stir well. Spoon into tomatoes. Place into a shallow pan. Sprinkle with paprika. Bake in a 375 degree oven for 15 minutes. Yield: 8 servings.

Jeanne Mears—St. Peter's Catholic Church
Beaufort, South Carolina

TOMATO CASSEROLE

1	CAN TOMATOES	2	TEASPOONS SUGAR, GRANULATED
1	LARGE ONION, SLICED	4	EGGS, BOILED AND SLICED
2	TEASPOONS SALT	2	CUPS FRESH BREAD, CUBED
1/2	TEASPOON PAPRIKA	4	TABLESPOONS BUTTER
1/8	TEASPOON PEPPER	1	CUP SHARP CHEESE, SHREDDED

Cook first 6 ingredients for 5 minutes on stove burner. Alternate layers in a casserole dish. Begin with tomato mixture, then sliced eggs, bread cubes, butter, and cheese. Top with cheese. Bake in a 375 degree oven for 30 minutes. Yield: 8-10 servings.

Polly Neal—First Presbyterian Church
Marion, North Carolina

Ritzy Vegetables

IRISH POTATOES, SLICED	RITZ CRACKERS, FINELY CRUSHED
ONION, SLICED	MILD CHEDDAR CHEESE
YELLOW SQUASH, SLICED	1 CAN CREAM OF MUSHROOM SOUP
BELL PEPPER, SLICED INTO RINGS	1 SMALL CAN EVAPORATED MILK
SALT TO TASTE	1 STICK (1/4 CUP) MARGARINE
PEPPER TO TASTE	

Butter a casserole dish. Sprinkle 1/2 the cracker crumbs on bottom. Layer the following vegetables over the crumbs—potatoes, onions, bell pepper rings, and squash. Place mild cheddar cheese slices over top layer of vegetables. Dilute 1 can of mushroom soup with 1 small can of evaporated milk. Pour over vegetable mixture and cheese. Sprinkle cracker crumbs over the top. Slice margarine (1 stick or 1/4 cup) thinly over entire top. Bake 2 hours in a 250 degree oven or 1 hour in a 350 degree oven.

Note: An Irish potato is any white potato used for baking or boiling. Use 2 1/2 or 3 quart casserole dish for 5 medium potatoes, 5 medium squash, 1 or 2 medium onions, 1 large bell pepper, 1 to 1 1/2 cups cracker crumbs, and 6 to 8 ounces cheese, sliced or shredded. Test potatoes with a fork for tenderness before removing from oven as you may need to adjust cooking time.

Marion Vaughan—Hampton Presbyterian Church
Hampton, South Carolina

Spring Casserole

3 SQUASH	3-4 TOMATOES
3-4 BELL PEPPERS	2 EARS FRESH CORN, CUT FROM EARS

Boil water and immerse tomatoes for a minute and remove skins. Chop all vegetables coarsely. Place in a greased casserole dish and dot with 1 stick of butter. Cover with bread crumbs. Bake in a 325 degree oven for 1 hour. Yield: 8 servings.

Mary Cope—Independent Presbyterian Church
Savannah, Georgia

Vegetable Casserole I

2 TABLESPOONS BUTTER	4 OUNCES PIMENTOS
2 TABLESPOONS FLOUR	1 LARGE GREEN PEPPER, CHOPPED
1 TEASPOON SALT	1 QUART COOKED POTATOES, SLICED OR COARSELY CHOPPED
4 OUNCES MUSHROOMS	
1 LARGE CAN GREEN PEAS	1 CUP CHEDDAR CHEESE, GRATED

Drain green peas and reserve liquid. Make sauce from butter, flour, salt, and liquid from peas. Place potatoes into casserole. Mix peas, mushrooms, pimentos, and pepper on top of potatoes. Add cheese to sauce and pour over vegetables. Add additional cheese on top and bake in a 350 degree oven until hot and bubbly. Yield: 10 servings. Freezes well.

Faye McGowan—First Presbyterian Church
Beaufort, South Carolina

VEGETABLE CASSEROLE II

1	CAN GREEN ASPARAGUS, DRAINED	6	EGGS, HARD BOILED AND SLICED
1	SMALL CAN GREEN PEAS, DRAINED		CHEDDAR CHEESE, GRATED
1	CAN CREAM OF MUSHROOM SOUP		

Layer all ingredients as listed in greased casserole. Top with butter and cracker crumbs. Bake in a 350 degree oven until hot and bubbly.

Mrs. Norman Olsen—First Central Presbyterian Church
Abilene, Texas

VEGETABLE CASSEROLE SUPREME

2	TABLESPOONS BUTTER	1	CUP MAYONNAISE
1	CUP ONION, CHOPPED	3	TABLESPOONS DIJON MUSTARD
2	(16 OUNCE) CANS MIXED VEGETABLES	1/2	TEASPOON SALT
1	(15 OUNCE) CAN WATER CHESTNUTS, CHOPPED	1/4	TEASPOON PEPPER
1	(3 OUNCE) CAN MUSHROOMS, SLICED	1	TABLESPOON DRIED PARSLEY
1	CUP CELERY, CHOPPED	4	TABLESPOONS BUTTER, MELTED
1	CUP CHEDDAR CHEESE, SHREDDED	26	RITZ CRACKERS, CRUSHED

In a sauce pan, melt butter and sauté onions until soft but not browned. Drain mixed vegetables, water chestnuts, and mushrooms and place in large bowl with onions, celery, and cheese. In small bowl, combine mayonnaise, mustard, salt, pepper, and parsley. Stir into the vegetable mixture. Spray Pam in a 3 quart casserole dish and spoon vegetables evenly into it. Top with a mix of butter and crackers. Bake in a 350 degree oven until bubbly. Will not freeze. Yield: 12 servings.

Maryann C. Abbott—First Presbyterian Church
Greenville, South Carolina

Vegetable Munch

1	BUNCH BROCCOLI, CHOPPED	3/4	CUP WHITE VINEGAR
1	HEAD CAULIFLOWER, CHOPPED	1	TABLESPOON DILLWEED
6	CARROTS, SLICED THIN	1/2 TO 3/4	CUP SUGAR, GRANULATED
3	CELERY STALKS, SLICED THIN	1	TEASPOON GARLIC
10	SPRING ONIONS, DICED	1	TEASPOON SALT
2	CUCUMBERS, PEELED AND CHOPPED	1	TEASPOON PEPPER
1	CUP VEGETABLE OIL		

Combine seasonings, oil, vinegar, and sugar. Pour over vegetables. Cover and marinate in refrigerator. Serve cold. Will keep for several days.

Phyllis Knight—United Presbyterian Church
Lenoir, North Carolina

Vegetable Scallop

4	TABLESPOONS (1/2 STICK) BUTTER	2	CUPS MILK
4	TABLESPOONS FLOUR	1	PACKAGE FROZEN CUT GREEN BEANS, COOKED
1/2	TEASPOON DRY MUSTARD	1	PACKAGE FROZEN PEAS, COOKED
1/2	TEASPOON SALT	16	SMALL WHITE ONIONS, PEELED, COOKED
1/8	TEASPOON PEPPER	1	CUP BREAD CRUMBS, COARSE AND BUTTERED
1/2	TEASPOON WORCESTERSHIRE SAUCE	1/4	POUND CHEDDAR CHEESE, GRATED

Melt butter in saucepan. Remove from heat and blend in flour, mustard, salt, pepper, and Worcestershire sauce. Stir in milk. Cook over medium heat, stirring constantly until sauce thickens and boils 1 minute. Add drained cooked peas, beans, and onions. Turn into an 8 cup buttered baking dish. Make a rim of bread crumbs around edge of dish. Sprinkle cheese over the area within the crumb rim. Bake in a 350 degree oven for about 30 minutes, until top is bubbly. Yield: 8 servings.

Wilma Verduin—United Presbyterian Church
Paterson, New Jersey

Part Two

Historical Vignettes

Chapter Fifteen

Ministry through the Centuries

AUCHTERGAVEN & MONEYDIE PARISH CHURCH, *Perth, Scotland*. Auchtergaven is the parish name for the village of Bankfoot. With a population of fifteen-hundred, the village is in rural Perthshire, about nine miles north of Perth. Moneydie is a hamlet close to Bankfoot. A church has stood on the site of the present building since before the Scottish Reformation in the sixteenth century. The current building is the third on the site and was erected in 1812. In the traditional style, the church has a belltower, and a horseshoe gallery and is surrounded by a graveyard outside.

PORTMOAK CHURCH, *Milnathort, Kinross, Scotland*. This church serves the parish of Portmoak which includes St. Serf's Island adjacent on Loch Leven. Ruins of a priory, dating from Pictish and Culdee times, about 700 A.D., still stand there. It is thought that the name, Portmoak, derives from, *port of monks* or, *St. Moak's port.*

The present church building is of stone, and has had a succession of ministers since 1574. Ebenezer Erskine, minister in 1703, was later banished by the General Assembly and led the secession. Michael Bruce, the *Gentle Poet of Loch Leven*, who composed many best loved Scottish paraphrases, is buried in the churchyard. Linked with the neighboring parish of Orwell in 1960, the present minister is the Reverend Robin Stewart. Portmoak Church is *Church of Scotland* and therefore, Presbyterian.

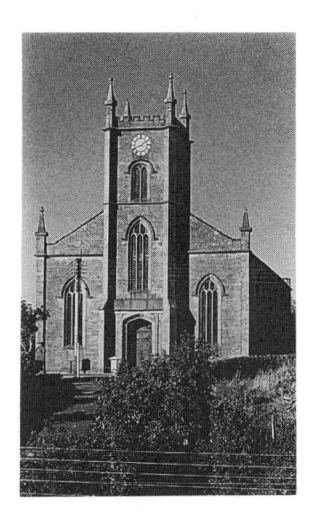

ISLE OF CUMBRAE PARISH CHURCH, *Isle of Cumbrae, Scotland.* Columban monks (Culdees) occupied a site on the island around 500 A.D. Viking raiders destroyed many records so a gap occurs in the church history, until 1318, when the Chapel of Cumray came under the jurisdiction of Paisley Abbey. In 1612, a post Reformation church was built, which had a Hebrew arched doorway with the following inscription, *Let thy Servants o Lord God be clothed with Salvation* (2 Chron. 6:41) written in Hebrew. The archway was incorporated into the present church which was built in 1837, on a hill above the town of Millport, near a holy site. Following tradition, it incorporates stones from the previous churches. It is the only church in the country with a Hebrew inscription within its wall. Also fixed to the chancel walls, are two dogs which traditionally, hold the devil at bay.

NEW WAPPETAW PRESBYTERIAN CHURCH, *McClellanville, South Carolina.* Colonial history records show that the Wappetaw Independent Congregational Church was established in 1697, by a group of settlers from New England. During the American Revolution, it was occupied by the British troops, who eventually burned the church and neighboring farms and possibly instigated the murder of the pastor at the hands of his slaves! In 1786, the church was incorporated as Wappetaw Independent Church. During the War Between the States, the church was occupied by Union soldiers, who burned the pews as firewood. After the war, with the structure in total disrepair, all denominations in McClellanville worshipped in an old schoolhouse. On August 23, 1872, the New Wappetaw Presbyterian Church was organized with the support of the Charleston Presbytery. This church was given the assets of the Wappetaw Independent Church including the Old Wappetaw Cemetery, Communion silver, and linen. The linen bears the date, 1831, and is still in use. The church was remodeled and enlarged in 1911. In 1989, *Hurricane Hugo* caused serious damage, and members of the First Presbyterian Church of Beaufort actively assisted in the restoration.

PLYMOUTH CHURCH IN FRAMINGHAM, *Framingham, Massachusetts.* The origins of Plymouth Church are deeply rooted in the history of America's first settlers in Massachusetts. The area, first settled in 1647, had by 1699, a community of 350 souls and 64 dwellings. A petition was presented to the court to establish a township. It noted that there was a meeting house and a pastor, Mr. John Smith, in place.

Framingham was incorporated on May 29, 1700, and the church formally organized the following year on October 8, 1701. The congregation grew rapidly over the next one hundred years. In 1830, due to doctrinal differences, a new parish, the Hollis Evangelical Society, was formed by *friends of orthodoxy.* On April 17, 1871, the congregation voted to adopt the name, Plymouth Church in Framingham.

Dedicated to God's work, Plymouth Church, throughout its history, has been responsible for the establishment of several other churches in the area.

THE PRESBYTERIAN CHURCH, *Basking Ridge, New Jersey.* The entrance of this church is highlighted by tall doric columns. A magnificent white oak tree stands in the churchyard. The original log structure was built about 1717 by Scottish and Irish Presbyterians. The present church was erected on the site of the log edifice. The congregation met continuously throughout the years and the churchyard has been a community burying ground since early in the eighteenth century. Many graves are overhung by the 140 foot spread of the limbs of the oak. The ancient tree stands 80 feet tall, has a trunk that is 18 feet in circumference, and is estimated to be five hundred years old.

Dedicated to the ministry of Jesus Christ, the congregation reaches out to people of all ages. Among its diverse projects are youth tutoring, support of the Elizabethport Community Center, Christian service in local jails, hospitals, and nursing homes.

PAXTON PRESBYTERIAN CHURCH, *Harrisburg, Pennsylvania. Paxton* (from the Indian word *pexteng*, meaning, *where the water lies still*) is the site of the oldest Presbyterian church building in continuous use in Pennsylvania, and the second oldest, in the United States.

Paxton Presbyterian was organized in 1732. Local legend indicates that there was preaching in private homes as early as 1716. Many of Harrisburg's founders are buried in the churchyard cemetery, John Harris, (1726-1791), four of the commissioners who planned the city, and William Maclay, (1737-1804), the first U.S. Senator from Pennsylvania.

The Reverend John Elder,(1706-1792), is also buried in the churchyard. Elder was the pastor during the French and Indian War and the Revolutionary War, and is remembered as the *fighting pastor*, and, organizer of the famous *Paxton Boys* featured in the book *Light in the Forest* by Conrad Richter.

The Reverend James Anderson of Donegal became the first regular minister in 1726. Formally organized as a Presbyterian church by the Presbytery of Donegal, the Reverend William Bertram became the first installed pastor.

Early services were held in a log building until the present stone church was built in 1740. The interior of the sanctuary was restored to the original design in 1931. The pews, which have doors on the ends to ward off drafts, are arranged in a U-shape to symbolize the church as a family gathered around a Communion table. The old pewter Communion set and lead tokens used as early as 1734, are on display in the archives room.

DEERFIELD PRESBYTERIAN CHURCH, *Deerfield Street, New Jersey.* In 1732, a log school house was erected in Deerfield Street to educate the people so they could read the Bible and have a place to hold religious services.

By 1737, there was need for a larger quarters, and a log church was built. In 1767, a permanent structure was built to replace the log church. A stone church was built at that time from sandstone that was readily available in the nearby fields.

HISTORICAL VIGNETTES											Eighteenth Century 291

PITTSGROVE PRESBYTERIAN CHURCH, *Daretown, New Jersey.* Located in a small village in southwestern New Jersey, this church is full of history from colonial days. The Pennsylvania Presbytery sent a preacher, Henry Hook to the area about 1720. Perhaps inspired by his ministry, forty-nine men signed a covenant in 1741, that established the Pittsgrove Presbyterian Church. The first sanctuary was erected in 1767. A new church was built by 1865. Many of the families who worship at this church are descendants of the original members. In 1932, as part of a bicentennial celebration of George Washington's birth, the church was restored *to its colonial beauty.* Today this old church is described by members as their *pride and joy.*

FIRST PRESBYTERIAN CHURCH, *Beaufort, South Carolina.* There were efforts of Presbyterianism in the Beaufort area dating back to 1684, when the Scottish Covenanters attempted a settlement near what is now residential Spanish Point. Spanish mauraders ended this settlement. The next formal thrust to establish a Presbyterian Church in this corner of South Carolina came in 1743, with the beginnings of a congregation at Stoney Creek. Though somewhat remotely located twenty miles from the successful 1711 settlement by the English of Beaufort, Stoney Creek remained the stronghold of Presbyterianism until First Presbyterian was formed in 1912. This new church grew out of a meeting in the home of Benjamin Burr. The first minister, Dr. N. Keff Smith, came as a supply pastor from the Bethel Presbyterian Church in Walterboro. The present church building was erected in 1929. The church has grown in membership, facilities, and service.

Note: The Stoney Creek Chapel is in custody of First Presbyterian, and services are held there twice each year. It is for this lovely old church, that this cookbook has been created and the proceeds dedicated to its maintenance and preservation.

PERTH NORTH CHURCH, *Perth, Scotland.* The congregation of the North Church, a Presbyterian church, was formed in 1749. Its parish serves the Hillyland and Tulloch areas. The original church was built in 1792, and replaced in 1877. The present church was dedicated on November 11, 1880. The current membership stands at about 2000. The Reverend Robert Swan is the current pastor.

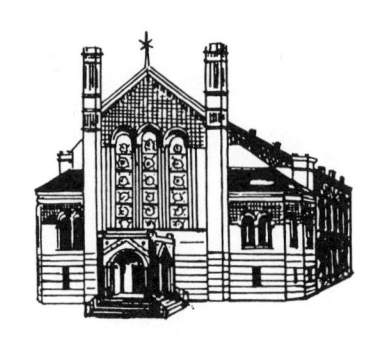

FIRST PRESBYTERIAN CHURCH, *Blackwood, New Jersey.* Organized in 1750, the church called Benjamin Chestnutt, as pastor, from the first graduating class of Princeton University. The present sanctuary is the third building to house the congregation and was erected in 1848. The present membership numbers 180 and is served by the Reverend David A. Davis.

SOUTH SALEM PRESBYTERIAN CHURCH, *South Salem, New York.* Known in its small historic community as the *Old White Church*, the history of the church is almost synonymous with the history of the town. From this area, once known as Lower Salem, forty-five patriots marched off to fight the American cause. Twenty-seven of these Revolutionary-War soldiers are buried in the churchyard. Organized in 1752, by the Reverend Solomon Mead, the church has served not only its members but all community residents. As the community grew, the church grew, and in 1826, a larger church was built to accommodate the congregation. On January 30, 1973, the church building was totally destroyed by a fire. Members rebuilt the church by 1975. Today's *Old White Church* resembles its predecessor, a simple country church in the style of rural New England, but it houses an up-to-date ministry that serves both congregation and community.

INDEPENDENT PRESBYTERIAN CHURCH, *Savannah, Georgia.* Scotsmen, landing with Oglethorpe at the founding of Georgia in 1733, carried with them a strong faith from the Church of Scotland. Independent Presbyterian Church, founded in 1755, as a branch of the Church of Scotland, was originally called, The Presbyterian Church of Savannah. The first church building, facing Market Square, was erected on property that was granted by King George II: *To the intent and purpose that a place of public worship be there upon erected and built for the use and benefit of such of our loving subjects...as are or shall be professors of the Doctrines of the Church of Scotland, greeable to the Westminster Confession of Faith.*

The original church was destroyed by fire in 1796. Another was erected in 1800, but damaged by a later hurricane. The church moved to the present location and had an impressive church built in 1819. The edifice created much favorable comment as to the design and elegant interior. President Woodrow Wilson was married in the manse, in 1885, by the Reverend L.S.K. Axson, grandfather of the bride, Ellen Louise Axson.

After fire destroyed the church once again in 1889, the present church was built immediately with the same design, and is called *Savannah's most notable building* by Savannah's own historian, Walter Hartridge.

FIRST PRESBYTERIAN CHURCH, *Statesville, North Carolina.* Although founded in 1753, records in the church's Historical Room tell of gatherings of the congregation for a period of ten years previously, each time meeting in a different place because of the danger from the Catawba Indians living in the area at the time. The members consisted mostly of Scotch and Irish Presbyterians who migrated from Pennsylvania to the Piedmont area of North Carolina. Today many descendants of the original families worship in the church. These same people were the founders of the city of Statesville, North Carolina. The church was first known as the Fourth Creek Congregation, taking its name from the fourth creek running near by. The church has a membership of approximately seven hundred members and is involved in many endeavors.

INDIANTOWN PRESBYTERIAN CHURCH, *Hemingway, South Carolina.* This church was founded in 1757 by a group of Calvinist settlers led by Major John James and Robert Wilson. The building was burned by the Tories during the Revolutionary War. The present sanctuary was built in 1830 on the approximate site of the first church. Its meeting house style remained unchanged until the 1900s, when a porch and basement were added. The Session House, a small building on the right side of the churchyard, is older than the church, and housed a school in the 1820s.

GREENVILLE PRESBYTERIAN CHURCH, *Donalds, South Carolina.* The church was founded in 1769 as a preaching point on the Saluda River, and as a member of Orange Presbytery. Land acquired in 1784, has been the location of three churches. The present church, erected in 1853, was built of materials and bricks made by parishioners on the property. Regular worship services have been held continuously since 1773.

THE OLD PRESBYTERIAN MEETING HOUSE, *Alexandria, Virginia.* This historic shrine of exceptional interest is known as the cradle of Presbyterian faith in the Alexandria area. Scottish and Scotch-Irish settlers built the sanctuary in 1775. A fire in 1835 destroyed the building except for the walls, but the congregation reconstructed the church and later added a bell tower. The Meeting House is associated with famous figures of the American Revolution. Memorial ceremonies for George Washington were held there. Buried in the graveyard at the rear of the grounds are founders of the church, heroes of the American Revolution, leaders of early Alexandria, and friends of George Washington. At the side of the burial ground is the Tomb of the Unknown Soldier of the American Revolution.

TIMBER RIDGE UNITED PRESBYTERIAN CHURCH, *Greeneville, Tennessee.* Beginning as the Sinking Springs Presbyterian Church, under the leadership of the Reverend James Balch, a log meeting house was erected in 1786 to serve the thirty families who had migrated into Tennessee from Virginia and Pennsylvania. When the church moved to its present site at the turn of the century, the name was changed to Timber Ridge. They erected a log church that was later replaced by a similar structure. In 1854, another building was erected. In 1886-1887 the original church buildings were replaced by the present church. Bricks from the older building were used in its construction. Since then, extensive remodeling has been done and an educational building has been added.

FIRST PRESBYTERIAN CHURCH, *Paris, Kentucky.* This church traces its roots to the 1787 establishment of a Presbyterian church before the town was named and prior to Kentucky statehood. On the edge of Paris, there is a large sinking spring by which the pioneers camped. It was natural for the church, led by Rev. Andrew McClure, to bear the name Sinking Springs Presbyterian Church until 1794, when the town was named Paris.

OLNEY PRESBYTERIAN CHURCH, *Gastonia, North Carolina.* Founded in 1793, Olney Church now supports Logos, an after school program for children and youth incorporating Bible study, worship skills, music, crafts, recreation, and fellowship. Logos is an outreach made possible by profits from a cookbook published by the church and dedicated to Martha Bess Holder. The book's foreword denotes the many changes Olney Church has endured in the over two hundred years since its founding: "From a brush arbor to a brick building; From open-air meetings to air conditioning; From a deep rural setting to industrialized surroundings; From a one room building set on rocks to a spacious facility with an elevator; From a congregation of farmers to a congregation of diverse occupations."

MARKET SQUARE PRESBYTERIAN CHURCH, *Harrisburg, Pennsylvania.* Celebrating its bicentennial in 1994, this church's first congregation initially met in the loft of Harrisburg's jail. Their subsequent home was the county courthouse. This did not distract them from the Higher Authority. In 1806, members built their first structure. They organized the first Sunday school in Harrisburg in 1816. A fire in 1858 led to the construction of a new edifice which today still serves as sanctuary and chapel. Its Gothic spire, 193 feet high, is prominent in Harrisburg's skyline. Market Square helped establish several Presbyterian churches in the city. In 1972, the church began a Korean ministry, calling a Korean associate minister and they also helped establish a center for Vietnamese refugee resettlement in south central Pennsylvania.

NATIONAL PRESBYTERIAN CHURCH AND CENTER, *Washington, D.C.* Unique among churches of the denomination, its beginning goes back to worship services held in a carpenter shop on the grounds where the White House was being constructed in 1795. The present church was formed by the merger of two historic congregations, the First Presbyterian Church in the District of Columbia and the Church of the Covenant.

FIRST PRESBYTERIAN CHURCH, *Columbia, South Carolina.* This was the first church organized in Columbia. The pastor, Rev. D. E. Dunlap, was ordained and installed on June 4, 1795. Services were initially held in the State House. In 1810, services were moved to South Carolina College Chapel where students sat on the floor and the congregation sat in the galleries. The first building was erected in 1813, and subsequently, replaced in 1853. An expansion in 1925 increased seating capacity from 800 to an impressive 1,250. The churchyard contains the graves of five soldiers of the American Revolution and many from the nation's subsequent wars. It is a place of interest to students of local history and includes the graves of President Woodrow Wilson's parents.

First Presbyterian Church, *Morganton, North Carolina.* Morganton is located in western North Carolina, in the foothills of the Blue Ridge Mountains. Founded in 1797, Morganton's original sanctuary was the town's first church. In 1959, the church moved from the original downtown site to a hilltop west of town. Services were held there in the fellowship hall until the new sanctuary was completed in 1965. One of their most successful building fund projects was a cookbook!

The Jewett Presbyterian Church, *Jewett, New York.* The church dates to July 7, 1799. Construction began on the first church building in 1803, with services there in 1804. The present building dates to 1848. In 1850 the congregation adopted their present name. Previous name changes occurred due to the change of names for their locale, a mountain area of New York State.

First Presbyterian Church, *Attica, New York.* Built of wood in 1809, this landmark was later replaced by a brick building with a clock tower whose clock sounds the hours. The church entrance has wide iron steps, imported from England. The sanctuary is enhanced by lovely stained-glass windows. An adjoining parish hall, added in 1955, serves both congregation and community as a meeting place.

First Presbyterian Church, *New Vernon, New Jersey.* Beginning as a Sunday school, this church was established in 1809. The Reverend Ulric Maynard was called as pastor June of 1833. The new church was built within a year, and has been in continuous use ever since. Classrooms were added in 1950. In 1981, a twenty-two-rank Casavant Pipe organ was installed. Dr. George E. Chorba, called in 1968, is the seventeenth pastor to serve the church.

FIRST PRESBYTERIAN CHURCH, *Easton, Pennsylvania.* In 1811, forty-three people petitioned the Presbytery of New Brunswick, New Jersey, and established First Presbyterian Church. A supply pastor, the Reverend Stephen Boyer, was sent in November and services were held in the Northampton County Courthouse for several years. The first sanctuary was built in 1819. The present building, with the adjoining church house was erected in 1896.

Twenty-eight pastors have served First Presbyterian in its 180-year history. The first woman to hold the position of pastor, the Reverend Carol M. Gregg has served the congregation since 1990. The church has a membership of 425, a 15-person lay board, and belongs to the Lehigh Presbytery in the Synod of the Trinity (PCUSA).

THE BETHEL REFORMED CHURCH, *County Durham, England.* The church had its origins in a group of Independents (dissenters from the Church of England) who held cottage meetings. In 1814, the first minister, Peter Rathbone, was called and a site and buildings were obtained for services. The original lay trustees were a millwright, a skin-dresser, a clogger, and two tallow-chandlers. Financial struggle dominates this church's records yet the small congregation has managed to persevere through such hardships as war (1914-18), and the distressing times of the 1930s, when the town had 8000 unemployed out of 11,000 insurable workers. In the Second World War, the church's schoolroom was used for a Forces Canteen, staffed by the ladies from local churches.

The Reverend Hugh Kember who arrived as minister in 1961, is credited with both a physical and spiritual renewal at the church on Chester-le-Street. Although membership has never risen above 100 communicants, the little church has responded magnificently to their present opportunities by undertaking a regular visitation in the town; by reshaping children's work; by sharing fully in the local Council of Churches; and by becoming financially self-supportive. The church has a thorough program of renovation and redecoration underway. The present minister, the Reverend Rhona Mitchell Jones, was called in 1987. The church recently celebrated their 175th anniversary.

HISTORICAL VIGNETTES *Nineteenth Century* 299

First Presbyterian Church, *LeRoy, New York.* Both in history and geography, this church is a close neighbor of the Stone Church Presbyterian Church in Bergen, New York, whose members also contributed to this book (see p. 302). First Presbyterian Church of LeRoy was founded in 1815, when its first elders were chosen. The church building was completed in 1826.

First Presbyterian Church, *Wyoming, New York.* The 112 members of the First Presbyterian Church of Wyoming, New York, are keepers of a landmark church. The little church was organized on June 14, 1817, when the village consisted of twelve log cabins, three frame dwellings, a grist mill, and little else. Despite the smallness of the area, the church grew and in 1830, the first building was constructed. The church was enlarged in both 1867 and 1928. Today it remains one of the most beautiful landmark churches in the country.

United Presbyterian Church, *Corfu, New York.* The town of Corfu is in western New York, about twenty miles from Buffalo. The church was founded in 1817. It has a very active mission and enjoys lots of pot luck dinners around the year.

The Presbyterian Church, *Cadiz, Ohio.* This church celebrated its 175th anniversary on October 17, 1992. The congregation was first organized in 1817. In 1967, the Grace United Presbyterian Church and Trinity Presbyterian Church joined to form The Presbyterian Church. The present church building was dedicated in 1871. A *Tiffany* window, entitled, *Resurrection Morn* adorns the sanctuary. A Moeller organ, installed around 1900, provides music for worship services. There are 420 members on active roll. The church has been served by the Reverend William H. Hudson for the past fifteen years.

FIRST PRESBYTERIAN CHURCH, *Charleston, West Virginia.* The exterior of this church is an exact duplicate of the former Madison Square Presbyterian Church, in New York City. The interior resembles the richly ornamented Italian Renaissance structure, St. Marks's Basilica, in Venice. First Presbyterian Church was founded in 1819, by the Reverend Dr. Henry Fuffner. The present sanctuary was built in 1915, restored from 1991 to 1992, and rededicated on September 13, 1992.

FIRST PRESBYTERIAN CHURCH, *Athens, Georgia.* Founded in 1820, this church erected a sanctuary in 1855. In 1964, an educational building was added. The pulpit in the sanctuary is carved of Italian marble and the pulpit furniture was a gift from the family of General T.R.R. Cobb. The original pine pews are trimmed in walnut, and are from Whitehall Plantation. They were designed to accommodate families of different sizes, and many of the original nameplates can be seen on them. The private pews have not been used in many years.

BETHSEDA PRESBYTERIAN CHURCH, *Camden, South Carolina.* This church was designed by the first Federal architect in the United States, Robert Mills. The building stands today in complete restoration as it was originally constructed in 1822, and was designated a National Historic Landmark in 1985. The sanctuary contains numerous memorial tablestand bronze markers honoring dedicated and loyal parishioners, many of whom were a part of the history and heritage of the state of South Carolina as well as the development of the United States. An obelisk was erected in front of the church in 1825 in memory of Baron Johann deKalb, who was killed in the Battle of Camden during the Revolutionary War. The Marquis de Lafayette delivered a eulogy from the church steps as the body of deKalb was reinterred beneath the monument.

WARM SPRINGS PRESBYTERIAN CHURCH, *Warm Springs, Virginia.* The heritage of this church was developing as early as 1783. On October 14, 1824, the church was organized at Dean's Meeting House on the Jackson River. In 1855, a new brick church was built by the congregation near the famous Warm Springs pools. On the pool property, stood the Old Warm Springs Hotel. Built in 1811, the hotel served guests until 1925 when it was torn down. The recipes that were donated by this church, came from the hotel's well known kitchen.

FIRST PRESBYTERIAN CHURCH, *Savannah, Georgia.* Founded in 1827, this was the first Savannah church to unite with the Presbyterian Church in the United States and is today, a member of the Presbyterian Church (U.S.A.). The Washington Street location is the third in the history of the church. It has been served by twenty-two pastors, three of whom are especially noteworthy: Lowell Mason, a charter member and well known American hymn writer; Dr. Charles Colcock Jones, remembered for his evangelical and educational work with African Americans, prior to the Civil War; and Dr. Benjamin Morgan Palmer, first moderator of the Presbyterian Church in the United States.

FIRST PRESBYTERIAN CHURCH, *Baton Rouge, Louisiana.* Organized by fifteen members in 1827, this church is the oldest Protestant church in East Baton Rouge Parish. A new church was built in 1926, to accommodate the growing membership of over sixteen hundred. Located downtown, the building is only a few blocks from the original site. The congregation is comprised of persons from throughout metropolitan Baton Rouge. The church has supported and furnished members for fourteen new churches and counts among the membership a former state governor and a moderator of the General Assembly. During one period, four members were enrolled in seminaries to study for the ministry.

COVINGTON UNITED PRESBYTERIAN CHURCH, *Pavilion, New York.* Located in western New York State, this rural church was formally organized in 1827. Today's congregation of 155 members, still holds services in the original white frame building, erected in 1828. Twelve pastors have served this church with Reverend Ray I. Lindquist, having just completed his twenty-fifth year. The church enjoys a very active music program, Sunday school, and groups for women and men.

STONE CHURCH PRESBYTERIAN CHURCH, *Bergen, New York.* This church with a seemingly redundant name, is located west of Rochester, New York. It was organized in 1828 as the Second Congregational Society of the Towns of LeRoy and Bergen. It was also received into Genesee Consociation of the Congregational Church. A stone structure was built for worship that year and the community became known as *Stone Church.* In 1882, the church was received into the Presbyterian Church in the U.S.A. Ironically, the stone building did not last. In 1864, was condemned, torn down, and replaced with the present wooden structure.

THE UNITED CHURCH OF ELLICOTTVILLE, *Ellicottville, New York.* This church began in the early nineteenth century, when the New England settlers started moving into western New York. The congregation was organized in 1828. In the 1830s and 1840s, the church was involved in the underground railroad under the leadership of Rev. Sylvester Crowles, a strong abolitionist. In 1852, the congregation erected its present sanctuary.

Today Ellicottville remains a small village in the Allegheny Highlands. Every winter, skiers flock to the area's downhill skiing resorts. In the fall, when the trees are brilliant in color, a festival is held which attracts over twenty-five thousand people from New York, Ohio, Pennsylvania, and Ontario. One of the favorite stops is the United Church of Ellicottville, Presbyterian Church (U.S.A.), where they can purchase hot turkey soup to keep them warm in the autumn chill (see recipe).

FIRST PRESBYTERIAN CHURCH, *Medina, New York.* This church was founded in 1829. During that time, Medina was part of the western frontier of America. The town prospered on the banks of the Erie Barge Canal, helping to open the way westward. Presbyterians and other Christian denominations saw the need for the support and ministries the church could provide. They established a Reformed witness. It has continued over the years, seeking to be a rock of faith amidst the ever changing face and life of western New York.

FIRST PRESBYTERIAN CHURCH, *Findlay, Ohio.* Located in the town of Findlay, about forty miles south of Toledo, in northwestern Ohio, the church was started in 1830 by ten people and an itinerate preacher. Today the church has 1,150 members and three pastors. The original church of Gothic style, built in 1901, was later destroyed by fire. In 1955, the present church was built as a replacement. The stately, brick structure is of colonial style.

VICKSBURG PRESBYTERIAN CHURCH, *Vicksburg, Mississippi.* In 1826, a Princeton Theological student, Zebulon Butler, began preaching to Vicksburg Presbyterians in the upper chamber of a temporary courthouse. In the basement, was a saloon! In 1830, the Vicksburg Presbyterian Church was incorporated by the Mississippi State Legislature. The first building, probably completed around 1833, had a tall tapered steeple that distinguished the red brick church, and a small sanctuary. In 1855, this structure was sold, and a second building was dedicated. In 1908, a fire gutted the old church the evening after its last scheduled service. Fortunately, a new building was completed by the time of the fire. As the church grew, an educational building was approved in 1928, and built that year. A new wing was added and renovation took place in 1990. Today the growing congregation is known for its strong youth programs for children of all ages. The church is active in many service projects, recycling efforts, and Bible studies.

FIRST PRESBYTERIAN CHURCH, *Fort Wayne, Indiana.* Today's city of Fort Wayne has a history dating back to the 1700s. The Miami Indians had their main village at the junction of the St. Mary's and St. Joseph rivers. The original fort was built there by the French soldiers, but it was later captured by the Miami Chief, Pontiac. In 1794, General Anthony Wayne recaptured the fort. It was rebuilt and later known as, Fort Wayne.

In 1831, First Presbyterian Church was organized by seven members, two of whom, were nieces of Little Turtle, an outstanding Miami Chief. The first minister was pledged $275. A building was built in 1837, but growth, and a fire in 1882, led to four subsequent structures. Today's large and active urban church is also home to a Korean language congregation that moved from nearby New Haven in 1984.

ERVIE-KIRKCOLM WITH LESWALT, *Stranraes, Scotland.* Many dairy farmers are members of this parish kirk, constructed in 1832. Kirkcolm means *Kirk of St. Columba* and people have been living in this area since before the Vikings. Ruins of the old kirk may be seen at the other end of the village, along with the historic *Well of St. Columba.* Water was sacred to the ancient Celts, so it has been a place of worship for a long time. In 1843, some members left the kirk and formed the Free Kirk, built at Ervie, 1 1/2 miles away. The two kirks were reunited in 1929, and are yoked to the next parish, Leswalt.

WESTMINSTER PRESBYTERIAN CHURCH, *Charleston, South Carolina.* This suburban church ministers primarily to the portion of Charleston city and county lying west of the Ashley River. They actively support *Habitat for Humanity* and *Charleston Interfaith Crisis Ministry.* A 1970 merger of a downtown congregation Westminster (founded in 1832) and Covenant (founded in 1964) formed the present church.

ELMIRA UNITED PRESBYTERIAN CHURCH, *Toulon, Illinois.* Founded by Scottish immigrants in 1834, the church was at one time, the only Gaelic speaking Presbyterian Church in the United States. The current building has been in continuous use for over one hundred years. It stands on a Presbyterian Reformed Historical site.

HISTORICAL VIGNETTES *Nineteenth Century* 305

FIRST PRESBYTERIAN CHURCH, *South Bend, Indiana.* Organized on May 3, 1834, the present structure is the church's fifth home. This monument to God is of Georgian colonial architecture. It is a four-unit plan grouped around a towering spire, topped with a shining Greek cross.

FIRST PRESBYTERIAN CHURCH, *Orangeburg, South Carolina.* The church was organized on May 2, 1835. The earliest congregation met in the town's Merchant House. The first sanctuary, built in 1844, was destroyed by a fire in 1857. The congregation rebuilt on the same site. In 1948, the present property was purchased, and the church was relocated there by 1950. First Presbyterian is a member of the Presbyterian Church(U.S.A.) and it continues to grow in membership and faith.

AVELEIGH PRESBYTERIAN CHURCH, *Newberry, South Carolina.* Located between Columbia and Greenville, the church was founded in 1835. Its name was chosen by one of the founders whose parents were members of a church in Ireland of the same name.

Note: Morgan and Julia Randell, active members of the First Presbyterian Church (Beaufort) were married in the Aveleigh Church. Julia Randell's great, great grandfather served as minister in the 1800s, and her great grandfather and grandfather served as elders.

DAHLONEGA PRESBYTERIAN CHURCH, *Dahlonega, Georgia.* In 1829, the nation's first great gold rush was well underway near the present site of Dahlonega, Georgia. To serve the influx of people, this church was organized in 1838. The first pastor came from Philadelphia as chief coiner at the new Georgia branch of the U.S. Mint. The congregation began the first Sunday school in the town that same year. The original frame church built in 1898, is still standing. The present brick building was erected in 1963, and the Reverend Frank G. Colladay, Jr., is the current pastor.

FIRST PRESBYTERIAN CHURCH, *Demopolis, Alabama.* The church was organized on November 11, 1839, with nine original members. By 1843, there was a house of worship and later, a resident preacher. The Civil War and Reconstruction exacted a heavy toll on the congregation. The church building was seized, and the congregation was deprived of funds, members, and pastoral care. A new building was erected in 1869. Extensive remodeling took place in 1905. The church joined the Presbyterian Church of America in 1985. Today a fellowship hall, classroom, conference space, office, and kitchen facilities have been added.

ROSWELL PRESBYTERIAN CHURCH, *Roswell, Georgia.* Located north of Atlanta, the town of Roswell was first settled by families from coastal Georgia communities, such as Savannah. This church was organized in 1839. The first minister, Dr. Nathaniel Pratt, married the daughter of prominent landowner, Roswell King, whose family donated land for the church, built in 1840. It was the first public building in town. Seventeen slaves worshipped from the balcony. During the Civil War, the sanctuary served as a hospital for Union soldiers. It was unharmed during the conflict, and has remained in use through the years. A larger structure was built adjacent to the original building in 1978. This church is listed on the National Register of Historic Places.

FIRST PRESBYTERIAN CHURCH, *Alexandria, Louisiana.* By 1840, a small Presbyterian church was built on Beauregard Street. Although it withstood the flood of 1844, it burned at the end of the Civil War. Presbyterians joined other Protestants at the courthouse for service. In 1893, the Reverend B.L. Price was sent by the Presbytery of South Louisiana. During his ministry, a church and manse were built and other Presbyterian congregations in Central Louisiana were organized. During World War II, the church cared for soldiers in camps nearby. In 1990, a new building was completed, and already an even larger sanctuary is being planned.

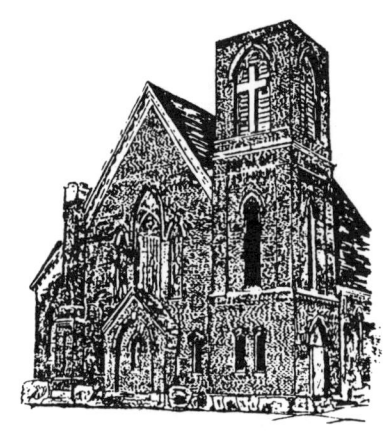

CENTRAL PRESBYTERIAN CHURCH, *Petersburg, Illinois.* This church is located in a town of Abraham Lincoln fame. In 1839, Petersburg was named the county seat. Abraham Lincoln lived in New Salem, and surveyed and plotted the town of Petersburg. Many of the early settlers from New Salem moved there, and started the Presbyterian Church. One of the founders, Dr. John Allen, of Vermont, served as a physician at New Salem. He was a close friend and a neighbor of Abraham Lincoln.

The church's fifteen members built and dedicated the small white frame church in 1842. After the Civil War, with membership of 170, a larger building was designed. The new brick building, with a one hundred foot steeple, was dedicated in 1874. The original stained-glass windows, are hand painted glass, the earliest type used in church windows in this country. In 1919, opalescent, leaded-glass windows were also installed, in memory of loved ones lost in World War I. In the chapel, is an authentic *Tiffany* window, installed in 1917. Petersburg is on the National Register of Historic Places, and the church is a part of the Historic District.

FIRST PRESBYTERIAN CHURCH, *York, South Carolina.* The church was organized by Bethel Presbytery in June of 1842, with only fifteen charter members. In 1862, the present sanctuary was completed. The building was brick with a stucco covering, and costs were $12,300.00. An adjoining educational building was later added, a gift from a generous member, Mrs. S.M. McNeel. The present 513 members take pride in the church. Its steeple is visible from the entire city of York, giving it the affectionate title, *the Steeple Church.*

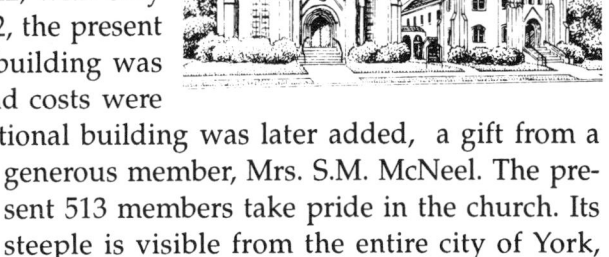

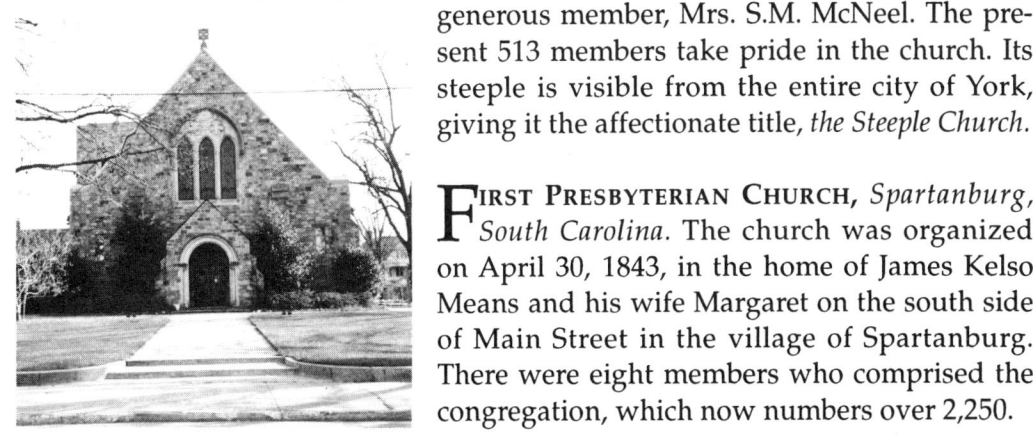

FIRST PRESBYTERIAN CHURCH, *Spartanburg, South Carolina.* The church was organized on April 30, 1843, in the home of James Kelso Means and his wife Margaret on the south side of Main Street in the village of Spartanburg. There were eight members who comprised the congregation, which now numbers over 2,250.

WESTMINSTER PRESBYTERIAN CHURCH, *St. Louis, Missouri.* Washington Avenue Presbyterian Church (founded in 1844 and later named Pine Street Presbyterian Church) and the Westminster Presbyterian Church (founded in 1846) merged in 1853 as Pine Street. During the Civil War, the Reverend Samuel McPheeters, who was an outspoken voice of moderation, was deposed from his pulpit, and banished from the state of Missouri. President Lincoln intervened, leading to an unsuccessful effort to recall the Reverend. With the growth of St. Louis to the west, the church also moved westward, becoming the Grand Avenue Presbyterian church in 1884. Another move occurred when the present structure was built in 1915. The name Westminster was then reestablished.

FIRST PRESBYTERIAN CHURCH, *Marion, North Carolina.* From writings of historian, Miss Elsie Keeter: *On the thirtieth day of August 1845, certain persons, members of various Presbyterian churches, met in propriety of organizing a Presbyterian church at this place. The project being unanimously agreed to, the church was organized by thirteen members. . . . The first building was erected in 1847, constructed of brick at a cost of $800.00. The present sanctuary was erected in 1922, using most of the bricks from the original building.*

FIRST PRESBYTERIAN CHURCH, *Waynesboro, Virginia.* The town of Waynesboro is located in the Blue Ridge Mountains, overlooking Charlottesville. The church was started by a group of people from the Tinkling Spring Church, and organized by the Lexington Presbytery in 1846. The sanctuary was built in 1911 with major additions in 1942 and 1960. The building was gutted by fire in 1983 and has since been rebuilt.

ST. PETER'S CATHOLIC CHURCH, *Beaufort, South Carolina.* The original church was built and dedicated in 1846 on land purchased by Michael O'Connor, who it is believed, personally assumed the building expenses. This beautiful little church is now St. Peter's Chapel, and a new church was completed in 1988 that serves more than 800 families in the Catholic parish.

FIRST PRESBYTERIAN CHURCH, *Greenville, South Carolina.* Organized in February of 1848, a church building was erected in 1850, and was later torn down. The present structure (1883), contains two walls from the original building. The sanctuary was enlarged, and dedicated on February 28, 1988. The congregation has been served by nine ministers, and provided large numbers to start other congregations. Present membership exceeds 3800 persons.

WAQUOIT CONGREGATIONAL CHURCH, *Falmouth, Massachusetts.* The first sermon at Waquoit Congregational was preached by the Reverend Silas S. Hyde. It was on the occasion of the dedication, February 2, 1848. Pews of the church were sold to parishioners to support the church. Later, a tax on the pews was also imposed for the same purpose. From 1890 to 1954, money was scarce, so the church often had services only in the summer. The Reverend Wayne Porter began the Sunday school in 1950.

FIRST PRESBYTERIAN CHURCH, *Cuero, Texas.* Three churches form this congregation. The first was Live Oak Church, so named because it was organized on July 8, 1849, under a live oak tree on the farm of Dr. Robert and Mary C. Trigg Peeble. A second church was organized at Concrete, Texas, in 1855. The First Presbyterian Church of Cuero, Texas, was the third, chartered in 1878. The consolidation of these three churches was approved in 1883. On March 8, 1970, the congregation moved to the present building and Reverend Harvey L. Friedal is pastor.

First Presbyterian Church, *Greenwood, South Carolina.* The roots of this church go back to 1850 when the Rock Presbyterian Church, near the growing hamlet of Greenwood Village, purchased the high school building as a more convenient location for Sunday school and prayer meetings. This became known as the Chapel. For the next thirty-three years, many members of the Rock Church worshipped at the Chapel until a first church was erected in 1875. In April of 1883, the Greenwood Church was formerly organized. The church continued to grow and another building was dedicated in 1899. The present sanctuary was dedicated in 1958. Today the church has 928 communicants. Fifty of the present members are direct descendants of the original fifty-nine charter members.

Carrollton Presbyterian Church, *Carrollton, Louisiana.* Originally a mission of the Presbytery in 1855, the church was kept alive during the Civil War years through the effort and energy of Mrs. Rosina Prague. Mrs. Prague held church meetings in private homes and provided religious education for her daughters as well as many of the community children. The Palmer Park Church and Carrollton Presbyterian Church merged in 1919. Together they built the present sanctuary on the corner of Panola and Carrollton Avenues. This church continues to witness to the stability of traditional Christian truths and values.

Piedmont Presbyterian Church, *Piedmont, West Virginia.* In 1856, approximately twenty-five people established the Piedmont Presbyterian Church to serve the tri-towns, Piedmont, West Virginia, Westernport, Maryland, and, Luke, Maryland. During the Civil War, membership dropped down to the low number of seven. However, the church prevailed and in 1883 the sanctuary was built at its present location. A new addition was made to the back of the church in 1956. Membership reached as high as 425 people in the early 1940s. Today enrollment is about 150 members.

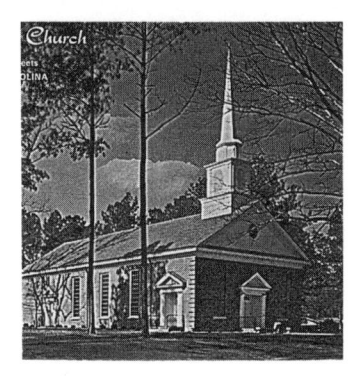

FIRST PRESBYTERIAN CHURCH, *Whiteville, North Carolina*. On February 10, 1856, The Fayetteville Presbytery organized the Whiteville Presbyterian Church. A building was erected in 1870, and was the first church edifice in town. After several relocations over the years, the present sanctuary was built in 1975. Two of the original pews and the Communion table are in the present church foyer. The same cup and bread plate are still in use, and the original bell is mounted in the courtyard.

ASH UNITED REFORM, *Kent, England*. Built in 1856, after a break from its sister church in Sandwich, a nearby market town, Ash United is situated in a village of three thousand people. The congregation of about forty, has weekday meeting's of women's groups, and Bible study. A monthly Saturday Coffee Morning helps to raise funds for the church.

FIRST PRESBYTERIAN CHURCH, *Belle Plaine, Minnesota*. Organized in 1858, the founders met at the home of Mr. H. B. Gates. The church was completed and dedicated in 1870. In 1948, the Fellowship Auditorium was added. The sanctuary was remodeled and, other improvements were made in 1958, as part of the Centennial celebration. The first organ was presented, and was used for the occasion. This small church has about 150 members.

FIRST PRESBYTERIAN CHURCH, *Aiken, South Carolina*. Organized in 1858, this congregation has strong connections with Stoney Creek Presbyterian Chapel. It was the "home church" of many early members of Aiken Church who played roles in First Presbyterian's history. The building of the Savannah River Plant caused accelerated growth and a severe shortage of space. These challenges were met in part by the construction of a new church in 1969. Presently, a new Family Life Center is under construction. The church is a part of Trinity Presbytery (PCUSA).

Honea Path Presbyterian Church, *Honea Path, South Carolina.* Eighteen charter members organized Honea Path on August 21, 1860. It is the oldest church in Anderson County, South Carolina. In 1869, the Methodists bought one half of the interest in the building and both congregations used it for seventeen years.

In 1886, it was decided that the property was to be divided. The Methodists built their own church. The two congregations remain close, sharing responsibility for Vacation Bible School and Christmas Cantata. Honea Path Presbyterian is part of Foothills Presbytery and currently has 120 members.

Armagh Road Presbyterian Church, *Portadown, Craigavon, Northern Ireland,* The Reverend Campbell Wilson states: *this church is relatively young in our terms, being built in 1860, to cope with the influx of Presbyterians at that time, (not everyone went to America).* Portadown is a largely industrial town and the church ministers to around 400 families.

Parkhead Congregational Church, *Glasgow, Scotland.* Founded in 1860 as a small Sunday school, the group staffed by deacons and members of Dovehill Church, met first in a weaver's cottage. Within ten years, growth necessitated the move to a larger building of corrugated iron. The congregation later relocated to the present church where worship has been held for almost a century.

First Presbyterian Church, *Rutherford, New Jersey.* In 1863, a petition was presented to the Presbytery of Passaic to organize a church in Boiling Springs. The petition was granted for fifteen members to move ahead. In 1868, the group incorporated as the First Presbyterian Church of Rutherford Park. The sanctuary was completed the next year. The present church building was completed in 1890.

HISTORICAL VIGNETTES *Nineteenth Century* 313

First Presbyterian Church, *Valdosta, Georgia.* Organized in 1864, the present sanctuary was built in 1908 and is now on the National Historic Register of Historic Landmarks. The fellowship hall and classrooms were added in 1958, and the Centennial Building was completed in 1964, in honor of the church's 100th birthday. Members of the church are involved in community service projects including *Break Bread Together*, a volunteer meals assistance program that the church began sponsoring in 1973, *LAMP* or, Lowndes Associated Ministries to People, the *Community Soup Kitchen*, and numerous other programs designed to serve the Lord.

First Presbyterian Church, *Paola, Kansas.* In the aftermath of the Civil War, a group of dedicated Presbyterians established the church in October of 1867. The structure housing the sanctuary was dedicated in 1905, with additions made in 1928, and 1966. Church members of the eastern Kansas community celebrated their 125th anniversary in October of 1992. The tradition they strive to pass on to future generations is grounded in the story of Jesus Christ and His love.

Helena Presbyterian Church, *Helena, Montana.* Members of this church note that the main street of Helena curves around the gulch named, *Last Chance Gulch*. The name is indeed reflective of the the church's early beginnings in Helena. In 1869, the Reverend Sheldon Jackson gathered a few people, some say twelve women, in the Last Gulch mining camps, and organized Helena Presbyterian Church. Elders and deacons could not be elected at the time due to the absense of male members. Thus, the church was not officially established until June 15, 1872. The present building was first occupied in 1892. Today the church accommodates a growing congregation of 532 members. Edna Hinman, a member since 1915, was the first woman moderator of the Presbytery. Two of Ms. Hinman's recipes were chosen to be featured in this book.

HARMONY PRESBYTERIAN CHURCH, *Crocketville, South Carolina.* Harmony Church was first planned in the summer of 1866, when neighbors of the Dry Swamp section of Whippy Swamp, a scattered rural community, met to organize a union church. The meeting took place only a few months after Lee's surrender at the Appomattox Court House. A ten year old girl, Lilly Gooding, described the Dry Swamp assembly: *People climbed out of farm wagons, carts, sulkies, buggies, gigs, a few stepped carriages, some rode old, poor horses; others walked. Seats and cushions from various vehicles afforded comfort for some, while others sat on the ground. The pulpit, was a wide board fastened between two trees at the proper height for a reading desk and long enough to hold the preachers hat, bible, hymnbook, pitcher of water, and a glass.* The church built at the Dry Swamp site was a great source of pride. Owing to a predominance of Presbyterian families, the church was a union church for only a short time. It was officially received by the Charleston Presbytery in 1870. In 1876, Harmony Church joined a group of Presbyterian worshippers in Crocketville to erect a centrally located building on a site donated by Major W. J. Gooding. The present edifice, the third to bear the name of Harmony Presbyterian, was built in 1907. An educational building was added in 1954, and the cemetery was later expanded. *Note: A granddaughter of Major Gooding, Nancy Gooding Gutheridge, is an active member of the First Presbyterian Church of Beaufort, South Carolina.*

BROWN MEMORIAL CHURCH, *Baltimore, Maryland.* The origins of this church are unique. The edifice was erected and then the congregation was organized! The church was built around 1870, by Isabella Brown as a memorial to her late husband, George, who had been an exceptional Christian and local citizen. Mrs. Brown never left her own church, First Presbyterian, which had actively supported the organization of the new congregation, initially of 60 members. Financial support came from the rental of pews, a practice that continued until the 1930s. Fine pastors, including Maltbie Babcock and Dr. T. Guthrie Speers, contributed to the significant growth of the church. Due to the unusual contract between Mrs. Brown and the original congregation, it was felt that the church should remain urban. However, in 1958, a second church was built in the suburbs, creating *one church in two locations.* This concept was continued for twenty years, until it was decided to divide the one church into two churches, Brown Memorial Woodbrook Church, and Brown Memorial Park Avenue Church.

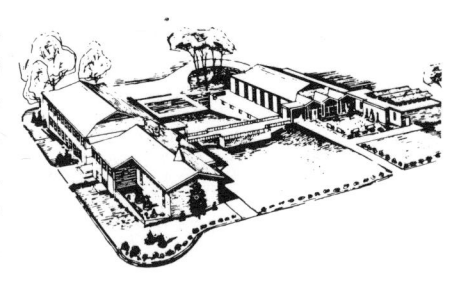

HISTORICAL VIGNETTES   *Nineteenth Century*   315

FIRST PRESBYTERIAN CHURCH, *Haddonfield, New Jersey.* This church's original founders met twice a month in the Town Hall of Haddonfield for thirteen years, before formally organizing. The years of delay were due to the problems and interruptions caused by the Civil War.

At the request of Joseph B. Tatem, the church was finally organized in 1871. Although the cornerstone of the manse was laid in 1873, the Panic of that year, slowed construction and the church was not dedicated until 1882. Since that time, many additions have been made to the church complex, and eight other churches have been established from the mother church.

FIRST PRESBYTERIAN CHURCH, *Dunedin, Florida.* Just north of Clearwater, on Florida's west coast, this church traces its roots to the 1868 arrival of the Reverend Joseph Brown to Dunedin. After initially holding services in a log house, Brown and his congregation organized as a Presbyterian church on 1871. The first sanctuary was completed in 1878. The church was named Andrews Memorial Church in memory of a young member who had been killed in an accident. In 1888, a new structure was built at a new site. Members worshipped there until 1926 and in that year, another church was constructed and renamed, First Presbyterian Church of Dunedin. The older building was donated to the local historical society, who moved it to a new site as the Andrews Memorial Chapel. Today it is on the National Register of Historic Places.

FALLSTON PRESBYTERIAN CHURCH, *Fallston, Maryland.* The church's history reveals a curious beginning: *The Reverend Finney suggested in 1872, the propriety of preaching in the neighborhood of Fallston occasionally on Sabbath afternoon. He secured the use of the bar room in an unoccupied hotel. Notice being given, Mr. Finney preached his first sermon in the bar room on January 17, 1872 to a good, large, and attentive audience.* The subsequent history includes that a more appropriate structure was erected in 1873, at the cost of $1,890.00. The following year, the church was formally organized. A new sanctuary was built in 1986 and is located fifteen miles northeast of Baltimore.

BRYN MAWR PRESBYTERIAN CHURCH, *Bryn Mawr, Pennsylvania.* This church in suburban Philadelphia, was organized in 1873. Its chapel was completed the following year. From its inception, the church had a strong commitment to missions and outreach. Its first missionary, Dr. William Wanlass, was sent to Miraj, India, in the late nineteenth century. This India location is still supported today. In 1886, a new brownstone church was completed, and eight years later, a Sunday school building. The present sanctuary was built in 1927, with a seating capacity of 1200. This number was double the congregation at that time. Growth continued, with the construction of a new education building in 1931, the Chapel, in 1941, and an activities building in 1967.

FIRST PRESBYTERIAN CHURCH OF APOPKA, *Apopka, Florida.* Apopka is located just northeast of Orlando and is known as *the foliage plant capitol of the world*. The Presbyterian church can be traced back to 1873, when a congregation first met in a local Masonic lodge along with Methodist and Baptist groups. The first structure was erected in 1887, and the church was initially served by an itinerant pastor. In 1950, a fire destroyed the building which led to the construction of the present one. This small church struggled early in the century. At one time, it was disbanded but in 1922, reorganized with four members. By 1932, the congregation had grown to forty-five members. Today there are 165 in the congregation, including Florida's longest office-holding mayor.

MENLO PARK PRESBYTERIAN CHURCH, *Menlo Park, California.* From 1874 until 1950, Menlo Park Presbyterian was known as *The Little White Church*, on the corner of Chestnut and Santa Cruz Avenue near Stanford University. Eighteen years older than the University, the church was organized in 1873, when thirteen pioneers united to create a new church. Jane and Leland Stanford attended services and did much for the church fellowship. The Stanford pew and an oil painting of *The Little White Church* can be found today in the Pioneer Room of the church building. Menlo Park was a quiet town, until the late 1940s when things began to boom and the little church began to grow. A larger sanctuary was soon needed. A new site was chosen and ground was broken for the new building in 1950. The first services were for Thanksgiving that same year. Since, the sanctuary has been expanded twice and additional properties have been purchased. Today the church has more than four thousand members and five services.

FIRST PRESBYTERIAN CHURCH, *Tampa, Florida.* One of the earliest founders of this church, Mrs.Ida M.Hale, came to Tampa in 1872 when there were fewer than eight hundred people in the town and even fewer Presbyterians. There were only a half a dozen buildings clustered on a block or so downtown, no city street lights, no pavement, no sidewalks, and, travelers still rode by stage coach. By 1878, with the help of Mrs. E.J. Cardy, Mrs. Hale arranged to start Sunday school classes in her home. A number of families wanted their children to have instruction in the Presbyterian Doctrine and worship. The efforts of Mrs. Hale and Mrs. Cardy brought together four teachers and seventeen students. The school prospered and by 1882, Mrs. Hale obtained signatures for the organization of the church in Tampa. Prayer meetings began in a private home, later, a court house, and an opera house. The Reverend W.G. Wallace was the first preacher. In 1922 many locations later, the first church was built. Women have always played a vital part in the church's activities and outreach programs. During its first hundred years, three women members passed the century mark. First Presbyterian continues to be supported, influenced, and sustained by the Women's Auxiliary, a major force in carrying out Christ's precepts.

BRYSON CITY PRESBYTERIAN CHURCH, *Bryson City , North Carolina.* First established in 1880 as Charleston Presbyterian Church, this church, resulted from a mission project of the Mecklenberg Presbytery. The present sanctuary was dedicated in 1891, the *hut,* in 1921. In 1961, an educational building was built, and a fellowhip hall was added in 1968. There are 103 members in the congregation. This active church has been served by thirty-four pastors in its over one-hundred-year history.

FIRST CENTRAL PRESBYTERIAN CHURCH, *Abilene, Texas.* A tent was the first home of Presbyterianism in Abilene when the First Presbyterian Church was organized in 1881. Since the first town lots were not sold until, March 15, 1881, two weeks later, the church is actually older than the town of Abilene. An historical marker, located on the Texas and Pacific Streets, sidewalk, identifies where the members first met. A small group of Cumberland Presbyterians organized on August 23, 1885, what was to become eventually, the Central Presbyterian Church, with the first services held, October 4, 1885. These two churches voted to join together and work as one congregation, in October of 1970.

The congregation kept the church property of First Presbyterian Church, adding a new sanctuary and additional educational facilities in 1979. Dr. Roy Zuefeldt, a native of Dallas, was installed as minister in special ceremonies moving the congregation from the old church, to the newly completed sanctuary next door. Dr. Zuefeldt retired as pastor this year, and the present pastor is Dr. Clifford Schweiber Stewart.

FIRST PRESBYTERIAN CHURCH, *Fairfax, Missouri.* The first sermon preached in the town of Fairfax, Missouri, was delivered by a Presbyterian minister in a depot building on October 3, 1881. On that same day a Sabbath school was established and operated as a Union Sunday School because other faiths had not established their churches at the time.

The original Presbyterian Church building in Fairfax was dedicated on June 18, 1882. This building was used for thirty-four years at which time memberhip had grown to 190 people, and a larger building was needed. The new building was dedicated on October 1, 1916. The impressive dedication was attended by a thousand people.

Today the congregation is a merged unit, having joined with the neighboring rural, English Grove congregation in 1976.

HISTORICAL VIGNETTES *Nineteenth Century* 319

FIRST PRESBYTERIAN CHURCH, *Rogers, Arkansas.* This church was established as Cumberland Presbyterian of Rogers, April 29, 1883. Most of the founders were homesteaders who came from Tennessee. The church's name changed to First Presbyterian Church of Rogers in 1904, when the two Presbyterian denominations of Rogers merged to join the Presbyterian Church, in the United States. An educational wing was added in 1966. Presently, plans are being adopted for a new church building.

MT. HERMAN PRESBYTERIAN CHURCH, *Hull, Georgia.* This church was organized on July 28, 1883. The present building was erected in 1912, and the Annex was constructed in 1959.

UNITED PRESBYTERIAN CHURCH, *Paterson, New Jersey.* United Church is an outgrowth of the merger of earlier churches in Paterson; Church of the Messiah, Central Presbyterian Church, and Madison Avenue Presbyterian Church.

Church of the Messiah was founded and attended by the city's leaders. Garret A. Hobart, Vice President to President William McKinley was a member.

Central Presbyterian Church was organized by German immigrants who settled in the area. United Presbyterian now uses the building that was formerly, Church of Messiah. The church is Gothic in style and was built *circa 1884*. The congregation is dedicated to the outreach of inner-city Paterson through programs directed at all ages and races. Members are from both urban and suburban areas.

Rocky Grove Avenue Presbyterian Church, *Franklin, Pennsylvania.* Eight miles west of Oil City, Pennsylvannia, are the adjacent towns of Franklin and Rocky Grove. This church is the outgrowth of a small Sunday school group known as the *Lilly Band*, organized in 1885. A wooden structure was built to serve as the church and public school of the area. This building, known as *the Chapel*, is still standing. Growth led to the construction of the present, stone church in 1889.

The group organized as an independent Presbyterian church in 1904, with eighty-nine members and became Rocky Grove Presbyterian. The word, *avenue*, was inserted into the name in 1912.

First United Presbyterian Church, *Lake City, Pennsylvania.* This congregation had its beginnings in the small town of Miles Grove in Erie County, in 1885. A church building was completed in 1886 at a cost of ten thousand dollars. The building is still in use today, for the worship of the very active, one-hundred-member congregation.

First Presbyterian Church, *Highlands, North Carolina.* This church was dedicated to God on September 13, 1885, thus making it the oldest church edifice in Highlands. The village is situated at one of the highest altitudes in western North Carolina and its population expands from one to eight thousand from spring through the *leaf change* in fall. The church reflects this expansion by a large attendance of part-time residents. The church rents property for one dollar a year, to the non-profit organization, Mt. Findings, who receive a variety of household donations. Profit from their sales is returned to community needs. The church has a busy children's day care center. Mission works have included, a clinic in the Dominican Republic, a project in Nicargua, journeys to Mexico, and disastor assistance for hurricanes, *Hugo* and *Andrew*.

Minister, Ron Botsford, maintains an active association with many ministers throughout

England, Scotland and Northern Ireland. This results in interesting pulpit exchanges. The most recent visiting pastor, the Reverend Keith Havers of Letchworth, England, exchanged with Dr. Botsford for two months last fall.

Note: The Stoney Creek Cookbook is grateful for the help of Dr. Ron Botsford and his assistant, Mrs. Anna Lou Beckes, for contacting the many foreign churches represented in this book. A member of the cookbook committee is a summer resident in Highlands and has observed a variety of community activities and programs this church is engaged in. This small church, with its Seven League Boots is greatly admired for the vitality of their outreach.

STONE'S CHAPEL PRESBYTERIAN CHURCH, *Berryville, Virginia.* This church is thought to be the oldest continuous church in its corner of northern Virginia. In 1785, a wooden church was constructed on land owned by Jacob Stine, of Germany. It was known as Stine's Church. Lutherans and Presbyterians both used the structure. The name was later changed to Stone's Chapel when Mr. Stine anglicized his name to, Stone. The present brick building was constucted in 1848, and remodeled in 1905. The church was an outpost of the Presbyterian Church in Berryville for a number of years until organized in 1886.

FIRST PRESBYTERIAN CHURCH, *Moorestown, New Jersey.* In 1887, the Reverend D.C. Porter, of the Presbyterian Church in Mt. Holly, New Jersey, wrote in a letter, *My visit at Moorestown was very satisfactory . . . , I really did not expect to find so many families strongly attached to the Presbyterian Church and I see no reason why a vigorous effort should not be put forth to gather them together for worship.* Rev. Porter's subsequent preaching services there, led the Presbytery of Monmouth to recommend the following year that the church in Moorestown be organized. Petitions that were circulated found that twenty-nine people were prepared to become members. The Presbytery officially constituted the First Presbyterian Church of Moorestown in September of 1888. The first building was constructed in 1891. This served the congregation until the 1950s, when a new church was built to accomodate the growing congregation. Today over 1,000 members worship in the sanctuary. The old building was sold to the Lutheran Church.

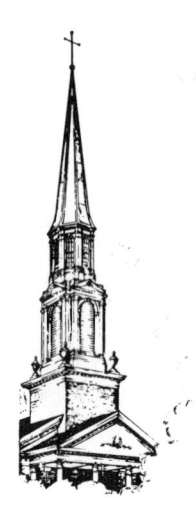

CENTRAL PRESBYTERIAN CHURCH, *Fort Smith, Arkansas.* Central Presbyterian was formed in 1888 and celebrated its Centennial in 1988. Dr. John D. Barklind is the current minister. He is assisted by, the Reverend Tom Boone.

FIRST PRESBYTERIAN CHURCH, *Kerrville, Texas.* This church was organized in 1888, when Texas was predominantly, frontier country. The present sanctuary was built in 1923. The congregation will soon celebrate the church's 105th anniversary. The culture in the Kerrville area is today, western in style, with pickup trucks, ranches, sheep, and cattle. It lies in the heart of the beautiful hill country of Texas where many professional people come to retire. The church therefore, serves a large retirement congregation of 900 members. The church is active and alive with wonderful music, Christian education programs, service to the community and the world at large. Members boldly proclaim the *Good News of Jesus Christ*. The pastor is Thomas W. Currie, a third generation Presbyterian minister.

THIRD PRESBYTERIAN CHURCH, *Birmingham, Alabama.* A highly regarded pastor, the Reverend James A. *Brother* Bryan served this church from 1889 until 1941. This extraordinary man, devoted his life to the service of the entire community, whether black, white, industialist, or convict. A journalist once called him, *the patron saint of Birmingham*. In an unusual tribute to his ministry, local citizens erected a marble statue of a praying Brother Bryan in the Five Points of the city.

WALDENSIAN PRESBYTERIAN CHURCH, *Valdese, North Carolina.* Unique among American churches is the Presbyterian Church whose history dates back to the twelfth century. Excommunicated from the Roman Catholic Church for nonconformity in 1183, the Waldensians of northern Italy were deemed heretics. They were inhumanly persecuted for over two hundred years. Intermittent persecution until the nineteenth century, and economic hardship, forced twenty-nine Waldensians to journey in May of 1893, to Burke County, North Carolina. Others followed, making Valdese the largest colony of Waldensians in North America. Led by the Reverend Charles Albert Tron, the church was the unifying influence and governing body of the group. Organized in 1893, the Valdese Church united with the Presbyterian Church in the United States in 1895. A major building program enlarged the church in 1991. In 1992 the Waldensian Museum was named one of the ten best museums in North Carolina. Last year membership stood at 587. A festival is held on August 14, the anniversary of the emancipation of the Waldensians by King Albert of Italy.

WESTMINSTER PRESBYTERIAN CHURCH, *Burlington, North Carolina.* In 1989, this church was formed through the merger of two predecessor churches; Westview, and East Burlington Presbyterian churches. Located between Greensboro and Durham, Westview evolved from the formation of Elmira Chapel in 1894, with the support of First Presbyterian Church. In 1913, they organized as Second Presbyterian Church, with eighteen charter members. They became Park Avenue Presbyterian Church after a later relocation. In 1962, a new sanctuary was built and the Westview name was adopted. The East Burlington Church was founded when fifteen charter members signed a petition at an open air revival. In 1921, they were formally organized by the Orange Presbytery. Their sanctuary was completed in 1926. After sixty-eight years of service, merger was sought with Westview due to declining membership. Today the church has 261 communicant members who worship and praise in the faith of their predecessors.

FORT HILL PRESBYTERIAN CHURCH, *Clemson, South Carolina.* This church is rich in community history and outreach to Clemson University. Organized on July 12, 1895, Fort Hill Presbyterian was the first church to serve the village of Calhoun and Clemson College. The congregation began with thirty-three charter members who elected three elders and two deacons. The first minister, the Reverend Benjamin Palmer Reid, conducted services in Boggs Store until the new church at the present site was occupied in1896. A fire destroyed the church in 1932, but it was restored within six months. The church continued to serve the Clemson students, and established the Foothills Presbytery Ministry to Clemson University in the 1960s.

FIRST PRESBYTERIAN CHURCH, *Casa Grande, Arizona.* Located between Phoenix and Tucson, Casa Grande has been known to many as the spring training ground for Major League baseball players. But a more sufficient national pastime came to town first. In 1896, when there were only three hundred residents in Casa Grande, the First Presbyterian Church was organized. First named, the Endeavor Church, it is usually referred to as the Union Church, being the only Protestant church in town, with Methodists, Baptists, Lutherans, and others all united in worship there. The congregation has outgrown the building twice. The current sanctuary was built in 1974. Today church membership exceeds five hundred. The spirit of the "Union" church continues. They want all who cross their threshold to feel at home.

GRETNA PRESBYTERIAN CHURCH, *Gretna, Louisiana.* The history of Gretna Presbyterian Church is closely entwined with a handmade quilt. The church was organized on December 12, 1897, with ten charter members. The following year, with the Spanish American War raging, a schoolteacher, Winona Robert, determined that war or no war, there should be a church built for Gretna Presbyterians. Ms. Robert organized the women of the church to create a quilt as a fundraising effort.

Sixteen ladies in the congregation each made a quilt square. So enthusiastic was Miss Robert's project, that virtually all of the town citizens participated by donating money to have their name embroidered on the quilt. More than $500. was realized. Miss Juanita Robert was awarded the quilt for raising the most in donations, $108.54. All of the donations were used as a down payment for the church, erected in 1901. The quilt was handed down through the Robert family and came into the possession of Agness Cross, the long-time organist, and her brother, Fred Cross. Through their generosity, the quilt has been restored to museum standard, and now hangs in Gretna's Fellowship Hall.

ESTILL PRESBYTERIAN CHURCH, *Estill, South Carolina.* The church was organized with eight members and admitted to the Charleston Presbytery on May 29, 1898. The original building was destroyed by a fire in March of 1934. The present building, on the same site, was rebuilt sufficiently for services in 1937. The remainder of the building was completed by 1947. In the years, 1958 and 1959, a fellowship hall, choir loft, Sunday school rooms, and office were added. The present manse with a handsome brick veneer, was built in 1958.

CHURCH OF THE HOLY SPIRIT, *Lake Forest, Illinois.* Church of the Holy Spirit was originally a mission of Trinity Parish. The church's founders first met on Palm Sunday of 1898. The site of the present church was purchased in 1900, and the building was consecrated on Whitsunday, June 11, 1905. As membership increased, major building programs were necessary in 1925, 1952, and 1963. This church, whose founders were devoted lay persons, has been characterized by a strong sense of lay responsibility and participation. Mission and outreach programs are significant in the work of the church.

HODGES PRESBYTERIAN CHURCH, *Hodges, South Carolina.* The church was founded in December of 1899, when forty-nine persons from Greenville Presbyterian Church, and one from Upper Long Cane Presbyterian Church came together to organize a new church. The church building was erected in 1901, and a Sunday school was organized the same year. Stained-glass windows were purchased for the church in 1955, as was an organ, in 1964. A manse was built in 1960, and an education building was built in 1970. This church is proud of the impressive number of young men who have gone out from their church to minister to the Lord.

Paint Gap Presbyterian Church, *Burnsville, North Carolina.* Organized on October 20, 1901, by the Reverend John Abner Harris, this evangelist was doing pioneer work under the Concord Presbytery of the Presbyterian Church in the United States. This beautiful white frame church was built on Horton's Creek, by the men of the community. It began with forty-six members. The sanctuary and two classrooms are on the upper level, more class room space, a kitchen, and other facilities are on the lower level. This church has maintained active programs serving the community, the country, and the world, through Sunday school, youth groups, and women's work.

Church of the Pilgrims, *Washington, D.C.* This church was organized in 1903, in a townhouse in what was then, the rural northwestern outskirts of the nation's capitol. The church's original name was the *Second Presbyterian Church (South) of Washington, D.C.* During the period when the denomination was distinctly divided into *Northern* and *Southern* parts, this congregation was known as one of the few *Southern* churches north of the Potomac. By 1919, Washington had grown into a significant international community. That year, the church became Church of the Pilgrims, declaring themselves a *way station* for life's transient *pilgrims* who were dwelling in the city for only a year or two. Originally, in the midst of simple homes and open farmland, they are now surrounded by embassies and townhouses. As an urban church, they are familiar with the many serious issues cities of today must face.

First Presbyterian Church, *Frostproof, Florida.* Established, March 20, 1905, as *The Church Among the Lakes*, this church became affiliated in September of that same year with The Congregational Church of Florida. Shortly thereafter, the church became a Union Church. In 1915, it was affiliated with the Presbyterian Church in the United States and and in 1924, joined the Presbyterian Church of the U.S.A., becoming in 1982, an Associate Reformed Presbyterian Church.

LETCHWORTH FREE CHURCH, *Letchworth, England.* In 1905, in the home of Miss Grace Stabb in Baldock Road, were the beginnings of what was to be a church with no denominational measuring rods. Among the group were Baptists, Congregationalists, Methodists, Presbyterians, and others whose vision was to build, with their own voluntary labor, what was to become a *Cathedral of Non-Conformity.* Before the end of that year, the first building was opened, on what is now the church parking lot. It held two hundred people and soon was too small. It was extended twice, but in 1918, a new building was planned to accommodate growth. The new church was officially opened in June 1924, by Miss Stabb in whose home the whole scheme had been conceived.

From early years music held an important place in the life of the church. The organ, installed in 1928, was designed and built, incorporating the latest techniques, under the guidance of the organist of Kings College, Cambridge. It has been a fifty year tradition for the church to present *Handel's Messiah* each Good Friday, augmenting with its own choir and friends from other churchs. The church has a tradition of fine preaching from men of scholorship and culture. By the 1930s, it was again overflowing, so that unless one arrived half an hour before the service time, one could not get in.

The present Free Church Hall, superseding the original church building, opened June of 1969, by Bishop the RT. Rev. Dr. C.K. Sansbury, General Secretary of the British Council of Churches. Today, the Free Church is a member of the United Reformed Church.

ASHLAND EVANGELICAL PRESBYTERIAN CHURCH, *Voorhees Township, New Jersey.* Established as a Sunday school after the turn of the century, this church met first in private homes. By 1907, they had grown to the point that the Ashland Chapel was built. Located in the New Jersey suburbs, east of Philadelphia, the church now has four hundred very active members of all ages.

SPARTA PRESBYTERIAN CHURCH, *Sparta, North Carolina.* This church stands today where the original church, Carson Memorial Presbyterian was built and dedicated in August of 1906. In the summer of 1900, efforts began to establish a Presbyterian church in Sparta. Mr. James Carson of Charlotte was contacted and agreed to finance the church building provided Orange Presbytery built a manse of equal value. Both the manse and church were complete by 1906, and the church carried the name of the benefactor. A new manse was built in 1938, and in 1952, a new church was erected to replace the old building. At that time, the name was officially changed to Sparta Presbyterian.

OAKLAND AVENUE PRESBYTERIAN CHURCH, *Rock Hill, South Carolina.* With the opening of Winthrop College, in the Oakland section of Rock Hill, in 1895, it was soon apparent that there was a need for another Presbyterian church. In 1909, Dr. Walter Lingle, departing pastor of the First Presbyterian Church, left the following directive: *A new church should be organized not as a secession, not as a competition, but as a new organization, the two churches are to work together for a common end, the good of the community.* This directive resulted in Oakland Avenue Presbyterian Church opening its doors for the first service on December 1, 1912.

Through the years, women have maintained active organizations. Their activities include Bible study and a monthly prayer service.

The church continues to show concern for the students of Winthrop. The Campus Christian Life Committee works closely with the Winthrop Presbyterian Campus Ministry to encourage the spiritual growth and welfare of the students. Music, and response to community are important aspects of Oakland's ministry.

FIRST PRESBYTERIAN CHURCH, *Coalinga, California.* Established in 1909, the present, modern sanctuary was built in 1952. The church is proud to have had a Chaplain of the United States Senate, Dr. Richard Halverson, serve as pastor from 1944 through 1948. In 1983, a major earthquake occurred, and the downtown center of Coalinga was completely destroyed. The First Presbyterian Church withstood the tremors, and became not only a symbol of God's presence but also, a distribution center for meals and disaster relief. It is interesting to note that the architect of the church who lived a hundred miles away, hurried to Coalinga after the earthquake to see if *his* building was still standing. *His* building and *God's house* was intact.

LILLINGTON PRESBYTERIAN CHURCH, *Lillington, North Carolina.* The roots of this church, in Lillington, half way between Raleigh and Fayetteville, date before the beginning of the century. A group of local citizens held worship services in a courthouse. Led by eight ladies from Lillington, the group purchased land for the church in 1907, for thirty dollars. By 1910, they organized as a Presbyterian church, and the sanctuary and a manse were constructed. The inside of the church is in the shape of the cross, and is described as *most impressive* by members.

HIGHLAND PRESBYTERIAN CHURCH, *Fayetteville, North Carolina.* This church was organized on June 5, 1911, by thirty-nine persons who transferred from First Presbyterian to form a new church. Soon after formal organization, the young church purchased a lot and building began. By 1940, expansion was necessary. Additional land was purchased but World War II delayed construction. The first phase of the present building, educational building, chapel, library, parlor, kitchen, offices, and fellowship hall, was completed in 1950. In 1954, the original building was torn down and a new sanctuary was built for worship by September 10, 1961. There are over 1100 members in the congregation and growth continues under the leadership of Dr. J. Ernest Johnson.

ALAMO HEIGHTS PRESBYTERIAN CHURCH, *San Antonio, Texas.* This church dates back to 1912, when the first communicants started holding services in their homes, and later, a school building. In 1916, the church was formally organized, and the building was moved to a new site. The new location was acquired in 1927, where the present structure was completed in 1931. Growth of the church continued and membership peaked to 921, in the 1950s. Demographic changes in the city brought a decline that has recently been reversed, with an influx of families. The listing of ministers at Alamo Heights includes one John Crockett in the 1940s. How appropriate for a church a few blocks from where Davy Crockett valiantly defended the Alamo a century earlier.

FIRST PRESBYTERIAN CHURCH, *Fort Lauderdale, Florida.* Nine of the one hundred souls, hearty enough to live in the pioneer village of Fort Lauderdale organized this church. In this part of Florida, you had to collect rain water to drink, and the mosquito ruled supreme. Ingenuity, perseverence, creativity and good humor, united with an abiding trust in God, brought the membership to forty-five, in the first year. As people arrived on Mr. Flagler's Railroad, the church continued to grow, by 1942, there were 275 members, and the congregation moved to the present site on Tarpon Bend of the New River. Since then, the buildings have expanded, the congregation grew in numbers and planted daughter churches all over Broward County. With the present membership at 2800, and completion of a new Christian Education Center, the church has programs for all ages. This is a seven-day and six-night per week church with an dedicated laity. The church sponsors an Adult Activity Center, Happyland Preschool, and owns and operates the Westminster Manor Retirement Residence. This Ft. Lauderdale congregation responds to the dynamic leadership of Dr. Richard M. Cromie, a dedicated, talented Christian professional staff, and above all, the grace of God.

WEST SIDE PRESBYTERIAN CHURCH, *Ridgewood, New Jersey.* In the fall of 1912, sixty-four charter members organized The West Side Presbyerian Church. The founders were for the most part, families who migrated from the city to the suburbs. They wanted a community church to serve their rapidly growing neighborhood. The first service was held on August 4, 1912. The church was formally organized in October of that year. The first pastor was Dr. Isaac J. Lansing, and the original building was formally dedicated and occupied on April 27, 1913. With a present membership of approximately 1500, The West Side Presbyterian Church is vitally *alive*, reflecting the vision of the charter members for Christian education, fellowhip, and service, worshipping, and working to serve God, together. Ridgewood, a *village of churches*, is a quiet *sleepy* suburban town located in the rolling hills of northeast New Jersey, twenty miles from New York City, with a population of 25,000.

SHANDON PRESBYTERIAN CHURCH, *Columbia, South Carolina.* This church was founded in 1916, with fifty-three charter members. The original church building was erected at Maple and Wheat Streets. The present sanctuary, on Woodrow Street, was occupied in 1930. Membership has continued to grow and Shandon Presbyterian now serves a congregation of over 1000 members.

CHURCH OF THE WAY PRESBYTERIAN, *Baton Rouge, Louisiana.* Organized in 1917, the church celebrated its 75th anniversary in 1992. The membership of around 100, are for the most part, older people. The small church has recently been served by a new minister. He began on January 1, 1993.

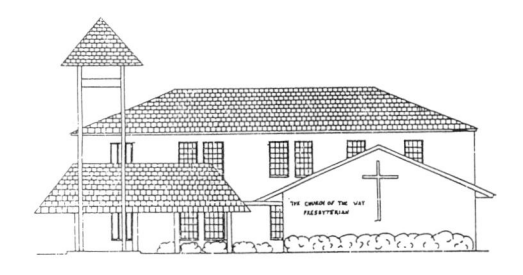

PEACHTREE ROAD PRESBYTERIAN CHURCH, *Atlanta, Georgia.* From a vision of a Sunday school for the neighborhood children, to a large physical plant and a membership of over 10,000, Peachtree Road Presbyterian Church came into being and progressed to its present state. There were many moments of hope, heartbreak and joy! On returning from the funeral of their infant son, Mr. and Mrs. C. S. Honour had a vision of a Sunday School in his memory. The first meeting was held on September 23, 1910, in a vacant store in Buckhead. It continued as a mission Sunday school until November 2, 1919, the date that Peachtree Road Church was organized. The first sanctuary was completed in 1926. During the construction, members often worshipped in the boiler room, the driest area of the building! During the depression years, the church temporarily lost its property through foreclosure. The church was actually sold on the courthouse steps. In the fall of 1937, the congregation repurchased the church for $32,000.00.

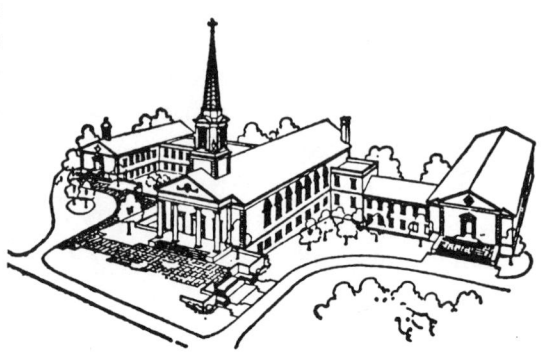

By the 1960s, continued growth necessitated further expansion, and the church relocated to Roswell Road, still in the Buckhead area. The first service in the new sanctuary was held on May 1, 1960. The present minister, Dr. W. Frank Harrington, became Peachtree's fifth senior minister in 1971. Since that time, the church has experienced great growth in membership, program and facilities. Dr. Harrington has said that *every generation is called upon to provide, and provide adequately for Christ and His Church, We must build in order to do the work that Christ has called us to do here.* This congregation continues the challenge to be *a church that cares* as they serve with joy!

Note: In an appropriate note for a cookbook, this church reports that they prepared 169,000 meals in their kitchen in 1992!

TRINITY AVENUE PRESBYTERIAN CHURCH, *Durham, North Carolina.* This church began as a Sunday school mission of the First Presbyterian Church of Durham before 1900. Their first building, known as the Pearl Mill Chapel, was erected in 1895. The congregation was recognized in 1921 as the Trinity Avenue Presbyterian Church. Construction of the present sanctuary was completed in 1925. An education building was added in the 1950s.

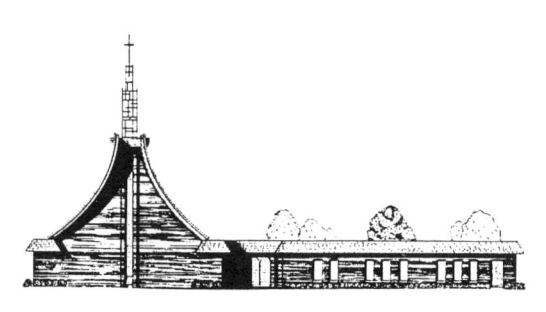

RAY MEMORIAL PRESBYTERIAN CHURCH, *Monroe, Georgia.* The only Presbyterian church in Walton County was formed on July 1, 1972, from Pannell Church (1923-1950) which had moved into town and become Monroe Presbyterian (1950-1972). The new name, was established by the Greater Atlanta Presbytery to honor the trust from Lavender Ray to establish new churches. So far, two churches are attributed to Lavender Ray's generosity.

ST. ANDREWS PRESBYTERIAN CHURCH, *Saskatoon, Saskatchewan, Canada.* In 1925, St. Andrews was founded by a group who wished to remain Presbyterian when the United Church of Canada was established. For twenty-seven years, the congregation worshipped in a basement church, until the present building was opened in 1953. The style of the church is Gothic with a brick exterior.

The stained-glass window in the chancel was dedicated to the glory of God and in memory of the first minister, the Reverend W.G. Brown, once a moderator of the General Assembly. Other windows were donated by members of the congregation in memory of their parents.

HIGHLAND PARK PRESBYTERIAN CHURCH, *Dallas, Texas.* On May 26, 1926, 190 dedicated and far-seeing Christians founded what was destined to become one of the largest congregations of the Presbyterian Church in the United States. Highland Park Church held its organizational meetings in the Highland Park Community House, and later, Highland Park High School. The cornerstone for the church's permanent home was laid in March of 1927. The first service was held in the building in 1929.

Today the church is served by senior minister, Dr. B. Clayton Bell, Sr. The congregation has 6,385 members, with a ministry encompassing world-wide and local outreach with ever-broadening services to community and members.

CROSSNORE PRESBYTERIAN CHURCH, *Crossnore, North Carolina.* Dr. Mary Martin Sloop, founder of Crossnore School, Inc., wrote wrote about this church in her book, *Miracle in the Hills.* Plans were prepared for the stone church by the architect, Leonard White, of Greensboro, at Dr. Sloop's direction. The building was constructed by Uncle Will Franklin, father of the pastor. Construction began in the summer of 1924, and continued in 1925. Rock was hauled from the nearby Linville river.

The stained-glass windows over the cross are in three sections, symbolizing the Holy Trinity. Scores of other Biblical symbols may be seen on the windows of the nave. Certain of the windows along the side aisles swing open on unique hinges. On the front of the pulpit, the builder placed a thick sheet of metal, bent in the shape of an open Bible. On each of the two flower pedestals he placed twelve raised stones to symbolize the twelve tribes of Israel and the twelve apostles. The ceiling is made of chestnut bark and the life-size hand-hewn cross is from a century old log of local white pine. The first worship service was held in the sanctuary on August 8, 1926. They have continued unbroken to this day. The church's current pastor is Dr. Paul Spaulding Smith.

TRINITY PRESBYTERIAN CHURCH, *Baton Rouge, Louisiana.* This church was organized as Northside Presbyterian Church in 1937, with 57 charter members. In 1955, the church moved to larger facilities on Fairfields Avenue and was renamed Fairfield Presbyterian Church. Later, property was donated on Greenwell Springs Road, the church relocated to its present site and became Trinity Presbyterian Church. A special service was held in 1987 for a 50th anniversary celebration.

GROSSE POINTE WOODS PRESBYTERIAN CHURCH, *Grosse Pointe Woods, Michigan.* The founders of this church held their first worship services in a school beginning on October 2, 1938. One year later, the Grosse Pointe Woods Presbyterian Church was officially chartered with 123 members. Another Presbyterian church in the area, Grosse Pointe Memorial, helped sponsor the church, by contributing $25,000 for the construction of the building. Two of its members also donated the land on which the church was built. Grosse Pointe Woods Presbyterian has been blessed with dedicated ministers over the years. Members continue their growing commitment to Jesus Christ and the work of the Lord.

WEST BATON ROUGE PRESBYTERIAN CHURCH, *Port Allen, Louisiana.* Founded in 1943, the congregation met for worship in the Sunday school building, until the church sanctuary was dedicated in 1956. Members celebrated the 50th anniversary of the church early in 1993.

TRINITY PRESBYTERIAN CHURCH, *Arlington, Virginia.* In 1943, the Home Mission Committee of the Presbyterian Church in the United States authorized the Reverend F.W. Haverkamp to organize a new church in the Westover area. The first service was held at a residence on N. Washington Boulevard, purchased by the Potomoc Presbytery on September 19, 1943. The Reverend Haverkamp acted as temporary pastor to a group of twenty persons. In less than a year, the congregation secured a petition of 123 signatures requesting the establishment of a church. On May 20, 1944, the request was granted and the charter members were organized as Trinity Presbyterian Church. In 1945, ground was broken for a new building. Today the church congregation has grown to 987 members with a church school enrollment of 165. At present there are six choirs for various age groups including two handbell choirs.

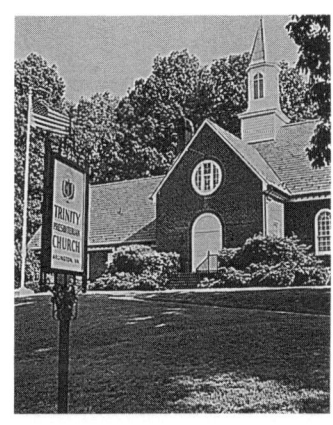

FAIRVIEW PRESBYTERIAN CHURCH, *North Augusta, South Carolina.* In the spring of 1945, a small church was started in a grocery store in North Augusta. The following year, this church was organized by the Congaree Presbytery. They started building a sanctuary in 1947. After nine years of growth, the members converted this building into a fellowship hall and constructed a new church with additional classrooms. The Fairview Church has developed a strong tradition of missionary work. They are particularly active in programs in the local Augusta area.

GUILFORD PARK PRESBYTERIAN CHURCH, *Greensboro, North Carolina.* In 1947, sixty-one organizers established a new church as an outreach program of Greensboro's Buffalo Presbyterian Church. First called the Fairfield-Kirkwood Presbyterian Chapel in recognition of its neighborhood, following organization, they took the present name. The original structure was built in 1947 and a new sanctuary was constructed across the street in 1956. At that time, as a labor of love, a group of wood carvers decorated the church with religious symbols. This tradition continues today and the congregation has grown to over 600 members.

WESTMINSTER PRESBYTERIAN CHURCH, *Greenville, South Carolina.* Westminster was organized in 1947, to provide a church home for young families settling in the Augusta Road area of Greenville. The church was founded after World War II, and the first services were held in a circus tent. The congregation has grown to twelve hundred members served by a staff of five ministers. The present senior pastor is the Reverend Ludwig Weaver.

FIRST PRESBYTERIAN CHURCH, *Chandler, Arizona.* This church was organized in May of 1949, under the leadership of Claude L. Morton, with thirty-three charter members. Services were initially held in borrowed space in a local building. In 1952, a sanctuary and education building were dedicated. New rooms and a kitchen were added in 1970. A fire on June 9, 1979 destroyed the sanctuary. A new and larger church building was constructed and dedicated within eighteen months.

PACIFIC PALISADES PRESBYTERIAN CHURCH, *Pacific Palisades, California.* This church held its first meeting in 1949, at the home of Dr. and Mrs. Benjamin Janes. Six weeks later, the congregation held the first worship service at the Presbyterian Conference Grounds in the Palisades. In 1951, the congregation moved worship services to a mansion at Sunset Boulevard and El Medio Street. The present chapel and other church buildings were erected on this same site in 1955.

ST. JOHN'S PRESBYTERIAN CHURCH, *Reno, Nevada.* St. John's was established in 1949 by 105 charter members. These founders volunteered their labor to build a church on a two and one-half acre apple orchard west of Reno. A larger sanctuary was constructed adjacent to the original building in 1969. A devastating fire destroyed the education wing and severely damaged the sanctuary in 1976. Within a year, the congregation rebuilt and restored their church, doubling the size of educational facilities. They also added a balcony to the sanctuary and renovated the pipe organ.

HIGHLAND PRESBYTERIAN CHURCH, *Winston-Salem, North Carolina.* Highland Church was a dream come true for the people of First Presbyterian Church in the Ardmore section of Winston-Salem. Land was purchased in 1949, and 106 persons from First Church were joined by thirty-two persons from other churches, and became the nucleus of Highland Church. The church complex was finished in the fall of 1950. On Thanksgiving Day, the first worship service was held. The congregation is very active. Outreach services include meals on wheels, crisis control, and child development center. The present minister, the Reverend Steve McCutchan was called in September of 1983.

EAST RIDGE PRESBYTERIAN CHURCH, *Chattanooga, Tennessee.* This church's founders first gathered for home prayer meetings in 1949. Their first worship services were held in the town hall. The church was formally organized in 1951. Through the years, the congregation has fulfilled the vision of charter members to create a *T* -shaped cluster of buildings, with an additional combination education and fellowship hall building extending from the top of the *T*. Work was begun in 1951, and the original design was completed in 1962. Two pastors, Rev. Jefferson T. Kesterson, and Rev. Leonard A. Bullock were the guiding forces throughout the building effort. Youth share vitally in the life of the church and their Christian experience is extended by retreats, conferences and exchange visits with sister congregations. Rev. Fred P. Zitzmann is the present pastor. Under his leadership a day care center, kindergarten, and missionary support programs have been established.

LITTLE FALLS PRESBYTERIAN CHURCH, *Arlington, Virginia.* Located in Arlington, just west of our nation's capitol, this church was organized in the 1950s, with a congregation of 100. Today the membership has grown to over 600. Colonel John Glenn (today, a United States Senator) was a member of this church at the time of his mission in space. In honor of his extraordinary achievement, the fellowship hall was named after his space capsule, *Friendship.*

NORTH COMO PRESBYTERIAN CHURCH, *Roseville, Minnesota.* This church was established in April of 1951, in Roseville, a first tier suburb of St. Paul. The church has an active membership of about 725 people from Rosewell and other suburbs. Two co-pastors, one woman, and one man head the staff. The congregation is of all ages with a variety of interests and talents. The church emphasizes worship and Christian education. Evangelism and outreach is also important. This church has a reputation for being active and caring.

TRINITY PRESBYTERIAN CHURCH, *Charlotte, North Carolina.* Trinity Church was organized in April, 1951, as an outgrowth of Myers Park Presbyterian Church. The sanctuary, fellowhip hall, education, youth, and kindergarten buildings are on twenty-two acres in Southeast Charlotte. Great emphasis is placed on Christian education and worship. The congregation has called only two senior ministers in its forty year history. Dr. Laurence Stell, (1951-1961) and the present pastor, Dr. Louis Patrick was called in 1962. The church has 1150 members.

FIRST PRESBYTERIAN CHURCH, *Naples, Florida.* A senior minister assisted by two associates, leads this busy congregation in more than 150 church activities and community programs.

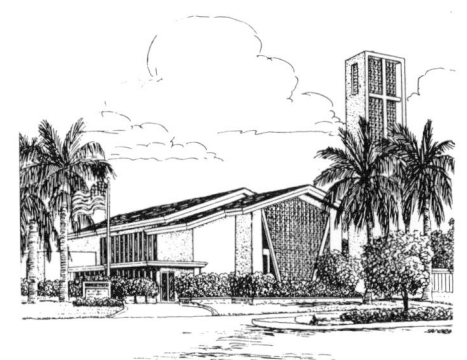

VALLEY COMMUNITY PRESBYTERIAN CHURCH, *Golden Valley, Minnesota.* Valley Church was organized in 1951 and now has approximately 660 members.

GLENCLIFF PRESBYTERIAN CHURCH, *Nashville, Tennessee.* Presbyterians in the Glencliff community began meeting in homes for worship in October, 1951. The present property located on East Thompson Lane was purchased by the Home Missions Committee of the Nashville Presbytery. The group held services in the living room of the house at that location and were chartered on Sunday, January 27, 1952. The church has been involved in three building programs. Construction began on the Christian education wing in 1952. The Fellowship Hall was used for worship until the sanctuary was completed in 1958. In 1967, a new manse was constructed; the first manse was sold and removed in 1981. The present pastor is the Reverend Dr. Alan V. Shields.

CLAIRMONT PRESBYTERIAN CHURCH, *Decatur, Georgia*. This church was organized on April 6, 1952, in the auditorium of W.D. Thompson School on the corner of LaVista Road and North Druid Hills Road in Decatur, Georgia, It was sponsored by the Decatur, Druid Hills, and Oakhurst Presbyterian Churches as a new congregation of the Atlanta Presbytery. The Reverend Max Milligan was Clairmont's first pastor called in 1953.

Dr. Scot Weimer has been Senior Pastor at Clairmont since September, 1991. Dr. Weimer and his family are a young and vital part of Clairmont's new growth of young families. For forty years God has faithfully led the people of Clairmont in vital ministry. "We are a growing congregation with a healthy balance of ages among our membership. We believe in Jesus Christ, the Head of the Church, who calls us to engage in Christian mission. To that end, we support and are actively involved in a variety of ministries to our neighbors in need throughout the Atlanta area and around the world."

HAMPTON PRESBYTERIAN CHURCH, *Hampton, South Carolina*. Hampton is a small southern town on the road to Beaufort and Aiken. This Presbyterian church was organized in 1953, under the auspices of the Charleston Presbytery. Fifteen charter members were received by letter from Harmony Presbyterian Church in Crocketville, South Carolina. In 1955, members opened and dedicated the building in which services are held today. The congregation has forty-five members.

NORTHMINSTER PRESBYTERIAN CHURCH, *Cuyahoga Falls, Ohio*. The founders of this church started worshipping together in a school in 1953. Their first pastor, the Reverend Richard Eshler, led the effort for the construction of a church building, which was completed in 1957. An addition for classrooms was dedicated in 1962 and in 1990, a new fellowhip hall and kitchen were finished.

FAIRFAX PRESBYTERIAN CHURCH, *Fairfax, Virginia.* For 175 years, there had not been a Presbyterian church in Fairfax, Virginia, site of the historic Fairfax County Courthouse. In July, 1953, a small but determined group established the Fairfax Presbyterian Mission, which gained full church status in September of 1954, and was admitted to Washington City Presbytery with 104 charter members. Subsequently, the church acquired an eight acre site and has had four building phases. The sanctuary was built during the third building phase and is an octagonal shaped structure. The 1200 member congregation holds two Sunday services. The church originally served an agricultural area. Today it is in the center of a bustling metropolitan and educational environment.

MEMORIAL DRIVE PRESBYTERIAN CHURCH, *Houston, Texas.* This church was founded in 1954 by thirteen people. The small group acquired the present site of the church, and after long meetings were formally recognized in February, 1955. First services were held on January 9, 1955, at Memorial Drive Elementary School. In the thirty-nine years since that modest beginning, Memorial Drive Presbyterian Church has grown to a membership of 5000 people. The present senior pastor, Dr. Thomas K. Tewell, challenges the church to *march off the map* into uncharted areas of ministry, service, renewal, and spiritual growth.

FAITH PRESBYTERIAN CHURCH, *Harrisburg, Pennsylvania.* In 1956, several families in the Colonial Crest area, met in their homes to initiate procedure for a Presbyterian church. Permission was granted by the Carlisle Presbytery and Rev. William A. Shaffer became the organizing minister. Services were held in a school until land was purchased. Architectural plans were made, and construction of the building was completed in 1961. Since then, the church has grown, paid off the land, and building. An additional space has been built for classrooms, a library, and a fellowship area. The largest active mission experience came in 1977 when members, Drs., Ted and Sharon Kuhn, went to Bangladesh as medical missionaries. More recently, some members donated financial contributions and hard physical work through Lend-A-Hand, to alleviate *Hurricane Hugo* flood damage in South Carolina. Four church members have been inspired to enter the professional ministry.

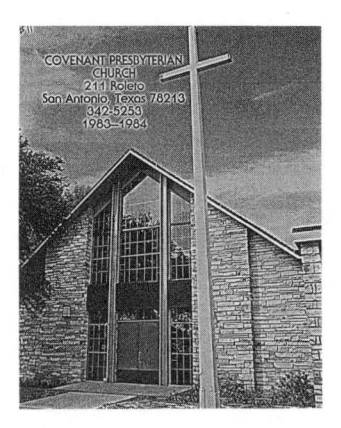

COVENANT PRESBYTERIAN CHURCH, *San Antonio, Texas.* Before the congregation had a name, they met for Sunday school and worship services headed by Dr. George Mauze in North Town Plaza. Their first Communion was celebrated on October 7, 1956. Officially organized on January 6, 1957, by year's end, the congregation numbered 158, and services were held at Castle Hills Shopping Center. The first building was completed in 1958 on land purchased by the Presbyterian Extension Council. Other buildings and improvements followed.

ST. ANDREWS PRESBYTERIAN CHURCH, *Jacksonville, Florida.* On March 13, 1956, the Home Mission Committee recommended that ten acres of land which was a chicken farm with a brooder house, be purchased for the development of a chapel to be named St. Andrews. In June, the brooder house was turned into a chapel that could accommodate 150 people. On January 20, 1957, there were seventy-six charter members. The Reverend William T. Baker was the first minister. The church has since built Sunday school rooms, a fellowship hall and added a narthex to the sanctuary. The present minister is Jeffrey W. Welch.

JOHN KNOX PRESBYTERIAN CHURCH, *Shelby, North Carolina.* John Knox Presbyterian is located in the western part of the city of Shelby, North Carolina. This church has experienced a decline in membership in recent years, yet maintains active worship services and outreach through Presbyterian Women.

FIRST PRESBYTERIAN CHURCH, *Oil City, Pennsylvania.* This church is located in an historic corner of northwestern Pennsylvania. Twenty miles to the north, is Titusville, where oil was first discovered in America in 1859. The extraordinary industrial growth that followed this event, led to the town of

Cornplanter to be renamed, Oil City. Today's First Presbyterian Church is the result of the 1958 merger of two predecessor congregations, the First Presbyterian Church, and the First United Presbyterian Church. The church's building is Gothic in style and was built in the shape of a cross.

St. Stephen's Presbyterian Church, *Scarborough, Ontario, Canada.* This congregation was first named Golf Club Road Presbyterian Church, and was organized in May of 1958. The group started meeting in Scarborough Golf Club Road Public School. Early the following year, the name was changed to St. Stephen's Presbyterian Church and immediately a search began for a permanent site for a building. While still a *mission charge*, the first building was a cement block, industrial-type facility. During the 1960s, with an expanding congregation, the present building was completed and St. Stephen's became self-sustaining. Beginning subtly in the 1970s, and continuing through the 1980s, due to the changing population, (retirements, moves, etc.), the membership declined. At present, St. Stephen's continues with a renewed mission reaching out into a diverse community.

St. Columba Presbyterian Church, *Belleville, Ontario, Canada.* In 1958, St. Andrew's Presbyterian Church bought property in the east end of the city of Belleville, and built a church house to be used as a church school. In 1960, a congregation was formed, and the church was built in 1963 in the parish of St. Columba, named after an Irish missionary to Scotland. In 1992, an addition the church provided offices and more classrooms. The present membership of the church membership is 210.

Wayside United Presbyterian Church, *Erie, Pennsylvania.* Founded thirty-four years ago, this church is a member of the Presbyterian Church (U.S.A.). The church has an enrollment of over 800 members and is continuing to grow in size and strength. They share a serious commitment to being a Christian community, and offer a full range of programs to meet the needs of the congregation and neighborhood.

GRACE PRESBYTERIAN CHURCH, *Lafayette, Louisiana.* This church was organized in 1960 by a group who saw the need for an additional Presbyterian church in Lafayette. Ground was broken for the new church the following year, and the first worship service was held on April 19, 1962. Classroom space was added three years later. The church purchased adjacent property and built a new sanctuary in 1978 to accommodate the growth of the congregation.

KINGS GRANT PRESBYTERIAN CHURCH, *Virginia Beach, Virginia.* Organized by a group of twenty people in 1960, the church was chartered on November 17, 1963 with sixty-six charter members. Of these, twenty-two are still active. Ground was broken in 1965, and the first building was dedicated May 22, 1966. The first pastor was Raymond Flitton, called in 1961. In 1985, a pipe organ was installed in the sanctuary. In 1991, an new wing was added to the building and renovation took place. Stained-glass windows were added to the church in 1992. The congregation as of 1991, has 425 members.

ST. ANDREW PRESBYTERIAN CHURCH, *Williamsport, Maryland.* Serving the community between Williamsport and Hagerstown, Maryland, and organized by the Winchester Presbytery in May of 1961, the church began with thirty-six charter members. A multi-purpose educational building was the initial structure where services began in December of 1961. This building was destroyed by fire in 1966. The congregation saw to the renovation within two months. By 1968, the plans for a new sanctuary were realized and the congregation dedicated the new building in January. Air conditioning and an eight rank pipe organ have been installed. Today there are nearly 200 members in this active church.

MAXIMO PRESBYTERIAN CHURCH, *St. Petersburg, Florida.* This church's special focus is the nurture and development of families bringing up children in the Christian faith, and the development of committed discipleship in all of their members. The church was organized December 16, 1962 with eighty-seven members. The founders first met at the Anchorage Club (a bar!), and then at Florida Presbyterian College, now Eckerd College. The main building and sanctuary, designed by architect, Alfred Browning Parker, was built in 1964. The church now has about 420 members.

PROVIDENCE PRESBYTERIAN CHURCH, *Fairfax, Virginia.* Friendliness and community service are hallmarks of Providence Presbyterian Church, founded in 1964. This congregation of 850 members is especially proud of their youth Christian education program for adults, youth, and children. Providence is involved in many community outreach programs. The church staff has two pastors, a full time Director of Christian Education, and additional supportive personnel.

UNITED PRESBYTERIAN CHURCH, *Lenoir, North Carolina.* Through a merge of two small Presbyterian churches, this church was officially organized by the Concord Presbytery on June 13, 1965, with eighty charter members. In 1969, a new church building was completed and dedicated. The growth of this church has been steady and they have continued a very active outreach program. The church contributes regularly to the Concord Presbytery, and receives yearly offerings for retired Presbyterian ministers and their dependents. They support Presbyterian missions and local mission causes. Presently, they support the work of the Yokeville Christian Center, Hospice, and Shelter Home, and sponsor Koinonia Apartments for the Elderly. Their building has been used for the care of handicapped children, and as a meeting place for a Girl Scout troop. The church supports the Lenoir Soup Kitchen, The Amazing Grace Ministry, and many other community efforts. The congregation's present minister is the Reverend David C. Kennedy.

PRESTON HILLS PRESBYTERIAN CHURCH, *Kingsport, Tennessee.* In 1963, a Presbyterian Church in the U.S.A. study recommended that a new church be established in the Hillcrest-Preston Woods area. This study was based on the projected growth of the Kingsport population. The chosen site for the church was the Preston Farm off Orebank Road. In 1965, eight acres were acquired, and prospective families were contacted. Organizational meetings were held, and the first service on the grounds in 1966, had 91 people in attendance. Elders were elected and the church was formally organized on February 26, 1967. The first Sunday school classes were held in the homes of the members. The first minister, the Reverend James Nichols was installed on 1967. The new church building was completed and services began in the new sanctuary on December 21, 1969. Today, the Reverend Bert Cramer serves as pastor.

ST. LUKE'S PRESBYTERIAN CHURCH, *Dunwoody, Georgia.* In 1969, Dr. E. Moss Robertson was commissioned by the Atlanta Presbytery to help form a new church in Dunwoody, Georgia. The first worship service was conducted at Dunwoody Elementary School on September 7, 1969. St. Luke's officially organized in May of 1970. Worship services began on May 12, 1974, in the newly constructed facilities. On May 12, 1985, ground was broken for the present sanctuary. Dr. Robertson retired in 1989, and Dr. Christopher Allen Price was called to serve as senior pastor in 1991.

CHRISTIAN ASSEMBLY, *Greenville, South Carolina.* Organized by seven couples in early 1970, the Christian Assembly first met at the home of Pastor, Lyman Richardson. The present membership of 150, now meet at a church on Wade Hampton Boulevard. Under the leadership of Pastor, Mark White, the church is popular among visitors to the area. Pastor White, now in his twelfth year of service, is well known in the area for his five minute radio program, *Fresh Start* which airs at 12:55 on station, WLFJ.

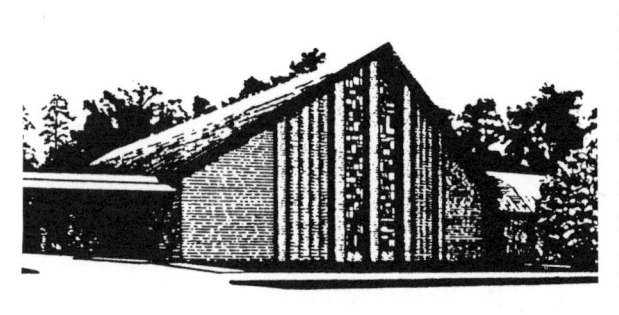

ALL FAITHS CHAPEL, *Fripp Island, South Carolina.* This neighbor of First Presbyterian Church, Beaufort, is located in an ocean front community about twenty miles east of Beaufort. Ministers and lay readers from St. Helena's Episcopal Church of Beaufort first met with small groups of residents in local homes. In 1976, the church became an all-faith group. Today, about twelve area ministers and military chaplains support the regular Wednesday evening vesper services. Ground was broken for a new sanctuary on Easter Sunday, 1980, and the first service was held in the chapel on Thanksgiving eve, that same year.

BURKE PRESBYTERIAN CHURCH, *Burke, Virginia.* Begun in 1978 and chartered in 1980, this church now has more than 600 members. The founding pastor was the Reverend Roxana Atwood. In 1984, the church had the distinction in the National Capital Presbytery, of calling the first woman as full-time pastor, the Reverend Beth Braxton. Under her leadership, this mission focused church has a thriving education program and creative, vital worship services.

WASHINGTON COMMUNITY FELLOWSHIP, *Washington, D.C.* This church, located nine blocks from the Capitol, was started in 1981 by the Reverend Myron Augsburger and forty founding members. The present interdenominational membership of 400 is affiliated with the Mennonite Church, and is committed to inner-city missions and neighborhood ministry.

THE KIRK OF THE HILLS PRESBYTERIAN CHURCH, *Fairfield Bay, Arkansas.* This church was organized in 1981. Kirk of the Hills is located on Greers Ferry Lake, in north central Arkansas, an area that is beautifully wooded. At present, the congregation has 145 members.

SEA ISLAND PRESBYTERIAN CHURCH, *Beaufort, South Carolina.* Until 1988, First Presbyterian Church was the only one of its denomination in Beaufort. With growth that was taxing its facilities, and with the church tradition of evangelical growth, it was decided by the Beaufort Church leadership and Charleston-Atlantic Presbytery that a new congregation should be established. Worship services were held in a school until 1991 when ground was broken for a new church building on Lady's Island, less than two miles east of Beaufort. The property is dominated by a magnificent live oak tree. In 1992, the structure was completed and the newest church in Beaufort began to grow rapidly. The present pastor is the Reverend Steve Keeler.

THE PRESBYTERIAN CHURCH OF BLOOMINGDALE, *Brandon, Florida.* In 1984, the Southwest Florida Presbytery and several individuals had a vision of starting a new Presbyterian church in Bloomingdale. The first service was held at a day nursery, August 10, 1986, with forty-six people in attendance. In 1987, Reid Isenhart was called to be the Organizing Pastor. As the congregation grew, their goal was to reach 100 members before taking their charter request to the Presbytery. On April 29, 1990, the church was officially organized. Ground breaking was held at the site on Bloomingdale Avenue, and the first service in the new church building was on May 26, 1991.

LOW COUNTRY PRESBYTERIAN CHURCH, *Bluffton, South Carolina.* The Presbytery of Charleston purchased the property for this church in the 1980s, knowing that the area was to experience growth. Frank R. Sells was called to be the Development Pastor in May of 1993. He began work in July, and the first worship service was held on September 12, 1993, in the Savings Bank of Beaufort County in Bluffton. Seventy people were in attendence. Since there was only limited meeting space in Bluffton, the church planned to build a 4200 square foot structure, with offices, classrooms, and space for a sanctuary. Construction began in 1993, and Dr. Sells began services in the new church in 1994.

INDEX TO RECIPES AND CHURCHES

INDEX TO RECIPES

APPETIZERS
See Hors D'Oeuvres.
BEANS
After Tennis Chili with Beans, 201
Ann's Baked Beans, 199
Baked Beans, 200
Dr. Pepper Baked Beans, 200
Fancy Baked Beans, 200
Frijoles con Chilies Y Queso, 201
Lentil Roll, 202
Baked Lima Beans, 202
Limas Supreme, 202
Stretch or Shrink Bean Dish, 203
Three Bean Casserole, 203
BEEF
Barbecups, 145
Cranberry Beef Brisket, 145
Westminster Brisket, 146
Corned Beef Hash, 146
Nannie's Plantation Hash, 146-147
Pepper Steak (Lot Ju Kair Ngow), 148
Rapid Roast, 147
Twenty-Four Roast Beef, 147
Beef Casseroles
Stay-A-Bed Stew, 158
Aardvark Tooth Casserole, 158
Applesauce Meatballs, 159
Beef and Macaroni Casserole, 159
Beef Noodle Casserole, 159
Beef-N-Noodles in Sour Cream, 160
Burns Burgers, 160
Cheese and Pasta in a Pot, 161
Chili, 161
Chili Relleno Bake, 162
Company Casserole, 162
Delicious Hamburger Casserole, 162
Enchilada Casserole, 163
German Meat Casserole, 163
Kathleen's Aunt Sharon's Beans, 164
Lumberjack, 164
One-Dish Dinner, 164
Marzetti, 165
Mexican Casserole, 165
Piccadillo (Spanish-Style Ground Beef), 165
Southwest Casserole, 166
Spaghetti and Beef Casserole, 166
Spaghetti Pie, 167
Taty Pot, 167
Texas Hash, 168
Togliarini, 168
Ground Beef
Hamburger Stroganoff, 148

Marilyn's Smothered Burritos, 148-149
Meat Loaf I & II, 149
Mother's Best Meat Loaf, 151
Wonderful Meat Loaf, 150
World's Greatest Meat Loaf, 150
Rice and Meatballs, 151
"Souper" Supper, 151
BEVERAGES
Coffee Frappé, 19
Hot Apple Drink, 19
Hot Percolator Punch, 20
Huldah's Boiled Custard, 20
Jingle Bell Punch, 20
Kris Kringle Punch, 20
Lime Punch, 21
Low-sugar Punch, 21
Party Punch, 21
Plantation Punch, 22
Presbyterian Champagne, 22
Presbyterian Punch, 22-23
Strawberry Punch, 23
Super Smoothie, 23
Russian Tea, 23
BREADS
Apple Bread, 35
Apple Harvest Loaves, 35
Angel Biscuits, 36
Basque Sheepherder's Bread, 36
Blueberry Monkey Bread, 37
Broccoli Bread, 37
Johnnie's Quick Cheese Bread, 38
Everett's Six Grain Communion Bread, 38
Cornbread, 38
Corn Spoon Bread, 39
Mrs. Dodd's Bread, 39
Easy Bread Sticks, 39
Hobo Bread, 40
Houston's Bread, 40
Lemon Bread, 41
Chinese Pepper Bread, 41
Pistachio Bread, 42
Pumpkin Bread, 42
Redeemer Bread, 42-43
Irish Soda Bread, 43
Oatmeal Bread, 43
Sourdough Bread, 44
Hearty Whole Wheat Bread, 45
Whole Wheat Quick Bread, 45
CAKES
Apple Cake (or Muffins), 51
Fresh Apple Cake, 52
Kay's Apple Cake, 52
Special Apple Coffee Cake, 52-53
No-Sugar Banana Cake, 53
Belgian Loaf, 53
Chukka's Blueberry Cake, 53
All-Bran Cake, 54
Bride's Cake, 54

Carrot Cake, 54-55
Pink Mountain Cherry Cake, 55
Chocolate Cake, 55
Chocolate Chocolate Chip Cake, 56
Chocolate Eclair Cake, 56
Chocolate Shortcake, 57
Chocolate Surprise Bundt Cake, 57
Date and Walnut Cake, 58
Chocolate Cake Icing, 58
Earthquake Cake, 58
Fruit Cocktail Cake, 58-59
Fruit Loaf, 59
Fluffy Gingerbread, 59
Ginger Bread, 60
Hawaiian Pizza Cake, 61
Hawaiian Wedding Cake, 61
Kentucky Jam Cake, 62
Lemon/Vanilla Tea Bread, 63
Lemon Stuffed Cake, 63
B. Huber's Mayonnaise Cake, 64
Miracle Cake, 64
Sunburst Miniature Muffins, 64
Oatmeal Cake, 65
Fresh Orange Cake, 65
Peach Glaze Cake, 66
Pineapple Do-Nothing Cake, 66
Pineapple Fruit Cake, 67
Poppyseed Almond Cake, 67
4- Banana Pound Cake, 68
Buttermilk Pound Cake, 68
Cold Oven Pound Cake, 68-69
Pound Cake, 69
Thelma Harvey's Sour Cream Pound Cake, 69
Pumpkin Cake Roll, 70
Punch Bowl Cake, 71
Recipe for a Happy Home, 60
Scripture Cake, 71
Shoo-Fly Cake, 71
Sultana Cake, 71
Kate's Upsidedown Cake, 72
Wine Cake, 72
CANDY
Bickenbach Candy, 73
Buckeyes Candy, 73
Black Walnut Divinity, 74
Tillie's Fudge, 74
Peanut Butter Easter Eggs, 75
Peanut Butter Fudge I & II, 75
Old-time Penuche, 76
Toffee Bars, 76
English Toffee, 76
Toffee, 77
CHICKEN
Another Chicken Casserole, 173

Aunt Kitty's Chicken and Corn Flakes, 173
Baked Onion Chicken, 174
Barbecued Chicken, 174
Broccoli Chicken Casserole, 175
Chicken A La Marsala, 175
Chicken Almond Supreme, 176
Chicken and Corn Casserole, 176
Chicken or Ham Supper Casserole, 177
Chicken and Spinach Casserole, 177
Chicken and Wild Rice Casserole I & II, 178
Chicken Artichoke Casserole, 179
Chicken Breast, 178
Chicken Broccoli Fettuccine, 179
Chicken Casserole, 180
Chicken Divan, 180
Chicken Enchiladas, 180-181
Chicken Lasagna, 181
Chicken Mushroom Casserole, 181
Chicken of the North, 182
Chicken Parmigiana, 182
Chicken Rice Casserole, 182
Chicken Spaghetti, 183
Chicken Sopa with Swiss Cheese, 183
Chicken Spectacular, 184
Chicken Tettrazini, 184
Easy Chicken Pie, 184-185
Easy Chicken Pie Casserole, 185
Gloria's Chicken, 186
Hawaiian Chicken, 186
Hawaiian Chicken Casserole, 186-187
Hot Chicken Salad I & II, 187
Hot Chicken Soufflé, 188
King Ranch Chicken, 188
Overnight Chicken Casserole, 188-189
Poppyseed Chicken, 189
Roberta Shepard's Chicken, 189
South Carolina Chicken Pie, 190
Cheddar Chicken Casserole, 190
Chinese Chicken, 192
Chinese Chicken Casserole, 192
Country Style Chicken Kiev, 190-191
Creamy Baked Chicken Breasts, 185
Crescent Chicken Rolls, 191
Curried Chicken/Rice/Broccoli Casserole, 191
COOKIES
Chewy Apricot Squares, 77
Australian Crunchies, 78
Basic Cookie, 78
"Mother's" Brownies, 78-79
Butter Squares, 79
Caramel Bars, 79
Caramel Cracker Cookies, 80

349

Chess Squares, 80
Chocolate Chews, 80
Chocolate Crinkles, 81
Church Windows, 81
Christmas Cookies, 82
Red and Green Christmas Ball Cookies, 82
Crispy Balls, 82
Coconut Macaroons, 83
Crumb Cookies, 83
Decadent 3-C Bars, 84
Empire Biscuits or Cookies, 84
Fennel Cookies, 84-85
Ginger Cookies, 85
Ginger Shortbread, 85
Graham Cracker Dessert Cookies, 86
Heath Bars, 86
Imperial Biscuits, 87
Mama's Ice Box Cookies, 87
Lemon Squares I & II, 88
Lethal Layers, 89
Monster Cookies, 89
Morning Cookies, 90
No-Bake Cookies, 90
Nut Crust Cookies, 90-91
Oatmeal Crispies, 91
Orange Cookies, 91
Parkins, 92
Peanut Butter Oatmeal Cookies, 92
Pecan Bars, 92
Pitcaithly Bannock, 93
The Practically Perfect Cookie, 93
Pumpkin Cookies, 94
Highland Shortbread, 94
Good Spice Cookies-Molasses, 94-95
Big Soft Sugar Cookies, 95
Streusel Fingers, 95
Survival Cokies, 96
Teatime Special, 96
DESSERTS
Apple Crumble, 97
Apple Fingers, 97
John's Boy Scout Blueberry Dessert, 98
New Orleans Bread Pudding, 98
Wonderful Bread Pudding, 99
Cheesecake, 99
Cheese Pie Dessert, 99
Charlotte Rousse, 100
Chocolate Eclair Dessert, 100
Chocolate Layer Dessert, 101
Cloutie Dumpling, 101
Coconut Torte, 102
Cranachan, 102
Cranberry-Apple Casserole, 103
Crown Jewel Dessert, 103
Easy Cheese Cake, 104
Fairy Torte, 104
Free Kirk Pudding, 105
Fruit Sherbert, 105
Lemon Delicacy, 105
Marshmallow Pineapple Dessert, 106
Mary, Queen of Scots, Tart, 106
Mint Mousse, 106
Peach Cobbler, 107
Pina Colada Dessert Squares, 107
Plum Pudding, 108

Layered Raspberry Dessert, 108-109
Frosty Strawberry Squares, 109
Trifle, 110
Welsh Cakes, 110
EGGS AND CHEESE
Mary Jackson's Cheese Fondue [Cheese Fondue for Two], 120
Cheese and Onion Pudding, 120-121
Red Apple Inn Cream Cheese Soufflé, 121
Supper Cheese Spread, 121
Chili Relleno Casserole, 122
Delicate Egg and Cheese Bake, 122
Easter Brunch Casserole, 122-123
Eggs Bettina, 123
Ortega Eggs, 124
Presbyterian Eggs (Breakfast Casserole), 124
Overnight Breakfast Casserole, 124
Easy Quiche Lorraine, 125
Breakfast Before, 125
Sausage Breakfast Cups, 126
Sausage and Cheese Casserole, 126
FISH
Grouper Mediterranean, 128
Kedgeree, 128
Oven-Fried Fish, 129
Salmon Loaf with Mustard Lemon Sauce, 129
Salmon Quiche, 130
Spinach and Salmon Terrine, 130
Filet of Sole Casserole, 131
Tuna Chow Mein Casserole, 131
Tuna-Potato Supreme, 132
FRUIT DISHES
Apple Chutney, 240
Cranberry Stewed Apples, 240
Baked Curried Fruit, 241
Brandied Peaches, 241
Fruit Cup, 241
Hot Sherried Fruit, 242
Pineapple Au Gratin, 242
Pineapple Bread Pudding, 242
Pineapple Casserole, 243
GRITS
Domino Grits Casserole, 127
Grits and Sausage Casserole, 127
Grits Souffle' with Cheese, 127
HORS D' OEUVRES
Anchovy/Celery Cocktail Dip, 24
Artichoke Dip, 24
Easy Artichoke Dip, 24
Aunty Kitty's Cheese Straws, 25
Avocado Dip, 25
Beef Balls, 25
Beef Sausage, 26
Cheese Ball, 26
Cheese and Frank Rolls, 27
Cheese Snacks, 28
Crabbies, 27
Crab Dip, 28
Curry Dip for Shrimp, 28
Dill Dip, 28
Glorified Onions, 29

Quick Paté, 29
Sausage and Cheese Balls, 29
Vegetable Pizza, 30
LAMB
Braised Lamb Shanks, 157
Lamb Cutlets in Oatmeal/Herb Crust, 157
MUFFINS
English Muffins, 45
Pat's Fresh Apple Cake/ Muffins, 46
Coffee Cake, 49
Corny Mini-Muffins, 46
Country Muffins, 47
Quick Holiday Muffins, 47
Delicious Low Fat Muffins, 47
Party Muffins, 48
Easy Breakfast Ring, 48
Orange Buttermilk Scones, 48
PASTA
Crock Pot Macaroni and Cheese, 203
Macaroni and Cheese, 204
Macaroni Topkapi, 204
Newberry Macaroni Casserole Speciality, 204-205
Super Macaroni 'n Cheese, 205
Manicotti Florentine, 205
Lasagna, 206
Presbytery Lasagna, 207
Super Easy Lasagna, 207
Vegetable Lasagna, 209
Inside Out Ravioli, 207
Betty Kirk's Turketti, 208
Turketti Spaghetti, 208
Baked Ziti, 209
PICKLES
Fresh Kosher Dill Pickles, 243
Frozen Sliced Sweet Dill Pickles, 243
Frozen Pickles, 244
Crispy Hot Pickles, 244
Mama's Peach Pickles, 244
Uncooked Pickles, 245
Zucchini Relish, 245
PIES
Ambrosia Pie, 110
Apple Crumb Pie, 111
Apple Pecan Pie, 111
Sour Cream Apple Pie, 111
Buttermilk Pie, 112
Miss Eva Keeter's Chess Pie, 112
Coconut Macaroon Pie, 112
E-Z Coconut Pie, 113
Coffee Toffee Pie, 113
Fudgey Pecan Pie, 114
Japanese Fruit Pie, 114
Lemon Pie, 114-115
Nantucket Pie, 115
Oatmeal Pie, 115
Peanut Butter Pie, 116
Pear Pie, 116
Pecan Pie, 116
New Orleans Pecan Pie, 117
Easy Pineapple Pie, 117
Refrigerator Fruit Pie, 118
Refrigerator Pie, 118
Rhubarb Cream Pie, 118
Fresh Strawberry Pie, 119
Southern Heavenly Pie, 119
PORK
Ham Balls and Green Rice, 152

Baked Ham Loaf, 154
Ham Loaf I & II, 153
Ham Loaf with Mustard Sauce, 154
Baked Pork Chops, 155
Barbecued Pork Ribs, 155
Pork Chops and Stuffing, 156
Pork with Apricots and Prunes, 156
Pork Casseroles
Chinese Pork Casserole, 168-169
Farmer's Casserole, 169
Party Ham Casserole,170
Pork and Hamburger Dish, 170
Baked Sausage and Rice, 171
Dr. Martin's Sausage Casserole Mix, 171
Fidget Pie, 170
Sausage Casserole, 171
Sausage Casserole With a Snap, 171
Tourtierre, 172
RICE
Crunchy Rice, 197
Louisiana Red Beans and Rice, 97
Red Rice, 198
Rice-A-Roni, 198
Rice and Cheese Casserole, 198
Rice and Vegetable Casserole, 199
Wild Rice Casserole, 199
ROLLS
Different Angel Rolls, 49
Yeast Rolls I & II, 50
Orange Buttermilk Scones, 48
SALADS
Chicken/Turkey Salads
Cabbage, Chicken, and Ramen Noodle Salad, 210
Chicken Delight Salad, 210
Chicken Salad, 211
Chicken Soup Salad, 212
Cool Chicken Salad, 211
Festive Turkey Salad, 212
Minnesota Chicken Salad, 212
Party Chicken Salad, 213
Salad by Committee, 213
Congealed Fruit Salads
Apricot Congealed Salad, 214
Arizona Salad, 214
Blueberry Jello Salad, 214
Cherry Pie Salad, 215
Cottage Cheese Fruit-Jello Salad, 215
Lemon Salad, 215
Pineapple Congealed Salad, 216
Pretzel Salad, 216
Reception Salad, 216
Red, White, and Blue Jello Mold, 217
Frozen Fruit Salads
Frozen Fruit Salad, 217
Frozen Peach Salad, 218
Pink Frozen Salad, 218
Fruit Salads
Fruit Salad, 218
Summer Fruit Bowl, 219
Pasta/Rice Salads
Light Garden Pasta Salad, 219
Very Easy Pasta Salad, 220
Fruited Rice Salad, 220
Pizza Rice Salad, 220

Culinary Favorites/Historical Vignettes

Seafood Salads
  Pasta and Shrimp Salad, 221
  Shrimp and Rice Salad, 221
  Shrimp Salad (from Connie Trask), 222
  Tuna Salad, 222
Slaws
  Apple Slaw, 222
  Blue Lake Slaw, 223
  Norwegian Slaw, 223
  Superb Slaw, 223
Pea/Bean Salads
  Blackeyed Pea (Soul Food) Salad, 224
  Kidney Bean Salad, 224
  Le Seur Pea Relish Salad, 225
  Marinated Vegetable Salad, 225
  Mustard Marinated Beans, 225
  Pea Salad, 226
  Pennsylvania Dutch Salad, 226
  Summer Salad, 226-227
  Pepperoni/Garbanzo Salad, 227
Potato Salads
  The Potato Salad, 228
  Potato Salad, 228
Congealed Vegetable Salads
  Beet Gelatin, 228-229
  Red Beet Jello Salad, 229
  Corned Beef Jellied Salad, 229
  Creamy Cucumber Salad, 230
  Cucumber Mousse, 230
  Horseradish Mold, 231
  Spinach Mold, 231
  Easy Tomato Aspic, 231
Mixed Vegetable Salads
  Eight Layer Salad, 232
  Layered Salad, 232
  Taco Salad, 232-233
  Broccoli Salad, 233
  Cold Broccoli Casserole, 234
  Easy to Carry, Broccoli Salad, 237
  Tart Carrots, 237
  Cornbread Salad, 234
  Marvelous Mess, 234
  Overnight Vegetable Salad, 235
  Stay Crisp Salad, 235
  Tossed Salad, 233
  Maryl's Spinach Salad, 237
  Mrs. Yoder's Spinach Salad, 236
  Sweet and Sour Spinach Salad, 236
SANDWICHES
  Chicken Salad Party Sandwiches, 30
  Chipped Beef 'n Cheese, 30
  Elmira B-B-Q, 33
  Fast Fillings for Sandwiches, 31
  Miss Elsie House's Sandwich Mix for Parties, 31
  Mock Crab Sandwich Filling, 31
  Orange Nut Party Sandwiches, 33
  Party Sandwich Loaf, 32
  Sloppy Joes for a Crowd, 34
  Stromboli Express, 34
  Tuna Party Loaf (Sandwich Spread), 33
SAUCES
  Basic White Sauces, 238
  Cheddar Curry Sauce, 238
  Harold Gooding's Clemson Sauce for Barbecuing

Chicken, 239
Dressing for Baked Potatoes, 239
Kentucky Sauce, 239
Mother Mather's Fudge Sauce, 240
SHELLFISH
  Clam Casserole, 132
  Crab a la Lorraine, 133
  Deviled Crab Casserole, 133
  Health-Wise Crab Curry Quiche, 133
  Low Country Deviled Crab, 134
  Very Best Crab Casserole, 134
  Scalloped Oysters, 134-135
  Oyster Pie, 135
  Scalloped Scallops, 135
  Bob Shephard's Shrimp Pie, 136
  Curried Shrimp Casserole, 136
  Fresh Shrimp and Crabmeat Au Gratin, 136-137
  Neptune Casserole, 137
  Overseer's Shrimp, 137
  Pickled Shrimp Appetizer, 138
  Pierre's Shrimp and Crab Gravy, 138
  Shrimp or Crawfish Fettucine, 140
  Shrimp Curry, 139
  Shrimp Gravy, 139
  Shrimp Harpin, 140
  Shrimp and Rice Casserole, 139
  Shrimp Wild Rice Casserole, 141
  Cioppina (Italian Fish Stew), 141
  Seafood Casserole I II, III, & IV, 142-143
  Seafood Supreme, 144
  Under the Sea, 144
SOUPS
  Bean Soup I & II, 246
  Cold Weather Bean Soup, 247
  Mission Bean Soup for 100, 247
  Savory Bean Soup, 248
  Broccoli-Corn Chowder, 248
  Cream of Broccoli Soup, 248-249
  Ann's Cauliflower Soup, 249
  Cheesy Chicken Vegetable Soup, 249
  Corn Chowder, 250
  New England Clam Chowder, 250
  San Francisco Crab Soup, 251
  Fish Soup, 251
  La Souppa, 251
  London Particular, 252
  Minestrone Soup I & II, 252-253
  Cream of Peanut Soup, 253
  Piccadillo, 254
  Baked Potato Soup, 254
  Red Riding Hood Soup, 255
  Hearty Tomato Soup, 255
  Tortilla Soup, 255
  Turkey Vegetable Soup, 256
  Vegetable Soup, 256
STEWS
  Chowning's Brunswick Stew, 257
  Five Hour Stew, 257
  Harriet's Tomato Beef Goulash, 258
  St. Phillip's Island Venison Stew, 258

TURKEY
  Maxine's Grilled Turkey Breast, 193
  Pam's Phake Chili, 193
  Low Country Fried Turkey, 194
  Smoked Turkey, 196
  Turkey Burgers with Salsa, 196
  Turkey Chunk Chili Tacos, 195
  Turkey Royale, 194-195
VEGETABLES
  Asparagus Casserole, 259
  Sweet n Sour Asparagus, 259
  Broccoli Casserole, 260
  Broccoli and Cauliflower Duet, 260
  Cauliflower, 260
  Company Carrots, 261
  Mandarin Carrots, 261
  Parsleyed Carrots, 261
  Pineapple Carrots, 262
  Marinated Carrots, 262
  Oriental Celery Casserole, 262
  Corn Pudding Au Gratin, 263
  Corn Pudding, 263
  Polenta, 264
  Succotash, 263
  Creole Eggplant, 265
  Eggplant Casserole I & II, 265
  Green Bean Casserole, 265
  Hominy Casserole I & II, 267
  Scalloped Green Beans (for 50), 266
  Sweet and Sour Green Beans, 266
  Layered Cashew and Mushroom Roast, 268
  Onion Pie, 268
  Scalloped Onions and Almonds, 269
  Vidalia Onion Casserole, 269
  English Pea Casserole, 267
  Hash Brown Casserole, 270
  Oven-Fried Hashed Browns, 270
  Gourmet Potatoes, 271
  Microwave Scalloped Potatoes, 271
  Stoved Potatoes, 271
  Potato Puffs, 272
  Candied Sweet Potatoes, 271
  Sweet Potato/Banana Casserole, 272-273
  Sweet Potato Casserole I & II, 273
  Sweet Potatoes Deluxe, 274
  Yam Puff, 274
  Miriam's Crunchy Sweet Potato Soufflé, 274-275
  Layered Spinach Supreme, 275
  Crustless Spinach Quiche, 275
  Spinach Casserole, 276
  Spinach and Artichoke Casserole, 276
  Spinach Soufflé, 276
  Spinach Potato Casserole, 276
  Fritatta, 277
  Deep Dish Zucchini Pie, 277
  It Can't Be Squash!, 278
  Posh Squash, 278
  Zucchini and/or Broccoli Casserole, 278-279
  Zucchini Arizona, 279
  Sweet Sauerkraut, 279

Fire and Ice Tomatos, 280
Mama's Tomato Pudding, 279
Mushroom Stuffed Tomatoes, 281
Tomato Casserole, 281
Charlotte's Tomato Casserole, 280-281
Ritzy Vegetables, 282
Spring Casserole, 282
Vegetable Casserole I & II, 282-283
Vegetable Casserole Supreme, 283
Vegetable Munch, 284
Vegetable Scallop, 284

INDEX TO CHURCHES

Full names (*italic*) are used for churches other than Presbyterian and those outside the United States. The first page number (**bold**) refers to that church's history; the page numbers which follow indicate location of recipes from that church.

UNITED SATES OF AMERICA
Alabama—BIRMINGHAM: Third, **322**, 100, 178; DEMOPOLIS: First, **306**, 34, 147, 184-185, 273
Arizona—CASA GRANDE: First, **324**, 82, 124, 265; CHANDLER: First, **336**, 196
Arkansas—FAIRFIELD BAY: The Kirk of the Hills, **347**, 182; FORT SMITH: Central, **322**, 70, 153, 270; ROGERS: First, **319**, 180-181, 225
California—COALINGA: First, **329**, 115, 156, 186; MENLO PARK: Menlo Park, **316-317**, 41, 52, 113, 277; PACIFIC PALISADES: Pacific Palisades, **337**, 29, 99, 147, 148, 186-187
Connecticut—WESTON: *Norfield Congregational Church*, 176
District of Columbia—WASHINGTON: Chevy Chase, 233; Church of the Pilgrims, **326**, 258; National, **296**, 104, 155, 203, 212, 247, 249, 275; *Washington Community Fellowship*, **347**, 20, 69
Florida—APOPKA: First, **316**, 114-115; BRANDON: *The Presbyterian Church of Bloomingdale*, **348**, 143, 171; DUNEDIN: First, **315**, 128, 151, 199, 204; FORT LAUDERDALE: First, **330**, 22, 117, 132, 184, 228-229, 231; FROSTPROOF: First, **326**, 217; HOMESTEAD: First, 24, 241, 243; JACKSONVILLE: St. Andrews, **342**, 124, 164; NAPLES: First, **339**, 143; ST. PETERSBURG: Maximo, **345**, 233; TAMPA: First, **317**, 165
Georgia—ATLANTA: Peachtree Road, **332**, 56, 239; DAHLONEGA: Dahlonega,

305, 92, 179, 252; DECATUR: Clairmont, **340,** 211, 226; DUNWOODY: St. Luke's, **346,** 225; HULL: Mt. Herman, **319,** 187; MONROE: Ray Memorial, **333,** 27, 51, 111, 133, 136, 205, 228, 233, 263, 265, 279; ROSWELL: Roswell, **306,** 262; SAVANNAH: First, **301,** 29, 43, 89, 101, 163, 270, 272; Independent, **293,** 282; VALDOSTA: First, **313,** 89, 213
Illinois—LAKE FOREST: *Church of the Holy Spirit,* **325,** 181; PETERSBURG: Central, **307,** 21, 80; TOULON: Elmira United, **304,** 33
Indiana—FORT WAYNE: First, **304,** 61; SOUTH BEND: First, **305,** 236
Kansas—PAOLA: First, **313,** 124
Kentucky—PARIS: First, **295,** 25, 173
Louisiana—ALEXANDRIA: First, **306,** 189; BATON ROUGE: Church of the Way, **331,** 234; First, **301,** 98, 146-147, 249; Trinity, **334,** 224, 270; CARROLLTON: Carrollton, **310,** 274; GRETNA: Gretna, **324,** 197; LAFAYETTE: Grace, **344,** 140; PORT ALLEN: West Baton Rouge, **335,** 163
Maryland—BALTIMORE: *Brown Memorial Woodbrook Church,* **314,** 23, 201; FALLSTON: Fallston, **315,** 150, 246; WILLIAMSPORT: St. Andrew, **344,** 58-59, 75, 271
Massachusetts—FALMOUTH: *Waquoit Congregational Church,* **309,** 115; FRAMINGHAM: *Plymouth Church in Framingham,* **289,** 24, 146; MEDFIELD: *First Congregational Church,* 81
Michigan—GROSSE POINTE WOODS: Grosse Pointe Woods, 334-335, 208
Minnesota—BELLE PLAINE: First, **311,** 86, 211, 266; GOLDEN VALLEY: Valley Community, **339,** 91, 251; ROSEVILLE: North Como, **338,** 199
Mississippi—VICKSBURG: Vicksburg, **303,** 265
Missouri—FAIRFAX: First, **318,** 39; ST. LOUIS: Westminster, **308,** 38, 39, 77, 87, 120, 146, 175, 184, 202, 206, 236, 240, 254, 257, 276
Montana—HELENA: Helena, **313,** 93, 152
Nevada—RENO: St. John's, **337,** 36, 48, 242
New Jersey—BASKING RIDGE: The Presbyterian Church, **289,** 159; BLACKWOOD: First, **292,** 47, 107, 260, 274, 279; DEERFIELD: Deerfield Street, **290,** 235; HADDONFIELD: First, **315,** 32, 190, 191; MOORESTOWN: First, **321,** 255; NEW VERNON: First, **297,**
49, 122-123, 131, 158; PATERSON: United, **319,** 37, 174, 201, 224, 284; DARETOWN: Pittsgrove, **291,** 73, 74, 75, 118, 169, 240, 256; RIDGEWOOD: West Side, **331,** 85, 178; RUTHERFORD: First, **312,** 148; VOORHEES TOWNSHIP: Ashland Evangelical, **327,** 177
New York—ATTICA: First, **297,** 66; BERGEN: Stone Church, **302,** 235; CORFU: United, **299,** 95; ELLICOTTVILLE: The United Church of Ellicottville, **302,** 198, 256; JEWETT: Jewett, **297,** 76, 81, 94, 105, 118, 179, 209, 271; LEROY: First, **299,** 115; MEDINA: First, **303,** 119, 135, 154, 161, 185, 208, 213, 221, 226, 250, 260, 261, 270; PAVILION: Covington United, **302,** 178; SOUTH SALEM: South Salem, **292,** 43, 52, 94, 161; WYOMING: First, **299,** 108-109, 250
North Carolina—BURLINGTON: Westminster, **323,** 144; BURNSVILLE: Paint Gap, **326,** 37, 70, 149, 162, 185, 223, 272-273; BRYSON CITY: Bryson City, **317,** 82, 94-95, 132, 151, 167, 248, 259; CHARLOTTE: Trinity, **339,** 125, 159, 214, 270; CROSSNORE: Crossnore, **334,** 38, 64, 91; DURHAM: Trinity Avenue, **332,** 68, 214; FAYETTEVILLE: Highland, **329,** 22-23, 78, 94, 96, 114, 155, 171, 188, 233, 243, 244; GASTONIA: Olney, **295,** 35, 36, 233, 234, 260; GREENSBORO: Guilford Park, **336,** 52, 124; HIGHLAND: First, 320-321, 218; LENOIR: United, **345,** 56, 154, 187, 200, 276, 284; LILLINGTON: Lillington, **329,** 40, 216, 234, 245; MARION: First, **308,** 19, 26, 31, 34, 39, 50, 76, 79, 112, 116, 117, 198, 214, 218, 220, 269, 281; MORGANTON: First, **297,** 125, 280; SHELBY: John Knox, **342,** 30, 55, 126; SPARTA: Sparta, **328,** 61; STATESVILLE: First, **293,** 33; VALDESE: Waldensian, 322-323, 251, 264; WHITEVILLE: First, **311,** 225; WINSTON-SALEM: Highland, **337,** 28, 124, 131, 144, 169, 175, 190, 206, 231
Ohio—CADIZ: The Presbyterian Church, **299,** 56, 278-279; CUYAHOGA: Northminster, **340,** 190; FINDLAY: First, **303,** 181
Pennsylvania—BRYN MAWR: Bryn Mawr, **316,** 142; CAMP HILL: Christ, 54-55, 141; EASTON: First, **298,** 88, 127, 177; ERIE: Wayside United, **343,** 102; FRANKLIN: Rocky Grove Avenue, **320,** 153; HARRISBURG: Faith, **341,** 20, 21, 53, 84, 129, 134-135, 160, 173, 193, 215,
220, 251; Market Square, **296,** 165; Paxton, **290,** 71, 271; Pine Street, 231; LAKE CITY: First United, **320,** 270; OIL CITY: First, 342-343, 194-195
South Carolina—AIKEN: First, **311,** 22, 70, 145, 162, 232; BEAUFORT: First, **291,** 19, 26, 35, 41, 42, 44, 45, 47, 48, 57, 61, 64, 66, 72, 73, 77, 78, 82, 87, 90, 99, 100, 102, 105, 106, 107, 110, 123, 127, 134, 137, 138, 139, 141, 142, 157, 168, 171, 176, 194, 196, 199, 200, 212, 215, 216, 222, 227, 229, 233, 237, 242, 243, 244, 258, 262, 266, 276, 277, 282-283; *St. Peter's Catholic Church,* **309,** 277, 281; Sea Island, **348,** 80, 122, 166, 209; BLUFFTON: Low Country, **348,** 75, 76; CAMDEN: Bethesda, **300,** 172, 232; CHARLESTON: Westminster, **304,** 136, 189; CLEMSON: Fort Hill, **323,** 27, 53, 58, 69, 80, 103, 136-137, 150, 223, 260, 261; COLUMBIA: First, **296,** 24, 29, 79, 221, 269, 278; Shandon, **331,** 203, 257; CROCKETVILLE: Harmony, **314,** 23, 27, 63, 68-69, 83, 92, 98, 107, 113, 139, 227, 238, 249; DONALDS: Greenville, **294,** 188; ESTILL: Estill, **325,** 118, 127, 135, 141, 180, 268; FRIPP ISLAND: *All Faiths Chapel,* **347,** 160; GREENVILLE: *Christian Assembly,* **346,** 99; First, **309,** 126, 283; Westminster, **336,** 110, 222, 263; GREENWOOD: First, **310,** 113; HAMPTON: Hampton, **340,** 21, 48, 88, 104, 105, 107, 116, 129, 164, 178, 203, 217, 218, 239, 266, 282; HEMINGWAY: Indiantown, **294,** 86; HODGES: Hodges, **325,** 25, 58, 210, 222, 260; HONEA PATH: Honea Path, **312,** 267; McCLELLANVILLE: New Wappetaw, **288,** 133, 158; McPHERSONVILLE: Stoney Creek Chapel, **291,** 280-281; NEWBERRY: Aveleigh, **305,** 204-205; NORTH AUGUSTA: Fairview, **335,** 42, 133; North Augusta, 137; ORANGEBURG: First, **305,** 30, 33, 46; ROCK HILL: Oakland Avenue, **328,** 65, 134, 140, 193, 197, 198, 202, 274-275; SPARTANBURG: First, **307,** 50, 207, 241; YORK: First, **307,** 183
Tennessee—CHATTANOOGA: East Ridge, **338,** 30, 40, 46, 49, 68, 88, 112, 144, 159, 188-189, 192, 220, 228, 247, 248, 278; GREENEVILLE: Timber Ridge, **295,** 97; KINGSPORT: Preston Hills, **346,** 23, 216; NASHVILLE: Glenclift, **339,** 20, 151, 174
Texas—ABILENE: First Central, **318,** 67, 80, 90, 106, 109, 165, 183, 205, 259, 273, 283; CUERO:
First, **309,** 111, 112, 166, 230, 241, 244, 267; DALLAS: Highland Park, **333,** 121; HOUSTON: Memorial Drive, **341,** 138, 178, 254; KERRVILLE: First, **322,** 200, 255; SAN ANTONIO: Alamo Heights, **330,** 57, 219, 232-233, 275; Covenant, **342,** 182, 212; *Fort Sam Houston Chapel,* 267; University, 42-43, 195
Virginia—ALEXANDRIA: The Old Presbyterian Meeting House, **294,** 38, 54, 60, 71, 84-85, 103, 119, 170, 253, 279; ARLINGTON: Little Falls, **338,** 192; Trinity, **335,** 180, 223; BERRYVILLE: Stone's Chapel, **321,** 263; BURKE: Burke, **347,** 116; FAIRFAX: Fairfax, **341,** 28, 45, 83, 89, 111, 162, 168-169, 186, 207, 242, 261, 270; Providence, **345,** 100, 122, 145, 148-149, 210, 219, 253, 255; WARM SPRINGS: Warm Springs, **301,** 45, 272; WAYNESBORO: First, **308,** 191; VIRGINIA BEACH: Kings Grant, **344,** 91, 226-227
West Virginia—CHARLESTON: First, **300,** 72, 229; PIEDMONT: Piedmont, **310,** 74, 76

INTERNATIONAL
Canada—BELLEVILLE, ONTARIO: *St. Columba Presbyterian Church,* **343,** 164, 182; SCARBOROUGH, ONTARIO: *St. Stephen's Presbyterian Church,* **343,** 90-91, 172; SASKATOON, SASKATCHEWAN: *St. Andrews Presbyterian Church,* **333,** 108
England—COUNTY DURHAM: *The Bethel Reformed Church,* **298,** 55, 78, 167, 204; KENT: *Ash United Reform,* **311,** 85, 120-121; LETCHWORTH: *Letchworth Free Church,* **327,** 54, 58, 60, 63, 65, 67, 92, 94, 96, 97, 110, 170, 238, 240, 252, 268
Northern Ireland—PORTADOWN, CRAIGAVON: *Armagh Road Presbyterian Church,* **312,** 25, 31
Scotland—GLASGOW: *Parkhead Congregational Church,* **312,** 202; ISLE OF CUMBRAE: *Isle of Cumbrae Parish Church,* **288,** 59, 84, 94, 95, 106, 121, 149, 156, 246, 271; MILNATHORT, KINROSS: *Portmoak Church,* **287,** 130, 245; PERTH: *Auchtergaven & Moneydie Parish Church,* **287,** 93, 101, 102, 105, 130, 157; *Perth North Church,* **292,** 31, 53, 71, 94, 101; STRANRAES: *Ervie-Kirkcolm with Leswalt,* **304,** 128
Zimbabwe—*Christ Church Borrowdale,* 237